THE FRIDAY PILOTS

First person stories of growing up and flying
the old airplanes in the "old Air Force" by the
Friday pilots of Tucson, Arizona. Come fly
with us. Strap-in, hold on. It's a wild ride!

Edited by Don Shepperd

authorHOUSE®

AuthorHouse™
1663 Liberty Drive
Bloomington, IN 47403
www.authorhouse.com
Phone: 1-800-839-8640

Published by AuthorHouse   11/22/2014

ISBN: 978-1-4969-5077-2 (sc)
ISBN: 978-1-4969-5065-9 (e)

Library of Congress Control Number: 2014919396

Other books by Don Shepperd:

Misty – First Person Stories of the Misty F-100 Fast FACs in the
Vietnam War – ed. 2002, 1ʳᵗ Books, Bloomington IN

Bury Us Upside Down – the Misty Pilots and the Secret Battle for the Ho Chi Minh
Trail – with Rick Newman, foreword by Sen. John McCain – 2006, Ballentine
Books, New York, Presidio Press, a division of Random House, Inc. New York

The Class of '58 Writes a Book – A collection of original stories by the Class of 1958, Wheat
Ridge High School – Wheat Ridge, Colorado - ed. 2008, AuthorHouse, Bloomington IN

Those Red Tag Bastards – their dreams, their lives, their memories - ed. 2012
AuthorHouse, Bloomington I

DEDICATION

To our fellow pilots, those who are with us and those who aren't. To the members of our Friday Pilots group who slipped the surly bonds of earth before publication of this book – may they "dance the skies on laughter-silvered wings"

Norm Sandell

Jim Record

"Dusty" Showen

Louis L. Wilson

Al White

"Boris" Baird

As shadows begin to appear on the western horizon, we want to share our stories. You are all part of them. We hear your laughter at Officers Clubs on Friday nights. We see you diagramming attacks in flight briefing rooms. We see your smiling faces in bars all over the world. You are forever young. We walk with you to your airplane and smell the flight line on a misty morning. We see you climbing the ladder and hear your engine start. We see your canopy slowly close and hear you check-in crisply on the radio. We see you take the active runway and feel the tremble as you hold the brakes against thousands of pounds of thrust, then release brakes and press back in the seat as your afterburner kicks-in with thousands more. Gear up, and you turn out of traffic climbing and climbing and climbing, headed west. Higher and higher you climb where the sky gets darker and darker and darker, until we meet again – flying.

The Friday Pilots

QUOTATIONS

Blue is up, brown is down – FLY THE AIRPLANE!

All this talk about lift and drag is scientific nonsense – airplanes fly on money.

I became a millionaire in the aviation business – How did you do that? – I started out as a billionaire.

The only time in an airplane when you have too much fuel is when you are on fire.

One of these things happens to every pilot – one day you will walk out to your airplane knowing it is your last flight – one day you will walk out to your airplane not knowing it is your last flight.

The worst day of flying beats the best day at work – said by someone who has never been in combat.

There is no reason to fly through a thunderstorm in peacetime – sign over an ops desk at Davis-Monthan AFB.

A smooth landing is skill – two in a row is luck – three is a lie.

Passengers prefer old captains and young flight attendants.

In aviation when your wife is happy, you're happy (this goes for much of the rest of life too).

In a tail-dragger, your problems start when you land.

God does not subtract from man's allotted time the hours spent while flying.

You've never been lost until you've been lost at Mach two.

The superior pilot is he who avoids situations requiring the application of his superior skills.

There are old pilots and there are bold pilots – there are no old, bold pilots (the Friday Pilots being an exception).

Never get in the backseat of an airplane with anyone braver than you in the front.

Did we land, or were we shot down?

The job of a pilot is to fulfill the dreams of the earthbound who only stare skyward and wish.

Contents

Acknowledgements

This book would not have been possible without Bob McMahon and his Tucson Prime Steakhouse Restaurant in Tucson. We gather there every Friday for lies, laughs, lunch and stories. Thanks to Bob and his superior staff for providing the atmosphere and great food and especially to Carrie Convertino who waits on our rowdy group and puts up with our addled senses of humor, poor hearing, bad eyesight and stupid menu questions.

Thanks to Terri Lundgren who, like Carrie at McMahon's, took care of us at Ric's before it closed.

Thanks to Rose "Rosie the Riveter" Shepperd for editing, advice (some even welcomed), proof reading, typing and not yelling, "GET OFF THAT DARNED COMPUTER!" too often during the long, aggravating assembly and publication process of an edited book with numerous authors.

Thanks to Bill Pitts, Rob Van Sice and Claudia Johnson for additional proof-reading assistance.

Thanks to Tyler Shepperd, a former USAF AC-130 gunship pilot and now Southwest Airlines captain, for his assistance with our cover and to his wife, Rebecca, who offered advice on handling photos.

Thanks to our families who provided support during our long absences, wars, temporary duty assignments, sometimes terrible living conditions and especially our children who often changed schools at inconvenient times. You lived with the danger that we found fun. We love you.

Thanks to those who taught us to fly. You provided the knowledge and experience that saved us from killing ourselves.

Thanks to our good bosses who mentored us to become better leaders and thanks even to the bad ones who provided examples to avoid.

Thanks to industry that provided our world class equipment.

Thanks to our Air Force who allowed us to fly their airplanes and spacecraft.

And most of all, thanks to the American people who allowed us to serve this great country. It was a higher calling and worthy effort. In fact, it was a blast.

FOREWORD

Walk into McMahon's Prime Steakhouse on a Friday noon and you will see a table of anywhere between 12 and 20 men. They are older, late 60s to mid-80s, balding, for the most part trim, some lean forward to hear. Viewed from a distance you would probably classify them as "duffers;" how wrong you would be.

Move closer, listen, meet them, shake their hands. The first thing you notice is laughter, camaraderie. Listen more carefully and you will hear stories; stories that amaze you. By any measure this is an exceptional group of men. They are pilots; pilots that flew in the old days, the old airplanes, the early jets. They have been to war. They have crashed and burned. They have run through jungles from the enemy and parachuted into oceans. They have been blown out of the sky, captured, imprisoned and horribly tortured. They have ridden huge rockets into space and orbited the earth. They have run large companies. They have been rich and they have been poor. There are pilots who finished their careers as generals, colonels, lieutenant colonels and majors. There are fighter pilots, bomber pilots, airline pilots, corporate pilots and astronauts, men who have owned airplane companies and been senior executives of corporations and on boards, and men who have landed gear-down and gear-up. They have landed on Navy carriers. They have been married, and they have been divorced. They have had children who are successful, some that were problems and some have lost children.

But, listen more closely. The stories are not about their flying, their wars, their accomplishments. There are heroes at this table, but none will admit it. They will tell you they have flown with heroes. The conversation is about the latest University of Arizona basketball victory, colonoscopies, Viagra jokes, trouble peeing, being bald, friends having a tough time, chemotherapy, wives and children that have passed.

Listen to their stories. These are stories about growing up in a different world at a different time when life was both simpler and harder. The airplanes were dangerous and there were no precision or stand-off weapons. Real men flew to far off places trying to win wars and dove down through AAA and avoided SAM missiles and paid for it mentally, physically and with their lives. Men blasted into space and docked with the Lunar Lander.

They do not look impressive but these are real men. They flew before political correctness, back when men were men and women were women and giants roamed the earth. They are oldtimers now, and these are their stories:

Come have lunch with us… "we few, we happy few, we band of brothers…"

The Friday Pilots

Introduction

It seems everyone at some point in life wants to write a book. There appears to be a desire to leave something for posterity, for one's family, for the grandchildren. Maybe it's as simple as wanting to say, "I was there. I did things. I mattered." Most leave photos, but few actually write a book. It is hard work and most people are not good writers. It is even harder to get published.

The Friday Pilots did something almost everyone talks about and few do: they wrote down their memories for their kids, grandkids, families and friends. These men reached back decades into history, times in our nation that were both difficult and different. Life and airplanes were hard. Some of the stories evoke joy and laughter; some bring back memories better left unvisited. The authors overcame addled memories, arthritic fingers and steam driven computers to write their stories. Strap in, hold on and you'll enjoy a look at aviation history through the eyes of those who lived it.

The idea for this book came at one of our Friday lunches in Tucson, Arizona. We meet every Friday and we kid each other, we laugh, we tell stories, some even true. We have become legends in our own minds. We decided to write a book, a collection of first person stories. Some will write about life, some about flying. Unless one is an author, they do not keep copious notes, but we all have memories. These are our memories. Enjoy.

CHAPTER ONE

67th Tactical Fighter Squadron, 2 March, 1965 – Mission to the Xom Biang Ammunition Depot

by Robert V. "Boris" Baird

Boris Baird was our friend, colleague and fellow fighter pilot. He attended our Friday lunches regularly. Unfortunately, as we collectively agreed to write this book about our flying lives, Boris was suffering from terminal cancer. As a tribute to Boris we are including a story he previously wrote about his FIRST mission into North Vietnam. We are certain Boris is reading his story and ours and we will all meet and laugh together again - Editor

It was March 2nd, 1965 that I found myself on foot in the very south of North Vietnam. My way there was paved by Jack Kennedy, Lyndon Johnson, Robert McNamara, and by John McConnell and his fellow members of the Joint Chiefs. They were aided by our weapons developers who thought CBU-2s were just the thing for flak suppression. Those of us in the cockpit share some of the credit for accepting the concept of flying over the target at low altitude in order to suppress (draw) flak.

The 67th TFS Fighting Cocks had deployed from Kadena Airbase, Okinawa to Korat Royal Thai Airbase (RTAB), Thailand in February 1965. From there, we had been escorting RC-121s over the Gulf of Tonkin and enjoying the ambiance of "Camp Nasty." Additional F-105s of the 12th TFS, also from Kadena, were at Da Nang on 2 March while F-100s from England AFB were deployed at Takhli RTAB.

Somehow, somewhere, March 2nd was selected as the day we would show the North Vietnamese what havoc three squadrons of Air Force fighters could bring to their ammunition depot at Xom Biang, 17 miles north of the DMZ.

The F-100s were the first to "suppress" the flak. For their trouble, they lost Hayden Lockhart who was shot down just as our squadron,

1

led by our commander, Robbie Risner, arrived in the area and switched radio frequencies to the "strike" channel.

I was flying on Robbie's left wing as we made a right hand descending turn to a westerly heading to drop our CBU-2s. As we leveled off at approximately 100 feet AGL, I spaced myself line abreast and about 200 feet off Robbie's wing. When he pickled off a string of bomblets, I would do the same. After a couple of these exercises, as I was looking forward to see what tree was higher than me, I saw what appeared to be black greasy smoke corkscrewing up from the trees directly in front of me.

In the split second it took to think, "What in the hell is that?" I knew what "that" was. In another split second, "that" became 23mm AAA, and it was impacting my F-105. In a very calm voice I announced to the world that I had been hit and was pulling off target.

As I assessed, also calmly, the damage to my "Thud," I noted one to two foot diameter holes in my left wing. I did not check the right wing as I now had smoke in the cockpit. The CIN PWR light and the COMPARTMENT OVERHEAT lights had come on, and the engine was compressor stalling. I was rapidly loosing airspeed. The FIRE WARNING light never illuminated.

I do not recall if I announced my ejection or just did so. As I am sure my squadron mates can attest, the entire sequence of events could not have taken more than a minute. In this short time, I never worried about fire or explosion but was concerned that the aircraft would slow to the point of stalling and go out of control.

Once my parachute opened, I found myself two to four miles west, southwest of the target at a moderate height. As I surveyed the terrain beneath me, my first inclination was to turn left so my landing would be on level, un-forested ground. A nano-second later, that idea was canceled as I realized the bad guys would march up the gentle slopes and "police" me up. With that thought in mind, I pulled down on the forward right hand riser and turned toward the hills to the west.

The noise of the battle behind me hardly registered as I concentrated on the forested ridge ahead of me. Later, when the noise was gone, the silence was quite deafening and quite lonely. With great good fortune, I cleared the ridge which was steep enough that I floated further from the target as I continued to descend down the far side.

As any good fighter pilot knows, the object that remains stationary when viewed through the canopy is the object you are going to hit or the aircraft you are going to intercept or join on. The same goes for trees as you descend in a parachute. I focused on "my limb" and decided I was going to grab it and hold on to preclude hitting the ground at a great rate of speed if my chute shredded or streamed on impact. The landing was bit rough, but I broke no bones and lost no teeth.

I will take a moment here to describe how fast a person's mind functions as one experiences something as stressful as a shoot down. It is much like a good instrument cross check – after you do your clockwise scan of your flight instruments, you check the aircraft clock only to find that the second hand has barely moved, and you wonder if a full minute has elapsed.

My mind was racing just like my eyes would be during an instrument approach with a 100 foot ceiling and a ¼ mile visibility. I was not yet dead – so far, so good.

As I clung to my limb, I used my G-suit survival knife to cut the lanyard attaching my survival kit and dingy to the chute harness. As they dropped away, I assumed (a gross and almost fateful error) they had fallen to the ground. I then looked for a way to reach the ground. I was about 30 feet above the ground, and my tree's limbs petered out just below my position, so I climbed into an adjacent tree that contained vines that reached the ground.

Once on the ground, I looked for my survival kit only to find it 20 feet in the air where the inflated dingy had snagged a limb. I hurriedly considered trying to go back up the tree to retrieve the kit versus "getting out of Dodge." I chose the later and was fortunate to discover that the heavy rains of the monsoons had washed a shallow gully under my tree that extended downhill to the south. This gully had created a low passage under the thick morass of trees and brush along which I began crawling.

Within 100 yards, the gully terminated at a small sand bar extending into a 20-foot wide stream which in turn created an opening to the sky. For those among the readers of this tale who are fishermen, the stream contained 14-inch trout.

As this adventure occurred before the advent of survival vests, I found myself somewhat short of communication and signaling devices. I began to improvise. I removed my G-suit, emptied its pockets, added wood and started a fire. I also removed my white T-shirt to wave frantically if someone friendly flew over. My last improvisation was to remove the ball ammunition from my snub-nosed .38 revolver, purchased at the friendly Kadena BX (I still have the gun), and replace it with tracers.

Having done about as much as I could, I sat down to wait and gather my thoughts. My view of the terrain during my descent in the parachute and the thickness of the "jungle" led me to believe that the bad guys could not get to me by coming over the ridge, but would be forced to come from the coast and up the stream. I felt this would require several hours if not a full day. As it was late afternoon, I planned to spend the night where I was and, if necessary, head south the next day.

In the days after my recovery, my squadron mates told me what was occurring in the sky over my head as I sat pondering my future and promising God that if He would see me through this mess, I would never fly again. I lied. As I recall the stories, Robbie and the remainder of my flight "capped" me for a time and called the HU-16 flying over the Gulf of Tonkin to come inland. He was reluctant but was persuaded with threats. After Robbie and the gang left the area low on fuel, the F-100 escorts for the RF-101 post strike reconnaissance remained in the area as long as possible.

As dusk approached, the silence, broken only by the sound of the HU-16's engines as it reached the western most point of its orbit, became ominous. After two hours and forty minutes on the ground and having reconciled myself to spending the night in North Vietnam, I heard the roar of big round engines mounted on the front of two A-1 Sandys. To this day, I do not know how they had me so accurately located, but with one to the left and the other to the right, they passed overhead. As they did so, I fired three rounds of tracers straight up between them in my imitation of the international distress signal. If they thought I was the bad guys, they must have also thought I was a poor shot for no sooner than the sound of their engines receded, I could hear the "whop, whop, whop" of the chopper's rotors.

As it came into view through the gap in the trees, the old fashioned "horse collar" was already being lowered. The pilot, Major Ron Ingraham, missed me neither right nor left, but came to a hover directly over the center of the stream. I waded to meet it and within seconds was being lifted by the winch and the rapidly departing helicopter. As the winch operator/door gunner grabbed me around the waist from behind and dragged me into the chopper, he yelled in my ear, "Are they shooting at us?" When I shook my head "no," there were grins and hugs all the way around.

On our way south, we were joined by the Sandys and another H-43. We were forced to land at Quang Tri to refuel and to leave the second chopper that had taken a round through a rotor as it participated in the attempt to rescue Hayden Lockhart. While at Quang Tri, I learned that two Marine H-34s had also participated in the rescue effort and that one of the four had actually landed and its rescue folks had actually called to Hayden and found his helmet, but could not make contact with him. I do not know how close or far we were from one another, but I would guess Hayden was on the bad side of the ridge. As a result, he spent eight years as a prisoner of the North Vietnamese.

The remaining flight to Da Nang was uneventful except for the racing of my mind as I began to realize what I had just experienced. I felt more irrational fear as we approached Da Nang than I had felt on the ground in North Vietnam.

When we landed at Da Nang, I was met by a group of folks that I cannot recall except for John Edelblute, an old friend and one of the F-100 pilots from Takhli, who had been on the mission along with Hayden. John stuck with me as I was checked by a flight surgeon and "debriefed" by an intelligence officer. From there, it was off to the Officers' Club (Da Nang Officers Open Mess) for steak and scotch. At the club, I was introduced to the communications officer who offered to connect me with Kadena so I might get a message to my wife, Shirley. This was done, and as no one was supposed to know what we were doing or where we were, the message was very brief: "No matter what you hear or who shows up at the front door, everything is OK."

Aircrew bunks were filled to overflowing at Da Nang, so I bagged-out in one assigned to a "Deuce" pilot who was on alert. In spite of good friends, good food, and a couple of stiff drinks, my nerves were so ragged that I tossed and turned all night thinking the F-102 pilot would surely turn up and want his bunk back.

The next morning, John met me for breakfast then took me to the flight line where his F-100F's light battle damage had been repaired. We launched for Takhli with a stop at Korat to drop me off.

While preparing for this flight, some of the 12th TFS pilots staging through Da Nang for another strike "up North" stopped by to say hello and to harass me for not being able to complete my first combat mission. Among them was John Morrissey who has remained a close friend for more than 40 years. This past March, John and Bill Hosmer helped me celebrate the 67th TFS Fighting Cock's first mission "up north."

EPILOGUE: Ron Ingraham received the Silver Star for his rescue of me. His two sons paid his way to Tucson a few years back, and we had a fine visit.

Boris' Tucson connections - Editor: Boris affected many people in the military and out. He was loved by friends and family alike. Mike Riggers was an especially close friend in Tucson. Mike got to know Boris when they were about 12 years-old in the early 1960s. Mike's uncle and Boris took their primary flight training in Tucson. Boris and Mike often went to Idaho to hunt and fish together in the fall. Mike was in the Army during Vietnam, Boris the Air Force. Boris "tried" to teach Mike the same lessons/wisdom that he expounded on with Mike's kids. "Some" of it was useful.

Mike's children grew up around Boris who offered them mounds of advice on life, liberty and particularly the pursuit of happiness. Mike's oldest daughter, Kristin McQuay, knew Boris from the time she was five years-old. Kristin wrote this for Boris:

"Please keep my sweet and beloved family friend, Boris Baird, in your prayers today. He is in his last days here on earth.

Living out his little boy dreams of flying, doing daring feats and becoming a hero, Boris spent 25 years as an Air Force fighter pilot retiring as a Lieutenant Colonel and Squadron Commander. Making his mark in the history books, on 2 March 1965, Boris was the second U.S. pilot shot down over North Vietnam during the first mission of

Operation Rolling Thunder. He spent five hours on the ground before he was rescued. This was the first mission of the 100 missions he would go on to complete flying the F-105. Among his many honors are the Distinguished Flying Cross with two Oak Leaf Clusters, the Air Medal with ten Oak Leaf Clusters, a Purple Heart, Meritorious Service Medal, Commendation Medal with two Oak Leaf Clusters, and a Presidential Unit Citation.

In retirement Boris went on to be an aerobatic pilot, managing the U.S. Aerobatic Team in the mid-late 1990s. As a child I remember walking into his living room in Tucson, AZ and being surrounded by exotic wild game trophies he had brought back with him from his expeditions in Africa. It was wild!

Boris, thanks for the wonderful childhood memories and for your wild and daring stories. You lived life to the fullest: adventurous and dangerous, unfettered and free - what every little boy dreams of growing up to be - the kind of man I want Tristin, my son, to become. Very soon you will be flying your stunt plane in the skies of Heaven, dazzling far-reaching crowds with loop de loops and inverted rolls. We part here on earth, but I know that one day we will meet again."

"It is not the critic who counts, not the man who points out how the strong man stumbles, or where the doer of deeds could have done them better. The credit belongs to the man who is actually in the arena, whose face is marred by dust and sweat and blood, who strives valiantly, who knows great enthusiasms, the great devotions, who spends himself in a worthy cause; who at the best knows in the end the triumph of high achievement, and who at the worst, if he fails, at least fails while daring greatly, so that his place shall never be with those cold and timid souls who neither know victory nor defeat." - Teddy Roosevelt

CHAPTER TWO

They Didn't Tell Me About THAT Part

by Robert W. "Bob" Barnett

Our Friday luncheon group is an amazing collection of aviators who have accomplished much in their lifetime. The group's roots go back about 20 years or so. I had retired from the Air Force in August, 1977. Before retiring, I had started a light airplane business. I bought a one-airplane Rockwell Commander operation. While operating my airplane business I met Col George Hupp. His two daughters had been ROTC cadets during my last Air Force assignment, when I was the Professor of Aerospace Studies (PAS) at the University of Arizona. George had a distinguished Air Force career. Among his many accomplishments he had flown a tour in Vietnam in F-4s and was a Squadron and Wing Commander. His final assignment was project officer for the A-10. Also, during this time I met Donald "Dusty" Showen. He had flown F-86s in Korea and F4s in Vietnam. The fourth member of our original luncheon group was Capt (U.S. Maritime Service) Milt Houpis. Milt had been a sea captain in the Merchant Marines. His ship was sunk off the coast of Brazil in WWII. For years he thought it had been a German sub that torpedoed him, but a few years after we started having our Friday luncheons, he discovered it had been an Italian sub. Milt was the Maître-D at the Palomino restaurant. Consequently, the Palomino evolved into McMahon's, where we lunch now. We have lunched at many different places. The Viscount Hotel, Palomino, Hidden Valley Inn, and TGI Friday's were all popular Tucson spots. Dusty usually coordinated the location.

Unfortunately, none of the original group can tell their stories. First, George succumbed to prostate cancer. When he passed away, we recruited my good friend, Lew Daugherty, to join us. Shortly thereafter, Milt Houpis passed on and Norm Sandel joined us. We moved to Ric's Cafe at the intersection of Craycroft and River roads. Norm had flown C-130s and KC-135s. Dusty Showen was the scheduler and named our group, "Luncho Buncho." We started to ask others to join as we enjoyed many lunches on Ric's patio.

At our age we realize we are not immortal. All of us have had many close calls and near misses. We have quite a few that have been our luncheon partners who have now "gone west" and are unfortunately not able to tell their stories. Of the original group, only I remain. George Hupp, Duty Showen, and "the Captain" Milt Houpis all had interesting and exciting lives. Over the years we have lost Lloyd Cain, a longtime friend with whom I had been stationed in the 50s. Lloyd had flown F-86s, F-104s and F4s in Vietnam. In Vietnam, his airplane was hit by ground fire and he was forced to eject.

And, there were others: Gen Lew Wilson passed away suddenly at age 91. He was a West Pointer. Lew flew P-47s in Europe in WWII. He had a distinguished career that included Commander of Air Forces in Vietnam during the fall of Saigon in 1975. Al White was a famous test pilot for North American and Rockwell. Norm Sandel flew missions in Vietnam in the C-130. Lt Gen Jim Record had been Commander of 12th Air Force. Jack Francisco, was an F105 pilot in Vietnam and in civilian life was the chief test pilot for Learjet. Boris Baird, F-105 pilot in Vietnam, was shot down on his first mission and bravely continued on to complete his 100th. When I went through F-105 training, Boris was one of my instructors. It is a small world, we fighter pilots. All the Luncho Buncho members who have passed would have related a life of excitement and accomplishment. I miss them. Somehow, I have emerged as the oldest member of our group. Only by the grace of God and good genes am I able recount a life that I would never have dreamed.

My dad and mother were both born in England at the end of the 19th and beginning of the 20th century. Both families migrated to Medicine Hat, Alberta, Canada, but at different times. My Dad joined the Canadian Army at 16 years of age and served in the trenches of France during WWI. After the war, he migrated to Los Angeles, CA. My mother joined him there, and they were married in 1923. Later, they became American citizens. I was the middle of three children. We lived in the same house throughout my school years, so my childhood was stable. I grew up during the Great Depression and WWII. When I graduated from high school in 1946, WWII had ended; however, there was still a draft and everyone I knew went into the service. Many of my schoolmates had joined the Coast Guard. So, a close friend and I enlisted in September '46 for three years. At 17, almost 18, I left home. First, I was on a Coast Guard cutter in San Diego for a short time. From there I went to Biloxi, Mississippi, but only briefly. From Biloxi I went to Groton, CT for Radio Operators School. When I finished the course, I was given the rank of Radioman 3rd Class. From Groton to Galveston, TX to Alexandria, VA, then to Juneau, Alaska to spend my last year and one-half onboard a cutter. I completed my three-year commitment in September '49 as a Radioman First Class.

With the GI Bill I was able to attend college, graduating from the University of Southern California in 1953. I had joined the Air Force ROTC in my junior year and was commissioned as a Second Lieutenant upon graduation. Between my junior and senior year I married Anita. After graduation, I had a slot to go to flying school, Class 54R. I attended Primary at Hondo AB, TX flying the Piper Cub and T-6. Following primary flying school I went to Laredo AFB, TX for jet training. There we flew the T-28A and T-33. Upon graduation in '54 I was presented my coveted wings. I was fortunate to receive one of six highly desirable slots for F-86 E/F training at Nellis AFB. At Nellis it was "every man a tiger," exciting times! Due to grounding of the F-86 and following restrictions on the aircraft, my entire class was assigned to commands other than Tactical Air Command. Fortunately, I went to Perrin AFB, TX to fly first as an T-33 instrument instructor, then over three years as an F-86L all-weather interceptor instructor.

My next assignment was a remote tour at Keflavik Air Base, Iceland in the 57th Fighter Interceptor Squadron (FIS) where I was a flight commander flying the F-89D. Then, it was from cold, snowy Iceland to sunny, hot Luke AFB, AZ in July of 1960. At Luke, I was assigned to the Phoenix Air Defense Sector. I flew the T-33 and F-86F as a flight instructor. My primary job was Fighter Officer and working with Air Defense Command (ADC) augmentation forces from Luke and Nellis AFBs. Among other things, I checked-out in the F-100C at Luke then flew the F-100A and F-100C with the Tucson Air Guard.

From Phoenix I received an assignment to Hamilton AFB, CA, just north of San Francisco. I was checked-out in the F-101B, to be assigned to the 83rd FIS as a flight commander. When the 83rd was deactivated in 1962, I went briefly to the 84th FIS. From there I went to the 28th Air Division as the T-33/F-101 Operations Officer. I was able to fly the F-4B at Miramar as an orientation because the F-4 augmented ADC. One day after returning from a trip, I learned Personnel Assignments at ADC was looking for someone to go to Ecuador as an advisor and to implement a program to introduce the F-86 to the Ecuadorian Air Force. I volunteered and was accepted. After a 24-week Spanish course at the Foreign Service Institute in Alexandria, VA Anita and I were off to Guayaquil, Ecuador. My detachment included three master sergeants and me. We lived on the economy and traveled 40 miles each way to Taura Air Base. I flew the T-33, F-80, Meteor Mark 8, T-28D, C-47, and C-54. After two years, I completed my very interesting tour and was assigned to ADC Headquarters in Colorado Springs, CO.

The Vietnam War was in full swing in the summer of 1966. I had volunteered for Vietnam to avoid the headquarters assignment after I returned from Ecuador, but my request was denied. When I arrived in Colorado Springs, I was assigned to Plans in the Bases and Units section. By this time I was a Major. I was sure the Vietnam War was going to end and as a fighter pilot I would not be a part of it. I was checked-out in the T-39. I again volunteered for Vietnam and after more rejections, I was able to backdoor an assignment to the F-105 Thunderchief (Thud). In December 1966, I went to survival school in Spokane, WA and then to McConnell AFB, KS for F-105 training. It was all that I hoped for and more. I loved flying the Thud and the training for combat was exciting and fulfilling. When I graduated, I received my assignment to Korat AB, Thailand. I left my family in Hawthorne, CA in an apartment with the idea I would complete my required 100 missions in seven to eight months. As it turned out, they lived in the tiny apartment for nearly six years.

At Korat, I was assigned to the 44th Tactical Fighter Squadron (TFS). After my initial checkout of five missions in the southern part of North Vietnam, I flew my first mission into Route Pack 6, a target just north of Hanoi. For planning and execution of the air campaign, North Vietnam was divided into six route packages, Pack 1 was in the southern panhandle from the DMZ north to Vinh and was assigned to the USAF. Route Pack 6 encompassed the Hanoi-Haiphong areas. It was later divided into 6A and 6B with the USAF having responsibility for 6A and the Navy 6B. So, the USAF ended up with Route Packs 1, 5 and 6A, the Navy Packs 2, 3, 4 and 6B. I was a flight commander and flying was exciting and rewarding. I was ticking-off my missions at a rapid rate. Probably the highlight was when I was mission commander and led 20 F-105s on a mission to attack the MiG base at Kep in North Vietnam, northeast of Hanoi. The mission was very successful, and I was awarded a Silver Star.

It seemed I would finish my 100 missions in seven months at the rate I was flying. There was a reorganization of the 388th Tactical Fighter Wing and I was reassigned to the 469th TFS as a flight commander. I didn't last long in the 469th. After only three days in the squadron, on 3 October 1967, on my 43rd mission, I was leading a flight of four in a 20-airplane strike against the same target I flown against on my first Pack 6 flight. Approaching the target, my aircraft was hit and heavily damaged by a surface to air missile (SAM).

I was able to fly "almost" to the coast of North Vietnam with my aircraft still burning. I lost hydraulics, and finally the engine seized. I was forced to eject just 10 miles from the coast and 11 miles ENE of Haiphong Harbor, bad country. Somehow during the ejection sequence my life raft became entangled with my parachute and I descended with a partially-deployed parachute. Fortunately, I fell into trees, my fall was broken and I survived. I had a fracture in my lower back, which went undiscovered until my return to the States after the war.

I evaded capture for three days and two nights. During this time I was nearly captured several times and the Navy attempted to pick me up with a helicopter, but the chopper was hit by ground fire and had to ditch in the Gulf of Tonkin. Fortunately, the crew survived. I was finally tracked-down by a dog while hiding under a bush. And so, began my nearly five and one-half years as a POW in North Vietnam. After a first night torture session and an unsuccessful attempt to use me as a decoy to lure other rescue forces, I was trucked into Hanoi to the "Hanoi Hilton" to start my long nightmare as a Prisoner of War (POW) – Whoa! They didn't tell me about THAT part. I spent the majority of my time as a POW in a camp called "the Zoo" which was just south of Hanoi. I went back to the Hanoi Hilton a couple of times and was trucked to another camp called "Dog Patch" with 212 other POWs in 1972. In January 1973, we were all transported back to Hanoi, and I spent my last couple of months at "the Plantation" in downtown Hanoi. Peace agreements were finally signed between the U.S. and North Vietnam in early 1973. In February the first POWs were returned to freedom. My freedom day came on 14 March 1973. We were flown from Hanoi to Clark AB, in the Philippines. After three days of checkups and debriefings, my group was flown to March AFB, CA with a stop at Hickam AFB, Hawaii. At March AFB, I was met by wife, Anita and daughter Lori, plus my family and many friends; a most happy day to say the least.

After some hospital time and many amazing homecoming events, the Air Force agreed to my request to attend the University of Arizona in a Master's Degree Program with a major in Latin American studies. As fate would have it, when I approached graduation, I learned the Professor of Aerospace Studies was finishing his tour at the same time. So, I applied for the job. After an interview with the president of the university, I was accepted and became the PAS. I served two years as the PAS, a very rewarding and interesting job. I received some pressure from the Air Force to take a job as an Air Attaché in Central America. I had started a small airplane business in Tucson, and built a beautiful home in the foothills, so it was time to move on. I decided to retire because I wanted to pursue my little airplane business.

In August 1977, I retired and became "Mr. Businessman." I started out with one airplane and a Rockwell Commander dealership. After nearly five years, I had built a Fixed Base Operation (FBO). With the help of my employees, our FBO had full aircraft maintenance facilities, a charter service, fuel services, a flight school, and a dealership for Rockwell Commander and Grumman American. We had 52 airplanes parked at my Tucson Commander facility. Fortunately, I received an offer to buy my business. After several months of negotiating, papers were signed, and I was liberated for the second time in my life.

After travelling six months in Europe, I returned to Tucson and was offered a job flying for a mine in Tombstone AZ. Along with a partner, I bought a Cessna 210 and flew for the mine for over a year. The mine shutdown and I was offered a job at Flight Safety

International as a simulator and ground school instructor in the Learjet.

I obtained my Air Transport Pilot (ATP) rating and became current in the Learjet. There were many highlights over the next 17 years where I worked first as a full-time then a part-time instructor at Flight Safety and also flew as a Learjet captain part-time. My dream job during this time was 14 months based in Geneva, Switzerland flying a Lear 36 for a wealthy financier. I made 30 Atlantic Ocean crossings, flew all over Europe and got paid for it!

In 1999, I retired completely and have enjoyed travelling and retired life ever since. Much has changed over the past year and one-half. Anita passed away on 24 December 2012. I sold our home in the foothills and bought a townhouse. I have met a wonderful lady that enjoys the same things I do, and after a time of sadness, life is once again good. Life takes many twists and turns. Some obscure occurrence can send it a completely different direction. I have been blessed and continue to be blessed. I have a loving daughter and son-in-law, four wonderful grandchildren and a brother and sister-in-law that stay very close.

The Luncho Buncho group that gathers on Fridays has been a constant for years now, and I am proud to be a part of it. I hope it never ends.

CHAPTER THREE

Cloth Airplanes, Straight Wings and Jets
by Wilbur L. "Pete" Carpenter

Many years ago in Chatham Louisiana, a small town (village), a country doctor assisted my mother in my arrival. That date of 24 March 1929 reveals my current age, but I prefer a simple one – the annual anniversary of my 39th birthday. My three older brothers, two younger sisters, plus Mom and Dad, made up a medium-sized family in those days. I had lots of "growing up advice" from older brothers, some of which wasn't always to my advantage. One thing I learned early on has stayed with me: "One learns a lot more by listening then with the mouth open."

Electricity came to our house in the mid 1930s. Prior to that, lighting came from kerosene lamps and a couple of Aladdin lamps, plus a battery-operated radio with a wind generator charger 30ft. in the air. The ice man delivered a chunk or two three times a week for our ice box "refrigerator." Then, electric power came, and we had light bulbs dangling from the ceiling in every room. The first electric refrigerator in town came to our house and was a "huge" six cubic feet.

Our garden provided fresh food and canning stored plenty for the entire year. We had a small farm one and a half miles away where we grew all types of food. When I was seven, we built our new house on the farm, and it seemed a hundred miles from town. I learned all the tasks of a simple rural life. Even though there were hired helpers, I learned the way things worked, like guiding a plow while walking behind a mule (he knew more of what to do than me). Finally, we bought a Ford tractor in 1943. Learning to drive the truck led to my driving on country highways at age 13. No driver's license was required until I was 17, and it was issued without testing of any sort for $1.00.

Of course, airplanes always caught my attention. In 1940 the Army had a huge training exercise involving all facets of the service including air support from P-40s; what a sweet sound. That sound made me forever want to fly the single seat thriller.

Then, came 7 December 1941, and life took a different path. An older brother enlisted in the Navy in 1940 and was aboard the USS Tennessee at Pearl Harbor anchored aft and inboard of the USS ARIZONA. We were visiting my grandparents and heard the news via auto radio. A couple of weeks later a post card arrived with a mark in the "I'm OK" box. I tried to convince another brother (who had recently soloed) that the two of us should get an aircraft with an armload of grenades, fly to Japan and burn all those paper houses.

As the war progressed, my other two brothers entered the Navy, one participating in the Okinawa invasion. A 1929 Model-A used for off-road hunting, was left in my care by one of my brothers. Gas was rationed for normal travel; however, farm fuel was not. My dad would not allow any gas to flow from the farm tank to the Model-A. Old manual gas pumps were still around. So, after stations closed at night, my buddy and I would visit and drain the hoses getting a cup or so for free. An alternative fuel, kerosene (not rationed) was available at five-cents a gallon, and with a manual-advance ignition, it worked well, just a little hard to start.

During school years I participated in basketball, baseball and softball (no football at our school). I wanted to enter the Navy V-6 program consisting of two years college, and then, pilot training. Being under 21 years of age, I required parental consent. My mom's response: "Three is enough," the answer is, "NO!"

After two years of college and a goof-off year, I was 21 years –old and hitchhiked to Shreveport (Barksdale AFB) and applied for Aviation Cadets. After a couple of days of testing and evaluation, I was accepted and soon offered a choice of three classes. I accepted the last date, which was class 51-E at Randolph, reporting 10 July 1950 for Basic Training. Pictures of the base were widely circulated during the war years, but not one picture compared to seeing it all first hand. Life for the next seven months wasn't exactly what I anticipated. The class consisted of about 75 percent West Point, Annapolis and ROTC graduates. We started with 47 cadets and graduated 27 for advanced training in jets, F-51s and B-25s.

My first flight in the T-6 frontseat was a challenge. It was my second time in an aircraft. As training progressed, my instructor,

Capt Alexander S. Hartley, and I headed for Martindale airport for landing practice. He advised that if I did a couple of good landings, he would let me solo. Wrong Words! First touchdown, then BIG bounce, but GREAT recovery. I taxied to mobile control, shut down, and he advised that I might learn something from just sitting and watching others land. After a few minutes, I strapped-in and thought he would also. I got a tap on the shoulder and, "Give me three good ones."

"What? Does this guy really trust me?" All went well on takeoff, and I entered a large square pattern with the other aircraft. Approaching base leg, mobile control advised all aircraft to continue in circuit as an aircraft had a collapsed gear on the runway. After a few circuits, my instructor asked if I could land in the first half of the runway. My reply was a firm, "Yes sir!" That was my best landing ever in the T-6. My instructor climbed in, and we flew back to Randolph. A one-landing solo complete, I became the last cadet to solo but the first to complete all final flight checks.

There were some Dutch and French students in 51-D and F classes. On the afternoon flying schedule, we were assembled for our march to the flight line, when a T-6, canopy open, came zooming across between "A" dorm and the admin/mess hall at 100 ft. with the pilot waving. An announcement advised all to remain in the dorm area. A French cadet, that had washed-out, snitched a T-6 and was having a great flight buzzing Randolph, Brooks and Kelly. His instructor attempted to intercept and get him back on the ground, but he totally evaded and lost the instructor. When out of fuel, he dove into trees about 50nm northeast of the base. Great flight, bad finish, Vive la France!

A movie was made while we were at Randolph and Williams AFB titled, "Aviation Cadet," with Gail Russell, Steve McNally and Rock Hudson. It opened in Phoenix after our arrival there. All we cadets were bused to the first showing.

At Willie, we went into the T-28 for three months. It was far easier and simpler to fly than the T-6. Nearing the end of the T-28 phase, we were scheduled for a night cross-country. The route was from Williams to Needles, CA, to Gila Bend, AZ and back home; simple enough. A couple of the students had instructors in their backseats to observe us crossing checkpoints. Passing Needles I noticed another bird coming up on my right wing. Between aircraft lights and a slight moon, I discerned it was a buddy in another T-28. Maybe he thought I knew where I was going? Nearing Gila Bend, another aircraft joined on the left wing. I assumed it was another buddy. It was, but he also had an instructor aboard. As "my formation" turned home for Willie, a clear voice came over the air: "AIRCRAFT 654! MAKE A 360!" That was the aircraft on my right wing, a solo student. When we landed, my IP, Capt Snyder, was waiting.

"What have you been up to?"

"Uh, uh, uh..." The whole class was invited to a debriefing, more of an interrogation. After a half hour of stalling, the jig was up, and the two of we "formaters" (and I was damned near innocent) confessed. It was a sleepless night. We figured we would be on our way home the next morning. Strangely nothing happened. I even noticed my instructor smiling. At a graduation student/instructor beer fest an instructor related it was seen as a "positive." I guess they could see aggressiveness rather than stupidity in our demeanor?

Then, came the F-80A and B, after one backseat and one frontseat ride in the T-33. Engine start in the F-80 was a challenge, so it was easy to tell a new guy from the noise on start. On my first F-80 flight at the takeoff position on runway, I ran the engine up and checked the engine gages. My legs were shaking trying to hold the brakes at full power - then - "What am I doing here???" When the gear came up, the whole world came to life just as beautifully descriptive as the poem "High Flight." Nothing could match the fantastic feeling of my first jet solo! The landing pattern was, throttle to idle from pitchout to touch down. Base leg was the last opportunity to make a go-around because of engine lag and the very slow spin-up time.

I lost oil pressure during one four-ship flight over Phoenix, and it created a severe vibration. I retarded the throttle back to 80 percent and headed for Willie with instructor and flight in tow. I flew the "flame out" pattern. The engine unwound to 10 percent. Using speedbrakes and slipping, I made the runway and even had a good touchdown. Mobile yelled that the aircraft was on fire and advised, "Pull the battery disconnect!" Huh? This was only a couple of weeks before graduation, Friday the 13 July 1951. The next day we were scheduled for a cross-country to California, and for fun, they assigned the same bird to me.

We had some great instructors: Junior Snyder (T-6 aerobatics demo pilot), M. Charlson, the famous Bruce Carr and Leon Gray (Group Commander). The big event: Graduation, Pilot Wings, 2nd Lt bars and an evening at the O-Club, all on 4 August 1951! Then, on to Nellis for tactics and gunnery training in the F-80B and C. After a tactical gunnery mission, our flight was jumped by a couple of other flights, which was not unusual. I couldn't convince lead that I was way past "bingo" fuel. So, I took a straight line for Nellis, solo. At 20,000 ft. I discovered I was over a gigantic target type circle. Whoops! Too late to avoid the forbidden gunnery range area, so on to Nellis and a normal pattern. I pulled into the dearming area and flamed out!

I spent a couple of weeks in the Nellis hospital with "mumps." That's another story – terrible – not fun. The pipeline was filling up with F-80 guys as units in Korea picked up F-84s ands F-86s, so most of our class was diverted to Clark P.I. and Naha, Okinawa for two months TDY. The 26th Fighter Squadron was using long-range 265 gal. no-baffle, underslung wing tanks as we sat day air defense alert.

The travel to Okinawa was by ship. It wasn't a bad vessel and we were assigned two guys to a stateroom. Meals were served in a dining room with activities such as cards, Bingo, and dancing. Wives and children were on board along with fifteen WACs and nurses accompanying we thirteen young fighter pilots. A thousand or more enlisted Air Force and Army troops were quartered below decks.

Each of we pilots were assigned duties for the trip. Mine was as "Provost Marshall," and I had no idea what that was. While playing cards and munching canned, fried potatoes, a four year-old looked on, and I offered him a couple. He grabbed two handfuls, stared at me, emptied his right hand and socked me in the eye. It got really black. I guess he had it in for Provost Marshalls? We docked in Honolulu for 36 hours, then on to Naha. A few miles offshore, we were greeted by a couple of F-80s from the 26th TFS. It wasn't a bad trip, but I never had a desire for another long boat ride.

I left Nellis for Suwon, K-13 airfield and was met at the aircraft by Black Matt Matthews, an old friend from Willie. He also led me on my first combat mission in Korea. My dad passed away unexpectedly after I had about 12 missions, and I returned to the States for 30 days. Back at K-13, I flew 100 combat missions, a couple up near the

Yalu River, but most were south of Sinanju, interdiction or close air support. It was not unusual to fly a couple of missions a day. I was once scheduled for five missions to Pyongyang, but we ran low on turn-around aircraft and I only flew three. During a close formation low-altitude 50 ft. pass, a gunner managed to punch 15 holes with .50 cal starting in my left wingtip and a string of holes two-feet aft of my cockpit, out through the tail section. My crew chief was very excited about the bad guys damaging his aircraft. By October 1952, I completed 100 missions and returned to the U.S, at Amarillo AFB Texas assigned to the 1739th Ferry Sq.

I had a couple of flights in a T-bird. Then on the morning of 15 December, I was told to prepare for a checkout in a P-47 that afternoon. My response was that I had never been closer than a mile to one. They said, "Here is a P-47 flight manual, a questionnaire and the answers." Another captain said I had to get some T-6 backseat landings before my P-47 check flight. Between him and me (mostly him) we logged the landings. Now we really had to rush because the two P-47s were scheduled to leave the next morning for Cuba.

My IP showed me the cockpit and helped start the engine (what could possibly go wrong?). We taxied as a two-ship, performed our runup and took the active runway. His canopy wouldn't close, so, back to the ramp we went and I shutdown. Unbeknownst to me, the crew chief moved the "control lock lever" to the "LOCKED" position. The control lock was a complicated mechanism. It was a small lever attached to the aircraft floor on the right side of the stick. When moved "aft" with the stick in the proper position, a metal rod slipped into a hole locking the stick. The rudder lock was similar but would only lock when the rudder was slowly moved through the neutral position. In this case the stick was never locked but the rudder locked when I neutralized the rudder pedals momentarily on takeoff at liftoff.

My IP's canopy finally closed and my crew chief assisted my restart. At take off position I ran up to full power, released brakes, neutralized the rudders and then got the tail up. When I neutralized the rudders, the flight control locking pin engaged, the rudders locked and I was along for the ride. At takeoff speed, I became airborne with a very rapid left drift due to the torque developed by the huge 2800 hp Pratt and Whitney engine. With no rudder control, I applied right aileron to stop the drift causing the aircraft to touch down on the right wheel hard, then a hard left wheel bounce that caused a gear collapse, and the aircraft started a low-angle cartwheel. The prop struck the turf, and the engine separated igniting the fuel system. We (the aircraft parts and me) slid to a stop, and the canopy wouldn't open. With helmet on, I hit the canopy with sufficient force that it cleared the wreck (I was always hard-headed). I jumped out, and one step later was off the tip of what remained of the right wing. I removed my chute and moved to the opposite side and away from the burning aircraft. A number of people from the commercial terminal made it to my position. The fire was raging, and the crash vehicles almost arrived when a couple of civilians asked me if the pilot had gotten out. To which I sheepishly replied, "I don't know. I just got here myself." I suffered no injury but had to spend the night in the hospital. This occurred long before SAC arrived to expand the base and extend the runway. I had always wanted to fly a WW II fighter. I did, but it was a VERY, VERY short flight.

Soon after my P-47 experience, I got an F-84 check out at Dover, then went TDY to Farmingdale-Republic on Long Island delivering new aircraft to the port 10 minutes away and to Warner Robbins AFB, GA. I got lots of flying time in the ferry business. Finally, I was assigned a trip to Europe via the F-84! At Robbins, I was to join jocks from Luke and other bases for the trip. The first I saw was "Black Matt" again. During that period in the ferry outfit, I met Robert Titus and Gary Willard with whom I still stay in touch today, 60 years later.

My "High Flights" in the F-84 and four subsequent F-86 crossings were by the northern route. The ferry route was through Bangor, Maine, Goose Bay, Labrador, BW-1 (Bluie West 1, Narsaruaq, Greenland), Keflavic, Iceland, Prestwick, Scotland, with refueling stops at each base, and on to European destinations. When I think back over those flights: bad winter weather, cold oceans with storms and angry seas below, unreliable navigation aids, no GPS, poor weather forecasts, lousy radios, no long range communications, doubtful air-sea rescue and poor survival equipment, it is a wonder any of us who made the flights are still alive. On only one flight did I have enough fuel to proceed to a weather alternate for BW-1. If the weather was below minimums, our procedure was to cross the radio beacon at a specified altitude, put gear and flaps down in landing configuration, establish 600 fpm rate of descent until "contact with the ice cap." Yeh, sure. A NOTAM on one trip: "Six inches of ice with four inches of snow on runway, iceberg near end of runway." We went. It was only a few days before Christmas.

Shortly after the Europe trip, I was transferred to 1738 Ferry Sq. in Long Beach, CA. Wow! - me a country boy with lots of stories from the California beaches. The Miss Universe Pageant was being held there, and I received an invitation to escort one of the young finalists. I had never seen so many beautiful, elegantly dressed and well-coiffured women from all over the world in one place. I escorted Libby Walker, Miss South Carolina 1953. We stayed in touch for a while, and I was invited to visit her and family.

At Long Beach I checked-out in the F-86 and made four quick trips to Europe; two to Bitburg, then one each to Chaumont and Manston England. The assignment was boring after a while, and someone suggested a school. Without any research, I was on my way to Communications Officer School at Scott AFB. It wasn't all that bad as I met my wife to be there, Honeyjean Roos.

My next stop was Shaw AFB in a Comm. Sq. After a couple of months, the deputy commander, a colonel, called me to his office. He opened the visit with, "The boss is away. I'm an old fighter pilot, retiring very soon, and I know you want to go to a fighter unit. You can go to England AFB (F-84s) or Clovis AFB (F-86Hs)." My choice was Clovis and the 86H!

After a year attached to 386 FBS, I was assigned to 430th FBS which was scheduled for a six-month TDY to Toul-Rosieres AB, France. On Easter Sunday, 1 April 1956 my girlfriend, Honeyjean, and I were married in the Base Chapel at Clovis, Cannon AFB NM. The date was always significant to us because being on "April Fools Day" I frequently kidded Honeyjean that it was all a joke and we weren't really married. I didn't get beat up too bad. It was a traveling marriage with an understanding wife. I checked out in the F-100 led a flight of eight to Europe in 1958 via Harmon direct, with no air refueling, to the Azores, then Europe (all in a six-tank configuration). In 1959, I deployed three times to Europe; twice to Hahn; once to Chaumont and once to Incirlik Turkey in 1960. I became Chief, 474th TFW Stan Eval just prior to the Incirlik trip.

Overseas deployments have become de rigueur. Today we effortlessly move flights of aircraft over oceans to far away places.

Lest anyone think it was always routine, let me describe how it was in the old days; the days before GPS, radar, modern tankers, accurate weather forecasts and long range communications:

On 11 Nov 1959, having returned to Cannon after completion of survival school at Stead, I was scheduled for an early air-to-ground gunnery mission. During the flight briefing we received a phone call recalling the entire squadron for deployment (life in a fighter squadron those days was comprised with a lot of "no-notice" drills). The squadron maintenance troops readied 14 birds, and we departed for Myrtle Beach AFB, SC around noon. Two aircraft required test hops, so a friend and I completed the checks and departed for the Beach arriving late afternoon. We rested overnight and headed for the morning deployment briefing.

I was looking forward to flying my personally assigned aircraft, #563 188, but the flight lineup placed me in an "F" with an unknown name in the backseat. So, after the briefing, I approached the commander and operations officer asking about my passenger. He just said it was an important VIP and to treat him well. My aircraft was number seven in an eight-ship section. I proceeded to the aircraft where the line chief advised me the ship was not ready because of a fuel leak, and it also needed a run up check. I had a Myrtle Beach pilot brief my passenger while I performed the preflight and told the line chief I would do a run up for the leak check. We barely caught the rest of the flight for takeoff. Lead had already rolled, but we rejoined the flight and headed for rendezvous with our KB-50J tankers a couple of hundred nautical miles east of Bermuda.

Tanker rendezvous at the time was conducted thru UHF DF steers from the tanker, plus time and distance computations, an often shaky system. I spotted the tanker cell. There were five tankers, one for each two receivers plus a spare. We moved in to refuel and hung on with partial flaps at 190 knots for almost 200nm, all IFR, guts ball.

We were dropped off in elements, still IFR. Each tanker had a separate refueling frequency, so we dropped off and climbed out in elements until on top. Lead then called for check-in and rejoin and our number two aircraft was missing. I checked with the tankers, and he was still hanging on and was 50 or so miles behind the rest of the flight. Lead asked me to drop back (solo) and retrieve the wayward new guy (yes, with my VIP passenger watching it all). After a few sharp turns and afterburner lights, a shrill voice said, "I see you!" I told my new wingman to rejoin in close formation and stay on my wing. We finally caught the flight near the Azores with my new wingman never more than two feet from my wingtip. After the next refueling came darkness, and then we went into high cirrus, perfect for disorientation. As we approached St. Sebastian radio beacon in Spain, it was impossible to get a good ADF reading (not unusual as both non-directional radio beacons and aircraft equipment were notoriously unreliable). We passed a brief clear area in the clouds, and I saw the coast and advised lead. His reply, "Are you sure?" and we continued inland.

I was running low on fuel. I requested permission to call the tanker that was scheduled to be near Bordeaux, France. They were on station and gave me a UHF DF steer to their position. I relayed the information to lead for a new heading. As we approached the tankers the cirrus cloud level dropped and there were those beautiful KB lights right where they should be. Things were looking good, but not so fast.

Our destination was Chaumont. But, upon contact with my tanker, I requested the Bordeaux weather in case I had to make an emergency divert if unable to air refuel. In 30 seconds his answer, "They are zero-zero with fog and rain." Damn! When it rains it pours. With 800lbs. fuel remaining and a mile behind the tankers my only thoughts were…GAS! Slipping into refueling position, my probe just tipped the basket. Then, I orally repeated the correct steps, and a voice from the rear cockpit assured me, "That's right, son." then CONTACT! and I took on enough gas to get to Chaumont. Number two couldn't get hooked up, so I backed off and slid under him to help if possible. He hooked up and called for a "toboggan" (a slow descent allowing more power for hook up). Now, down we go into IFR. Can it get any harder? Yep.

After refueling, we found the Chaumont weather also crumped, so we dropped off the tankers and headed for Chateauroux Air Base, France, our mission planned alternate. As we approached the fix I planned an ADF penetration and GCA pickup. It was my turn with number two on the wing. We planned a teardrop with GCA contact and a formation landing. Great plan, but then we hear, "Go to your alternate, aircraft in the barrier."

My reply, "Negative, not enough fuel." No response. I switched us to tower frequency. The weather was, "250 – 300 ft. with rain, visibility poor." I told the tower I was continuing my ADF approach with two to land, no reply. Number two hung tight, and we broke out right on centerline. "What!!!" aircraft lights from other end of the runway shining at us. Touchdown! Two good drag chutes. Whew! We taxied-in, and I opened the canopy for my VIP passenger to exit into his staff car. My VIP passenger who had viewed all the weather-induced goat rope was Maj Gen Maurice "Mo'" Preston, DO HQ USAF, who later became four-star General Preston and commander of USAFE. He patted my shoulder and gave a "thumbs up." Well, I guess at least "he" enjoyed the white-knuckle ride. He later sent a letter complimenting me on my "professional conduct of the mission under adverse conditions." He later stopped by Cannon and invited me to join him at the O-Club for dinner.

The aircraft lights on the runway were the flight lead's wingman who went into the runway overrun and was taxing back. After 10:15 airborne, it was time for the bathroom and adult beverages.

Three of our flight diverted, and my personally assigned aircraft #563 188, in which I was originally scheduled, lost the drag chute on the rain slick Chateauroux runway. The fuel tank jettison system failed, thereby preventing barrier engagement with the old web barrier. He continued off the end of the runway into a ditch, collapsed the nose gear and severely bent the intake. One of the KB-50 tankers took off from Chateauroux with only three of four recip engines turning along with his outboard jets in that terrible weather to refuel other aircraft that had no place to land. I can't say enough for tanker crews. Please don't think all overseas deployments in the old days were this bad – some were much worse.

In July 1961, Honeyjean and I were reassigned to the 417th TFS Ramstein Airbase, Germany. Early in 1962, I was selected as aide and pilot for 17th AF commander. I maintained combat ready status with 417th and flew as IP in F-100D and F and also flew the T-39 throughout Western Europe, North Africa and the Mid-East. I visited and associated with staffs and units. I attended commanders' briefings and visited "the cave" (Command Post). On one trip, I visited RAF Wattisham, and they gave me a ride in an RAF Lightning. It had great performance but some unique engineering quirks. In 1964, we returned to Maxwell AFB for Air Command and Staff College. I met some great seminar friends and classmates that made the year less painful. Two moved on to four stars, one being Jerry O'Malley.

After ACSC, it was on to 19th Air Force as Fighter Plans Officer. I made a deployment to Norway with an F-4 squadron from MacDill and operated the Command Post near a ski resort close to Oslo. While on duty there, a Norwegian Lt Col tapped me on the shoulder and said "the King" wanted to meet me. "What?" I wondered what I had done wrong. King Olav V was a real gentleman, and we talked for a few minutes. I have no idea why he wanted to speak with me but not many fighter pilots have rapped with a king.

I was then sent to Research Analysis Corp. for four months to represent the USAF in a "Controlled Fragmentation Munition" (COFRAM) study of a new munition. The munition was being developed for use in "Igloo White," a Top Secret operation along the Ho Chi Minh Trail. My suggestions were not incorporated. After that, came the journey to Davis-Monthan for an F-4 checkout prior to leaving for Vietnam. Then, it was off to Da Nang, and after getting settled, Lt Col Robert Titus offered me an Ops Officer job. Just a couple of days later, I was notified of orders to 7th AF. Damn! I traveled down to 7th and was told, "We selected you for this." After much complaining, I was promised 7th would release me back to Da Nang for my Ops Officer slot in three months after project completion (it was the damned "COFRAM" project that had rejected my suggestions). I returned to the States for two weeks TDY at Elgin and met some other folks, including Brig Gen William P. McBride, scheduled to command a new Top Secret facility at Nakhon Phanom, Thailand.

Back at 7th AF, my next problem surfaced as my host boss departed without notice, and I was stranded. His promise to return me to Da Nang was forgotten and suddenly a gall bladder operation, old style that sliced down my belly with a three-month non-flying recovery made my return to Da Nang out of the question.

Then, came" Tet!" I lived off-base in Saigon by myself and was awakened early in the morning by rapid gunfire on 30 January 1968. I opened the drapes and saw a C-47 flare ship and helicopter nearly overhead with tracers from the ground streaking up at them. This, the first Battle of Saigon, was a ferocious attack. The NVA and Vietcong launched a nationwide series of attacks. Thirty-five battalions of

Vietcong in Saigon were attacking the ARVN headquarters, the Presidential Palace, the U.S. Embassy, the National Radio Station, Tan Son Nhut Airbase, Long Binh Naval Headquarters and several other selected targets. Meanwhile, across the country other NVA and Vietcong units attacked other airbases, cities and provincial capitals. The whole country was on fire, and it seemed like it was all taking place right outside my window. I had a front row seat on history.

Firefights erupted nearby and I was HELPLESS - no gun, and I couldn't find my survival knife, so I waited for daylight. Freshly-shaved (a soldier doesn't want to die looking bad), I headed for my motor scooter. My landlady came out yelling, "NO GO! VC ALL AROUND! COME ON ROOF AND YOU CAN SEE!" On the roof I ran into an old friend, Col Speed Keller, plus another Air Force guy, and they had four weapons. Bullets were flying all around and we could see a G.I. throwing grenades over a roof peak half a block away. The other Air Force guy had a jeep, and I finally convinced him we should race for the base about one and one-half miles away. We passed some military barracks that had been blasted by anti-tank rockets and made it to the Tan Son Nhut base gate looking at a tank pointed right at us. No vehicles were allowed because they might be caught in the line of fire, so we had to walk. I slept on my desk for a week. One of my captains was due to rotate out the next day and was trapped off-base. Cecil Calhoun and I borrowed Gen Jonsey Bolt's jeep, brought an M-16 along with our newly-issued .38 revolvers and proceeded off-base to pick up my captain and two other guys. I was really scared after someone told me we had driven right through the worst of the bad guy areas. We also took a speedy route to my quarters for some clean clothes. There was so much confusion, no one knew who was shooting who, or why. There was gunfire everywhere. Over Tet many bad guys tried to get through the base barbed wire defenses and paid the price, when AC-47 gunships provided constant night coverage. It was quite a sight from the O-Club deck for several days.

Then, came Khe Sanh. The isolated Marine outpost in northern Quang Tri province was essentially surrounded and isolated by elements of at least three NVA divisions. The North Vietnamese wanted to turn Khe Sanh into another Dien Bien Phu, while Gen Westmoreland wanted to hold it at ALL COSTS. The only way in and out for resupply was by air and the main defense was airstrikes by Air

Force, Marine and Navy fighters and B-52s launched from Guam. I was tasked to put together an Air Ops plan for Khe Sanh defense. It took a solid two days and nights of hard work, but the plan passed by all the stars with little change. Gen Bolt and I flew to Da Nang to brief the Marine Commanding General, who hadn't been adequately briefed on the number of NVA troops, artillery and tanks coming into the South and headed for his hill. The plan was simple: keep all kinds of aircraft, bombers, fighters, recce, FACs, airlift on alert and ready to strike in an instant. It was a very flexible and responsive plan that paid good dividends to those on the hill. Khe Sanh was finally ordered abandoned by Gen Creighton Abrams, the new commander in Vietnam, in July 1968 as Tet wound down.

I had been promised to return to Davis-Monthan upon my return from SEA. It was not to be. My orders didn't even get me to CONUS. HQ PACAF at Hickam was to be my home for four years. I was assigned to Ops Requirements in the Fighter/Weapons division. I traveled to the east coast almost monthly with fast turnarounds. I had great bosses, Col Bill Colgan, Gen Moose Hardin and Boots Blesse. After PACAF, I PCSed to 9th AF at Shaw AFB in Ops Plans.

From Shaw I was sent once more back to SEA and 7th Air Force as Tactical Air Command's Liaison Officer. Yep, it was back to Tan Son Nhut and more inbound rocket attacks. While attending an evening ops briefing for Maj Gen Carlos Talbot, a high priority TWX was delivered saying, "GO GET 'EM!" and the 1972 December bombing air campaign against North Vietnam, "Linebacker II," was underway. The campaign led to the signing of the Vietnam Peace Accords and the return of our POWs in early 1973. I returned to 9th AF and Shaw AFB in March 1973 and worked with more outstanding bosses including Hoot Gibson and Maj Gen Levi Chase.

We retried to Merritt Island FL in 1979 with the prospect of purchasing an airport fixed based operation. Thank goodness that didn't work out, so we headed for Tucson. My wife, Honeyjean, was especially pleased. I went into real estate, first as an agent, then as a broker. I dabbled in property investment with my old friend and former Thunderbird leader, Hoot Gibson. I also dabbled in the restaurant, deli and catering business.

My wonderful wife, Honeyjean Roos, was born 30 April 1930 in Abington and grew up in Collegeville, PA. She was a beautiful woman and a model at Stix, Bayer and Fuller in St. Louis when we met. She was also an excellent steno, typist, receptionist and a professional interior decorator. She was a volunteer dental technician at Hickam, but first and always, a loving wife and mother. I drug her all over the world, some of it smiling, some crying. It was a tough but wonderful life. Our daughter, Cricket, was born in Tucson in 1968. She was adopted and came to our home 32 hours after birth and has been loved and brought joy ever since.

In 1999, Honeyjean developed a serious medical problem, a brain tumor. After an operation, she faced a tough rehabilitation. At first there was only eye movement, followed by almost total recovery with my constant encouragement; then, the disheartening discovery that the untreatable condition had returned. The most difficult time in my life was caring for her during her last months. After 46 years together, I lost my one and only in 2002.

During this time, our daughter had a serious back injury leaving her with a permanent disability. It was a difficult time, and I learned the importance of good friends. Friends were always there for me, especially my best friend, Hoot Gibson until his untimely passing from a fall while showing a real estate property.

Just three months prior to Honeyjean's passing, Cricket and her husband, Raymond, gave us our only grandchild, Sebastian, also born in Tucson. Sebastian spends Saturday nights with me and is a great traveling companion. A month ago we drove 3500 miles together, talking all the way through Arizona, New Mexico, Texas, Arkansas and Louisiana. On the return home, as we approached San Antonio, I elected to take the bypass that runs next to Randolph AFB. We entered the base and I was able to find my old cadet quarters, even my old room. Sebastian was impressed. Then, we proceeded to Randolph's bas centerpiece, the "Taj Mahal" tower. The sight of it is still special to me.

Korea was my first war, Vietnam my last. My career was not typical, but eclectic, exciting and rewarding. I traveled the world, flew great airplanes maintained by wonderful people, lived in exciting places and made lifelong friends. I came a long way from Chatham, Louisiana retiring as a colonel in 1979. I never served a day in the Pentagon. Between a rewarding career and a wonderful wife, daughter and grandson, I lived my dreams.

CHAPTER FOUR

Sandy

by Lewis S. "Lew" Daugherty

My dad was a dairy farmer in upstate New York. We did all our field work with horses. Dad didn't buy a tractor until I was in high school. In 1943 or '44, I was plowing with a team of horses on a blustery November day when a DC-3 passed overhead. I was sick and tired of getting up at 5:00 AM to milk cows and thought to myself that flying would be a beautiful way to make a living. As it turned out, when I got to be a fighter pilot, I was frequently up at 4:00 AM to make a 6:00 AM mission.

On VJ day 14 August 1945, I had a birthday party and was taking my buddies on a hayride. Everyone in town was singing. Cars flew by honking horns to celebrate the end of World War II. I had a heck of a time holding the horses in check.

Cornell University is the land grant college of New York State. I entered the Agricultural College in 1948. While a student, I had a job on a horse farm near Ithaca and earned room and board. There were still some returning WW II veterans that made tough competition in class work.

After graduating from Cornell in 1952 and getting an ROTC Commission, I entered active duty in the Air Force as a 2nd Lieutenant. I was unable to pass a flying physical due to a slightly disabled left arm (result of a farm accident) and was assigned as a maintenance officer. I was sent to the Aircraft Officer's Maintenance Course at Chanute AFB. While attending the school, I met Caryl in nearby Champaign, Illinois. We married when I completed the maintenance officer training. My next assignment was the B-36 Wing at Biggs AFB, El Paso, TX where I was a flunky for the Chief of Maintenance. In 1954, my two-year active duty commitment was nearing completion. I took a last ditch flying physical. I passed (via devious means). There were several of us taking the physical that day and I maneuvered to a place at the end of the line. When we went thru for vitals, I put my skivvy shirt over my left arm to hide the scars and had blood pressure taken from my right arm. No medic or physician detected my disability, and I passed the flight physical. During primary at Marana and basic at Laredo, I had numerous physicals and no one ever looked at my left arm AND no one ever reviewed my medical records to see the first physical record at the bottom that detailed the limitation of my left arm. I received my wings in December 1955 as an Air Force Pilot. They retained a couple of us at Laredo as basic instructors in the T-33. Allegedly, returning Korean veterans were teaching "bad habits." We new pilots had no "bad habits." After Instructor Pilot training at Craig AFB, I returned to Laredo as an instructor. While instructing students, I became acquainted with our flight surgeon. When I applied for a regular commission, he gave me the physical exam. I came clean and showed him my scarred arm. He just shook his head in a quandary. He delved back through all my physical records and found the first that described my injury in detail. Since I had over a thousand hours and no problems controlling a T-33, he passed me and I became a regular officer in the Air Force.

In 1957 Air Force policy changed requiring those getting pilot training to agree to a five-year service commitment. Almost immediately, numerous student pilots departed and there were more Instructor Pilots than students at Laredo. Someone picked up my service as a maintenance officer and I became a flightline maintenance officer with 50-some T-33 aircraft on the flightline. In 1959, I went to Wethersfield, England and was assigned as the maintenance officer for the 55ᵗʰ Fighter Squadron of the 20ᵗʰ Fighter Wing. Lt Col "Red" Stewart wanted ALL his pilots to be bomb commanders (including his maintenance officer). I had an "In-Theater" checkout in the F-100 at Wethersfield. On my first ride in the F-100F, my instructor, Bill Gillette, said we had to burn some fuel before we could shoot landings. When he asked if I had ever seen the White Cliffs of Dover, I had to say, "No." I still haven't seen the cliffs. Bill was flying from the back seat and he was so close to the water that I could see spray from the jet's exhaust in my mirror. I just looked straight ahead with my hand hovering around the stick

I had gunnery training at Wheelus Air Base in Tripoli, Libya. All fighter squadrons in Europe went TDY to Wheelus for gunnery at El Uotia range. Speedy Pete Everest was the commander of the training detachment at Wheelus. The 20th Wing Commander, Jay Robbins, called him the "range officer." Everest didn't appreciate the title. Training consisted of strafe, skip bomb, dive bomb and nuclear deliveries, both LABS (over the shoulder) and dive. For whatever reason, there was a requirement for a dive bomb nuclear delivery. The tactic was to roll in at 35,000 feet and release at 18-20 thousand. The first time I made this maneuver, I forgot to come out of afterburner and was supersonic at release. Who knows where the practice blue bomb went? I do know that the sonic boom woke the range officer.

Throughout my tour at Wethersfield, I worked as a maintenance officer and flew the Super Sabre, gunnery with the 55th squadron and test flights for the Wing. Subsequent to the overseas tour in 1962, I was assigned to TAC HQ as a staff maintenance officer. Also, I was a T-33 instructor at Langley base flight. In 1964, the word was out that volunteers for the A-1 Skyraider in Vietnam would get choice of base upon return. I volunteered. After jungle survival in Panama, water survival at Homestead AFB and escape and evasion survival at Stead AFB, I checked out in the A-1 Skyraider at Hurlburt in May 1965. This was my first experience with a tail-dragger and a round engine. Before takeoff we rolled in right rudder trim to compensate for the engine torque when full throttle is applied to the big 3350 Wright Engine. Then, when the throttle is pulled back on base and final, left rudder trim is cranked in. On an early touch-and-go landing I forgot to take out that trim prior to pushing up to full throttle for takeoff. The big mother veered left until I got the right rudder all the way to the firewall. I can still hear the Instructor screaming obscenities in my ear. We never made any take off with a heavy load during check out, but the Instructor advised that when going with a full load it expedited lift off if you picked-up the tail to streamline the airplane. The first time I took off with a full bomb load in Vietnam, I remembered to "pick-up" the tail. When I landed, I found that I had curled the tips of all four propeller blades. Obviously, I had overdone the streamlining.

I arrived at Bien Hoa AB, Vietnam in June 1965. During weekdays, we instructed Vietnamese pilots in gunnery in the A-1. Nights and Sundays we flew close air support and interdiction as needed in the Mekong Delta. In August 1965, I took my flight and six airplanes to Udorn, Thailand for two weeks and initiated the SANDY mission recovering downed aircrews. The Navy had started using the AD

(Navy designation for the Skyraider) for finding downed aircrews and covering their pickup by choppers. There were few facilities at Udorn, and we stayed in a hotel downtown. Interestingly, the hotel had insulated, sealed windows to facilitate air conditioning; however the air conditioning was inoperative. Hot! Hot! in August. On my return to Bien Hoa, the Vietnamese training had moved to the States and the 602nd Fighter Squadron moved to Nha Trang and eventually to Udorn. Until we moved PCS to Udorn, we always had an alert flight stationed there covering the SANDY mission. Also, throughout the latter part of 1965, we kept a detachment at Qui Nhon.

Dafford "JUMP" Myers was the detachment commander at Qui Nhon. He had been in the class ahead of me at Hurlburt. He had completed the checkout in the Skyraider and was soon to be off to SEA. I bought an old station wagon from him in order to have wheels for the 60 days at Hurlburt. I later sold it for the same price I paid. I was frequently with him at Qui Nhon. When Jump Myers had to belly his A-1 on a PSP strip after taking a hit while defending a Green Beret outpost in the A Shau Valley, Bernie Fisher landed and picked Jump up. Bernie was awarded a Congressional Medal Of Honor for this heroic act. Later, after Jump resumed command of the Qui Nhon detachment, he and Big Daddy Billingham were in the Qui Nhon MACV club bar with a couple nurses. When the bar closed at 2200, they had several drinks lined-up. Apparently, the MACV commander observed the frivolity at the bar and closed the compound. When Jump and cohorts tried to leave the compound in his Scout, the sentry had a concertina wire barricade across the exit. Jump said, "We're just going around the perimeter road to our villa, so please open the gate." When the sentry refused several pleas, Jump crashed through the concertina wire. In June 1966 when I was at Than Son Nhut overnight awaiting departure from Vietnam, my roommate in the quarters was Jump Myers. He was awaiting a Court Martial. I later learned that he took an Article 15 and was fined a month's pay. Rescues in North Vietnam were a dicey business. The SANDY tactic was for four airplanes to orbit over the JOLLY GREEN choppers while they refueled at Lima Site 36, a remote CIA-maintained site that "did not exist" in northern Laos near the North Vietnamese border. We stayed overhead while strike missions were underway in the North. When aircraft went down, we were flushed to find downed aircrews. Typically, a wingman would vector two Sandys to the vicinity where a bailout had occurred. The lead Sandy became the "on-scene commander" and assumed control once contact was made with the downed pilot. When the aircrew on the ground was spotted and the nearby area sanitized, the other two Sandys escorted two JOLLY GREEN choppers to make the pickup. Frequently, the mission didn't follow the planned tactic and we encountered resistance; however, we saved a lot of airmen. Once in early 1966, we were escorting the Jolly Greens out of North Vietnam after a successful pickup, when the chopper pilot called (I should say SCREAMED), "MiG!" I was about a mile off his left and spotted the MiG overshoot the formation. We jettisoned the centerline tank and charged the 20 mm cannons but never saw the MiG make another pass, and we called for fighters. The choppers went into the undercast. Apparently, there had been a delay in the F-4s coming off the tanker, and there was a lapse in top cover. I remember we were damned near killed when the fighters overhead jettisoned their fuel tanks. Squadron aircrews not scheduled for the Sandy mission flew attack and/or interdiction missions in Laos or north of Mu Gia Pass where NVA infiltration was taking place. Later in 1966 we had some missions as Forward Air Controllers (FACs) against fragged targets in the southern part of North Vietnam and in Laos.

One day, I was checking-out Lew Smith as flight lead on a FAC mission north of Mu Gia Pass. En route to the target area we spotted a derelict truck near the top of a hill in Laos. On completion of the FAC mission I asked Smitty, who was in the lead, "Shall we go get that truck?" When he spotted it thru scattered clouds, he rolled-in to drop a bomb. At the time there was a shortage of ordnance at Udorn. He was carrying 260-pound frag bombs in addition to white phosphorous rockets, for marking targets, and I was carrying 5-inch rockets inherited from Navy stores. I went down thru a hole in the clouds and missed the truck by a truck length. Smitty was coming down for a second pass as I climbed out. As I jinked-up thru the scattered clouds. Smitty called, "I'm hit, boss - I gotta' get out, the cockpit is filling with smoke!" When I dove down below the clouds, I spotted his aircraft crash and saw him in his chute just before he went into the trees. I called for choppers and strafed where troops were approaching, coming up a path. In less than thirty minutes, a

Jolly Green arrived from Nakhon Phanom and lifted Smitty out of the weeds. The Sandys and I escorted the choppers back to NKP. He debriefed with Intelligence. We had a beer, refueled my Skyraider and I took Lew Smith back to home base at Udorn. The derelict truck was obviously set up as a trap. My Stupid!

In 1966, it seemed that half the Air Force was in SEA. I was concerned that the "choice of assignment" promise was at risk. I called Dudley Foster at Randolph. He and I had been in the same sewing circle at Squadron Officer School. He said he would take care of me and he did. When I returned to my wife and three girls in Tucson in 1966, I couldn't get a direct flight to Tucson, so I called Caryl to fly to Phoenix where we would meet and drive to Tucson together. Caryl flew to Sky Harbor on a commuter, Apache Airlines. Her pilot didn't put the gear down and landed wheels-up closing the runway. My flight from San Francisco had to circle for over an hour until the runway was cleared. I had flown a year in Vietnam without mishap, and Caryl crashed.

After a TDY at the Armed Forces Staff College, I reported-in to the Deputy for Operations at DMAFB, Chappie James. He shook his head. He needed returning F-4 veterans as Instructor Pilots, and I had lost jet currency. He was tasked to train eight RAF pilots, since the Brits were buying the F-4. I entered the training program tailored for these pilots. Sixty days later, I was an Instructor in F-4 Combat Crew Training at Davis-Monthan AFB. I worked my way up to Operations Officer of the F-4 Instructor Training squadron; best assignment ever – gunnery missions to Gila Bend Range on weekdays and every weekend off. My next assignment (great assignment) was as commander of the 307th Fighter Squadron in the 401st Fighter Wing at Torrejon AB in Spain. Caryl and I took our three girls over in December 1969. In January 1970, I returned to the States to pick up the first F-4E for Europe. The 307th achieved OR status and commenced nuclear alert at Incirlik AB in Turkey. The USAF could not have nukes in Spain, and no USAF units were allowed to be permanently stationed in Turkey. So, once the two sister squadrons at Torrejon achieved OR status, each squadron in the Wing pulled a one-month nuclear alert at Incirlik and two-months home station at Torrejon. In 1971, I was promoted out of my job and reassigned to USAFE Headquarters as War Plans Officer in OPS. I elected to retire from the USAF in 1972.

My early retirement was ill-conceived. I bounced around Tucson for several months. When I checked out with the Davis-Monthan Aero Club, my instructor was J. D. Brown. I had known him when he was squadron commander of a sister squadron conducting F-4 Combat Crew Training at Davis-Monthan. He left the Aero Club and started flying for Cochise Airlines, an Arizona commuter line. Soon thereafter, he called to ask if I wanted to fly for Cochise. I was checked out in the Cessna 402 by the Operations Officer, Jerry Brannon. Ten days later I was an airline captain. Cochise covered all communities in Arizona, plus Las Vegas. Many passengers were soldiers with their families at Fort Huachuca. Many were tourists going to the Grand Canyon. I recall once when I entered downwind west of Tucson International Airport, the tower called and said I was cleared to land on the east-west cross runway. I put the 402 in a falling leaf, dropped the gear and flaps and landed. Troop passengers from Sierra Vista sucked-in their breath but nobody got sick. We flew a lot of hours for very little pay. J.D. stayed with Cochise, but after a couple years I decided to do something else.

I checked-out in a Piper Pawnee and started spraying pesticides on cotton in the Eloy, Arizona area. Early in my tour working for Finis Booker, I was flying across a field when I spotted Finis in his pickup speeding down a parallel farm road waving directions. While trying to interpret his instructions I flew through a power line that crossed the field to a pump. Finis found an APS crew working in the neighborhood, bought them a case of beer and they repaired the power line to the pump. We taped a small tear in the wing and I was off to the next field.

My next fiasco was running out of gas: The fuel indicator for the Pawnee was a cork bobbing in front of the windscreen. I wanted to make one more pass and obviously overlooked that the cork had quit bobbing. I was halfway across the field when the engine quit. I pulled up over some wires and sat it down on a parallel county road. I couldn't get stopped before an intersection and my right wing clipped a stop sign. We couldn't fix that damage with tape.

The next year I went to work for Ed Thomason in Eloy. I was the number three man behind a couple of gents that had sprayed cotton since World War II. Slim didn't have a tooth in his head, but I have seen him eat a steak. He could make a turn at the end of a field at minimum altitude. A couple times I was teamed up with him. I'd get as close to him as I dared on the first pass across a field. He'd turn so low, practically dragging a wing, while I got a "little" altitude for the 180-degree turn. After two or three turns, he would be right behind me. When we landed to refill the tank, Slim would slap his shirt pocket and say, "I left my cigarettes in the car," and go to his Mustang. He would slug down a couple fingers of vodka and light a cigarette and then jump back in his airplane.

The two "big kids" would get the fields with a mile and a half run. I'd get the smaller fields with wires on three sides. We sprayed mostly at night, commencing at 2:00-3:00 AM so as to be finished before the temperature hit triple digits. Supposedly, there was an "inversion" at night and the pesticides better-enveloped the cotton plants. We always studied the fields in daylight and knew where the wires were. The "'flaggers" used flashlights to guide us. This was long before GPS.

In 1977, I went to the University of Arizona and earned a Master's Degree in Agricultural Economics. After I completed the course, the Department Head hired me as a research assistant.

The land grant colleges in each state are tasked to provide data on commodities produced and the costs of production for those grown in that state. My primary job at the U of A was to develop costs of production for commodities produced in Arizona counties. Crops included cotton, wheat, alfalfa, citrus and vegetables. I toured the state talking to growers to identify equipment used in production and to get a typical sequence of the operations and seed, fertilizer and other inputs required. Then, I surveyed vendors to get typical prices for the inputs. My predecessor had developed a primitive computer program that I used to develop a budget for each commodity grown in each county. The budgets depicted the sequence of typical field operations, and the inputs used by most growers. The bottom line was the cost of producing an acre of the commodity.

In addition, I taught a farm management course each fall for freshmen and sophomores. This course taught records-keeping, financial management, business analysis and related subjects.

I retired from the Agricultural Economics department at the University of Arizona in 1997 to enjoy family. Caryl and I recently celebrated our 60th wedding anniversary. We have three daughters, 11 grandchildren and 10 great grandchildren.

Life is good, VERY good.

CHAPTER FIVE

The Zipper - Upside Down Is Better

by Robert K. "Bob" Dundas

My interest in flying started at age 14 or 15. A man was installing linoleum in our kitchen at Great Falls Montana. When he mentioned that he had a Curtiss Robin airplane at the city airport, my curiosity got the best of me! Being young and pugnacious, I asked if he would give me a ride. He agreed, if my mother would bring me to the airport that weekend. She agreed. I was "hooked!!"

In the 1940s, the USA was giving Russia a lot of combat aircraft. Since Malstrom AFB was under construction at Great Falls, the city airport was used as a refueling stop on the way to Alaska and then to Russia. I must have seen 500 to 1000 P-39s in those years. Also, we saw many P-40s and B-25s. Occasionally, the city would get buzzed, and that was great. The city airport (called Gore Hill) had a good drainage system. The concrete piping was large enough for small kids to get into the airport without a problem. I remember one windy day a tied down P-38 nearly got airborne with the wind gusts.

When in college at Montana State University in Bozeman, I enrolled in AFROTC, and with that came ROTC Summer Camp at McCord AFB Washington. I lucked-out and got to fly the rear seat of an F-94C. The pilot was a real "wimp!" When I asked him to do a roll, he refused. The best he would do was a 30-degree banked turn. Needless to say, I was extremely disappointed!

While attending college, I met and married Jean, a fellow classmate, in September of 1951. By the time we graduated, we were the parents of one daughter, Sheryl Anne, with another on the way. I was assigned to Marana Air Base west of Tucson AZ, as a 2nd Lt to begin my pilot training (January 1954).

We started in the PA-18, a small Piper aircraft, learning how to take-off and land, spin the bird, etc. Next, came the T-6. We flew about 20 hours in the PA-18 and 150 hours in the T-6 (class of 55-G). Then, it was off to Williams AFB. At Willy we flew the T-28 and

T-33. What a great time we had with our first jet. Next, I was assigned to Nellis AFB near Las Vegas, NV. Most of our instructors had just returned from Korea and were really wild compared to our civilian instructors. The F-86 was really easy to fly and they taught us "air-to-air" combat over the "green spot," an area close to Nellis. If you showed up there, it was assumed you wanted to hassle.

The next assignment was Korea for a year. We were allowed a 30-day leave, so Jean, Sheryl, Mary (Mary was born in Tucson) and I were off to Montana for R & R. Really it was I & I ("intoxication & intercourse" for those not in the know). Jean taught home economics and science at West Side Jr. High while I was gone. My mother let us know immediately that she would not be available to be a full-time baby sitter; bless her heart for being honest. With two such adorable (?) children, we had no problem finding a nearby neighbor who was looking for extra work, and who loved children. Jean drove them to her house every school morning, which was no big deal, except when the streets were icy.

Our squadron commander was Lt Col Bud Anderson, who looked as young as the rest of us. Bud was an "Ace" with 16 kills during WWII in his P-51, and what a pilot he was. I recall doing barrel rolls in finger-tip formation at 15,000' in high cirrus clouds. If you fell out of formation you were the bad guy. He really taught us how to fly.

During this time, the squadron went to Taiwan to pull alert with the Chinese, who were flying straight-winged F-84s. We ate lunch together and it was amazing how fast the Chinese could inhale that rice with chop sticks. Bud decided we should check out the Sixth Fleet, so every F-86 was loaded with rolls of toilet paper in the speedbrake wells. All of that TP was left on the deck of a Navy carrier (I can't remember the name of the carrier). As far as I know Bud never got in trouble over that incident. Ah, fond memories of those days.

The Chinese threw a party for us. There were about 10 courses to the meal and after each course, was a toast. It was not too long before we were all drunk! Several weeks later we hosted them, and the drink of the day was the martini. Our NCOs were the bartenders. We drank water and the Chinese got the real martinis, so we had to carry them home (now, that's how to get even). That year in Korea was really fun. The war was over, but every so often "Bed-Check

Charlie" would fly down from the north and we would be scrambled. As soon as the North Koreans saw us on their radar, Charlie would head back north.

In 1956, I was assigned to George AFB, CA. The first three years we flew F-100Cs. We were all "Green Card" (instrument rated) pilots, but the weather at George was always good. We never flew in bad weather until 12 of us were picked to ferry F-100Ds to France.

On the American Airlines flight to the east coast they seated us in an area where two cases of beer were stored. By the time we got to the coast, all the beer was gone. You can't trust those young fighter pilots.

As I recall we each got two flights in the D-model to get used to the flaps. We departed for Harman AFB Newfoundland the next day, and were we ever surprised. We were past the "point of no return," when we got word that Harman was socked-in. They called the weather, 100-foot ceiling with a half-mile visibility. Larry Brehm was on my wing. I did not see the runway until Larry said, "Lead, chop it, we are over the runway." All 12 of us made a safe landing, so it was off to the club for a few drinks.

The next three years flying the F-104C were even more exciting. I had two four-month rotations to Moron Air Base Spain, near Seville in the southern part of the country. We refueled from KB-50s in those days. On one rotation Col "Rudders" Rudell, the wing commander led a gaggle of 16 (we called him Rudders because, when he got excited, he kicked the rudders). The weather was forecast wrong, and it appeared we would not make the rendezvous. Rudell called Ocean Station Echo and asked if they could call the KBs to head our way. The lead of the 50s had a loud southern drawl. As they picked us up on their radar, he said, "Come on down here boys, we have what you need." There were four 50s and each could refuel three birds at a time. No one missed the hook-up, as the alternative was to go for a swim in the ocean. We arrived safely at Lajes Field, Azores before heading to Spain.

The four months in Spain were lots of fun as TAC headquarters was far way, and we were free spirits. Every 104 on the line could go Mach 2, and our radar site guys wanted us to see how fast the 104 would really go. I took one to 2.4 mach on one of my runs. The J-79 engine in the 104 had a tendency to stall occasionally. I was on Max Jesperson's wing on takeoff. When he nodded to come out of burner, my engine stalled. At that time, the procedure to restart the engine had about eight steps, I went through as many steps as I could with no luck. I punched-out at 1,000 ft. in a downward ejection seat, made one swing and hit the ground. A Spanish guy with a small donkey walked up and asked if I had a cigarette. I still smoked at that time, so we lit up and watched the 104 burn. The 104s were being modified to an up ejection seat. I was the last guy to punch-out in a down configuration. I don't recommend it.

A week later, I was pulling alert with George Ziegelhoffer, when we were scrambled after a target that was at 65,000 ft.. The radar on the 104 was worthless, but the target was pulling a small contrail. That was the only way we could keep it in sight. We got behind it by about 30 miles, got our speed up to 1.8 mach, and went for it. George didn't come up there with me, but as I went by the B-57D it appeared to be going backward. My mach was still high and the 104 became difficult to handle at that altitude. I finally rolled it over and split–Sed down to 35,000 ft. and joined up with George. We were not wearing pressure suits, so I would probably have died if the canopy had blown.

Our third daughter, Roberta, was born at George AFB in April 1960.

The next four years were really great flying the F-105 at Spangdahlem Air Base Germany. The 49th Tactical Fighter Wing was composed of three squadrons, the 7th, 8th and 9th. During the Vietnam War years, two of the Thud drivers from the 49th wing were awarded the Medal of Honor; Merlyn Dethlefsen, 10 March 1967 and Leo Thorsness, 19 April 1967.

In 1962, the Russians brought missiles into Cuba; JFK was President. I was on nuclear alert, and we were listening to Kennedy's speech. It sounded like we might go to war. We were playing Bridge in the ready room, so I got up, put on my G-suit, strapped-on my .38 and went to my aircraft, so I could be the first one airborne. That was one disaster that, thank God, never happened.

The four years in Germany were wonderful. We did a lot of gunnery at Wheelus Air Base, Libya. Socially at Spang, the Officers Club was active, food was good and off-base the small towns had good restaurants. Both of our parents visited us in 1965. My mother took the older girls on trips she had planned to Oslo, Norway and Rome, Italy. The time in Europe was quite a learning experience for the family. We were only an hour from Luxembourg City and they had a very good movie theatre. I remember seeing *The Sound of Music* there.

For our country, the four years 1962 to 1966 were very active. Eisenhower was President in 1962, Kennedy was assassinated in November 1963, and LBJ became President. In 1965 things became active in Vietnam and it appeared the F-105 would be used as the prominent air-to-ground fighter.

I got orders for my next assignment to Korat Air Base, Thailand in May 1966. From July to December 1966 the flying schedule was heavy and many of us finished our 100 missions in about six months. North Vietnam was very well defended with SAMs, MiGs and AAA. Bob Brinkman was one of the best Wild Weasel pilots in the wing. I remember one mission in particular. We refueled over the water and entered North Vietnam south of Haiphong looking for SAM sites. We got a launch and headed for the deck. I ended up in trail at about 500 ft.. The first missile was high and between us. The next one had my name on it. When I finally saw the missile, it was to my left, I pulled up hard and the missile blew just past me. Not one hole in my bird, perfect timing, thank God.

The 421st TFS was my squadron and in November 1966, Hollywood guys showed up to film us. It turned out to be a pretty good title, "THERE IS A WAY." That title reflects what we as pilots said to each other whenever we had a hard mission coming up. We would kiddingly say, "THERE AIN'T NO WAY."

On 4 December 1966, I led 12 aircraft to hit JCS-19, which (to the best of my knowledge) had never been hit. JCS-19 was the main rail yard in the northeast part of Hanoi. This was my 96th mission over the North and we all made it back to Korat. Four more easy missions to 100, and it would be time to go home.

I was a major at that time. After Vietnam, quite a few of us were assigned to the Pentagon. At "Studies and Analyses," I was selected to be on a special study held at the Arba Vita study facility in Los Angeles CA, close to LAX. Gen Bill Chairsell led the study, but Lt Col Jasper Welch ran the place. Welch was a PHD with connections to most of the defense contractors in the country. The only active duty Air Force guys were Chairsell, Welch, and myself. The rest were PhDs with defense connections. Every morning when I came to work, I would kiddingly ask our cute secretary if the White House had called for me. A week or so later a Col at the White House called to let me know that LBJ would be presenting Merl Dethlefsen the Medal of Honor and asked if I could attend. Most people think that LBJ was a huge man. I was six-feet at that time and about half an inch taller than LBJ. I have a picture to prove it.

On our way to Washington D.C. for Merl's ceremony, Jimmy Stewart happened to be on the same flight. Since I was in uniform I went up to him, saluted, and said, "How you doing, General?" Stewart was a Air Force Reserve Brigadier General. He was met by his wife and two daughters at Dulles, as my wife met me. They were very friendly. We must have spent five minutes in the terminal chatting. The Stewarts were heading to Quantico where his son was an active duty Marine.

After several years at the Pentagon, I volunteered for a second combat tour. In Tuy Hoa, Vietnam I was a F-100 squadron commander for the year and got 200 more combat sorties. I now had 300 combat missions, five Distinguished Flying Crosses and 23 Air Medals. I retired a few years later with 20 years of service. I am 83 years old now and think of my 20 in the USAF as the best part of my life!

Chapter Six

From First Crash to the Thunderbirds

by William J. "Bill" Hosmer

I was raised in a small town in North Dakota. The population was about 700. It was a rural community just 13 miles south of the Canadian border, midway between Montana and Minnesota. Life was simple, growing up there in Dunseith. I was the oldest of three brothers. My Dad was a rural mail carrier, and my mother was a nurse employed in a nearby hospital. They eloped in 1929 with another couple in a car borrowed from another couple who were secretly married because the woman could not reveal her marriage. In those days female schoolteachers had to be single. It was a weird state law.

I was born in 1930, went to school my first seven grades and then for the first time, left home to live with relatives. The reason for this is interesting and something for which I will always be grateful to my parents. It began in 1936, when my Dad's youngest brother graduated from West Point. When he came to our town and wore his uniform, I was convinced that is what I wanted to do - get a nice uniform like his.

My uncle eventually transferred from Infantry to the Army Air Corps, and got his wings. On two instances, he flew to Dunseith in the trainers and observation planes of that pre-WW II era. He buzzed our town, and we all ran out to the pasture which had a windsock, to greet him and bring him into town. It was then that I knew I also wanted to fly. I was about nine when I made that decision.

My Dad routinely asked me what I wanted to do when I grew up. It was always the same answer, West Point and Air Corps. As time went on it became clear to my Dad that in our little school with the academic level of our teachers and limited curriculum, if I wanted to be qualified for West Point and flying, I needed to go to a bigger city, where algebra, geometry, science, etc. were offered.

WW II was underway when, in 1943, my mother and I took a train to Seattle where I was to live with my grandparents and where we figured I could get the academic exposure required. My grandfather was working at a shipyard that built Navy destroyers. I lived in Seattle for two years, after which I lived with the uncle whose career I wanted to follow. He was at the University of Minnesota in an academic program sent by the Air Force to get an advanced degree in Psychology. He had chores for me to help with my room and board. He had three children, the oldest being a brilliant grade school lad named, Brad Hosmer. Part of my job was to babysit him and his siblings when their parents were out (more about Brad later).

I graduated from high school in 1948 and learned that if I were in the service, I could attend the U.S. Military Academy Prep School since I had received an appointment to West Point for entry in 1949. So, I like many others, joined the Army, showed the enlisting officer my appointment letter and was off to Stewart Field, NY for Prep school. I would not have passed the entrance exam without it.

I entered the academy in 1949. I met men as a Plebe with whom I still have contacts 65 years later. Some of us served in the same Company for all four years. Later, one of our wives called us "Horny Toads," a term that still stays with us. Those of us on this side of the grass meet once a year. I'll get back to the "Toads" later.

I graduated from West Point in the class of 1953 and took my commission in the Air Force. I married a woman who was a nurse in Montana whom I also knew when we were infants back when our parents made their living in North Dakota. We are noted for having slept together before being married, a mortal sin in those days. When our parents visited one another for social events, we were placed in the same crib with a baby sitter supervising our behavior to keep it decent. Her name became Patricia Small Hosmer.

We lived as a couple through flight training at Malden, MO in the T-6, and Greenville, MS in the T-28 and T-33. After pilot training, being assigned to Nellis AFB in Las Vegas, was my choice, and the F-86 E/F aircraft was my aim. The training concept at Nellis, as I understood it, was, "We expect losses in this program." The squadron commander, at our initial "welcome briefing" included such statements as, "Half of you will not succeed in completing this program. Also there will be those of you who won't live through the course." With those words of encouragement, we all paid rapt attention.

My first F-86 flight was with a chase by my Instructor Pilot (IP). We flew two missions without a glitch, and I thought I had the world by the balls. Because of a Labor Day holiday and three days of no flying, my next mission was a solo flight. My IP told me to go do aerobatics and come home in an hour and, "I WILL BE AT MOBILE CONTROL, AND IF I SEE BLACK SMOKE ON DOWNWIND, MEANING YOU'RE ADDING POWER, IT WILL BE A FLUNKED RIDE!"

My flight was great. I came into the "Brown Spot" which was an entry point for turning initial to the landing pattern. I heard a radio call, "Solo over the Brown Spot, could you do a 360? I've got a flight of four low on fuel." I rogered it, came around and got another call from a guy who said, "Solo over the Brown Spot, how about a 360? I've got three planes low on fuel."

After another 360 with a high fuel flow, I thought I'd better get home. I forgot whether I was flying an E or an F, but the E fuel gauge was in gallons, and the F gauge was in pounds. I had "250" of something and decided I didn't have enough for a go-around, so I needed to look good. I pitched firmly onto the downwind. As I started to turn base, I could see that I needed to pull it in a bit tighter, but also had to keep a few knots above normal. As it became obvious I needed power, I pushed it up, but it took 12 seconds for that old axial flow engine to spool up, and it did so just as I hit the ground.

Since I was able to hit in a three-point attitude, I did not get major injury, but was pretty much unconscious when I heard some one yelling through the canopy to, "Lean over, I'm going to break the canopy!" which he did. I couldn't see because I had injured both eyes which were cut and bruised in a big way. That guy lifted me out of the cockpit and said, "When your feet hit the ground, run!" I did and got intercepted by someone I couldn't see, and put into an ambulance. At the hospital, I asked, "Who was the guy who lifted me out of that bird?" Someone said, "The biggest guy you've ever seen."

After being taken to my room, my wife, Pat and our friend, the wife of one of my classmates, who I was told also just had an accident, said that they were going to see him when they could. When they came back, they were both crying, and said my classmate was to be evacuated to Travis AFB, where there was a major hospital. I was wheeled down to tell him a goodbye. He was paralyzed from the neck down in a stryker frame holding his body rigid to prevent further damage during the evacuation. He said, "You are the ugliest thing I've ever seen." When I looked at my face in the mirror, I agreed. I looked pretty bad, squinting through one slit of an eyelid.

My classmate had aborted on takeoff because of a loss of thrust. His aircraft continued out into the desert. When the fireball came over the canopy, he came to a stop and ejected. He landed in the seat right next to his burning bird. He was dragged away from it in his seat by the same guy who pulled me out of my wreck three or four hours earlier. Ironically, he, I and another classmate were in the same carpool and drove to work together that morning. It was a "bad day at Blackrock." The man who drove home alone that evening thought, "That squadron commander was sure right about losses." Another classmate was killed about a week later when his wings came off in the recovery from a rocket pass. So, we learned that the F-86 wings needed to be beefed up.

My recovery time had me joining a following class about six weeks later. While I was still making visits to the base to have my eyes checked, I stopped for a beer at the club before heading home. I was at the bar and saw a giant of a man and his woman come into the bar. I said, "Major, did you have anything to do with an accident on 7 September? He looked down at me and said," Is that you, boy? How in hell are you doing?"

I said, "Fine. Can I buy you a drink for pulling me out of that burning airplane?" He accepted, and I learned he was a copilot of one of the B-25s on the Doolittle Raid. His name was Jake Manch. He was the Base Operations Officer and towed targets for aerial gunnery in the B-25. When I asked him how he got to me and to my friend so fast, he said, "On first solo day in this program, I always hang out at one end of the runway or the other. You're not my first save." Damn, when I think of it, I get humble. By the way, "Manch Manor" is a family base housing area on the west side of the highway from Nellis.

Two years later when I was assigned to Nellis to be an F-100 IP, I ran into Jake. He told me of getting into jet flying and was being trained in the T-33. He told me it was a tight fit and he worried about losing his kneecaps in an ejection. Painfully, I remember that he was on a T-Bird flight in the back seat when they entered traffic over the Brown Spot, site of all my 360s in the F-86. Their bird flamed-out. The frontseater got as high as possible in a zoom, tried several airstarts that did not work and told Jake to eject. Jake delayed ejecting. The frontseater got out just in time. Jake's chute didn't open. He was too low and I can envision his scooting as far back in the seat as possible to save his knees, and took up too much time. Tragic.

I was an IP and eventually got into the Fighter Weapons School at Nellis. I was preparing for an overseas assignment. In 1960 President Eisenhower declared, "No more dependent travel overseas." Since I already had a remote F-86 tour to Korea at K-55 in 1956-57, I didn't want to put Pat and my first three offspring through another one of those. I talked to Pat about trying to get on the Thunderbird Team. At least I'd get home once in awhile. She agreed, and I was accepted.

In 1961, President Kennedy was inaugurated. Just as I was beginning training with the team, the President cancelled the, "No more dependent travel overseas" rule. So, we didn't get an accompanied overseas tour, but flying with the Thunderbirds was an exceptionally gratifying, and adventurous experience. I was honored to be able to serve. I flew 189 scheduled airshows during 1961-63 and had some exciting incidents.

After my T-bird tour, I trained in the F-105 at Nellis and was assigned to the 18th TFW at Kadena, Okinawa. Getting oriented, finding an off base house for my family (now including five offspring), and getting qualified for the mission took a few weeks. Our life included nuclear alerts, TDYs to other locations in the PACAF arena and typhoon evacuations to Japan and Korea. We got the planes to safety, reloaded for nuclear alerts, and left our women and children to fend for themselves. They survived and were never hit directly by the storms during our tour.

In late 1964, some of the F-105 squadrons were being deployed to Vietnam and started getting their first taste of combat with targets mostly in Laos. My squadron, the 12TFS, was preparing for a Feb 1965 PACAF ORI and was the designated "deployment squadron." We deployed 18 Thuds and pilots to Da Nang AB, Vietnam. Pat asked how long I might be gone, and I told her it was usually about three or four days. We were gone for two months and began flying missions from Korat AB, Thailand.

We got our first taste of being shot at and for the most part did what had to be done without any fatalities in our squadron. There was a shoot down in a sister squadron on the first mission into North Vietnam by the USAF. I led a flight into the same target dropping CBU-2, which I was better at than dive bombing. On an aside, Boris Baird, part of our Friday Pilots group in Tucson, was the pilot from our sister squadron who was shot down. He became an F-105 IP at McConnell AFB, KS. He had a student, Bob Barnett who is also part of our Friday group. Bob was a POW for five plus years, and tells us that Boris taught him how to get shot down. This is one of my favorite humorous stories from that lousy war. Sadly, Boris passed away before publication of this book.

Later in 1965, we again deployed to Korat, and things escalated. We were attacking targets closer to Hanoi. Some of the missions were an attack on the Than Hoa Bridge, which had resulted in at least one aircraft from the Air Force or Navy getting shot down on every mission. I was flying #3 with the squadron commander leading a five-ship flight. #5 had a camera mounted on the centerline to take pictures of our impacts on the bridge. We were carrying the first 3000-pound bombs of the war. Since the SAMs had not been placed that far south in North Vietnam, we rolled-in from 24,000 ft.. I was on an offset run-in heading from lead and had about a 20-degree angle on the bridge longitudinal axis. When I released and pulled off, I noticed I was supersonic, which caused my bombs to separate from the intended flight path and land one on each side of the wide bridge. I killed thousands of fish and got the bridge wet. As fate would have it, the camera got my bombs in living color. No one got shot down, but the AAA started as soon as we rolled-in. About this time, I thought I'd rather do more CBU deliveries than trying to bust bridges. I later changed my mind.

I led an eight-ship flight from Korat on the first mission tasked to attack SAM sites in the North. There were 46 Thuds flying out of Takhli AB and Korat that day, 27 July 1966. The two bases were to fly low level, below 1000 ft. to "negate the ability of the SAMs." That put all of us in the range of every AAA weapon, plus granddad's peashooter. The two sites being attacked were about seven miles apart, just east of the Black River and west of Hanoi about 30 nautical miles. The results were the loss of six Thuds; three pilots KIA; two pilots captured who became POWs for 7 1/2 years; and my wingman who was hit in the target area on the deck during the high speed run-in, ejected and was later rescued.

On the run-in, we were loaded with rockets and guns. I called for my wingman to break left, climb, jettison everything and head for the high country to the west of the Black River. I watched him throughout the maneuver and eventual ejection over the foothills of those high karst peaks. He lost control, ejected and I established radio contact with him on the ground. He said he was OK.

I sent the other four fighters back to the tanker to get fuel to relieve me when I reached "Bingo." They reported the tankers were all gone, so I told them to RTB. There was no other option. I called the lead of another flight from Takhli, asking if he could afford a couple to relieve me since I knew the exact position of my wingman and had radio contact. It worked well.

The other flight had refueled before the tankers left but were still a long distance away. I identified the piece of terrain in terms that described it perfectly, and which stood out from the other foothills. I said, "He's in a hill mass that looks like a 'pussy'," figuring every fighter pilot knew what pussy looked like.

The flight lead said, "Roger, Got it." and after a length of time my wingman was picked-up and taken to a Lima Site in Laos to spend the night before returning to Korat the next day. This rescue is documented in several aviation magazines, and one of them is the "Smithsonian Air & Space" magazine, dated July 1997, in an article entitled, "Tullo and the Giant." It was a harrowing experience for Frank Tullo. When he got into the horse collar, the Jolly Green headed for Laos, but the winch did not work,. It took a long time to determine it would never work, so they landed in NVN, and Frank jumped aboard. Several small arms hits were taken on the climb out and departure.

One of the pilots captured that day was a man named Robert "Percy" Purcell, assigned to my flight in the 12TFS. He was flying with the squadron commander against support buildings and barracks near one of the SAM sites. I found out talking to him after his release in 1973 the reason the other wingman in the napalm formation didn't see a chute when Percy's bird rolled-off to his left and impacted the ground in the target area. He said about two miles before the target, he lost control of his aircraft and ejected. He was immediately surrounded and captured. We thought he was killed in the crash. We even had a memorial service for him and two others killed that day.

As fate would have it, one of the men who was in my flight that day, was shot down a week later at the Than Hoa Bridge. He broke both arms in several places, rendering him helpless for a long time while he was imprisoned. After the war, he told me that he was in a holding cell at the Hanoi Hilton and saw the nickname "Percy" and "7/27" scratched on a wall. He said, "Damn, I was the only guy on earth who knew Percy survived, and I couldn't do a damned thing about it."

As a sad note, the two other pilots we memorialized at Korat were killed while performing a post-strike damage check. One of the birds did a "hard over" with a flight control malfunction and they had a mid-air collision. Both pilots had "streamers." A truly bad day that has stayed with me all these years.

After returning to Kadena, I was informed I would be PCSed back to the States early because I had been selected to attend the Armed Forces Staff College. I told my boss that I'd already taken the Staff College by correspondence. He said, I was going to the AFSC because that's where "generals" have gone. I said I'd like to refuse and finish my tour in the Thud. The tour length had not yet been set by our glorious Secretary of Defense, Robert McNamara. My boss said, "Get the hell out of here!" So, I flew 60 Thud missions over a combination of targets in Laos and North Vietnam. I never wore the coveted "100 Thud Missions North" patch.

After AFSC I was assigned to HQ Tactical Air Command. I was in the Fighter Requirements office with the office symbol of "DORQ" pronounced appropriately, "DORK." I had 13 fighter pilots working for me in the Fighter Test branch. We worked hard because we were all SEA returnees dedicated to getting tests accomplished that improved fighter avionics, modifications, munitions delivery capabilities and other associated requirements sent from the war zone as pressing needs.

To show we still had a sense of humor, one of the requirements we received was for "battle proof tires." One of my Thud drivers brought me the first blush of how we were approaching this requirement. We had to respond within 24 hours. My astute officer drafted a response as follows: "TAC is meeting this requirement by converting to concrete tires and rubber runways." Hilarious, and if I'd sent it, I'd have been strung up in the parking lot. But, such kept us sane under the constant pressures of deadlines and wartime needs.

One thing my office did before I returned to SEA was get major commands and HQ USAF to approve the final version of the "Required Operational Characteristics" (ROC) for the F-15 and F-16, a MAJOR accomplishment. How I would have loved flying either or both of these wonderful machines.

In 1969, I returned to SEA after a re-checkout in the F-100 at Luke AFB. I'd asked for either the Thud or F-4, but the stated rationale was, they needed experienced HUN drivers. So, back to the HUN it was. I was assigned to the 31st TFW at Tuy Hoa AB on the coast of Vietnam. I was honored to be selected as commander of the 308th TFS. The DO was a famous aviator named Bruce Carr. Bruce was an "ACE" with 14 kills in WW II.

I finished nine months at Tuy Hoa in May of 1970. I flew 180 combat missions in the HUN. The most memorable was the one on which I was directed by a Misty FAC in Laos. He and his backseater came upon a crew of an estimated 1000 people repairing a bombed-out road on the side of a mountain. My wingman and I had 500# high drag bombs. Jack Doub, the Misty FAC, asked if I could see the dust being raised toward the setting sun from his position. I affirmed it, and he said, "I'm not going to mark, just put your load in the middle of that dust." I did, and he liked it and told my wingman to hit my smoke. We had to head back to Tuy Hoa because we were low on fuel, having been diverted from a pre-fragged target.

The BDA report I received from Intelligence the next day before the Stand Up briefing for the Wing Commander was "an estimated 300-400 KBA (Killed By Air). The high number was a result of the road repair site collapsing and carrying many of the workers down the mountain with the dirt. This is documented in a book about the Mistys put together by one of our Friday group named Don Shepperd. Voila!!!

After Vietnam, I was assigned to Lakenheath AB, UK, the 48th TFW equipped with HUNS. We were programmed to get F-4s in 1970, so I was there for the "Last of the Huns" celebration, an all-nighter in the great O-Club at Lakenheath, and an unforgettable celebration with many from across USAFE in attendance. I was the Wing DO before I left Lakenheath, a great place peopled with tremendous fighter pilots.

Leaving Lakenheath in 1972, I had a slot at the Air War College (AWC) in Montgomery, Alabama. Because I was the most senior in my class of 1973, I was told by the Commandant I was to be the Class President. Wow! My wife just wanted to hibernate while I was a student. When I told her the bad news, she shrugged and said, "Well, I'll just have to be out of my home more than I wanted to be during your school year, but I'll try." She became a well-known and well-liked woman by the other wives. She made me proud.

After AWC, I was assigned to Davis-Monthan AFB in Tucson. I was to be the 355th TFW Vice Commander. I reported, got checked out in the A-7 and eventually became the Wing Commander in 1974. That was a huge responsibility, and the challenges took energy, time, patience, and humility. I was not promoted to brigadier general after this tour and was faced with the prospect of some unwelcome and unwanted assignments. I elected to retire after 24 years of service, including my enlisted time. I was asked what I was going to do? I replied that, "I'm going to Montana, grow a beard, make my own beer and get a flying job." So I did.

My beard was starting to get white whiskers, my beer was excellent, and I needed to get a multi-engine rating in order to get a job. So, using the GI Bill, I got licensed to fly multi-engined airplanes. I could not get a flying job in Missoula but I was eventually hired by Cessna Aircraft Company in Wichita, KS to be a Demonstration Pilot in the Citation business jet. I flew for Cessna 12 years, and worked for a fighter pilot named, Bob Fizer, an SSS member now retired in Wichita. I shaved my beard, kept my mustache and started a 12-year mind-bending global aviation adventure with great people I will never forget. I was one lucky guy to get into that program.

Cessna allowed me to travel to places the Air Force would never send me. I flew in all the countries of South America more than once. I flew to Europe and visited all the western nations and finally got to spend a night in Moscow on a demonstration trip from Helsinki, Finland. I delivered Citations to Japan, China, South Africa and New Zealand. I landed the Citation in every state of the union except my own home state of North Dakota. Damn.

My last paying job was flying a Citation III for a Japanese businessman I met when I delivered his airplane to Tokyo in 1989. We flew all over the Pacific and to the States with he and his family. He bought a home for Pat and I to use in Honolulu just to make it more convenient for all of us. It was a little bit of heaven. Then, he asked why we had to "island hop" and not go direct. I told him that would take a bigger airplane. He ordered one, a Challenger 605 with a range of 3500 nautical miles vs. the 2000-mile range of the Citation III. So, now we had two airplanes. Wow! But, soon the Japanese stock market dropped from 24000 to about 9500 and he lost his money, his airplanes and waved goodbye to his pilots.

Since I was getting somewhat deaf, I retired from everything and "snowbirded" between North Dakota and Arizona until my dear wife Pat passed away in 2010. I sold my North Dakota place but still go north to visit friends and relatives. Lately, I stay pretty close to Tucson.

I need to add a few comments about the "Horny Toads" mentioned in the first part of my story. We were West Point "Plebes" in 1949 and spent our four years in close quarters. Most of us went Army and two of us went Air Force, which was allowed until later when the AF Academy started to graduate cadets, including my young cousin Brad Hosmer. I used to live with Brad who became the number one graduate in the first USAFA class of 1959. Brad was also a Rhodes Scholar, an Air Force pilot who fought in Vietnam, and eventually became a Lieutenant General and the first Air Force Academy graduate to serve as the Superintendent. We Hosmers came from good stock.

In 2011, I met the younger sister of one of my Horny Toad classmates at a "Toadarama" at his home in San Antonio. She and I have been seeing one another since that time. Her father was a graduate of West Point in the 1920s. He was a survivor of the Bataan Death March and imprisonment by the Japanese during WW II. Her older brother was an upperclassman at West Point. He was killed while serving as an infantryman in Vietnam. My classmate, her younger brother, was a Battalion Commander in Vietnam, and is still with us Toads.

My friend is Elizabeth Smith, and when she was a little girl living in the Philippines, her father worked with General Jonathan

"Skinny" Wainwright. Sometimes the General would give her father a ride home, and Elizabeth would run out and get a hug from that well-known soldier. She was evacuated with her brothers and mother before hostilities began. I consider myself in the company of beauty, friendship, history and tradition most never experience. I am blessed with another beautiful life adventure that includes a lot of love.

I want to reflect on a couple of things about life as a Thunderbird: There were a few incidents and airshows of note. I flew left wing in the diamond formation for the whole two years and 189 airshows backed-up with practice airshows over a dry lake bed north of Nellis that included two full airshows a day for the entire time we were at Nellis between trips. I don't know how many of the whole routines I did but over two years plus a couple of months, we flew at least two or three hundred shows on top of the 189. It was an exciting life but a grueling schedule.

The only ejection I experienced was in 1961 as we were arriving at Quonset Point NAS, RI. We were setting-up for some arrival maneuvers for the next day's show. My leader, Hoot Gibson, called, "Let's push it up." We were a few miles away from the base and down on the deck. I pushed it up, and my engine quit. I pulled-up, checked things out and started to try some airstarts.

I was at a place that I could not get to "Low Key" for a dead stick landing, and the engine would not start. On the downwind leg I rolled-out, aimed for a vacant field at my 12 o'clock, and ejected at about 600 ft. in a decent, not good. I spent about five seconds in the chute and was descending onto a highway with heavy car traffic. I thought I'd be run over for sure, so I slipped the chute and landed in a tree right next to the roadway. I was about 20 ft. off the ground. The cars stopped, and people gathered around my tree trying to help. I told them to back off, because I didn't want to drop anything on them. The spectators formed a wide circle around my tree. I really needed to urinate, but figured peeing on my would-be rescuers was bad form and was able to delay it. I made it out of the tree and to the base, just across the road, where I found my teammates and took the longest pee of my life. We flew the show the next two days with me in the spare, which I used for the rest of my tour. Since all my clothing went down with my bird, I borrowed clothes until I could get a change of underwear, as a minimum.

We did a T-bird tour of South and Central America for six weeks later in '61. That was a stupendous experience with many hours and many airshows at sites such as Quito, Ecuador, elevation 9600' with a 10,000 ft. runway. We did high air shows at that elevation that were a challenge because of the nature of the beast. We were flying, Hun Cs with no flaps. At high altitude control response was sort of mushy. We also did a show at an elevation of 13,485 ft. in La Paz, Bolivia. We could not land there, but staged out of a base in Chile. We had to carry external tanks and did a "flat show," all rolling maneuvers with no over-the-tops. It was indeed mushy at that altitude but we made it. On some days during that tour we flew more than one show. We had a few days off which were cherished, but we "time hogs" loved the idea of additional cockpit time.

I must finish by telling about the only air show I performed over my hometown in North Dakota: We were scheduled to perform a show out of the newly- established Minot AFB. On the day of our arrival, we were flying from Minneapolis, Minnesota, where I graduated from high school, to Minot ND, a leg of about 500 miles. As we were passing over North Dakota, our leader, Hoot Gibson, transmitted, "Hoz, didn't you live around here in this vicinity?" I rogered and said it was about 32 miles north of where we were. Hoot cancelled our clearance, let down on a perfect weather day and asked if we were on the right track. I told him to stay on the highway we were over and it would lead to Dunseith, my hometown. Then I broached discipline and said, "Sir, don't make just one pass, because they will all wonder what the noise was."

Hoot said, "Solo, set up for an opener." We only had one solo that year, so what we did over my hometown of about 700 people was about half of our high show. We didn't do the bomb burst because Hoot didn't want to give away our entire show format. Our show line was the main street where I grew up. When Hoot said, "Let's get to Minot," I asked if I could break-off and make a low, slow pass down the main street to see who was there. He cleared me for it and I was low, with speedbrakes out doing about 170. As we got about two blocks down our four block main street, the right wing man flew UNDER me, lit the burner, did a roll and beat me back for the join-up. I nearly shat, and there were other reactions that my hometown people still talk about after all these years.

As I look back, my Thunderbird tour was sort of a back-up decision to avoid a second remote tour, But, the tour gave me a rare gift that few experience and I will always treasure. I salute Pat Hosmer for going along with my logic those many years ago. She always gave, never demanded, was a mother beyond comparison, and a loving wife I will not forget.

We had 57 years, WONDERFUL years.

Chapter Seven

From Intercepts to Airlines

by Terry D. "Terry" Johnson

Being involved in writing even one chapter in a book, was the furthest thing from my mind when I got involved with the Friday Pilots. But, it does force one to blow the dust off the old yearbooks and take a stroll down memory lane.

I was born and raised in Duluth, Minnesota, a small town on the western end of Lake Superior made famous by Gordon Lightfoot's song, "Ballad of the Edmund Fitzgerald." I actually worked on the SS Edmund Fitzgerald while it was dry docked for refitting and lengthening several years prior to it's sinking. My childhood was fairly typical of the 1950s and 60s suburban lifestyle, pre-drugs, protests and Vietnam. I played sports as a kid, but wasn't good enough to make my high school hockey team who were state champions two out of my three high school years. My lack of hockey skills led me to pursue alpine snow skiing, a sport at which I was reasonably competent in high school and college. Traveling to downhill and slalom competitions in the Rocky Mountains and as far west as Washington state was where I discovered there actually was sun and warm weather during the winter months.

As a senior at Duluth High School, I remember fellow students who had twenty-year plans for their lives. I, on the other hand, had no clue what direction my world would take. That would change when I was a junior in college. What was a carefree summer afternoon ride in a Cessna light aircraft with a childhood friend and neighbor, would become the experience that changed the direction of my life. I was muddling along in college with the idea of getting a degree in business, then like several of my friends, going on to law school following graduation. After being exposed to 30 credits of undergraduate law courses and all the accompanying reading, I discovered I would not enjoy being an attorney. Upon returning to school in the fall, I got involved in Air Force ROTC and actually passed my private pilots written exam having never flown an aircraft. If my friend could learn to fly, so could I.

Prior to my college years, the only exposure I had to aviation was taking off in a Cessna, but not landing in it. Rick Balzer was a lifetime friend that I had met in Alta, Utah where we spent a winter semester ski-bumming. As dumb 19 year-old kids, we decided to try sky-diving. One of our older and more mature friends, Herb Nolan, was a former Marine fighter pilot, who volunteered to pilot the plane. I remember thinking after letting go of the plane's wing strut, that I had made the biggest mistake of my life. After the chute opened, it was actually really neat up there, until the landing. I managed to land back at the airport – not on the grassy area, but on the concrete. Not so good, but I was 19 and in good condition, so no long term damage. That was my one and only parachute experience. One was enough. I have since shared the story that it was like practice bleeding.

Ten years post high school, I was standing by the ladder of an F-101 interceptor trying to be a good representative of my Duluth Air National Guard unit and the USAF at a base open house and airshow. One of my former high school English teachers and his two sons walked up. In the process of showing the kids the cockpit and speaking with my former teacher, both he and I realized I had changed demonstratively in the post high school years. Here stood a fighter pilot who as a boy had barely passed his English class. The challenge of military pilot training had a way of forever affecting how a young person deals with not only the challenge of flying, but life in general.

I'll pick up my story in the spring of my junior year of college: My Dad had given me a $1,000 college graduation gift a few months earlier that I could spend however I pleased. I chose to invest it in learning to fly. Finding time in between awful summer jobs (if you want to encourage a young man to finish college, make him work in a sheet metal shop or unload freight cars for a few summers. It is certain to influence his decision), I got my Private, Commercial, Instrument, and Flight Instructor ratings.

One of the aircraft I was flying was leased to the flight school by a radiologist who was also a Flight Surgeon in the Minnesota ANG. I took all the USAF pilot qualification tests, and after I graduated, he helped me get a slot in pilot training. While waiting for my number to come up for pilot training, I spent a summer in northern Wisconsin with the doctor and his family teaching him to fly. His job as a radiologist took him from his home to several small hospitals within a 150-mile radius, a route he had been driving daily. This came to a bad ending with a car accident that nearly killed him when he fell asleep at the wheel at the end of a long day traveling between hospitals. That's when I got involved. By using the aircraft and placing an old, reliable car at each airport where a hospital was located, we were able to cut about four hours off his workday. He flew that same aircraft 20 some years without an incident, adding years to his life and immeasurable time with his family. I must have done something right. I will be forever grateful for the trust Dr. Kundel placed in me to instruct him to fly, and the effort he put forth to get me into Air Force flight school.

After I became fully qualified and had been flying for a few years with the Guard, I dreamed of taking the doctor for a ride in a fighter. Alas, it was never to be. We just couldn't seem to put the pieces in place. He would have loved a max performance climb in an F-101, and I would have enjoyed giving him the experience.

Before I headed off to the USAF, I did have one quite interesting incident while piloting the doctor's six-passenger Cherokee. I was given the opportunity to attend the "Ice Bowl," the coldest outdoor football game ever played, as the 1968 NFL final between the Green Bay Packers and Dallas Cowboys came to be known. The stadium announcer for the Packers was Marsh Nelson, a friend of Erv Goldfine, owner of a large multi-department store chain for whom I worked writing advertising during my college years. Goldfine's was very innovative for the times being one of the first stores to incorporate diverse "departments" under one roof. He was announcing the game and a seat on the 50-yard line was offered; not a bad deal. I flew from Duluth to Green Bay with five souls on board (Marsh Nelson, Erv Goldfine and his two children, and a friend) early in the day to allow the announcer time to prepare for the game. As a result, the aircraft sat on the ramp at the airport from about 11:00AM until 5:00PM in -20 degree temperatures. Predictably, the aircraft wouldn't start when it came time to head back to Duluth. The ground crew applied 100-degree hot air to the engine. After lots of spitting and backfiring, it started up and we were on our way. Little did I suspect the significance of the coughing and spitting.

On our flight home, a clear, minus 30-degree January night in Wisconsin with high winds out of the northwest, I made a rookie decision from which I learned a good lesson. I thought that rather than buck 50-knot winds at 10,000', I would fly at a lower altitude (at night, in a single-engine aircraft over miles of wilderness terrain). That is not a bad decision providing everything works, but not so good if you are about to experience engine failure. About three-fourths of the way home, the engine began to run rough to the point we could not maintain altitude. My plan was to land at an airport in Ashland, Wisconsin with which I was familiar. I was following a road that would have put us on a 45-degree angle to the airport's main runway, when the motor quit altogether. Now, we were in the dark; no generator equals no lights. As luck would have it, a car was on the road ahead of us illuminating the path. I managed to land right over the top of the vehicle using his headlights to light the way. The only damage to the aircraft was a dent in one wingtip where we struck a mailbox.

The announcer was also a sportscaster for one of the local TV stations. The first thing he did when we were safely on the ground, was call-in "breaking news," which interrupted the evening news and almost gave my dad, who was watching, a heart attack. The next day, we determined the cause of the problem: a clogged air intake caused by the backfiring which had dislodged a filter. I flew the aircraft back to Duluth and left five people with a story to tell their grandchildren.

The following spring, I was off to Williams Air Force Base outside Phoenix, Arizona for undergraduate pilot training. I remember driving through Flagstaff, Arizona in a snowstorm and two hours later arriving in Phoenix to 70-degree weather and clear skies; my first taste of what an interesting and beautiful place Arizona can be.

The initial phase of flight training was flight screening in the Cessna 172 (or T-41) which for me was a piece of cake having already flown quite a bit in light aircraft. The second phase was the T-37 (the "Tweet"), a faster aircraft for sure, but nothing overwhelming. That all came to a screeching halt with my introduction to the T-38 (the "White Rocket"). I don't think there is an Air Force pilot trainee that doesn't remember his or her dollar ride in the T-38. Strapped to the front of this needle where for the first time you can't see the wings, in an aircraft that climbs through 10,000 ft. while your brain is still back on the runway, is your introduction to becoming a real military pilot. After six months of hard work, we finished a year that probably none of us would willingly repeat, but wouldn't trade for anything.

After the year in Phoenix, it was off to Houston, Texas for F-102 (Deuce) school at Ellington Air Force Base. Deuce training was preceded by a few weeks of Air Force instrument school in the T-33 and water survival training at Perrin Air Force Base. To my surprise when I showed up at Perrin for survival training, I was given a two-bedroom suite at the Bachelor Officers Quarters (BOQ). I thought there must be a mistake- this is Lt Johnson, not Lt Gen Johnson. It turns out I had spent a couple of days with five NASA guys from the astronaut program and they just figured I was one of them.

F-102 school began on a chilling note: a student two classes prior to mine was killed on a low-level night mission over the Gulf of Mexico just two weeks before I arrived. On one of my first rides in the "TF" two-seater (trainer version of the single-seat F-102), I remember my instructor looking me in the eye and saying, "This aircraft will kill you if you give it half a chance." I didn't. He was right. The102 was a very busy aircraft. I now had to not only fly, but also operate the radar, acquire a target, and run the weapons system over water, at night, or in the clouds, often times in unusual attitudes. One had to pay attention to business.

The training at Ellington took about seven months. After approximately one year and seven months of active duty with the USAF, I returned to the Duluth ANG, "Combat Qualified" in the F-102. But, as any new entrant in an occupation knows, I still had a lot to learn. The initial local checkout was interesting. Our Ops officer (a senior pilot I always considered one of my mentors) and I went out in the TF. Following the normal checkout, we climbed up on top of an overcast. He asked me to do a series of aileron rolls 100 ft. above the cloud tops. We were using the clouds as "the ground." He knew young guys would do this sort of thing close to the ground, so he made damned sure I knew how to do it correctly. There were many stories of AF pilots creating a smoking hole in the ground while their friends and family watched.

The time I spent in the Deuce was great. I learned a lot about every aspect of flying and gained the confidence that comes with flying a single-seat aircraft. The F-102 remains to this day my favorite airplane.

After spending a couple of years on alert (we had a 24-hour air defense commitment with four aircraft), flying every chance I could, the F-102 era came to an end. It's replacement was the McDonnell Douglas F-101B (the "Voodoo"), a beast of an aircraft which would go like a rocket in a straight line, but required a couple of zip codes to make a high-speed turn. The first few flights were probably a bit nerve-wracking for the Radar Intercept Officers (ROs) in the backseat. All the pilots coming out of the single-seat F-102 environment and an aircraft that could turn, would hear comments like, "What was that all about?" coming from the backseat after shuttering the airframe through turns a bit tighter than the aircraft liked. I guess I was fairly typical of single-seat pilots in that I wasn't overly enthusiastic about having a backseater. I recall one incident where we got into a thunderstorm, at least in part, because I no longer had a radar up front.

One situation has always bothered me; something I'll never know the answer to: One cold January day, a flight of four of us briefed, strapped-in, had the engines running ready to go, and because of poor runway conditions, decided to scrub the mission. I went home and along with another pilot friend, left with our wives for Aspen, Colorado for a week of skiing. A few days after we had been in Colorado, my Dad called to tell us about an F-101 that crashed on takeoff the day after we left town. Two friends were killed that day; the pilot (a guy I flew F-102s with) and the RO whom I had gotten to know over the past year. I always wondered: Had I been strapped into the same aircraft that crashed when we aborted our mission the previous day? It was determined that the crew had a catastrophic engine failure at liftoff taking out the hydraulics, leaving them with no control. They never had a chance. Another friend from my F-102 squadron in Texas was killed in a similar incident with the North Dakota Air National Guard. I'll never know the answer.

With the "Voodoo" came a reduction in the alert aircraft from four to two. That, combined with me not getting any younger, led to a decision I have thought about my entire life. I loved military flying, the guys I worked with, everything about it. But (and it was a big BUT), I had to consider the future. Claudia, my girlfriend from Phoenix, and I had married. She had been warned about those pilots with the fast cars and fast lifestyles but married me anyway. With no opportunity for full-time employment with the Guard, I took a job as a production test pilot at Gates Learjet in Wichita, Kansas. It was a great job. Who wouldn't like to max perform Learjets from 8AM to 5PM, be home every night and get paid to do it; however, more change was about to come.

I had only been at Lear about six months, when I got a call from North Central Airlines asking if I could make a new hire class date in about three weeks. Once again, we agonized over what to do, but finally realized that an airline career was just too good to pass up. I actually missed an opportunity to be in a class several months prior, but North Central was unable to contact us. If that would have happened, I could have stayed in the ANG and skipped the whole Learjet experience. You never know the direction your life will take, you just make the best decision you can.

One of my classmates at North Central was a fellow Guard guy from my unit. He elected to stay in the Guard and left the airlines when he was able to get a full-time technician's job. He had the opportunity to fly several versions of the F-4 including the RF-4 and the F-16. He retired as a Lt Col. Which career was better? I don't think either was bad, just different. Certainly, he flew more interesting aircraft.

Seven classmates and I began training in the Convair 580, a 50-passenger twin-turbine aircraft. Of the eight of us, five were fighter pilots, familiar with high-speed and high-altitude flying. We were now being thrown into a low altitude, non-precision ADF environment (quite a change, but certainly one from which we all learned and were the better for). After a few years in the 580 and a couple of interesting engine failures, we were senior enough to fly the DC-9, a great aircraft, but a very busy one for the first officer.

The DC-9 was the aircraft I flew for the majority of my career, with a short time on the Boeing 727. That choice was, once again, determined mainly by where we were living. About 10 years into my career, North Central Airlines and Southern Airways merged to form Republic Airlines which went on to acquire Hughes Airwest.

That opened the door for us to go back to Arizona after 10 years in the frozen tundra of Minneapolis. Claudia was thrilled. The pilot domicile that Hughes had in Phoenix was the largest in the airline, so we figured it was a safe move. Not so fast. A guy by the name of Alfred Kahn had the idea to deregulate the airline industry, the goal being that more competition would reduce the cost of airfare for the consumer. In reality, it led to 20 years of confusion with many disrupted lives and careers. Forty years later, the industry is essentially back where it was with the strong carriers surviving and the rest falling by the wayside.

I would have loved to fly the 747 or the DC-10, but I made the decision fairly early in my career that there is more to life than your job. Besides, the view out the window is the same in a big jet as a small one. You only get one shot at being with your kids growing up - a small, fleeting window of time that if you miss it, you won't get another chance. I would have been quite junior on either of the big aircraft which would have meant being in Tokyo, Hong Kong or some far away place when the school play was on or a soccer tournament was being played. I have never regretted that decision.

We now had three children (Brent was seven, Shanlee was five and Kellee was three), when Northwest Airlines came into the picture and bought Republic. Overnight, I and everyone else at Republic, went from one of the best workplaces to one of the worst. Republic was a great, small airline with a wonderful working environment. Northwest was plagued with labor disputes and unhappy employees. Northwest slowly improved with the involvement of outside investors and changes in management. Today, as part of Delta, it is one of the best places to work.

I was directly affected by the Northwest purchase of Republic when they proceeded to close all of the west coast and southern pilot bases. This left the choice of commuting (living somewhere other than where you were working), or moving to Minneapolis, Detroit, or Memphis. Most of the west coast and southern pilots made the same choice I did - Memphis. Memphis was a nice enough place to live aside from the terrible tornadoes and thunderstorms that made flying interesting at times. At least no one had to shovel rain.

I checked out as a DC-9 Captain as soon as we got to Memphis, and remained on that aircraft until retirement. Commuting just wasn't in the best interest of family life. Of course, within months of my airline retirement, the Airbus 320 was moved to Memphis.

Towards the latter part of my airline career, I decided to get back into a sport I had been involved with briefly back in college, Sports Car Club of America (SCCA) road racing. I did that with Claudia's support for 10-11 years. I raced for three different auto manufacturers: Mazda, Nissan and Chevrolet. They supplied us with parts as well as technical assistance. We also had our tires, lubricants, uniforms, etc. supplied by sponsors, but the expense was still quite high. Considering the costs (plus a few attention-getting incidents on track), I decided it was best to give it up. Another contributing factor to ending my racing career was, both girls were on competitive soccer teams that traveled to weekend tournaments. The boys would race and the girls would play soccer, which divided our family on weekends. I did manage to win the SCCA Midwest Division five different years. I also finished in the top three position four other years which qualified me to compete in the national championship runoffs nine times. Like a national championship in any sport, there were some very good racers. Several went on to race in major national series like IndyCar and NASCAR. I was glad just to be a part of it.

Racing is a very selfish sport. The driver gets to have all the fun while everyone else does a lot of hanging around. Claudia was always more of a participant than a spectator. Brent as a teenager accompanied me on lots of race weekends, and got his racing license. We shared the Chevy Camaro for a few years. He would run the regional races on Saturday, and I would race the nationals on Sunday. I think his exposure to mechanical things and natural gifts influenced his decision to pursue engineering at the University of Tennessee a few years later. When we stopped sports car racing, we went directly into another sport Claudia and I had done briefly when I was in the Air Force, and she was in college, motorbikes. I was 14 and Claudia was about 12, when we got our first motorized two-wheelers. Mine was a Vespa. Hers was a Honda 50.

Careers, along with raising children, have a way of interfering with recreation. We did some dirt bike riding as a family in Tennessee at a wonderful cabin we owned on the Tennessee River about one and a half hours east of Memphis. Several families rode motorcycles in the winter and enjoyed water sports in the summer together.

After our children were out of the nest, we decided to really learn how to ride motorcycles. I was an instructor in SCCA sports cars, so I felt I had a basic understanding of vehicular dynamics, but I had much to learn about two-wheelers. After a few years of attending different riding schools as students, we got involved with a well-known school famous for training several world class riders, as corner workers. By now, we had either raced cars or ridden motorcycles on most of the major racetracks east of the Mississippi. Both Claudia and I had lots of bumps and bruises and a few broken bones over the years, but we've also seen a lot of the USA and Europe via motorcycle, met some wonderful people and had a great experience with both street and dirt bikes. The discipline you acquire in the flying business had a direct affect on the sports we enjoyed. To be completely focused was very important, not only in racing and biking, but also in tennis, a game Claudia and I have pursued for 40 years. You tend to approach competition in the same way you do flying. Of course the consequences of bad decisions are never quiet as high.

We are currently enjoying our lives in Tucson. Our children are all law abiding citizens with our oldest son in Chattanooga in the heating/air conditioning business; middle daughter in DC who owns Little Birdies, a new and consigned children's clothing boutique; and the youngest daughter who has a business here in Tucson. After many years of having no grandchildren to brag about, we are expecting our first grandchild. Life is good, and we are excited about our new role.

Thanks for the opportunity to step into this time tunnel, a journey which all of us travel alone and seldom discuss. It has been an honor for me to be accepted into a group of men for whom I have the highest respect and admiration, whose word is as good as their handshake.

Courage has many names - bravery, confidence, nerve. The difficulty of a job defines it. Demands of competition inspire it. Danger can arouse it. Whatever one calls it, courage is really the inner strength and the determination to hang in there. It is something all the Friday Pilots have. I'm glad to have the opportunity to reflect a bit on my life. I really feel fortunate to be included in a group of honorable men that I respect and admire.

CHAPTER EIGHT

Career Limiting Capers (CLCs)

by James A. "Jim" McDivitt

In the late 70s, long after retiring from NASA and the USAF, I was introduced to a new acronym --- CLC! I thought I had been exposed to every possible acronym in NASA and the Air Force, but this was a new one --- and interesting.

I was a senior executive and board member of Pullman Inc. I ran the railcar building business, Pullman Standard, and also had some engineering and construction divisions reporting to me. I had just finished having breakfast with the other board members at the Duquesne Club in Pittsburgh. As I was leaving the Club, I ran into a young man who worked for me. It was his job to coordinate the transportation for the board members who were all going in different directions. I asked him how it was all going, as he was lining up the limos, trying to get member A going to HIS destination and not to member B's. He said, "So far, so good, but you know this is a 'CLC'." Trying to act "smooth", I didn't ask him what it meant. Later that day, when I gave up trying to figure it out, I called him and asked. He responded like I was really out of it, saying, "I thought everybody knew 'CLC' means 'Career Limiting Caper!'" I responded with a meaningless comment, but I never forgot CLC.

Looking back at my time in the USAF, NASA and business I can point out too many CLC opportunities. Because of the limited space for our "Friday Pilots" book, I will limit myself to just a few. To clarify how I picked them, I should mention that I consider decision making an essential part of each CLC episode with a large potential downside for the decision.

The first one, and probably the craziest, happened when I was a 1st Lt stationed at DOW AFB in Bangor, ME, and it came in two parts. I was the assistant ops officer of the 49th FIS. It was my first assignment after returning from Korea, and I'd been there only a few months when we got a new Squadron CO. He was not the typical fighter squadron CO. He just didn't seem to fit in. He was an older guy, nice, but very quiet. I often left the Ops office late at night and passed the orderly room on my way home. I often saw him sitting at his desk with his head in his hands. He just seemed a little different to me --- very "up tight." One Monday when the Ops officer was on leave, I put the flying schedule together and took it over to the CO's office for his info. When I got there, he wasn't there, which surprised me since he seemed very conscientious, and it was mid-morning. I asked the adjutant who shared an apartment with the CO, where he was. He replied he didn't know. I left the schedule and went back to the Ops office. The more I thought about the CO's absence, the more odd it appeared. I went back to the orderly room and asked the adjutant when he had last seen the CO. He said he thought it was Friday afternoon. I then asked him to make certain the CO wasn't on leave. He assured me he was not. Since the ops officer, a major, was on leave I went to see the maintenance officer, also a major, and told him I was concerned. He quickly told me he was the maintenance officer and looking after the CO was not in his job description. No help! After stewing over this until about noon, I had decided, based on the CO's odd actions, that he had probably committed suicide! What followed was a CLC that only a 1st Lt without much to lose --- except my Air Force career, could do. I called the Wing Commander who was at Presque Isle, our Wing HQ, and told his secretary I needed to talk to the colonel. She said he was in a meeting and didn't want to be interrupted. I told her I thought he would want to hear what I had to say. He came to the phone and said, in a not too friendly tone, "Lieutenant, what do you want?" I told him our CO was not in and I thought he probably committed suicide. There was a VERY long pause and he finally asked me why I thought that. I explained my logic and told him I thought I could use some senior help. After another long pause, he said he would send a couple of colonels to help, and I should call the state police. I did! Fortunately for me, but not the CO, the police found him dead in the trunk of his car with a hose from the exhaust into the trunk. As I look back on this, I think I was the one that was nuts to do what I did. What if the CO was just having a long weekend?

Part two of this CLC happened when I was in Korea. I was the Ops officer of the 35 FBS. I was a spot 1st Lt (but really a 2nd Lt) I was the Ops officer only because all the higher ranking pilots had been shot down or quit. I also had the most combat time in the squadron.

We briefed for an eight-ship mission, four from the 36th and four from the 35th, with the Ops officer of the 36 FBS, Maj John Bell leading both flights of four. We briefed together with a start engine time and a taxi time which was standard procedure. I was checking out a new flight leader in our squadron. We started on time and tried to check in with the leader from the 36th with no luck. After 10 or 15 minutes, we had burned a lot of fuel, so I told the flight to shut down while I got a couple of fuel trucks to top us off. As I was doing that, I saw the 36th FBS pilots just walking out to their aircraft. There wasn't time to top off. As soon as the 36th flight checked in I told them we'd been running for about 15 minutes and were short of fuel, so we might have to turn back if the winds weren't right. Well, we made it. But, as soon as we landed, I leaped out of my airplane, ran down the ramp and chewed out the major who was leading our eight-ship formation. We were both ops officers of our respective squadrons and so I, the 1st Lt, had the responsibility to straighten out the major, and I did so, big time. Possibly a major CLC.

Back to Maine and Dow AFB: The Wing Commander said he would send a new squadron CO in a couple of days, and I should just keep running things. A couple of days later I got a call from the Wing Commander, telling me the new squadron CO would arrive that afternoon. A T-33 landed and taxied to our ramp, and in it was our new squadron CO, Maj John Bell, the very major I had chewed out in Korea just a few months before. It all turned out OK. Maj Bell never mentioned it, and of course, neither did I. We became good friends. I left Maine about six months later, and never looked back.

I was in a couple of other squadrons and then back to school to get a degree. I attended the University of Michigan where I got a degree in aeronautical engineering. Then, it was off to the test pilot school at Edwards AFB CA. After graduation, I stayed on at Edwards AFB in Fighter Test. After a few days to find my locker, parachute and the coffee pot, I was assigned to the T-38 program as the number two pilot. It was fun with lots of flying. As the program wound down, one of my bosses, Maj Walt Daniel for fighter test, or Lt Col Clarence (Andy) Anderson head of all flight test pilots, called me in and informed me that I had a great opportunity --- the USAF was starting the "Aerospace Research Pilot School" and I had been selected as the first (and only) student. I very politely told him that I appreciated the opportunity, but that I must decline (CLC). I liked flying and didn't really want to go back to school. We had a little back and forth on the subject when he firmly said, "Goddammit, you are going to that school!" Having now been properly motivated, I saluted and said, "Yes Sir, I volunteer." And so, I went back to school. It was fun. There were four of us who taught each other and developed the requirements for the hardware (simulators and airplanes), put together the academic curriculum and developed the flying program. We all worked on everything, but I did most of the flying. I enjoyed it.

Back to flight test – Hooray! After working on a number of programs, my bosses told me I had been selected to fly the X-15. Bob White, the number one USAF pilot, was leaving, and Bob Rushworth, the number two, would move up to number one, and I'd be the new number two. They also told me I had been selected to be the USAF PRIME pilot for the Air Force F-4 program. I was in airplane heaven. Before I started on those programs, my boss called me in again, and said I was going to France to evaluate the French Mirage IIIC as a candidate for the Military Assistance Program (MAP). There would be three pilots, Stability, Control and Flying Qualities – me, and an air-to-ground pilot, and an air-to-air pilot. He also told me there was going to be another Astronaut selection and asked if I wanted them to put my name in for consideration. I said, "NO!" I wanted to stay at Edwards and fly airplanes. Was that a CLC?

So, off to France for a month. I flew the Mirage IIIC a lot, along with 15 other French airplanes they were kind enough to let me fly. The Mirage was a fine airplane, but like most European airplanes, it didn't carry much fuel. I flew it once with a rocket engine -- it went high and fast, but not for very long.

After I got back to Edwards, I was getting some X-15 simulator time and getting fitted for my pressure suit and doing a lot of X-15 close chase support. However, a CLC was brewing. I began to feel guilty about not volunteering for the Astronaut program. The USAF had sent me to the University of Michigan, Test Pilot School and the Aerospace Research Pilot School. I did exceptionally well in academics. I was a very good pilot and I was a risk taker. Finally one evening, I called Bob White and went to his house to talk over the issue. I was certain that he had recommended me for the X-15 program, and I didn't want to let him down. We had some long, serious talk over a few beers. He said I wouldn't be letting him down, and I finally decided it was OK to apply for the Astronaut program. I should mention that the USAF time for applications had closed a month or so earlier. Bob and I met at Test Ops at 5:00 AM. He called the USAF HQ to see if they would still take my application. They agreed, and he, the Lt Col, typed up the application for the Captain. I then took it to the Colonel, who was the Director of Flight Test, for his signature. He wasn't in, so I asked his secretary to have him sign it and send it off, since they were waiting for it in Washington D.C.

About 10 minutes later, as I was sitting in my office filling out a flight test card for a flight I was about to make, the Colonel stormed into my office, threw my application on the floor and told me I had to withdraw the application. After some discussion, during which I told him I couldn't, he called me a traitor to the USAF and took me off both the X-15 and F-4 programs. A *major* CLC!

Fortunately, I was accepted by NASA and became an astronaut in 1962, along with eight other selectees. I reported to NASA in September of 1962 for the grand announcement of the new astronauts. We were told that we could tell no one, other than our wives, about our selection, because NASA had planned a big press conference for the announcement. We were supposed to go to the Rice Hotel and ask for "so-and-so" by name. We thought he was some top NASA guy in on the secret. Neil Armstrong, Elliot See and I flew in together. In the taxi on the way to the hotel, we passed a giant billboard that read "Come to the Rice Hotel and ask for the same "so and so" name we had been given. It turned out this was the *hotel manager*.

The next day was the grand announcement and press conference with lots of pictures and interviews -- and then -- it was all over. We just went back to the hotel. Ed White, Neil Armstrong and I were on our way to dinner at the hotel, when we noticed a party in full swing in a ballroom filled with people from a truckers' convention. I thought it would be a good place to have a few free drinks and talk over the day, so we signed in as "Acme Trucking." After about 30 minutes a REAL trucker came over and said, "I know you guys aren't truckers, but you're welcome to stay; however, get those loud-mouthed guys over in the corner out of here before I call the police."

Those "guys" were Pete Conrad and Jim Lovell. I advised them we should all retreat! We did. It could have been a very short astronaut tenure for us all.

After a few months of rudimentary academics and a lot of travel to aerospace contractors, where they all wanted to show us their computer rooms, our group of nine was given engineering assignments. Mine was guidance and navigation. During our travels around with a lot of interviews and photos, we created a fictitious 10th astronaut -- Joe Blitzfitz. Whenever we had a group picture, we always gave the photographer 10 names for his picture. The best photos were the ones where we wore hard hats. We would get an extra hat, put it on a stick and hold it up in the back row -- so there were 10 hats, but only nine heads. We had a good group of guys -- all different, but good. We had fun.

In the mid-sixties, an interesting thing happened. We got a message that Deke Slayton, Al Shepard and I were to go to Washington D.C. to meet with "Tiger" Teague. Tiger, a congressman, was chairman of the House committee that dealt with space. We arrived at his office and did the usual social things. Then, out of the blue, he asked how astronauts should be paid. What a surprise! We responded, one at a time with the same unrehearsed answer, that we thought we should be paid the same as any other military officer. How could we get paid more than the guys in combat in Vietnam? As for the civilian astronauts, NASA already had a pay scale for their pilots, and that's what the civilian astronauts were getting. He seemed surprised at our answers, but then after thinking it over, he congratulated us on our good judgment. Pay problem closed (CLC).

We finally got around to flying. I was assigned as the commander of Gemini IV, along with my best friend, Ed White. We were the third and fourth Air Force pilots to fly in space. Our back-up crew was Frank Borman and Jim Lovell. They were a good pair. We did a lot of spacecraft testing on the ground at McDonnell Douglas in St Louis. While we spent a lot of time in meetings or spacecraft testing, we did have some spare time. Someone made arrangements for us to play handball at the St. Louis Jewish Community Center. We played a lot of handball at the Manned Spacecraft Center and thought we were pretty good. The first time we went to the Center to play, they put us in the number one court. It had a glass wall, but we didn't pay any attention to it. When we finished, they turned on the lights and we saw we had an audience of about 50 watching from bleachers behind the glass wall. As we were leaving the courts, some guy came up and said, "You guys might beat the Russians to the moon, but whatever you do, don't play them in handball." Some time later, Ed and I arrived at the Center to play, but they had lost our reservation and all the courts were full. Finally, an attendant mentioned that one guy was in court 5 and would probably like to play with us. We went to court 5 and met the guy who was about 50 years old, short, and kind of chubby. After warm-ups we suggested we play a couple of round robin games. He said, no, that we would play us both. Being our macho selves, we said that would not be fair. He assured us it would be. After a long "fairness" discussion, he said we wouldn't get a *single* point. We took the challenge! After FIVE games we hadn't scored a single point…so much for our handball ego. I found out later that he had won the national championship the previous year.

Finally, it was time to fly. We launched on June 3, 1965 for our four-day flight. It was to be the longest flight to date, with a lot of medical interest. Some of the pessimistic doctors thought we would die after landing and sitting in a vertical position, because our hearts would be so de-conditioned after four days of zero Gs that they could not pump blood upward to our brains. After landing in the Atlantic Ocean, we quickly checked to make certain the spacecraft was not leaking. I then asked Ed, "How do you feel?" He said he felt fine, I said I did too and, "I guess we aren't going to die after all."

An important part of the flight was to be the first EVA (Extra Vehicular Activity) by an American, and Ed was going to do it. On our first orbit we dumped the cabin pressure to a vacuum and tried to unlock the hatch so we could open it. The unlocking mechanism didn't work. We'd had a similar problem in St Louis during an altitude chamber test. In that case, we were able to unlock it OK, but were not able to relock it after the test was over, so we just completed the rest of the test in a vacuum. Later, after I had changed clothes, I watched a technician work with the mechanism, so I had some understanding of how the internal gears and cogs worked. I told Ed, I thought I could get it unlocked and later relocked. But I was not certain. We discussed it for a couple of minutes and decided to try it. *Now this is truly a CLC because if I could not get it relocked, we would burn up on reentry.*

Since I am writing, you know we were successful with the unlocking and relocking. Ed's EVA was quite successful and I was able to take some great photos of him floating around outside the spacecraft.

Our computer failed during flight, but using our back-up procedures we had a successful reentry and landing, although we landed about 40 miles from the carrier, the USS Wasp. Our procedures were such that the recovery forces knew exactly where we were and we had the helicopters circling us while we were still in the chute. Shortly after reaching the carrier, President Johnson called to congratulate us -- very nice of the President. We stayed on the carrier for three days to make certain we got the mission report done. During this time we had a great time with the ship's crew. We docked near Jacksonville, Florida. As we, the two Air Force guys, were about leave the ship, the Admiral said, "In the Navy, when leaving the ship, we always salute the ensign! That's the flag. It's on the stern. That's the back end of the ship, and it's to your left." I loved the Admiral. He was a great guy.

Upon arriving back in Houston at Ellington AFB, the President called us again. He invited Ed and me to spend the weekend with him at his ranch. Since Ed and I had discussed going to the White House, I thanked the President, but said we would rather go to the White House if he didn't mind (surely a CLC. Do you really decline a Presidential invitation?). He said that would be fine. Boldly, I added that Ed and I had not done this mission alone, and that he really ought to come to the Manned Spacecraft Center (MSC) and thank all of the people who made it all work (this too is a CLC, telling the President what he should do). He responded with, "Goddamn, Jim, I think that is a great idea. I'll do it!" Ed and I then told Bob Gilruth the Center Director, we had just invited President Johnson to MSC, and he was coming. I thought Dr. Gilruth was going to have a heart attack. The President did come. More later on that visit.

What followed was a series of fantastic parades and dinners. Ed and I addressed a joint session of Congress. The Congress loved us and both parties wanted us to run for public office on their ticket. We declined. The most memorable moment in all of this Hoop-La was a parade in Chicago. When we turned onto LaSalle Street, we were stunned!! Confetti streamed down from the office buildings, thousands of people cheered and waved, people were standing 10-15 deep along the street. In the front row was a man in bib-overalls holding a live, white goose – what a sight! During these events we had Vice President Humphrey with us. He was a wonderful man. He kept asking if we wanted to go to the Paris Air Show. Of course we said, yes. Until then, no U.S. astronaut had gone outside the country. However, that year the U.S. government failed to support the contractors at the air show so there was little U.S. presence and the Soviet Union was making a major effort with numerous new aircraft. So, now we have the setting for our trip to the White House.

As I vaguely remember, we arrived in the morning, Ed with his family and me with mine. We both had little children -- mine were eight, seven and five and Ed's about the same ages. Our parents were also there. The ceremony was in the Rose Garden. We had been invited to spend the night in the White House, so during the rest of the afternoon, the kids swam in the indoor pool (built for President Roosevelt but it is no longer there). In the evening Ed and I were to give a talk about the flight to the entire diplomatic corp. This was scheduled for the State Department auditorium where we and our wives stood in a receiving line to greet the members of all the foreign embassies. About half way through the allotted time for the receiving line, VP Humphrey came over to Ed and me, and told us we were leaving for Paris that night. Photographers put our wives in front of a plain wall to take passport pictures. NASA HQ got pictures for Ed and me and quickly made some diplomatic passports for the four of us. Later, Lady Bird Johnson invited our wives back to the White House to pick out some formal gowns from her wardrobe. Since we thought we would be in Washington for only two days we were not prepared with clothes for a week in Paris. At the conclusion of our talk, the President took the stage and announced that we were going to Paris that night. Later, back at the White House, we found the kids, who were having a great time being entertained by Lucy Johnson, and told them we were leaving that night for Paris, but *someone* would take care of them. We put them to bed and got repacked for our trip. Off we went to Paris! -- I'm still uncertain who took care of my kids.

We were a big hit at the Paris Air Show and helped to repair our country's prestige in the eyes of the political and aircraft worlds. For Ed and me it was exciting and interesting. We met with Yuri

Gargarin, the first man in space, a couple of times. He seemed like a good guy.

Now, for a quick segue back to Edwards AFB...I mentioned the Director of Flight Test colonel who called me a traitor to the Air Force. In a way, that was a widespread belief in parts of the Air Force. There was a brutal fight in progress between NASA and the USAF about which was going to lead in manned space. This fight was similar to one between the Army and the Air Force over which was going to lead in rockets. In the NASA-USAF battle, the lead combatants on the Air Force side were the field grade officers. The company grade officers, (lieutenants and captains) were <u>very</u> supportive of the USAF/NASA astronauts as were the general officers, but not the field grade officers (majors, lieutenant colonels and colonels).

I was promoted rather early to captain. At the time, "time-in-grade" was used as a major promotion criteria. Just as I was coming up for possible selection to major, the rules were changed from time-in-grade to "commissioned service time." That delayed any promotion consideration for me for some years. However, later, when I was a NASA Astronaut and did become eligible for below-the-zone, I did not get promoted. The second year of eligibility, I again was not promoted. By this time I had been a captain for nearly 10 years. Captain is the best grade in the Air Force, but I must admit, I was tired of it. One day while in Washington, I went to the Pentagon to review my records. They were very good. I asked a nearby sergeant who I could talk to about my records. He told me I was in luck since the colonel in charge of the majors' selection was just on the opposite side of the room. I walked over and introduced myself to the colonel, and asked him if he could tell me what the problem was. He looked over my records, nodding his head in agreement until he got to he last page that had the location of my present duty. When he saw "NASA," he frowned, turned to me and said that I was under-educated, was in the wrong career field, and a few other not nice things. In conclusion, he said I had no future in the Air Force and that I should get out. I must say, I was shocked. I returned to Houston, thought about it, wrote my resignation and sent it through NASA channels. All this took a fair amount of time, so that when it came back from NASA approved, we were getting fairly close to flying on Gemini IV. After thinking it over, I decided I would not forward my resignation to the

Air Force until after I flew because it might look bad for the Air Force for me to resign right before the flight. Shortly before the flight, Ed and I were promoted to major, but not below-the-zone. This is a long preamble to good news.

As mentioned earlier, I had invited President Johnson to visit the Manned Spacecraft Center. Shortly after we got back from Paris, the President arrived at the Center. Ed and I escorted him and had a good time with him. At the end of the tour, he was going to give a talk. My mom and dad were there along with my wife. Ed's family also attended. At the conclusion of his talk, to the best of my recollection, the President said, "I am the President of the United States. That makes me the Commander-in-Chief of our armed forces. Since I'm the Commander-in-Chief, I can do whatever I want." Then he said, "Jim, get up here!" I was stunned, to say the least. I had no idea what he had in mind. As requested, I popped to my feet and went to the podium. "Jim," he said, "You are now a Lieutenant Colonel," and gave me a set of silver oak leaves. Since I was in civilian clothes, I couldn't pin them on, but they certainly felt good in my hand. He then also promoted Ed and Gus Grissom. A great day for the three of us, but I think it was good also for the Air Force because I think that single event stopped the bickering and back stabbing over who was going to have the lead in manned space flight.

When the President was leaving the MSC, he invited Ed, Dr. Gilruth and me to ride out to the airport with him. I was sitting in the back with him. We had a lively conversation on the way. At one point we had a lull. The President quietly said to me, "I wonder how I would feel today if Lucy and Linda were boys?" After some moments of silence, I asked why. He said he had just authorized a very large (I think 50,000) troops to be sent to Vietnam. His public image was one of toughness, but I know he was really concerned about our military and the potential of death for the men he was sending into combat.

After Gemini IV, I went back to astronaut engineering work on the Apollo program and tried mightily to make certain that the man was considered in the spacecraft design. Shortly after that, the first Apollo Crew was named: Gus Grissom, Ed White and Roger Chafee. I was commander of the backup crew. My crewmates were Dave Scott and Rusty Schweickart. I had a good crew.

It was tough getting the spacecraft and procedures ready for flight. By now I was a Colonel. One night about 3:00AM I got out of the spacecraft we were testing and was sitting on the test stand steps with a technician who was probably making three times what I was making. He said, "Jim being an astronaut isn't nearly as glamorous as I thought." I do believe he was right. Unfortunately, Gus, Ed and Roger never got to fly that spacecraft. The fire killed them all. I lost my best friend, Ed White.

We did finally fly the first Apollo in 1968. President Kennedy said we were going to the moon in "this decade." He said that in 1961, which gave us about eight and one-half years. We were getting close to running out of time.

My crew and I were assigned to fly Apollo 9, the first flight of the Lunar Module and the first full-up lunar combination. Being a test pilot, there is nothing better than making a "first flight" in a vehicle. I had the pleasure. We had a great flight! Everything went as planned.

Then, came another very important CLC. I had to decide whether to stay in the Astronaut office and fly a lunar flight, or shift over to the Apollo Spacecraft Program and run it. I decided to run the program. It was challenging and I enjoyed it. I was responsible for Apollos 12,13,14,15 and 16, most of the lunar missions.

As the Apollo Program was winding down, I had some more tough decisions to make:

1. Stay with NASA and run the Shuttle program. This was a non-starter since the program was grossly over-promised and under-funded.
2. Go back to the Air Force. This was what my heart wanted. I had been promoted to Brigadier General with just slightly over 19 years of commissioned service, and I probably had a fairly bright future; however, I had been out of the main stream of the service for a long time and I foresaw a future of many service related moves. I had spent a lot of time away from home working for NASA and I thought it was time to think more about my family which was very important to me.
3. Retire from both NASA and the Air Force. I decided to retire and spend more time with my family. I announced I would

retire in September of 1972. I had cleared this with the Air Force Chief of Staff and he gave me his approval and blessing.

At the end of September 1972, I left the Air Force with a heavy heart and shed a few tears during my retirement parade at Bolling AFB in Washington D.C.

At the time I announced my retirement I didn't have a job. I felt I couldn't go into an aerospace company since I had every aerospace company in the U.S. working on the Apollo program and thus for me. I felt it might appear as a conflict of interest and I'm a real stickler for "conflict of interest." Therefore, when offered a job in a large gas and electric utility company, I accepted. I learned a lot but worked for a very unpleasant CEO. I left after a couple of years and joined Pullman Inc. I ran the railcar building division and later had the engineering and construction division reporting to me. We were taken over by another company and I left and joined Rockwell International, a great company. I finally retired completely in 1995.

I must say, before I close, that the Korean War was the best thing that ever happened to me. I was rudderless and had no plans for the future. I was struggling to earn enough money to continue my college education. When I graduated from high school, I worked for a year in a water heater factory to get enough money for books and tuition at a junior college. When I finished junior college, I had a scholarship to Michigan State University, but it only covered books and tuition. I needed more money, so I got a job with Dow Chemical Co. I was to start on June 26, 1950. The Korean War started on June 25th. I received my draft notice shortly thereafter. Since I liked to hunt and fish, campout and hike in the woods, I thought the infantry would be fine. Bad idea!! CLC. My mother liked the Navy uniforms. I had read a lot about flying but I had never been in an airplane. However, that was my choice. After a lot of lucky breaks, I was accepted for Aviation Cadet Training, and my entire life changed. Fortunately, I was a good pilot and did well academically. Upon graduation, I was offered a regular commission. Without knowing exactly what that was, I graciously accepted. Thus, my USAF career started. Most of us from Williams AFB were sent to Luke AFB for gunnery before going to Korea. It was a great time. We could do almost anything. How could they punish us? We were 2nd Lts and on our way to a war. What could anybody do to us?

Arriving in Korea, I found that it was interesting and exciting. After I flew my 100 missions, I extended for 25 more. At 125 missions I extended for 25 more. My parents were supportive, but after a C-124 R&R transport crashed in Japan (I was supposed to be on it), my parents leaned on me to retire. I received their tear-stained letters just after we had briefed for my 131st mission. So, that was the end of my combat. The last mission makes you think, if I get back from this one, I can go home. I told the Squadron CO that I was retiring. Unfortunately, I was one of only two group leaders in our squadron. When it was our squadron's turn to lead the group every third day, if the Squadron CO couldn't do it, I got leaned on to un-retire for one more mission. This continued on until I flew my last mission two hours after the armistice was signed. So -- I had 15 "last" missions. That's a little hard on the nerves, but I survived to have the opportunity to face up to many more CLCs.

CHAPTER NINE

Everybody Loves a Tanker Pilot

by Andrea A. "Andy" Muscarello

Associating with such a group of aging warriors has been a privilege. For the most part the makeup is generally fighter pilots; however, my career span has been in multi-engine aircraft. When I graduated from Air Force pilot training, my graduation certificate said "Tactical Pilot Single Engine Jet." Inasmuch as my class standing was in the middle of the class, and we had few fighter assignments, I was awarded assignment to advance training in the Boeing B-47 Stratojet. The prospect of becoming a fighter pilot was dim at best. Thus, I began my Air Force career as a "Strategic Air Command Pilot," a SAC-puke!

Perhaps this was my entre to being accepted into this august group. Since I have not experienced combat, my stories do not have a riveting edge to them. Consequently, I will have to fill my pages for this book with emergency situations and some humorous stories associated with my career as an Air Force and airline pilot. It is a privilege to have lunch each Friday and listen to the adventures and risks experienced by my fellow airmen.

I entered this world in Evanston, IL in April of 1934. One year later, my father died, and my mother and I moved to Chicago where I grew up in my maternal grandfather's home. It was a two-story house on the north side of Chicago. My grandmother died 15 days before I was born, so my grandfather was now a widower. My grandfather, August Schwab, was a tool and die maker and commuted to Elkhart IN, coming home on weekends. My aunt, Cecil, along with my mother, was also a widow. She had two boys, seven and 10 years older than me. She took care of us. My mother, a beautician, had her own business. An aunt and uncle lived on the second floor.

To better understand my environment, I need to present a broader overview of those times. My mother had her beauty shop down the street where my father was a barber in his father's barber shop. This is how the relationship developed:

My maternal grandfather immigrated to the United States from Danzig, Germany when he was 16 years-old. My paternal grandfather immigrated to this country from Alta Vista, Italy just down the coast from Palermo, Sicily at about the same age. At this time the people that emigrated and settled in Chicago created pockets of like nationalities; i.e., Italian, German, Irish, Polish, etc. Since both of my parents were born here, I was a second generation American.

Most importantly, I had the greatest relatives for which a boy could hope. I was remembered on holidays and my birthday. I was taken to sporting events and various activities. I never felt deprived by not having a father. My mother saw to it. I never lacked for anything and had an aunt and uncle that were childless. My uncle helped me financially while in college. He was a World War I vet and was proud that I was an Air Force pilot. Actually, this uncle got me interested in airplanes at the age of seven. He would take me out to Chicago Municipal Airport (now Midway Airport) to watch planes arrive and depart; Douglas DC-3s and Lockheed Lodestars for the most part. The planes taxied right up to the fence and you could see the pilots and watch the passengers deplane. At the airport there was a flying service called, Monarch Airways, that gave rides over Chicago. My first airplane ride was in a "Bamboo Bomber," a World War II multi-engine trainer. My second, a year or so later, was in a DC-3 from the same flying service. We flew down Archer Avenue in Chicago and circled Soldier Field where the annual Tribune College All-Star game was in progress. I was hooked and determined to be a pilot. This prompted me to build model airplanes, and I still do to this day.

Growing up a Catholic, I attended St. Bonaventure grammar school and was taught by the nuns. I attended DePaul Academy, an all boy high school. I studied pre-engineering and managed a B average. As a freshman, Latin was required. When I finished the final exam at the end of the year, Father Cook called to me, "Muscarello, don't show up for second year Latin." I received the message loud and clear, so I took his advice and took Spanish the following year. I now wish that I could tell Fr. Cook that somewhere deep inside me was a Latin scholar, since my son, the physician, won the state of Illinois award for Latin in his high school senior year. I played freshman and junior varsity football until my grades began to decline; however, I was on the swimming team for four years. The ability to swim afforded me the opportunity for summer employment working for the Chicago Park District as a lifeguard. I spent four summers as a lifeguard at Montrose Beach on Chicago's lakefront.

My mother, being a beautician and having a trade, felt everyone should have a trade. Consequently, during the summer between my sophomore and junior year of high school, she sent me to barber school. I was 16 years-old and the barber school was near downtown Chicago in a less than desirable neighborhood. The street outside the school had prostitutes soliciting and drunken Native Americans falling out of the many taverns and fighting on the sidewalks. The other students were Korean War veterans and would take me along when they went for lunch at the tavern next to the shop. In there was a "26" girl who ran a dice game. I later found out she had additional talents. Interesting enough, I used to ride home with her on the bus thinking what a nice lady she was. This talent of cutting hair allowed me to make spending money while in college.

For college, I selected University of Detroit since they had Aeronautical Engineering and Air Force ROTC. The only thing I excelled in was ROTC. In fact, I won the Chicago Tribune Silver Medal for my ROTC activities. The remainder of my college experience, mainly the educational aspects, conflicted with my social activities. I made sure I didn't miss out on any "fun stuff." I parked cars for the football games and was responsible for one of the cars to be raffled at the spring carnival. I went from warning, to probation, to required to withdraw in three semesters. I petitioned the Dean and having convinced him I would do better, he reinstated me. I managed to prove his judgment to be lacking. Once again I was required to withdraw. It is hard for me to imagine that I was "thrown out" of the same school twice. I guess they were not visionaries and could not see my potential. About this time I also began to question my interest in being a student. My son a physician, cannot get over the fact his father got "booted twice" from the same school; perhaps this is somewhat of a record.

I knew my wife Ginny, since I was 16. Actually, my mother knew her before me. My mother's beauty shop was across the street from

Ginny's father's fruit and vegetable store. Ginny worked for her father after school and weekends when my mother became acquainted with her. A girl across the alley in Chicago where homes have alleys, went to Immaculata Catholic Girl's School, and was a classmate of my wife. One day, when I went over to see the neighbor girl, there was Ginny, and I was taken with her. Of course my mother liked her and encouraged our budding relationship. After my second year of college, we planned to marry. I was to go to school and she would work. The marriage was planned for the summer right after receiving my "walking papers" from the University. What the hell was this girl thinking of marrying me? She obviously saw the potential others had missed.

We were married in July 1955, and our honeymoon consisted of flying to St. Louis to enroll me at Parks College of St. Louis University. The aviation school was located in Cahokia, IL across the river from the main campus. Ginny obtained a job at Monsanto Chemical, and we were able to rent an apartment quite close to school. Since I was married, we associated with the married veterans that were older than us. These same veterans were there for the education and kept the curve up. I was now motivated to study. I was on the honor role every semester until graduation. It is amazing how a good woman can make a better student.

During my last year in ROTC, the Air Force provided us with 40 hours of flying time, enough to acquire a private license. The head of the flight line flying school flew B-17s over Germany when he was 19. My instructor, Charlie Parrish, learned to fly in a Jenny JN-4 in 1923 and instructed aviation cadets during the war at Parks under a military contract. His favorite expression was, "Son, you're not f-----with a bicycle." We were instructed in a Cessna 170, a four-place aircraft. It had a spring steel gear, and I was having a problem mastering the wheel landing. So, Charlie sent me over to Parks Metropolitan Airport, adjacent to the college airfield. On Saturday of that week, I took an hour instruction in a Piper Cub and soloed. The following Monday, Charlie soloed me in the 170.

Upon graduation in 1957, I was commissioned a 2nd Lt USAF. I was awarded a diploma stating I had a Bachelor of Science Degree in Aeronautics with a major in Aircraft Maintenance Engineering. This also provided me with an Airframe and Powerplant license. At graduation, my mother aunt and uncle were present. Ginny could not attend because she had returned to her father's home expecting our first son. I requested to be called to active duty in the third quarter after graduation, since I had been hired by Ford Motor Co. Aircraft Engine Division in Chicago. Ford was building the Pratt and Whitney J-57 jet engine under license. When Ginny and I were home for Christmas prior to graduation, Ford interviewed me, took me to lunch in the "executive dining room," gave me a tour of the plant, showed me where I would be working in the engine test cells, and later followed up with a letter offering me employment. I was sent to their J-57 engine school that covered the afterburner and water injected engine.

Our son, Vincent, was born in August 1957. A few months later I was informed that Ginny was expecting once again. Wow! I was working for Ford and now going to Air Force pilot training with a family. Maybe not the best idea, but too late. In April, the orders arrived stating that I was to report to Lackland AFB on 25 April 1958. Shortly after arrival, we received our primary base assignments. I was assigned to Bartow Air Base at Bartow, FL. After a month at Lackland, I traveled to Bartow to begin flying. I arrived on 4 June just in time to get dinner at the mess hall. When I finished and came out, they were night flying. The sky was filled with T-28s. This, along with the fact the next morning when I looked at the T-34 with the star and USAF on the wing, I realized that I was to be trained to defend the USA through air power. I was in Class 59H. We started out in a Beechcraft T-34, followed by the North American T-28A.

When I arrived for class the following morning, we were assigned our instructors. These were civilian instructors mostly RIFed (reduction in force) officers from active duty who had wanted to remain in the Air Force. I was in a class of 76 1st Lt navigators that had been on active duty for at least five years. There were thirteen of us 2nd Lts out of ROTC.

I was assigned an instructor, along with three other 1st Lts. In short order, it became apparent my instructor had no use for ROTC students. The Air Force sent out correspondence indicating if you wanted to fly, you had to sign for five years. Naturally, I signed even though the previous commitment was for three years. Apparently some of the ROTC students my instructor had at that time refused to sign and opted to get out and remain in the Reserve. His bitterness was something I had to deal with. Fortunately, I had the previous flying training afforded me by the Air Force. Try as he might, he had no grounds to wash me out. In fact, I was the first at my table to solo the T-28. In fairness to him, he graded me on my ability to perform and not on his preconceived views of ROTC students.

After several students washed out, there was only need for one instructor for every three students. My life improved 100% with my new instructor, a big Texan, with whom it was a joy to fly. In July our daughter was born at the Winter Haven Hospital. Upon completion of primary flight training, the class was asked for 13 volunteers to hold over. I volunteered and then departed for Laredo, Texas the first week of January 1969.

Upon arrival at Laredo, once again late at night, the sky was filled with T-33s night flying. We were able to secure lodging at a local motel. The next morning, after checking in at the base, the first order of business was securing living quarters. We found a large home near downtown Laredo that was divided into two apartments. Another student lived in the adjoining apartment. We were only a block from the Rio Grande.

I was now in Class 60A, the "Thunderbird" squadron. I was fortunate to have an instructor who had previously flown the F-84F, and who was a superb pilot and credit to the USAF. On my first flight with him, I was in the frontseat, he in the rear. He made the takeoff and as we were climbing through 20,000', I was mentally still on the runway. He took us out to show me the area, particularly the aerobatics area. Next thing I knew, we were dog-fighting with a Navy Cougar from Kingsville NAS. I was so far behind the airplane, I became nauseated. I did not "lose my cookies," but what an uncomfortable feeling, and what a "first ride."

I progressed normally meeting all the requirements and could not wait to solo. The day finally arrived and my instructor said, "Andy I would solo you today if I thought you could get the Bird to the runway." It seemed I had a penchant to cock the nose gear and a mechanic would have to grab the nose and rock the airplane until the gear streamlined. My IP relented and soloed me anyway.

Midway through the training I applied to become a regular officer, which was shortly granted. One day, when flying solo, I decided to practice some of the acrobatics the instructor had demonstrated. I first did a series of stalls, the last one being "dirty," gear down. This was followed by diving for airspeed to do a Cuban-eight. I couldn't figure out why I was having trouble getting the entry airspeed until I realized the gear was still down. I retracted with some concern hoping the gear doors were not wrapped around the wheels, since I knew I had exceeded the gear down limit speed. To my amazement all was well until I landed and went to insert the seat pin for the ejection seat, which I "forgot to remove before takeoff." The ones that you get away with stick with you forever.

On my last solo flight in the T-33, I flew over my house for the first time and then out to the practice area. Wow! What a feeling to know I would soon be receiving the coveted wings of an Air Force pilot. The graduation went well, except one of the student pilots and his father went over to Nuevo Laredo to celebrate, and got thrown in the "Mexican slammer." The base commander was not particularly happy that he had to make arrangements for their release.

My orders assigned me to combat crew training at McConnell AFB, KS. Before reporting, I had to go to Reno Nevada for survival training at Stead AFB. Now this is where a city boy meets the wilderness with some trepidation. Although I was a Cub Scout and Boy Scout and had camped numerous summers with the scouts, this was now the "big league." The first phase of the training consisted of classroom work. The evenings we "sashayed" into Reno for food and beverage. We received a watered-down version of POW training. It seems a couple months prior to our arrival a student died and a congressional investigation was underway.

Finally, the day arrived where they trucked us out to the Sierras for the trek and escape and evasion training. The first few days were with a group. They gave us a live rabbit. The fellow charged with transporting it as we moved along, decided to put it in a pilot chute and tie the cord around the rabbit's neck. The rabbit strangled the first night out. The country boys in our group skinned it and roasted it the first night. When I was offered a piece, I declined. A few days later I would have gratefully eaten the whole rabbit. The last day and night was an E and E exercise. We deployed to a prearranged location in pairs at nightfall. We struggled through the manzanita bushes at the higher elevations and stayed clear of the roads. Through some miracle we arrived at the correct location early in the morning. What a welcome sight when a truck arrived with coffee and rolls.

The fellow that I was paired with and I drove to Wichita in his car. When I arrived, I rented a house in Derby Kansas close to McConnell AFB. I then flew to Chicago, picked up my family and drove to Kansas to begin B-47 combat crew training as a co-pilot. Early on, I was paired with an aircraft commander (AC) and destined to report to Davis-Monthan AFB in Tucson, AZ. after training.

The course lasted several months with the AC receiving the bulk of the flying time. Although I was along on every training sortie, I rode in the nose until perhaps the last hour and then got the chance to fly. I believe I only had two or three opportunities to land from the backseat. On completion of flying training, we attended nuclear weapons school prior to reporting to our assigned base. I guess what amazed me was, a nuclear bomb actually looked like a bomb. I don't know what I expected to see when the weapon was first presented. While at McConnell, our second son, John, was born. Now, it was off to Tucson.

We arrived in Tucson on 4 May 1960. I had never been this far west and was amazed driving into town on the Benson Highway (now I-10) how austere the landscape was. Where is the grass and trees? We found a rental where we lived for five months. Since I was a mere 1st Lt, there was no base housing available. We eventually purchased a home in a new subdivision on the far east side. It was at Broadway and Spanish Trail. None of the roads east of this location were paved. It was a four-bedroom home costing $13,800.00 with an enormous $112.00/month mortgage payment. This required adjusting our budget.

After reporting to DMAFB, our navigator/bombardier arrived and we were now officially a crew. The training continued until we finally became Combat Ready. We became part of the 358th Bomb Squadron (The Black Eagles), 303rd Bomb Wing, Strategic Air Command. SAC had spot promotions at that time. Consequently, the crews were heavy with rank since many of the crewmembers were highly experienced WWII veterans. A newly arriving 1st Lt was hardly noticeable.

In 1962, we participated in an exercise called, "Double Eagle." Several B-47s rendezvoused over the Pacific Ocean, the target being

Los Angeles. The B-47s were to simulate a Quail drop, a decoy missile that B-52s carried to fight their way into a target. We could readily see B-58s at high altitudes pulling contrails. Fighters were using 90 degree beam tactics to intercept. It was fascinating to watch the B-58s "walk away" from the fighters using their superior speed.

Most training missions in the B-47 lasted about seven to eight hours. They consisted of a refueling, a navigational leg and then several bombing runs on a RBS (Radar Bomb Scoring) site. On some missions we dropped training chaff and fired the 20mm guns over the ocean.

Many of the bomb runs were at low level. The navigators were never fond of this sortie since their ejection seat went downward and did not permit enough time for a parachute to deploy. It was also disconcerting to look out at the wings during daylight low level over the hot desert and see the wings flexing. The wings were designed to flex 17 feet. I hoped the structural engineer who designed the wings was not a "C" student. Low level at night required strict adherence to altitudes for the various segments of the route, since at that time there was no terrain following equipment. While I was stationed at DM, we lost a stanboard crew that impacted the top of a mountain at night. I knew the copilot very well. In primary, he washed out and was granted reinstatement into training.

As a copilot my duties were to maintain a fuel log, pre-comp with the navigator in selecting stars for celestial navigation and "shoot" the stars with the sextant in a port in the canopy above the copilot's seat. In addition, the copilot dropped the chaff, jammed the RBS site when the APS 54 indicated a lock-on and recorded bombing results radioed back from the RBS site after release.

The copilot's seat swiveled around to fire the tail guns. The guns were equipped with a radar that could supposedly acquire the fighter threat and commence firing at 1000 yards. The ground trainer we were required each quarter worked like a champ. It simulated an intercept by a fighter; however, in the airplane the system did not work well. We could adjust the screen gain and brightness to no avail. We were simply unable to track the threat. I had no confidence whatsoever in the equipment – low bidder crap.

The bomb release system was a team effort. During an EWO (Emergency War Order) when the "GO Code" was received and verified by the AC and Nav, the copilot controlled the release handle of the bomb shackle assembly. This would then permit the release of the bomb electronically. Our navigator/bombardier was tops in bombing and navigation. We were acknowledged by 15th Air Force and our crew received an award. Shortly after, the aircraft commander and navigator received a spot promotion to major. We were now select crew S-75. I was still a 1ˢᵗ Lt. Another aggravation - SAC did not permit touch and go landings. The landings had to be full stop. Thus, copilots got very few landings. Whenever I got one, it was after the first landing. A new brake chute was installed, and I was given the second landing, very frustrating.

After becoming combat ready, we stood alert at DM a week at a time and flew about three times a month in between. Our turn arrived to Reflex to Elmendorf AFB, Alaska. There, we would stand alert for a month before redeploying to Tucson. In the four years I was based at DMAFB, I made several trips to Alaska. There were six B-47s and six KC-97s standing alert. We were all housed together in a large hangar. In the event of an actual EWO launch, we had 15 minutes to get all the aircraft airborne. The Russians had missiles at Anadyr with an eight-minute time of flight to Elmendorf. Do the math.

Deterrence was the objective during the Cold War, and "Peace Is Our Profession" was the mantra of SAC. Usually, we had an opportunity for a free day or two during the month in Alaska. A fish camp was set up on Sheep Creek off the Susitna River. We took the Alaskan railroad and got off at the 100-mile post. There was no station, just the middle of nowhere. A sergeant arrived with a weapons carrier to pick us up and drive us to the camp. It was summer and daylight all night. One "night" we were fishing for salmon and experienced a couple of surprises.

Along the tree-lined river, taxied a Seabee push-puller float plane. It taxied up to the banks, a man got out and asked how was the fishing? He then presented his badge and checked if we had a license. Of course we did. We could not hear the aircraft land and only heard him when he rounded the bend of the river.

The second incident involved a large bear coming down the bank of the river about 20 yards from where we were fishing. We had some salmon laying on the ground and the bear did not consider ownership negotiable. It was "feet don't fail me now" time.

During one deployment to Elmendorf AFB during the winter, the ceiling at our destination fell below minimums. All six aircraft had to divert to Eielson AFB at Fairbanks, Alaska. The next morning Elmendorf cleared and we attempted to redeploy. Unfortunately, the temperature at Eielson was minus 65F. Of six B-47s with six engines (J-47s) each, only one engine out of 36 started.

Eielson AFB supported Operation Chrome Dome with KC-135 tankers. The tankers refueled the B-52 bombers overflying Alaska that were part of the airborne alert concept. The tanker force had many Herman-Nelson gas heaters to pre-heat tanker aircraft engines to prevent launch delay. Eventually, the ground support people were able to free up the necessary heaters to heat the engines of one of our B-47s at a time and send it off to Elmendorf. By late in the afternoon, all the aircraft made it back to Elmendorf.

A second more serious incident occurred on redeployment to DMAFB during the summer. We took the runway and the aircraft commander advanced the throttles for takeoff. He released brakes and went to max power. Immediately a deafening pulsating roar occurred that could be heard throughout the base, The AC retarded the throttles (in jets they are called thrust levers) and began braking. We received clearance to taxi back to takeoff for a second attempt. We had a mechanic riding in the fourth man's seat, an improvised seat on the way up to the copilot's seat. He chimed in that it was an "off-idle compressor stall."

The second attempted takeoff had the same results. The AC taxied off the runway. When we deplaned, we discovered that the engine compressor blades in the first three stages were bent like pretzels. We required all the engines to be changed, causing an additional week at Eielson. It was determined a bad batch of water/alcohol was the culprit.

One day at Eielson I was told to see the 55Th Strat. Recce. Wing Commander. I received no particular details except, apparently a crew had aborted a mission. Aborts had occurred twice from the same crew. It was no secret that they flew over Kamchatka peninsula in the USSR, Sakhalin Island and on to Japan for recovery, a risky venture. I was told by the detachment commander when the crew returned, we would fly the same aircraft to see if the reason for the aborts could be duplicated. We could not duplicate the aircraft anomaly and apparently there were no further aborts.

On one of my off days, I asked the tanker detachment commander if I could ride along on a refueling mission. He consented, and I was scheduled later in the day. We took off in the afternoon and headed for the refueling track designated, "Cold Coffee." We orbited for a short time and headed down track with the B-52 in the observation position ready to hook-up. I went back and laid next to the "Boomer" to observe the refueling. The B-52 hooked-up and took on 125,000 lbs. of fuel in 22 minutes without a disconnect. That was impressive! The B-52 had two Hound Dog missiles painted red, one on each wing. With the sun going down it was a sight to behold.

We redeployed to DM the day before the big Alaskan earthquake of 1964. Our replacements said the B-47s sitting on the ramp with EWO weight of 220,000 lbs. were jumping up and down like toys on their struts. They indicated it was a frightening experience.

In October1962, the Cuban Missile Crisis was upon us. After hearing President Kennedy speak to the nation, our wing commander generated the force before official orders from SAC headquarters arrived. This permitted him to disperse the fleet when the order to generate was given. We were out front of all units because of his initiative. I believe he received his star because of this action.

Our crew deployed to Edwards AFB, CA. along with two others. We deployed with two MK-28 nuclear weapons on board and ATO (assisted take off) bottles on the horse collar rack. The horse collar attaches to the side of the aircraft and the ATO bottles are attached to the collar and can be dropped when their thrust is exhausted. We spent a month at Edwards on alert until another crew replaced us. We then flew back to Tucson, had a week off and flew to Alaska to relieve crews there. SAC nuke alert was a TDY merry-go-round.

One day at Edwards, when I arrived with my crew for lunch, I spotted a college acquaintance. In the course of our conversation, he told me he worked for McDonnell Aircraft. I happened to mention that I saw an F-4 taking off in the morning while performing our preflight. I thought it to be an innocent statement. Later, I learned he was contacted by the OSI and asked if I told him why we were there and did I tell him what we were carrying? I guess the OSI was on the job. At Edwards, I also got to play handball with Joe Engle, one of the

X-15 pilots, and met the second tier of astronauts while there. I guess we scared the Russians. The missiles came out of Cuba.

On one of our checkrides we had a standardization pilot aboard that could be quite caustic. It was night and I was to shoot the stars with the sextant. I put the sextant in the mount and apparently wound it around so that it caused a spark and a shock. He looked up at me in disgust and motioned me out of the seat. He climbed into the seat and grabbed the sextant. When the calves of his legs touched the front of the ejection seat, he got quite a shock. Thank God I had on an oxygen mask, because I was grinning from ear to ear.

While at DM on alert, I took the Squadron Officers School (SOS) course and Aircraft Maintenance course by correspondence. Although I now had the time to upgrade to aircraft commander, the wing commander refused to send any copilot to PUP (Pilot Upgrading Program). I also requested to attend SOS in residence at Maxwell AFB to no avail. Our third son was born at the DMAFB hospital in August 1961.

In April 1964, we received orders to Plattsburg AFB, New York. I tried to finagle an assignment to Forbes and the 55th Strat. Recon. Wing to no avail. We departed Tucson on 4 May 1964 exactly four years to the day after we arrived. On arrival in New York, we were able to get base housing in a two story complex of four units. Shortly after being paired with a crew, I saw that I was on the upgrade list and anticipated being upgraded to AC.

From Plattsburg we "Reflexed" to Brize-Norton, a former RAF base in England. On off days, we traveled by train to London and stayed overnight at the Columbia House Officers Club across from Hyde Park. At Brize our alert quarters were quonset huts very close to the runway. Once a week a KC-135, followed later by a RB-47, departed without lights on a mission along the Baltic coast. Their departure really made us sit up in bed fearing the aircraft were coming through our huts. In the year and a half at Plattsburg, I made four trips to England to stand alert..

On arrival back from a deployment, I went in to see my squadron commander about upgrading. The three of us that arrived from DM were no longer on the list. It seemed obvious that the plan was to upgrade those that had been based at Plattsburg for some time, and they would be given preference regardless of flying time or time-in-grade. The squadron commander was indifferent to my questioning but followed up with, "had I got seat belts installed in my car?" During fire prevention week our quarters were inspected and had no write ups. I was on alert when they wanted someone from my family to attend a lecture on fire prevention at the base theatre. My wife failed to attend because of a sick child. I received a caustic letter for our "failure to attend." Later, the tanker force was relocated elsewhere and the Capehart housing quarters became available. These were ranch style one-story buildings. The base commander would not permit those of us in the four unit complexes to relocate to the Capehart housing; however, he let 1st Lts with no children move into them from off base.

These aggravating incidents set me to believe I did not have a career in the Air Force. I began to investigate the airlines. I loved the Air Force and my wife was a perfect Air Force wife. She never complained about my frequent deployments or home base alert.

While on Alert in England another pilot told me American Airlines was to start hiring. In June of 1965, I received a letter from American indicating that I should report to LaGuardia airport for an interview and testing to determine my suitability to become an airline pilot. When I returned to Plattsburg, I received a telegram offering a pilot position at American. This took some soul searching. I was a regular Air Force officer with four children and a check arriving twice a month. The airlines at times laid off personnel. What to do?

I liked the Air Force, and so did my wife. With five years of college, a complete aviation background and yet I could still not be upgraded to aircraft commander? This became the tipping point. I replied to American's letter and received a class date.

I sent a letter to the Wing Commander resigning my commission. He requested I report for an interview. He explained that I had made captain in four years; however, this was virtually automatic unless you had some sort of disciplinary action. He addressed that I "had the advantage of these two fine schools at no cost to me." He was referring to Squadron Officers School and Aircraft Maintenance School, both of which I took by correspondence. He finally said, "I am approving your resignation. The Air Force doesn't owe you anything and you don't owe the Air Force anything." Somehow I did not feel very good after this meeting. At personnel I requested a Reserve commission, which I received. They also asked me to give them 90 days before being discharged. I did. With that I was taken off the crew and given the job of opening and closing a building for the painters; so much for "mister nice guy." I was discharged on 30 October 1965. I left the Air Force with a heavy heart and some trepidation.

On 1 November 1965, I reported to American Airlines Lockheed Electra School in Chicago. We were trained as flight engineers, then copilots. I flew as an engineer on the L-188 Electra for three months, then as a copilot for seven.

I had finished my copilot training when crew schedule sent us out to get 25 hours of observation time. I choose a flight that went from Chicago to Tulsa, Oklahoma City then on to Dallas. When we reboarded the aircraft and I entered the cockpit, I noticed the copilot was seated in the jump seat behind the captain. The captain said to me, "Get in the copilot seat." I had simulator training but had not yet been on a training flight. He taxied to the takeoff runway and said, "Take us to Dallas." That's way back when a captain made decisions with little chance of reprisals from management. Today, all the training is done in the simulator with full visuals. The first time the newly qualified captain or copilot fly the airplane is on the line with passengers and a check airman in the other seat. At American, the only time a pilot receives an actual airplane training flight is when a copilot is to fly American equipment for the first time. Thereafter, all training is in the simulator.

In January 1966 I applied to join the Illinois Air National Guard based at O'Hare IAP. I had been told they would only take previously qualified KC-97 pilots. A couple of months later I walked into the Guard offices and was addressed by a gentleman in blues, but no blouse, so I did not know his rank. He introduced himself as Col Bristow, the Wing Commander. I stated the reason for my visit and he invited me into his office and interrogated me about my experience. When he heard I had taken the Aircraft Maintenance Officers course, he decided to take me into the unit. In the Guard we attended a "drill weekend" and also flew three times during the month. You could also be scheduled to fly on the drill weekend. The weekend was used mainly to take care of training requirements

I was sent to the Minneapolis Air National Guard unit to train on the KC-97L as an aircraft commander. When I returned to O'Hare, I was attached to maintenance as the Functional Check Flight Officer. The Boeing KC-97L was powered by four Pratt and Whitney 4360-59B reciprocating engines and two General Electric J47 jet engines, "Four Turning and 2 Burning." Without superb maintenance by the ground crews it would have been difficult to keep them in the air.

By fall of 1966 I was scheduled by American Airlines to train on the Convair 990. I received a call from crew schedule and suggested I should go to Boeing 707 school in Los Angeles. I questioned this since I did not think my seniority was yet in line for the B-707. He convinced me I would be just fine. So, I was trained as a copilot on the B-707.

My first trip back in Chicago from training, I was paired with the most senior captain in Chicago. It was a non-stop to Los Angeles and back. My reaction was WOW! Sure glad I took the B-707 assignment. That was the last passenger trip I had for some time. For five years, the only trip I could hold was on B-707 freighters, that wonderful all-night flying.

We had some captains that were hired in1938 and were captains in six months due to the war. This group thought only "they" could do the flying and had little trust in the "new hire" copilots. I enjoyed flying with the WW II vets the best. I flew with guys that flew B-17s over Germany; a pilot that flew a P-38 over the beaches of Normandy on D-day; a pilot who flew F4U Corsairs in the South Pacific.

The ex-military pilots always traded flying legs with the copilot. One captain said to me, "Ok, Andy, your leg. Just don't get me killed or fired." One of the 1938-hired captains flew seven legs himself before he gave me a leg, and then it was "cook book" flying with him offering complete supervision. Finally, I said to him, "If you don't trust my flying ability, I'll just answer the phone and you do all the flying." One thing you learned early on was to take mental notes of the captains you would emulate for their flying skills and command presence in the cockpit.

Night flying and winter in Chicago was always a" joy." There was often snow to contend with. One night we arrived by company car at the freight dock with a light snow falling. I did the walk around and notified the captain that the airplane should be deiced. His reaction was, "Naa, not necessary. It will all blow off." In those days the captain was God. My thought was, this guy could get us killed, but

I trusted his judgment, sorta. We were to depart with a B-707-300 freighter, intercontental model, grossing 330,000 lbs. on an 8000' runway. He made the takeoff. When he rotated, we had just entered the last 1000' of red lights and climbed out at 300'/min. I guess the snow blew off.

"Standardization" began to enter into the lexicon of airline training. There was some resistance from older captains. Those of us that had military training were already exposed to its value in crew coordination. Consequently, we began to speak up when a captain was deviating from the operating manual. I was told a long time ago of the necessity to fly an airplane within the performance envelope. When you exceed those limits, you become a test pilot; not a good idea with passengers onboard.

One captain I flew with would not use reverse thrust to slow the aircraft on landing. He used only brakes because the reversing was "so noisy." Finally, I told him, "When we end up in the grass at the end of the runway, it will take some creative explanation on your part to explain how we ended up there."

Another captain would start back pressure on takeoff roll to get the weight off the nose gear, and would continue until we received the stick shaker warning of an impending stall. I finally told him if we lost an engine at that point he would cartwheel down the runway. The airplane would break ground before V1, the speed that you could safely abort and stop on the remaining runway, and below V2 where you could safely control the airplane and climb out.

In 1967, the Air National Guard was charged with supporting Air Force units in Europe. It was called, "Operation Creek Party." The intent was to allow fighter units, particularly in Germany, to maintain refueling proficiency. Ten Air Guard units rotated to Rhein-Main Airbase, co-located at Frankfurt International Airport over a 10 year period. Our unit the, 108th Air Refueling Squadron, with our KC-97s, was one that participated.

My first deployment was in Oct 1967. We departed O'Hare and flew to Goose Bay, Labrador, stayed overnight, then flew non-stop to Frankfurt Germany. We spent two weeks until relieved by another refueling squadron. The return trip was from Frankfort to Keflavik Iceland, then non-stop to O'Hare.

In Germany, we refueled fighters from Air Force bases at Hahn, Bitburg, Ramstein and Spangdahlem. On occasion we fueled fighters from England over the English Channel. On one of my missions I refueled a flight of four F-4s. When they completed refueling and departed, they flew through another flight of F-4s causing a collision with the loss of two aircraft and associated lives.

I made a trip every year from 1967 until Feb 1976 to satisfy the active duty requirements. On my first trip I was still attached to maintenance, but as an aircraft commander, I was in command of one of the six aircraft deployed. As the years went by I became an Instructor Pilot and evaluator. Eventually, I became head of Standards and Evaluation for our unit with a secondary job as simulator officer. Before I was installed in the job of Chief of Standards and Evaluation. I had to attend a Combat Evaluation Group school located at Barksdale AFB.

I was in class with all active duty pilots. The instructor, to add some levity to the first day of class, began to bend down and glance under the tables. It seemed a little strange, then he said, "I just wanted to see who had the white socks on to determine a Reservist or Guardsman." Of course everyone laughed.

I was fortunate on two of the trips to Germany to have the chance to fly a mission out of Torrejon Airbase in Madrid, Spain. On the first trip I refueled a flight of F-4s on a track adjacent to the Rock of Gibraltar over the Mediterranean. After the refueling, we descended to low level and flew along the Coasta Del Sol.

The second time I was sent to Torrejon to participate in an air show. I rendezvoused with a couple of F-4s and flew across the airdrome at a low level; not very exciting; however, it permitted me an evening in downtown Madrid. I had dinner at Casa Botin's on the Plaza Mayor and saw a flamenco performance; a great evening.

On one of my deployments to Germany I had a four-day weekend. I met my wife, her sister and father in Rome and we flew to Palermo Sicily, Italy, my ancestral home. My father-in-law's family is from Cefalu on the coast just past Alta Vista. The family name is "Portiera" (Muscarello/Portiera – are we Italian, or what?). My wife's uncle was the mayor of Cefalu. An uncle was the town architect and another uncle had a business. I thought I was going to visit among peasants. It turns out I was the peasant. My wife's relatives lived extremely well, an apartment overlooking the sea, cut glass in the interior doors and we slept in crochet linen. The chandlers were ornate, and so was the wallpaper.

On Sunday I had to return to Frankfurt. The relatives drove me to the airport in two cars, in one of which rode the mayor. I asked to stop in Alta Vista. When we pulled into town, the people were hanging out the windows. They recognized the mayor but wanted to know who I was. A beautiful park was at the entrance of the town with a tremendous view. Across from where I was standing I saw a fellow bring out a horse from a stable. I remarked to my wife that he looked like my uncle Joe. It turned out he was a Muscarello. Later, an old man peered from around a building. He turned out to be my grandfather's youngest brother. My grandfather, Andrea Muscarello (I was named after him as is the custom of the first born grandson), owned olive groves outside the town. I later learned he left them to this brother.

While in Germany, I was scheduled to refuel the Thunderbirds on their way to the Netherlands for an air show. En route, an engine failed and we "feathered" the prop. I elected to continue and complete the mission. When the two J-57 engines were added outboard to the KC-97, an increase of our refueling speed to 230 knots made the refueling much easier for the fighter drivers. We could also "toboggan" by starting a slow descent to increase speed for the refueling. I was confident we could achieve the speed the Thunderbirds needed to complete their refueling.

The only incident I experienced in the KC-97 that could have been quite serious was the ingestion of a flock of birds. I was departing on a refueling mission from O'Hare and was second in line behind an American Airlines DC-10. The DC-10 was cleared into position. Instead of the captain taking the runway from the taxiway where we were lined up, he choose to taxi further down and take the runway from the next taxiway. With that delay, the tower asked if we were ready for takeoff. We were cleared for an immediate takeoff. I made it a rolling takeoff and as we began to roll, I could see what l looked like a mirage at a dip in the runway. As we progressed it became apparent it was a flock of seagulls. I initiated the abort but plowed into the midst of them. I was able to get the aircraft stopped by the end of the runway. When the tower asked the reason for the abort, he closed the runway. An inspection vehicle reported at least 2-300 dead birds covering the runway. The damage was excessive on the lights, engine cowlings and forward fuselage skin. Fortunately, none came through the windscreen. Several hundred man-hours were needed to repair the aircraft. I have often wondered what would have happened to the DC-10 if he had initiated takeoff.

To put airline seniority in prospective: When I started with American my seniority number was 2233. To be a captain your seniority number had to be in the 500s. There was little movement unless someone retired, died or the airline acquired a new route. American served 44 cities and generally speaking you landed at most of them. Consequently, when checking out as a captain, you had knowledge of the airports, runways and taxiways.

I was a copilot for 12 years, 10 of which were on the B-707. So, when I checked out as captain on the B-707 at American or the KC-135 in the Guard, it was little challenge. By the time I retired there were captains with seniority numbers at 3300 on the DC-10. Of course, there were 10,000 pilots on the list by then.

By 1978 at American, I had cycled through the Electra, B-707, and DC-10 as a copilot. It was time to check out as a captain on the B-727. This afforded me the ability to fly with my "favorite" captain every month, Ha! Ha! During training we new captains were introduced to all departments of the airline, from operations to maintenance and everything in between. We called it, "charm school." I then flew the B 727-100 and B 727-200 (stretched version) for two years. During this time I became an "L-type" airman. This meant I conducted the line checks required of every captain once a year.

Being a check airman afforded me the privilege of displacing captains to fly a trip if I desired. Additionally, I had the ability to interact with crews often. I was called one day to "deadhead" to LaGuardia to route check a captain that was letting his flight engineer fly. Arriving at LaGuardia, I boarded the airplane with the crew in question. I knew the captain who had been a Navy pilot. As I walked into the cockpit I immediately saw he had the flight engineer in the copilot's seat. I greeted them all and told the captain I was going to the back to hang up my coat. When I returned, all were in their proper seats. Another problem solved.

At O'Hare, there was also a C-119 Air Force Reserve squadron. One of the pilots from the Reserve unit had been with American since 1957 when they last hired. He was now American's B-727 fleet manager. Since he knew I was Chief of Standards and Evaluation at the Guard unit, he called and asked if I would come to work for him at the American Flight Academy just south of the Dallas-Fort Worth airport. At the time I was scheduled to go to captain school on the B-707. He assured me I would get the 707 rating if I came to work in training on the B-727.

Thus, I became an "X-type" check airman. X-types worked the line and simulators, L- types were line check airmen only. It was an education for me. I would pick up a crew in training after they completed their ground simulator instruction. They would have four rides in the simulator with me as instructor and one "pump-up" ride prior to the rating ride in the airplane. Then, with an FAA Air Carrier Inspector on board, we flew out to a satellite airport for their rating ride. The FAA would request the maneuvers he wished to see while I would be in the right seat acting as the candidate's copilot. After the rating ride, I usually offered the FAA inspector the chance to fly the airplane back to DFW. They did not fly much, so it was welcomed.

I was also given the task to give an occasional proficiency check. At that time a captain came for training every six months. The first time was a practice session in which you could demonstrate or allow them to practice certain maneuvers in the simulator; the second time was the proficiency check.

There were pilots that would arrive all psyched up thinking you were there to fail them. The opposite was in fact true. Every consideration was afforded to passing them. I had a pilot from San Francisco whose proficiency check was not going very well. During the post flight critique, I was saving the bad news until the end until he confided in me that his 13 year-old son was dying of cancer. I am sure he knew the ride was unsatisfactory. Consequently, I told him I would record this simulator session as a practice ride so that when he felt comfortable, he could be rescheduled.

One weekend I was called to report to LaGuardia to give a copilot an evaluation. I flew two days with him and had three pages of unsatisfactory performance write-ups. What surprised me was how he ever got hired. When we arrived back at LaGuardia, the chief pilot met us at the plane for a report. American had acquired Caribbean Airways where the pilot was a flight engineer. He had a commercial license with minimum time, and elected to transfer to American as a pilot instead of a flight engineer. Two check airmen from New York rode with him and failed him previous to my evaluation.

A year later I testified at his hearing with regard to his termination. A company attorney and a union attorney were present. I testified that he was incapable of getting an airplane from altitude to a landing airport in the event the captain was incapacitated. That sealed his fate. A month later I found out his termination was upheld mainly because I had not been told ahead of time about his lack of experience and had no preconceived idea of his ability. At a break in the hearing, in the hallway, he was confident that he would continue with just some more simulator training and asked me if I would be his instructor. I was stunned.

I instructed for two years and then got my rating to captain on the B-707. I flew the B-707 as a captain for a year until American began to retire them. I worked in the school and every third month I would fly the line by displacing a captain. This was a plus because I could choose the trip I desired.

In November 1976, the Air National Guard received the KC-135s. Instructors were brought in from Castle AFB, CA. All training was local. A simulator was brought in and housed at Glenview NAS in a railroad car, where we traveled for training. I was able to qualify in the shortest amount of time owing to the amount of time I had in the B-707.

In order to make an EWO tanker takeoff (max gross weight) we had to fly to Grissom AFB, IN. There, we were refueled and required to demonstrate the max weight takeoff. Simulator training was also conducted at Grissom. Our tanker unit soon acquired an alert commitment in support of a B-52 unit. This also required me to stand alert a couple days a month at O'Hare. I knew I was back in SAC.

I flew the KC-135 for two years and during this period I retained the position as Chief of Standards and Evaluation. Two of the Castle instructor pilots left active duty and joined our unit as fulltime Air Technicians. The unit now mirrored an active duty unit and not a "flying club." I was working at the American Flight Academy and flying with the Guard; two fulltime jobs. I decided it was time to retire from the Guard. In 1978 I retired with eight years active duty and 12 with the Air National Guard. I had a total of 4800 hours military flying.

I left the Flight Academy and requested to return to fly the line. After a few months, I went to DC-10 school at DFW. After I received my rating and flew the line for 100 hours, I was once again made an L- type check airman. For a while the schoolhouse philosophy was to have captains from each of the bases work there for a time. I was the only one in Chicago that ever worked at the Flight Academy.

The American Chief Pilot in Chicago petitioned me to take the job of International Chief Pilot. At this point ego got in the way of good judgment, and I accepted. It soon became apparent that it consisted of meeting after meeting. In the morning I went to offices where the previous day's f---ups were hashed out. God forbid, you bring up an obvious deficiency in another department; this was heresy And, here I thought we were all on the same team. The attitude was, "just fly them from A to B, we will handle the rest." Then, there were the constant trips to DFW for boring meetings or sitting in when the company doctor came in once a month to allow the alcoholics to pour out their souls. If you wanted to fly you had to do it on weekends. I preferred working in the trenches and did not have a penchant for administrative work. I submitted my resignation to return to the line.

My wife and I decided to move to Tucson. I transferred to Los Angeles flying the DC-10 and commuted until American received the MD-11. I transferred back to Chicago to fly the MD-11. Since all the flying was international I only commuted to Chicago three or four times a month. After a few months, I was contacted by the fleet manager of the MD-11 program and asked if I would consent to instruct on the airplane.

American bought 18 MD-11s and they were being delivered rather rapidly. Three of us agreed to instruct, but I added a caveat. I would only work until they were caught up with the training because I was two years from retirement and wanted to end my career flying the line. I spent two different months at Gatwick Airport in London. American leased simulator time from British Caledonia Airlines. One of the months my wife accompanied me which provided her a fine vacation.

On returning from England, I had an A-1 pass (company business) which in theory the agent could displace a passenger to give me a seat. Realistically, as a pilot, you would take a seat in the cockpit. My wife had an upgraded pass but the airplane was full. So, we both stayed back. The agent advised me a trip from DFW arrived late the previous day and it was going back late that afternoon, empty. That afternoon he met us and arranged to take us to the airplane that was parked on the tarmac. My wife did a considerable amount of shopping; we had boxes upon boxes. The agent graciously loaded them on board (what service). We traveled back to DFW with 14 flight attendants and just us. Two of the girls lost the toss and worked the trip and serviced the rest of us.

While flying the MD-11 our flight attendants went on a short strike. My monthly schedule was a trip nonstop to London Heathrow. American decided that they wanted the equipment in London and did not cancel. We had no passengers due to the strike. Onboard were only we three pilots. At O'Hare, on departure you are "capped" at 5000'. The controller noticed our climb rate and asked if we could maintain a 2000 fpm rate of climb. I told him we could do better than that. He cleared us unrestricted to 39,000'. The three General Electric CF-6-80 engines developing 61,900 lbs. of thrust permitted an extreme deck angle in the climb. At last, I was flying a fighter.

Finally, the momentous day arrived. There are two things that happen inevitably in a pilot's life: one, you walk out to your airplane knowing it is your last flight; two, you walk to your airplane not knowing it is your last flight. This was my happy/sad occasion - I would be flying my last trip as an American Airlines Captain. It was April of 1994. I had a six-day trip that went from O'Hare to Heathrow, overnight, then to New York, overnight, back to London, overnight, then, back to O'Hare. My wife rode to London and stayed there until we returned to O'Hare. Two of my sons are captains for United Airlines. Son, John, rode in the cockpit with me to London then deadheaded back to O'Hare. Son, Michael, deadheaded to London and rode in the cockpit with me to O'Hare. I had my wife come up to the cockpit and sit on the jump seat for the final landing at O'Hare. In London, a large cake was put aboard that was shared with the first class passengers as well as the crew. On arrival in Chicago my cousin, a Chicago fire department lieutenant based at O'Hare, was able to film my arrival on the International gate. In operations there was an additional celebration with cake and beverages.

While employed by American, I had the opportunity to fly to London, Frankfurt, Madrid, Brussels, Buenos Aires and Tokyo Narita internationally. In addition I flew into all the Caribbean cities American serviced as well as domestic locations.

Because of the reliability of the jet engine I only shut down an engine once on each aircraft on which I was qualified. This in the operating manual is not considered an emergency. I enjoyed weather approaches because it challenged my proficiency and the training I had received.

I finished my career flying 20 years with the Air Force and Air National Guard, 29 years with American Airlines and accumulated just over 25,000 total flight hours. After retirement I flew my Beechcraft Bonanza V-35B until selling it in 2004.

I have been blessed with a wonderful wife of 59 years, four children and 12 grandchildren. I am proud that I have one son, a physician, two sons that are captains with United Airlines and a daughter that has her own business. I could not have had a better life.

CHAPTER TEN

Cheesehead Goes Airborne

by Martin J. "Marty" Neuens

I was raised in a small town, Aurora, in northern Wisconsin, a great place to grow up with a river and lots of woods in which to play. My dad died when I was in the second grade, so we were quite poor. But, Mom was a trooper, and we always had food on the table. I worked as a paperboy, delivered milk, bundled newspapers, and was a grocery clerk to help out. I went to high school across the river (also the state border) in Kingsford, Michigan. I played football there, and was the smallest guard around (Coach made me wear rib pads, not for protection, but so I would look bigger).

I always had an interest in airplanes, but not an avid one. I just stopped and looked up every time a DC-3, Gooney Bird, flew over our house on approach to the airport across the river. So, when my high school Principal called me to the office and told me my Congressman was going to be nearby, and I could have the day off to go see him about going to the Air Force Academy, the day off sounded good. My biggest problem was that every time I got paper work (lots and lots of it) to submit, it arrived a day or so after the "no excuses" deadline for submission. Somehow, I ended up in the USAFA Class of "64" anyway.

At the Academy, I survived "Doolie Summer" despite not being able to do push-ups or pull-ups at the level of most others. I did have stamina going for me though, so I struggled through. I ended up on the USAFA Ski Team for the last three years competing primarily in Nordic events, jumping and cross-country. Cross-country skiing requires a little bit of masochism, and jumping requires a lot of insanity. A case in point: I crashed and burned during my senior year while jumping on a rather large hill at Steamboat Springs, Colorado and ended up with amnesia. Apparently after the fall, I got up and jumped again before the concussion started to take effect. Later, someone found me wandering around in the parking lot not knowing where my skis were or what my name was. I have no memory from about half way through breakfast to around dusk, when I became aware of a doctor standing over me in a motel room asking how many fingers he was holding up. This was the sixth concussion in my young life (branch broke in an apple tree and I landed on my head as a child; hit my head on a rock wall while wrestling with a friend in grade school; got kicked in the head by a friend on a rope swing at the river during high school; hit my head on a raft while playing "King of the Hill" in the middle of the lake at night; and in soccer at USAFA, I tried to head a ball and someone else tried to kick it...he didn't get the ball, but he almost scored my head). Unfortunately, every time you get a concussion it is easier to get another, and it tends to be more severe. That's my excuse!...for a lot of things. I also observed that the masochism and insanity required above turned out to be good traits for a fighter pilot.

The amnesia became an issue when I wanted to go into flying after the Academy. The Academy sent me to Fitzsimons Army Hospital in Denver for an EEG (brain wave test). Fortunately, the old Army doctor I saw asked me if I wanted to fly. I said, "Yes," and he decided not to do the EEG because he felt the Air Force put too much stock in them, and that the test would certainly show some affect of the concussion with so little time elapsed. Instead, he gave me visual, sensory, and cognitive tests and said I was OK. So, I got an assignment to pilot training.

I went to Reese AFB, Lubbock, Texas for pilot training, where I became fond of a line from a popular song at that time that said, "Happiness is Lubbock in your rear view mirror." When I finished ground school, that old amnesia became an issue again. I was grounded while everyone else was starting to fly, and there was talk of sending me to Brooks Medical Center for an evaluation. However, after about ten days, paperwork came through clearing me to fly. I didn't ask any questions, but years later found out that all record of my amnesia had disappeared from my medical record...THANK YOU, UNKNOWN PERSON!!!

I didn't know it at the time, but my first IP was a FAIP (First Assignment Instructor Pilot) and four of us students were his first class. He turned out to be a very good IP. After we moved on from the T-37 to the T-38, he became a good friend that we went skiing with in Taos, Santa Fe, and Ruidoso, New Mexico. I am still in touch with him and the one other remaining student from our pilot training table of four.

The main excitement, other than learning to land in the ever-present cross-winds at Reese, was when it became popular to join the "Ten Mile High Club." To be admitted to the club, you had to climb over 52,800 feet, which wasn't allowed because it was required to have a pressure suit to go over 50,000 feet. It was also above the aircraft's service ceiling; therefore, you needed to shut off your IFF so you wouldn't be observed. Several students who had tried didn't make it since they had an engine flameout as they got close. I've always been a sucker for dares, so I decided to try. It took waiting to be in the right flying area that was big enough, and had sufficient maneuvering space to stay in the area. Just as I got to the ten mile altitude, one engine flamed out, and immediately so did the other one...oops. The canopy iced over instantly because pressurization was lost. Also lost were almost all my instruments. I was getting a little nervous now since I was above 50,000 feet, where they say blood boils without pressurization. I scratched a little peephole in the ice (probably really frost) after nosing over and went over the restart procedure. I tried to restart each engine repeatedly, to no avail, and was starting to have visions of a bailout as I got lower and lower. At long last one engine started, and then the other...WHEW!...I later noticed a small note in the manual that said that an engine might not restart until right about the altitude where mine started (wished I had been aware of that).

Out of pilot training, I was fortunate to get an assignment to F-105s at Nellis AFB, Las Vegas, Nevada. That was the most fun flying I've ever done: real low-levels at 50 feet, rolling inverted at the crest of each peak; having to pull up to get over a train; flying up Death Valley with the altimeter reading below sea level; pulling up to get over Joshua trees; and range missions almost every day with strafing so close to the ground, if you waited to see your bullets hit, you hit with them. Oh, did I mention flying over the Grand Canyon?

From there I was assigned to Takhli Air Base, Thailand to fight in Vietnam. I was fortunate to be able to fly an F-105 accompanied by three others across the pond to Hawaii and then to Japan. This good fortune also allowed me to avoid going to Jungle Survival

School (known as Snake School...need I say more). My second most interesting mission during the war was a four-ship mission that separated into two two-ships because of bad weather. We were to look for targets of opportunity in Route Pack 6. On the way home we were informed that a pilot, Fred Flom, was down, so we air-refueled and went back to look for him. We saw his chute but could not make contact and assumed he had been captured. On the way back home again, we were informed that Fred's lead, Jim Kasler, had also been shot down, so we refueled and went back again. Jim had made it across the river into the mountains, and we made contact with him on his emergency radio.

Jim was on a piece of karst (a sharp-edged, limestone, rugged hill), but the North Vietnamese were getting close.. We called to start the rescue mission, although things didn't look promising. We went back-and-forth to the tanker several times, most of which was in the weather. At Jim's location, the valley was clear, but the mountains on both sides stuck up into the clouds. I was having my own problems, as my "Stab-Aug" system (helps keep the plane steady) wasn't working making flying on lead's wing in the weather and refueling very squirrelly. Also, my TACAN (navigation system) wasn't working properly, so I was never sure of our location unless I could see the ground. I never did figure out how lead could let down in the clouds and end up in the valley without hitting the mountains. More important to me: when we were on top of the clouds, I took spacing for SAM missile defense, but when lead let down, I was on my own to decide how far down I was willing to go hoping to pop out in the valley. Fortunately, I didn't find any rocks in the clouds. The Gooks did get to Jim as anticipated, but there was also a miracle: an F-101 recce pilot who had disappeared the night before, came up on the radio in the next valley, and we were able to get him rescued. All-in-all, a very, very long, tiring, but rewarding mission.

My most interesting mission (unfortunately) was shortly thereafter, when I got shot down and joined Fred and Jim and several other people I knew in Hanoi. We were going against a factory that made 50-gallon oil drums on the south side of Thai Nguyen, which is about 50 kilometers north of Hanoi. We came off a ridge to the north, and as we popped up there were numerous small arms firing right off to my side (I could see the muzzle flashes and barrel movement).

Shortly, my engine "FIRE" and "OVERHEAT" warning lights came on (indicating an engine fire). Another flight member transmitted, "Two is hit!" (he probably saw flames coming from my aircraft). I jettisoned my bombs and came out of burner, and shortly the nose started to pitch down. I was losing hydraulic fluid and hence control. The nose pitched down sharply, and I was looking at dirt. I grabbed the ejection handles and consciously pulled my butt into the seat since I was pulling negative Gs and the shotgun shell ejection seat would break my back if there was any gap between my butt and the seat. I pulled the triggers and began a new flying career.

I tumbled with my arms and legs flailing, thinking I have to get them in for the opening shock, remembering that others said the opening shock was the first thing of which they were aware. So, I realized the automatic chute-opening feature hadn't worked (a great blessing, because I surely would have been severely injured since I was doing around 600 knots). I came down in a rice paddy next to a village, and the next day they took me into Hanoi. It was to be a long tour (six and one-half years).

The things that got me through my POW years were my faith in God (He has a plan for me), my faith that our country wouldn't leave us there (though sometimes I wondered), the faithfulness of my friends (I would trust them with my life) and their sense of humor (to brighten up my day). One example of the later: the little trap door in my cell door opened and a guard looked in and pointed to his eye (to show me the new English words he had learned). He said, "I'm," and I nodded to say you got that right. Then, he pointed to his ear and says, "queer." I nod again, but inside I was feeling only joy - a nearby POW friend had just sent me a little cheer!

Our group of POWs was released in March 1973. What a great day it was to walk up the ramp of the C-141. There were flight nurses aboard and one gave me a big hug...you have no idea how good she smelled...I still remember her name, "Mickey Mantle."

After recouping at Wright-Patterson AFB, Dayton, OH and at home in Wisconsin, I got my "Freedom Flight" and flying rehab in T-38s at Randolph AFB, San Antonio, TX. I then went to check out in A-7s and fly in an operational squadron at Davis-Monthan AFB, Tucson, AZ. There I met my future wife, Cindy, at a ski club meeting (I skied, she didn't, but she learned). By the way, one of the members of our Friday

Luncho Buncho is Col Bill Hosmer, who was one of my commanders at D-M (that's probably why he retired). When the A-7s converted to A-10s, I didn't have enough total flying time (due to my prison years) to be an IP, so I trundled off to The Naval War College, Newport, RI to complete Command and Staff School. Following Rhode Island, Cindy and I were married, a GREAT decision...on my part.

Next, came O-2 training at Patrick AFB, Cape Canaveral, FL. Cindy and I got to watch lots of space shots from our front porch. A tour at Bergstrom AFB, Austin, TX, followed, first working in the wing, then at HQ 12th AF on the General's Briefing Team. Air Force Operational Test and Evaluation Center (AFOTEC), at Kirtland AFB, NM came next. It was an interesting tour working on the testing of new air-to-ground weapons systems.

Ever the world travelers, we next headed for Tech Training Group at Chanute AFB, Rantoul, IL working with young airman training in electronic fields, and finally my hardship tour: ROTC at the University of Miami, FL. This was my favorite job, working with young men and women. It was really great to see that there were some wonderfully capable young people out there who were willing to serve...all is not lost.

My greatest achievement in the Air Force was avoiding the Pentagon (everyone I knew that went there aged tremendously).

My greatest joy in life is my wife, Cindy.

My greatest discovery in life is that God came to earth to suffer and die for my sins, and that I just have to accept that gift to spend eternity in heaven.

CHAPTER ELEVEN

Luckier Than a Three Horned Billy Goat

by Earl T. "Earl" O'Loughlin

"How did you get there?" is an oft-asked question and one hard to explain. Born in Bay City, Michigan of parents struggling during the Great Depression of the 30s, we were fortunate my dad, a refrigeration repairman, had a job. When I was five, we moved to a small town in the northeast portion of the lower peninsula of Michigan on the shores of Lake Huron, called East Tawas. This meant leaving my grandparents' home where we lived and moving into the north woods also referred to as "God's Country." As a small boy, this was a great place to grow up; a caring town of about 1,800 folks all of whom loved the area. It provided me with an excellent childhood. Despite the fact we didn't have much, no one thought of themselves as poor because most were in the same boat. We always had plenty to eat, a warm bed and anything new was a treat and usually unexpected.

I attended grade school and did well. Little did I know at the time the Japanese attack on Pearl Harbor was going to influence my future career choices and destiny. I remember getting my first job as a Special Delivery Letter boy. At 15 cents a letter and about 10 deliveries a week I was richer than "God." In addition, I delivered the Detroit Free Press to about 40 customers and that was another $2.00 per week. This money kept me in shotgun shells and fishing gear. I spent a lot of time hunting and fishing. My mother would give me 25 cents for two-dozen minnows and tell me she needed 50 perch, and off I'd go. She didn't like me to hunt alone with a .410 shotgun, but Dad said it was okay and a couple of grouse in the kitchen sink would soften Mother's feelings. We seemingly always had a deer hanging in the basement. Dad called it "government beef," and the Game Warden never bothered us. Times were hard, but we survived.

At age 11-12, I got a job in the local hardware store in sales – what a great job for a kid. I learned to thread pipe, cut glass, learned a 6/8/10 in. "flat bastard" was a file, a number 2 mantle fit most oil lamps and all sorts of useful things, all for $5.00 a week after school and Saturdays. At age 13 I went to work for the City Department of Public Works digging new sewer lines, building sidewalks, hauling garbage and working each summer through high school. I made $1.05 an hour. Moonlighting on my uncle's summer garbage route added another $1.00 an hour, and I packed it all away for college. A highlight of my moonlight job was picking up garbage at Ethel's Steakhouse where I also got a piece of pie and a "squeeze" from Shirlee, who had caught my eye in school. There is more to that story later.

During this time, the nation was waging WWII and my exposure to and interest in aviation was growing. East Tawas was located about 15 miles from what was then known as "Camp Skeel." Skeel was a gunnery range for the Army Air Corps out of Selfridge and the air on any given day was full of P-40s, P-47s, T-6s, P-39s and later P-51s, zipping over Tawas Bay, headed for the range. We often watched the aircraft come-in over the water and strafe the field targets and drop small ordinance and zoom off. During that time the 99th Pursuit Squadron of Tuskegee Airmen fame trained there. On Sunday, the sharply-dressed black pilots attended church at the Christ Episcopal Church where I was an alter boy and my mother played the organ. Two things remain vivid in my mind – first, the Tuskegee Airmen looked very sharp in their uniforms, and they were black. We had no black families that far north, and it was all interesting to me as a young boy. Later, many Air Force pilots trained at Skeel and the base became "Oscoda Air Base," later renamed, "Wurtsmith AFB" under the Strategic Air Command. The base was closed during the Base Closures (BRACs) in the 1990s – more about Wurtsmith AFB later.

Throughout the 40s until I graduated in 1948, the war was very important to me. My dad would often be on the base and talk about the captains, majors and even lieutenant colonels he met. Since I was known to have an interest in the service, people advised me to apply for a "service academy." This thought appealed to me as I knew my parents weren't in a financial position to afford college. In the fall of 1948 while attending Bay City Junior College on a partial scholarship with money I had saved working two jobs each summer, I received an "alternate" appointment to West Point. Unfortunately, or fortunately, the primary accepted and later blew the whistle on the football coach, Red Blaik, in a huge tutoring and cheating scandal. After all that,

I continued at Bay City in a mechanical engineering curriculum. I played basketball and pursued that waitress from Ethel's Steakhouse, who was also my classmate.

After graduating from junior college in 1950 and knowing that finishing my degree was financially doubtful, I still wanted to join the military and fly. So, in September 1950 with two years of college and an associate degree, I went to Selfridge AFB and took all the exams, met the board of review and returned to Tawas to see what came next. In about two weeks I received a letter saying I had been accepted for pilot training and would receive notification of a class date.

The Korean Conflict was in full swing and the services were jammed with draftees and the Air Force with enlisted personnel. Lackland had even established a "Tent City" to handle the backlog. I received a letter saying my pilot training was delayed and to insure I kept my slot, I should "enlist" as soon as possible! I did. In between receiving the letter and my enlistment, I became engaged to Ethel's (remember Ethel's Steakhouse?) daughter and was happier than a clam.

In February 1951, I took the oath of enlistment at Fort Wayne in Detroit and the next day left by train for Sampson AFB, NY, a new installation taken over from the Navy. Upon arrival, I learned why the Navy gave it up. It was February in upstate New York and colder than a well digger's ---. We were told we would live in a dormitory, not tents like Lackland. We were marched in the dark to our dormitory, 14 of us to a room, and most rooms had window glass missing. We were issued seven army blankets, a fart sack and told to get to bed. Four of the blankets were used as a mattress and the other three went on top for warmth.

After two weeks, we were issued a pair of fatigues, an Army olive-drab (OD) overcoat and brown rawhide brogans that had to be black and shiny the next morning - out came the canned heat, black polish and elbow grease. About one-third way through the 12 weeks of basic training we were issued Army OD uniforms. I received a green Army Ike Jacket, an off-green Army garrison hat, pants and a new pair of Air Force black low-quarter shoes. We looked like something from the foreign legion.

We graduated from Sampson, and I received orders for Perrin AFB, Texas reporting to an OMS Squadron as a "431xx" – this was a whole new world for me. After arriving on a weekend, I was to report to the First Sgt. in full dress uniform. So, early the next morning, I stood before his desk. "PFC Earl T. O'Loughlin reports as ordered, Sir." He took one look at me and said. "Where in the hell did you come from? And, don't call me Sir." I informed him of where I had come from and he picked up the phone and called another Sgt. and said, "I've got a job for you." He then said to follow him and asked me what I had in my barracks bag. I told him my OD overcoat, etc. He said, "Find the nearest dumpster," as he didn't ever want to see any more ODs. We went to the Clothing Sales Store, and after stripping to my shorts, I received a blue blouse, a blue Ike Jacket, blue shirts, blue hat, blue pants and new shoes. For the first time, I felt Air Force.

I worked the flight line with some outstanding Staffs, Techs and one Master Sgt. who had Command Pilot Wings – he had become a MSgt in the wartime drawdown after having been a Command Pilot with 15+ years in order to retire at 20. It was a great experience. I learned a lot in a hurry, worked on B-25s and T-6s and then received my orders to Class 52-D at Spence Field, Moultree, Georgia, a civilian contract school run by Beverly (Bevo) Howard, a renowned Acrobatic pilot. All of the flight instructors were civilian and ex-military. Many were also crop dusters. Of course the military was in charge of checkrides and final acceptance. Moultree Spence Field was different than northeast Michigan. "Tha-at" was a two-syllable word, watermelon was plentiful and the town mothers were always bringing their daughters to the Cadet pool. I was still deeply in love with Ethel's daughter and flying and ground school were challenges that kept me humping.

Each instructor had four students. My instructor washed-out three and was after me when we bent a wing tip at an auxiliary field (Tipton, GA). The next day I received a flight check by the flight leader, and he soloed me that day - what luck to save my --- (remember the three horned Billy Goat). I finished easily after that and got my assignment to Enid, Oklahoma, supposedly to fly T-28s; however, upon arriving, I found they were all grounded and sitting at the end of the runway with no props. It seemed the T-28s were shedding props at about 500 hours engine time, so we were put into B-25s.

With the washout rate at 50 percent or better in Basic, we found out that the military pilots were going to do everything possible to get us through. We even had one cadet buzz Norman, Oklahoma, hit some trees and knowing he had brush in his gear, intentionally ground looped on return to Enid. His aircraft didn't leave the runway and he met an FEB that only washed him back a class; however, the Honor Board got him for lying and he was history.

After I progressed at Enid, Ethel's daughter decided to move to Enid and got a job in the telephone office. She had one bedroom in a family home, and we got to see each other on Friday nights and some weekends until I became a first classman, when I had some weekends free. She quickly informed me that if I was thinking of spending weekends at her place there was going to be marriage involved. Long story short, we finally found a place in Huntsville, Arkansas where a justice would do the deed. It was a short, quick ceremony. "I now pronounce you man and wife – kiss and be happy and $10.00 please." This was of course against Air Force policy for Aviation Cadets to be married, and we had that problem to solve until the June graduation.

In April 1952, I received word the Commandant wanted to see me and I reported as soon as I could. He said, "You lucky SOB, I received word you've been accepted to West Point." My heart sank. I asked what does that mean and he said, "You resign your Aviation Cadet status and report to West Point." I asked what if I flunk the entrance exams (no prep school) he said, "Then you'll return to the Air Force at your highest grade (PFC)." I told him I had passed my instrument check and my contact check and I was six weeks from graduation and I was not going to accept the appointment. After questioning my sanity and intelligence, he dismissed me in total disgust. Shortly thereafter, Shirlee went home to prepare for the "big" wedding her folks were planning. Surely I would have been found out along the way at West Point and I felt already luckier than that Billy Goat to have gotten through pilot training. I married the girl of my dreams "again," and my folks and hers all went to their graves never knowing we were married twice (our secret).

Upon graduation from Enid, I received orders to Randolph Air Force Base, San Antonio, Texas to become a B-29 Eagle Crew Pilot. Awaiting the class, I was vectored to Ellington AFB, Houston, Texas to fly B-25s and C-47s at the Navigator Training Wing. Finally, after about three months, I reported to Randolph, met my fellow assigned crew members and prepared to fly missions over North Korea. We went through the usual transition, bombing, navigation and gunnery, then finished final training at Reno, Nevada, Stead AFB. I was lucky to be trained with a former B-17 aircraft commander from WWII with a lot of experience. He shared his experience with me. We were a good team in the cockpit and escaped many potential disasters during our tour together, both in training and over Korea. It was unbelievable that the same B-29s I watched as a kid in theaters dropping bombs over Japan in 1945, I would now be flying over North Korea only seven years later. Time flies.

In an attempt to depict the tour in B-29s over North Korea, one mission comes to mind, and while worse than most, describes what it was all about: All of our missions were at night and this mission, about my 20th was over the Uegu-Sinuegu complex north of the Yalu River. The strike consisted of 24 B-29s at three-minute intervals on takeoff from Yakota AB, Japan loaded with 40-500 lb. bombs. The strike was planned for four aiming points that would put six aircraft over the target in trail in a six-minute period – this tactic used radar bombing and was key to keep from dropping on a wing man because we were stacked up in a block altitude from 27-28,000 ft. (often we put six bombers over the target at night in four minutes). Flak throughout was heavy, and we wondered how in hell we were going to make it through, only to find it heavier as we turned off the target on egress. When the flak stopped, the searchlights came on, and we "yelled" over the intercom to our tenth crewman, an Electronics Warfare troop with his black box to, "GET ON THEM!" The electronic box caused the radar-controlled lights to stop tracking and go random. The lights were accompanied by fighters, usually Yak-23s. This night the lights came on and the flak stopped. That meant fighters were in the area. We were usually covered by Marine A-3Ds flying CAP. All of a sudden, there was a huge explosion on my right wing and I thought due to the heavy buffeting, we were hit. It appeared an F-94 was going thru the bomber stream, pulled-up through the line of bombers and saw a Yak-23 on our wing trying to silhouette us in the lights. The F-94 fired a rocket and blew him out of sky (remember the Billy Goat).

After recovering and heading for Yakota, we were in the letdown, when the base went below minimums. We were told to try Itazuke AB Japan. The whole fleet turned and upon reaching Itazuke found it was also below minimums. Needless to say, about this time, HQ Far East Air Material Command (FEAMCOM), had started to calculate losses (due to our flying time and fuel). Radio contact (VHF) was lousy, and we were left to our own devices. My Aircraft Commander, the Flight Engineer and I began to calculate fuel range at cruise control speeds and altitude. We decided to return to South Korea and K-14 which was above minimums. We made it and as we taxied-in, the outboards quit due to trapped fuel (again that lucky Billy Goat). This mission while full of excitement was typical of the dangers encountered by a 200 mph heavy bomber crew in those days: terrible weather, flak, fighters, search lights and airborne decisions in the cockpit that became routine. In my one year out of pilot training the learning curve was steep.

I returned to the U.S. after the Armistice signing, having flown my last mission over the North the night before. This completed my tour (29 missions). It was a relief to look forward to the next chapter of my Air Force career; no more flak; no more surging turbos; no more search lights; no more 2.75 balls of fire across our nose; no more leaning-out engines to reduce exhaust glow; now to escape by being assigned to the B-36 bomber, an aluminum overcast that stayed up for days.

Again, luck prevailed, and I received word that B-47s at Lockbourne AFB was my next destination. After returning to the States, I was again in the arms of Shirlee, my main squeeze and wife. We headed for Ohio where I would be assigned for the next ten years. Lockbourne in 1953 was really my first SAC assignment. Although the 98th Bomb Wing I flew with in Korea was full of SAC people, we were under Command of FEAMCOM. Under LeMay, SAC was definitely different. For the next ten years I was a SAC hired killer. This was undoubtedly the most important period of my military career, from 1st Lt to Major.

I started as a B/RB-47E co-pilot, but returned from the Korean conflict with 1150 total hours of flying time. I needed 50 more hours to be on a B-47 crew – I got the 50 hours on one KC-97 deployment where I augmented a crew refueling the first B-47 deployment of the

91st Strategic Reconnaissance Wing, our sister wing at Lockbourne. Our receiver aborted and we diverted to Bermuda (Kindley AFB), refueled him the next day, recovered into MacDill AFB, then returned to Lockbourne and "voila," magically 55 hours of flying time, and I was B-47-ready.

I left after the holidays in January 1954 for Pinecastle AFB, FL, later McCoy AFB and now Orlando International, with my now pregnant wife. We returned to Lockbourne after B-47 transition ground school, and I was assigned to the 10th SRS of the 26th Strategic Reconnaissance Wing, a newly-formed wing and squadron. We waited for our new aircraft to be delivered from Boeing. The 10th SRS was the last squadron to be formed in the wing. As a result we received all the leftovers the other three squadrons had sluffed-off. It was fortunate for me because all the "rank" was in the other squadrons and our youth, eagerness and fresh experience allowed us to "whip ass" in competitions. I was fortunate to have a good squadron commander and became the first 1st Lt aircraft commander to be checked out in 8AF (maybe all of SAC? - remember the Billy Goat).

In September 1954 while TDY on the first B-47 deployment to the UK after the wing was declared combat ready, I was notified that Shirlee had a baby girl and all were doing well. On another TDY to Thule AFB April 1956, she had a baby boy – this was beginning to be easy – but paybacks were to come. Shirlee, like many SAC wives, was a trooper, and a very important part of my career. She was a great mother, homemaker, my right-hand, took care of things during extended deployments, nurtured the children and put up with me – more later about her.

Needless to say, experience gained in a growing command caused me to start thinking about my future. The USAF was coming out of the Korean conflict having become a new and separate service in September 1947. The new Air Force was trying to sort-out the remnants of those who remained after WWII and also those from the Korean War. I was interested in only one thing, a 20-year career. I had no thoughts of returning to Michigan where the auto industry was about the only big chance for a job – or even if my former employer as a youth wanted me to return and run/own his hardware store.

The officer corps at this time was made up of mostly reservists who were extended or had limited contracts. Regular Officers were, I quickly assessed, the only ones guaranteed 20-years. We had three regulars in our squadron: the squadron commander, a navigator and one pilot, all majors. It was important to continue building flying time if I wanted to check out as an aircraft commander. The B-47 presented a formidable challenge to a lot of the former reciprocating engine pilots. Many couldn't convert to a doubling/tripling of ground speeds and the associated duties up front with the fuel panel (formerly a flight engineer problem/duty). My former aircraft commander washed out of the transition program in the B-47 and went to a personnel assignment (grounded, and he was no dud).

One day reading the Air Force Times, I noticed the USAF was going to accept 400 regular officers and those interested should apply. The criteria was: three-years commissioned and good standing in your unit. So, I applied by filling-out the request and waited. In about three weeks I received notice to appear at the local training operations to take a 100-question exam and meet a board. This I did and waited again. Several non-regulars thought I was nuts. With a reserve commission, the benefits were considerably better than a regular commission, something I never mentioned to my bride. Basically, if you were killed as a 1st Lt in an aircraft accident, the reservist's next of kin received over $400 a month for life. As regular officer, a surviving spouse received approximately $90 per month. Weighing this risk, a monthly stipend vs. a 20-year career, was easy for me. Who at 25 years-old isn't invincible? I was accepted and awarded a regular commission, one of 400 out of 800 applicants.

Even though this was considered dumb to do at the time, two-three years later the USAF offered 30,000 reservists regular Air Force commissions and changed the survivor benefit laws. It was dog-eat-dog in the squadrons fighting to get a regular commission – me? I sat back, grinned a lot (remember the Billy Goat) and watched the back-stabbing. I was now "guaranteed" a 20-year retirement.

I was sworn-in as a regular officer during a 1956 deployment to Thule AB, Greenland by Brigadier General Hewitt Wheless, my Division Commander, who gained fame as lead B-24 aircraft on the first Ploesti raids in WWII and mentioned in one of FDR's fireside chats. General Wheless was called "Shorty" Wheless, our

Wing Commander was "Shorty" Ming, our Squadron Commander "Shorty" Fields. So, if you were in their company, a 5'11" 1st Lt had to hunker-down. During this period, I was given the additional duty as a reports analyst for the squadron and I was busy. I was selected to train as a B-47 IP, which meant that I was in the backseat again. I then became Assistant Operations Officer for Major John (Bud) Burkhart and made Captain in 1958, still flying with my lead crew and gaining experience. Soon after assuming duties as Assistant Operations Officer, Major Burkhart received orders to B-52s at Warner Robins AFB. Lt Col Bob Bachtell with Colonel William Reddel's, my wing commander's, approval made me the Squadron Operations Officer. This, for a young captain, was unheard of in SAC. The fighting spirit of the 10th SRS continued to "whip ---" during every ORI. After two years as the Operations Officer, I was given a select crew, went to stand-board, was promoted to "Spot Major" and enjoyed life. In the meantime, Shirlee presented us with two more children. I learned what happens when labor takes place at 4am. In reviewing my 10 years at Lockbourne AFB, one can see it was a very important assignment.

A couple of incidents during my tour at Lockbourne stand out as milestones: shortly after I checked out as an aircraft commander, I was still a "combat ready" 1st Lt. I was assigned a Naval Academy 2nd Lt co-pilot, Eugene Poe, and a 2nd Lt Navigator, Tom O'Neal. We were selected to lead a six-ship cell on a "Leap Frog" mission to the UK. All the aircraft commanders were majors with one Lt Col Needless to say, I was apprehensive. We took-off joined-up, met our tankers and proceeded to the UK, landing at Brize Norton, RAF base. The Brits were behind the U.S. in navigation aids and still operated many radio ranges. This complicated the letdown as we penetrated over the Brize VOR. We had to cross several radio range legs at specific altitudes, and that added complexity. We landed from a GCA and relieved that we were on the ground, taxied-in and parked. About that time, a blue staff car with the biggest white star I've ever seen appeared in front of the airplane. My first thought was, "Did we screw up the letdown procedure, or what?" Out of the car got the biggest one-star general I had ever seen. As I sat there going over the letdown, the crew chief went down the ladder, then the navigator and co-pilot and I shortly followed. I saluted the general, and he took a look up the entrance hatch and asked, "Who's flying this thing?"

I replied, "I am, Sir." He said to let the crew chief take care of the airplane, and he would see us all at the O-Club for supper. I know this was an effort by my Wing Commander, Bill Reddell, to give us recognition. The next day we flight planned a mission, typically an EWO format, down through France, Spain, Italy, and return to Brize and the next day home. The one-star was Brigadier General Butch Blanchard, later a four-star Air Force great.

I can't let one more story go untold: it occurred during a deployment to Thule AB Greenland during the spring of 1956. At the time of making regular officer, having a new son and continuing a check-out program to aircraft commander, I flew with an aircraft commander who was one of the three regulars in the squadron. In those days we actually penetrated Soviet airspace and overflew Russia on airborne reconnaissance missions in the RB-47. This was before the advent of the U-2/SR-71 and high resolution satellites. These were truly dangerous missions. We had a long over-flight of the USSR scheduled the next day. The a/c for the mission was known as a gambler (poker) and quite a drinker. Our mission over the heartland of Russia was scheduled for a 0700 take off with a flight time of approximately 12 hours. Our station time was 0500, and I became concerned because when I left the O-Club at 2200, the a/c was just sitting down to play cards with his cronies and talk was he had a lot of paper out (checks), and was in a bad mood because he had learned his wife had just written a $3,800 check for a new car. Needless to say, he was underwater. He reportedly returned to the VOQ about 0400 to make the 0500 station time. The navigator and I got to the aircraft on time, started the preflight (temperature well below freezing) and the a/c finally showed up at engine start time. Takeoff was normal with an icy runway. Usually, the hold line was decision point because as heavy as we were, stopping, or aborting on takeoff wasn't an option. We got airborne and headed for the North Pole to meet our tanker. We picked up the KC-97's beacon and arrived in the refueling observation position as scheduled - then, the crap hit the fan! We needed every drop of fuel due to our mission length. The a/c had trouble hooking-up. After several disconnects, he asked me to hold the airplane while he got the water out of his mask. I did and took-on our 35,000-pound offload from the back seat. After disconnect, we flew on without a word and continued our flight plan to coast into Russia at about the entrance to the Tiksi River area on the Arctic coast of Russia. Our route bypassed Nova Zemlya and the weather over our targets was clear. The targets were a large airfield, missile sites and anything else of opportunity as we proceeded down river.

As we proceeded inland I saw and reported to the a/c that we had two fighters (MiG-15s) on our tail. I could see them pulling contrails. Outside air temperature (OAT) is the key to keeping out of contrail levels. Minus 29-degrees OAT to minus 49-degrees is the temperature range to avoid. At minus 29, contrails are light. At minus 49, they become heavy. Our flight altitudes were planned to avoid these areas if possible.

The MiGs continued, and the a/c initiated a 98-percent RPM climb and turned east. We climbed rapidly thru 40,000 ft. and then nursed it to 49,000 ft. our limit without pressure suits. This was also the days before reliable heat-seeking and radar missiles. The MiGs couldn't stay with us and stalled-out and rolled-over at about 33-34,000 ft. Now our problem was fuel! We were at decision point – a quick calculation on my fuel performance chart said we couldn't make it to Thule, so the navigator struck-up a course for Eielson AB, Alaska and we went into max-range cruise control. We entered the Alaskan ADIZ and made a straight-in from 150 miles out. As we turned-off the runway, the outboards flamed out – whew! Upon arrival at our hardstand, we were met by representatives from the 544th Recce Tech squadron out of Omaha. A Capt Popovitch picked-up our film. The name seemed ironic after having probably just flown thru and over his ancestors' homeland. I later ran into him at the Tan Son Nhut O-Club while in Vietnam.

We crew-rested and returned to Thule the next day. Shortly after we recovered, I was told the Squadron and Wing Commanders wanted to see me in their office. I reported and was asked how the mission went. I said we had a problem having to climb to escape the MiGs and were short on fuel but thought we got good coverage of the targets. My Squadron Commander said, "OK, who got the fuel?" I then realized there was an observer in the tanker boom pod and whoever had debriefed indicated the co-pilot was the one who got the fuel. Our commanders had been watching the a/c's gambling and drinking. I was thanked for my efforts and that probably accelerated my check-out to aircraft commander. For my participation on the mission I was awarded the Distinguished Flying Cross by General Curtis LeMay along with other squadron participants in a closed-door ceremony.

I would be remiss in not mentioning one individual who deployed with us from SAC Weather Division at Omaha. His name was Hyko Gayaken, a young captain, who developed the use of pressure patterns over the continents to determine single-heading flight plans. We would often fly his computed headings for six-seven hours over the Pole with rapidly converging latitude and longitude lines and be within two-five miles of planned destination. Grid navigation over the Poles is always difficult, especially in twilight; no sun, stars, etc to take sextant shots and polar ice that doesn't allow accurate Doppler navigation. Hyko retired as a colonel and was a real genius in my book, an unsung hero.

I enjoyed the rest of my assignment at Lockbourne AFB serving as an IP and especially enjoyed teaching air refueling to those with little experience. In 1963 I was selected for Air Command and Staff College, a real plumb for SAC guys. General LeMay wasn't in favor of his crews going to school. Having taken Squadron Officers School by correspondence and working on classes to someday finish my Bachelors degree kept me competitive academically to captain. Beyond that I needed to get more education on my record. Someone finally convinced General LeMay he was hurting his troops by not allowing attendance at the professional schools. He relented and allowed the USAF to select SAC combat crews. In 1963, I attended ACSC and was promoted below the zone to major with spot time and pay back-dated (remember the Billy Goat). While at ACSC I received a phone call from the Wing Commander at Robins AFB, GA, Colonel James Keck, and Lt Col John Burkhart. They asked, "What are you doing during Christmas break at ACSC?" I replied I was working on my thesis, and they said get up to Robins during the break and fly the B-52G a couple of times as part of "your check out." They then said, "You are coming to Robins to be the Operations Officer." I went to fly the B-52 and it was everything the B-47 wasn't; however, tragedy struck when my father was killed in a car-train accident. SAC honored my request for a humanitarian assignment to Wurthsmith AFB, MI so I could assist my family.

Upon graduation from ACSC in June 1964, I served as a B -52 Aircraft Commander and Instructor Pilot with the 379ᵗʰ Bombardment Wing at Wurtsmith. From 1965 to 1968, I was Chief of the Programs and Scheduling Branch for the 379ᵗʰ Bombardment Wing. In January 1968, then a major, I was assigned as B-52 Arc Light Air Operations Officer with the U.S. Military Assistance Command, Vietnam (MACV) J-3, Saigon, Republic of Vietnam. In January 1969, I returned to Wurtsmith as a Lt Col and Commander of the 379ᵗʰ Organizational Maintenance Squadron. From January 1970 to November 1971, I was assistant Deputy Commander for Maintenance and Deputy Commander for Maintenance with 379ᵗʰ Bombardment Wing working for my old friend, Colonel John Burkhart. Believe me, working for an old friend when he is Wing Commander, isn't always great – many things can go wrong and put you both in a bad light. The work was long, hard and rewarding. Burkhart was promoted to Brigadier General, and I made colonel below the zone. We left Wurtsmith shortly thereafter. During my tenure as Deputy Commander for Maintenance, I was chosen to lead a 379ᵗʰ B-52 Bombing Team to the United Kingdom to represent Strategic Air Command in the UK Blue Steel Trophy competition. Our team finished first, and we returned to the United States with the trophy.

My next assignment came as a complete surprise. I figured I would finish out my time at Wurtsmith until attending the Army War College in July 1972. At the time I was a colonel below the zone. I received a call from my former 98ᵗʰ Bomb Wing Squadron Operations Officer of Korean War days informing me I was going to SAC Headquarters to work for him, Major General "Cucho" Felices, the SAC LG. He said, "You have to have a major command-level assignment on your record to go higher, so get your --- up here!" He assured me I would be released in time to go to the War College at Carlisle Barracks, PA. So, from November 1971 to August 1972, I was assigned to Headquarters Strategic Air Command, Offutt Air Force Base, NE as Chief of the Maintenance Management Division. I then entered the Army War College. After graduation in June 1973, I became Vice Commander of the 97ᵗʰ Bombardment Wing, Blytheville, AR.

While at the Army War College I received a call from then Lt Gen James Keck, Vice Commander of SAC. He wanted to know if I was in the Bachelors degree program. I told him I was taking courses but they had no Bachelors program, only a Masters program. He said the CINC won't give a wing to anyone without a degree, so you are going to Blytheville, AR where they do have a degree program. It was obvious I was being groomed for higher command.

I got to Blytheville, checked out in the B-52 and KC-135, enrolled in night classes and in December 1973, received my degree and was assigned as Commander, 310th Provisional Wing two days later. The 310th was the "Young Tigers Tanker Task Force" for the war in Southeast Asia - (the lucky Billy Goat again).

As the new Commander of the 310th Provisional Wing at U-Tapao and a former B-52 IP commanding all those TDY KC-135 crews, I continued to be a flying colonel. My DO was a former B-52D IP with a great history as a "Charlie Tower" expert. Charlie Tower was the SAC equivalent of a TAC "Super SOF" (Supervisor of Flying) located in the tower at Guam to make critical go-no-go decisions. He had a discrete frequency to discuss aircraft problems, provide advice, etc. The aircrews viewed him as "the Wizard." The DO and I decided we needed to beef-up tanker navigator expertise and we recruited a Lt Col Radar/Navigator from the 19th Bomb Wing to head our navigation section. The KC-135 had poor capability in its radar-nav suite, and I wanted to make sure the young navs learned from a bombing-nav pro how to maintain orbit and be at the ARCP on time. The Radar/Nav did a great job. The tanker crews got better and the procedures paid real dividends in the winning of the Fairchild Trophy when I was later Commander of the 380th Bomb Wing at Plattsburg (another story). I left the 310th with great respect for the crews and their accomplishments. By building them up in prestige, they drove the bomber guys out of the Officers Club bar and all returned home more experienced and proud. It was my pleasure to work alongside Colonel Jerry O'Malley, my ACSC classmate, as he commanded the Consolidated Maintenance Wing. Our friendship continued until his fatal accident in a T-39 in 1985.

I returned to the United States in April 1974 to command the 380th Bombardment Wing at Plattsburgh Air Force Base, NY. During my assignment, the FB-111/KC-135 wing received the Fairchild Trophy as the best bombardment wing in the annual bombing and navigation competition. The next assignment was working for General Russ Dougherty, CINC SAC, as Deputy for Maintenance, Engineering and Supply in the Office of the Deputy Chief of Staff for Systems and Logistics at Headquarters U. S. Air Force, Washington D. C. (the Pentagon) from July 1975 to June 1977. I then became Vice Commander of the Oklahoma City Air Logistics Center at Tinker Air Force Base, OK.

General Bryce Poe named me Deputy Chief of Staff for Contracting and Manufacturing at Air Force Logistics Command headquarters in December 1978. I was assigned as Deputy Chief of Staff for Maintenance in June 1979. Transferring to Kelly Air Force Base, Texas, in March 1981, I served as Commander of the San Antonio Air Logistics Center. In July 1982 I was named Vice Commander of Air Force Logistics Command and assumed command of Air Force Logistics Command in September 1984 as a four-star general. I retired in September 1987.

I finished my career as a command pilot with more than 7,000 flying hours in 22 different types of aircraft.

In thinking back over the nearly 37 years in uniform, I have to remember all the great icons I was associated with, worked for, or influenced me during those years:

Major General William Reddell	Lt. General Richard Nelson
Major General Hewitt Wheless	Lt. General Richard Hoban
Colonel Robert Bachtell	General Jack Catton
General Russell Dougherty	General David C. Jones
General Bryce Poe II	General P. K. Carlton
General Bruce Holloway	General Robert Dixon
Lt. General James Keck	General Bill McBride
Major General John Burkhart	General Mike Rogers
General Dutch Huyser	General James E. Hill
General Jerry O'Malley	General Charles Gabriel
Lt. Colonel Lloyd Fields	General James Doolittle
General Creighton Abrams	

I learned one hell of lot from these men and most of it good enough to emulate. I also learned a lot from others and what not to emulate.

I must give credit to my wife of 51 years, Shirlee, whom I lost in 2003 to ovarian cancer. We had four children, two boys, two girls; the four "Ks," Kimberly, Kevin, Kelly, Kristin. I could not have done it without Shirlee's support, devotion, love and understanding. She made it all work. I am happily remarried to a long-time family friend, Thelma, and life is good once more. My children love her.

To the Friday Luncho Buncho Pilot Group: I would fly wing any day with them, and as before, remember that lucky three Horned Billy Goat.

CHAPTER TWELVE

Bosshawg

by Charles W. "Bill" Pitts

Vietnam determined my destiny. The A-10 Warthog redefined my personality. The Air Force restructured my character and refocused my determination. In combination, these made me who I was intended to be in life.

I came home from high school one day in my senior year, and everything seemed as normal as the day before. Things were about to change though. At the dinner table, my mother and father made their exciting announcement. "You were selected as a first alternate appointment to the Air Force Academy – we received the letter today." I couldn't believe how excited _they_ were. How had this happened? I hadn't even applied to the Air Force Academy – I actually thought there were only two colleges in the country – Auburn and Alabama. Fortunately for me (and the academy), the primary took his appointment, and I went to Auburn University.

My parents had asked a local judge, who was friends with one of the U.S. Senators from Alabama, to get me an appointment to the AF Academy. That first alternate appointment had now ensured that I would at least be in the Air Force ROTC program at Auburn, not Army. What a blessing – DESTINY.

There I was, a pre-dentistry student in my first quarter. This curriculum required seven or eight chemistry or related courses. I didn't do well in my very first chemistry course, so I knew I was in trouble. I was now in my second quarter as a _business administration_ major not having any idea where that would lead, but there was no chemistry requirement in that curriculum. I now had no plan at all.

Late in my second year, SSgt McGrath called me into his office. He said to me, "You did quite well on the Air Force Officer Qualification Test and especially well on the aviation portion. How would you like to become an Air Force pilot?" That sounded exciting to me as I had never even touched an airplane. Later in my life, I reflected back on all the pilots that I met along the way who either had a family member in the military, a father or uncle who was a pilot in WW II or Korea, or learned to fly at an early age, or lived close to an airfield and knew that flying was in their blood, or just went to an air show somewhere and said to themselves, "I want to do that one day." Not me – SSgt McGrath said, "How would you like to be an Air Force pilot?" and I said, "Why not?"

So -- born in Alabama, grew up in Alabama, had traveled to two adjoining states in my life to date – where do you think I was sent to pilot training? I had joined the Air Force to see the world and now I was in Selma, Alabama at Craig AFB 100 miles from home.

The year was grueling to say the least. We had started with a class of 73 and 32 had either washed out or quit – 43% didn't make it. I had competed well. I wasn't the best in my class but not bad for a rural red neck kid who had never touched a real airplane before April 1969. As graduation approached, we all knew that our standing in the class would determine what airplane we flew. The system simply listed 41 airplanes, and numbers one through 41 picked their assignments in order. We expected only one or two fighters and got only one – an F-100. I knew from bar talk what the handful of pilots in front of me wanted, so I was very comfortable with my first choice. I wanted to be a Forward Air Controller (FAC) in Vietnam. I wanted to fly the OV-10 Bronco.

After basic survival school, OV-10 training, water survival, and AT-33 gunnery school to become an "instant fighter pilot," I left the states for jungle survival in the Philippines in route to Vietnam. I arrived at Cam Ranh Bay, South Vietnam, for theater indoctrination and base assignment in December, 1970. I wasn't in Alabama any longer.

I was one of the lucky guys – don't know how it happened – don't care. I was assigned to the 23rd Tactical Air Support Squadron at Nakhon Phanom, Thailand, better known as NKP. This was by far the best of the bases in theater for FACs. Those of us new FACs going to NKP also got a Christmas present – a week in Bangkok before we reported for official duty. It was one hell of a week, but those stories are for another time.

There I was – a First Lieutenant, 23 years-old, in a foreign country far away from Alabama, and in the middle of a war. That dental degree wasn't looking so bad now, but too late. After drinking my "hammer," the squadron initiation drink, which I recommend to no one (you had to have a "hammer" in order to be a "Nail" FAC), I became Nail 27.

The first week is worth a short story. We started with theater indoctrination again. All of our missions from NKP were over Laos and the Ho Chi Minh trail. Days 1 and 2 were filled with local orientation and briefings. Several on sexually transmitted diseases, many of which nobody in the states had ever heard about. We were shown GRAPHIC photos of what could happen. *Man – they should have given this briefing before I went on Christmas vacation!*

On day 3, we were in the middle of classified intel briefings when the loud speaker in the building abruptly interrupted. A Raven FAC had just been shot down over northern Laos. He had crash landed in an open field and another Raven was overhead. The downed pilot was injured badly and could not get out of his O-1 Birddog. Air support and SAR forces were scrambled. We could hear over our speaker system the airborne Raven talking to Cricket, the Airborne Command and Control Center (ABCCC) aircraft. The conversation went something like this. "He's injured and can't run. There are enemy forces shooting at his airplane from the tree line. He has been hit. He has been hit again, and says he is not going to make it. He wants us to destroy his plane because he has classified on board." Not much time passed until fighters arrived on scene and did as directed. The room had become eerily silent. Through my tears, I saw the others, virtually everyone, wiping wet eyes. When the speaker went silent, we were released. That brave pilot, who I never knew, was my age for the last time that day.

Day 4 – more intel briefings until.... The speaker system interrupted once again. An F-4 with battle damage was inbound for an emergency landing. Moments later, the F-4, with no hydraulic pressure, landed gear up on our runway, came to a screeching halt, the pilots ran from the smoking wreckage, and the plane burned. These pilots were safe!

Day 5 – more intel briefings until.... The speaker system interrupted. We had a Navy A-7 with battle damage inbound. The flight control system failed him eight miles from the field, and he ejected safely and was picked up. I guess we'll be celebrating at the club tonight.

Day 6 – I was scheduled to fly my first mission. **Holy s...!**

It only took a month or so of FACing to become an old guy, not a newbie anymore. I caught on quickly and was enjoying the mission. I was good at this. We were shot at every day whether we had fighters on station or not. If they could hear our airplane, they would shoot through the clouds just to keep us away – it didn't work very often. I found it very easy to recognize which gun they were using by the airburst or tracers. Most of what we saw was from double barrel 23mm, 37mm, the occasional 57mm, and maybe once or twice from an 85mm which was radar controlled. We put red circles on our maps around known gun positions and in some places on my map, the circles touched for four or five miles.

Each day before we took off, we were briefed by intel on any unusual or interesting activity, preplanned missions for the day, and the occasional Arc Light mission. In my area, there were two interdiction boxes, "Charlie" and "Delta," adjacent to Mu Gia and Ban Karai passes leading into North Vietnam. At one point in time, these had been triple canopy jungle undercut by a maze of roads from North Vietnam, through Laos, to the south. Now, they were three-mile by two-mile mud boxes filled with tens of thousands of bomb craters, frequently glistening with water. Generally at night, the NVA used bull dozers and hundreds of soldiers or road repair teams to keep the roads open. I mentioned Arc Light missions for a reason. Of course, there is a story.

An Arc Light mission consisted of three B-52s, each carrying 108 Mk-82 500 pound bombs. Their targets were generally preplanned interdiction points. The B-52s dropped in Charlie and Delta boxes routinely. We were told to avoid the drop coordinates by five nautical miles. We were *always* given a warning call on "Guard" frequency that they were inbound. We knew the area to avoid and did so until we saw the bombs exploding, and then it was time to see what damage they had done, most often just more road work for the NVA.

Then came the day. No pre-planned, pre-briefed Arc Light. No call on guard, therefore no warning, and no area to avoid. The day was beautiful, filled with sunshine and blue sky. I was enjoying myself. I hadn't found a target of opportunity yet, but knew I would before the day ended – I always did. Without warning, my OV-10 violently went out of control – upside down – right side up – sideways – I was along for the ride. I believed that I had been shot at and possibly hit by a large anti-aircraft weapon, maybe even a radar controlled 100mm from across the border in North Vietnam. I regained control after maybe 15 of the longest seconds that I remember, and looked around for airbursts. The only thing that I knew for sure was that I wasn't dead. I thought I heard unusual noises. The OV-10 was so noisy that I had never thought that before. I scanned my surroundings and suddenly saw explosions on the ground to my left, to my right, in front, and behind me. My first reaction was to look up. I saw what I usually saw from four or five miles away. There were three B-52s, contrails trailing, at about 35,000 feet, in a left hand turn, on their way home. I had just flown through an Arc Light – 324 500 lb. bombs falling all around me and disrupting the smooth and critical airflow that my airplane so desperately needed in order to fly. After filing an airborne hazard report with ABCCC (which, by the way, does absolutely no good in a war zone), I went home to drink beer and realize, once again, that "if you *are not* on the list, there is nothing you can do about it." By the way, if you *are* on the list, there is nothing you can do about that either.

The OV-10 was a great airplane. It was easy to fly, very stable, with super visibility through a bubble canopy. Its downfall was that the canopy reflected most of the cockpit lights while flying at night. That could be very disconcerting. For that reason, we flew only day missions. The O-2, with either another pilot or navigator in the right seat, flew the night missions with a Starlight scope. Nail FACs covered "the Trail" 24/7/365.

I mentioned no night flying because there is a story worth telling. It was a beautiful day over Laos. The skies were perfectly clear, and I was at the end of my mission, the day's last sortie. My replacement, an O-2 FAC, had not yet checked in. I was flying westbound along Route 9 toward Tchepone. Little did I know that in the next half hour I would once again test my flying skills to the absolute limit.

As always, I scanned the jungle and route structure for targets through my binoculars. Our minimum altitude in this area of Laos was 6,000 feet AGL because of the AAA threat. Suddenly, from just east of Tchepone, three trucks pulled onto Route 9 headed east toward Khe Sanh, inside South Vietnam. They each appeared to be fully loaded. I called Hillsborough, ABCCC, for fighter support. There was a flight of Navy A-7s maybe 15 minutes away. The sun was setting, and I was supposed to have left the area *right now*. I had enough fuel, so I decided to stay. Chippie 404, a flight of two A-7s with Mk-82s and flares checked in 10 minutes out. I decided that if I didn't stop the trucks, they might not be there when the fighters arrived. I rolled in and fired two white phosphorous (willie pete) rockets, both hitting close to the road maybe 50 to 75 meters in front of them. Both trucks stopped, and I saw their drivers run north into the jungle. I was talking to the Chippies now, as they were headed to the rendezvous point. The light was quickly fading, so I decided to put down more smoke in the trees close to the trucks.

I digress just to explain how some of us OV-10 pilots maneuvered to mark a target when directly overhead. I pulled the nose of the aircraft up abruptly, kicked in rudder, rolled off to the side and down almost vertically, aimed and fired. This was a quick and generally pretty accurate marking technique. Of course, there is an immediate requirement to recover to something close to level flight.

Now, back to the trucks. The A-7s showed up overhead, and we acquired sight of each other. They set up an orbit maybe 2-3,000 feet above me. I explained about the smoke lingering in the trees, and they actually saw it. In order to keep the target illuminated, I requested that they drop flares on their first pass. We all agreed, and I cleared lead hot. I held directly overhead the trucks so I could see the A-7s throughout their passes. Lead called off south having dropped two flares. We waited but neither ignited. I advised them to hold high and dry while I set up for another mark. Night had arrived – full darkness. When I say "dark," imagine the depths of a cave with no flashlight. Without forethought or hesitation, I pulled the nose up abruptly, kicked in rudder, rolled off to the side, headed downhill vertically, aimed at what I thought might be a hint of smoke remaining in the tree line, fired two willie pete rockets, and pulled up in maybe a five-G recovery. I immediately realized that if I didn't see the rockets splash, I wouldn't be able to give a correction to the fighters, so I rolled a bit to see the rockets hit the ground – it was too late. I suddenly felt very uncomfortable. I looked at my attitude indicator – it was spinning. I could see no horizon. I looked at my airspeed indicator – it was one second from hitting zero. I attempted to move the stick but immediately went into an inverted spin. Don't ask me how I knew that I was inverted at night, but all my one and one-half years of aviation sense told me so.

I now digress to the OV-10 Dash 1. Spinning the OV-10 was a prohibited maneuver. So spinning the OV-10 inverted must be at least *four times more prohibited* since there was no inverted oil reservoir for the engines. I did remember step 1 in the inverted spin recovery procedure – **shut down both engines**. I used a total of maybe two seconds to rule that one out. I knew, (without practice), that the spin recovery procedure was similar to that of the T-37 which I had been required, without enthusiasm, to practice many times. The process is supposed to be very deliberate. I accomplished all the steps in perhaps 2.5 seconds. However, the end result was positive. I was now in an upright spin. I took a deep breath, keyed my mike button to say, "Chippie 404, hold high and dry, the FAC's in a spin."

It is redundant to say that lieutenants are stupid. I had gone into night time in a heavily defended area of Laos without turning off my outside lighting – quite obviously, the least of my worries right now. The next call was from Chippie lead – "Roger FAC, tally ho." He could see red/green, red/green, red/green going round and round. I slowed down to give my brain a moment to sort things out and accomplished the spin recovery procedures as I remembered them. Amazingly, I felt the OV-10 suddenly dip nose down, pick up some airspeed, and become responsive to my touch. I had recovered!!! I had started at over 6,000 feet AGL and was now at 2,500 to 3,000 feet AGL but in a climb.

I keyed my mike button and said, "Chippie 404, you can drop your bombs anywhere you want to, the FAC is going home." (I do actually remember using blunt expletives when making that call.) Chippie lead's reply was a hoot – "Nice recovery there Nail 27 – only about a four or five turner, wasn't it?" Those Navy guys had a great sense of humor.

From early February through late March,1971, there was a campaign called Lam Son 719. South Vietnam invaded eastern Laos in order to interdict the Ho Chi Minh trail. I was sent to Quang Tri, SVN to support that mission which happened to be directly inside my normal area of responsibility. I was now Hammer 271. FACs from around Vietnam came together to support this operation. We lived in Red Horse built rectangular plywood buildings with enough room for maybe 8 pilots, but we managed to pack in 16. Sometimes we just double bunked since the OV-10 guys flew daytime and the O-2 guys flew at night. Our sheets were brown but nobody cared. We had a shower that only trickled water. You had to stand in it and move around for about five minutes to actually get wet. You could only use minimal amounts of soap because it took too long to get it off. Most of us just eventually wet a bath cloth and cleaned the best we could. We had no dining hall. We mostly ate C rations or whatever some pilot may have found that was better – most things are better than C rations. We constructed our own outside five-holer toilet, which had absolutely no privacy. We did have three refrigerators full of beer. Unfortunately, none of the refrigerators actually worked, but hot beer beats no beer. About the third day we were there, my bunkmate, an O-2 pilot from another base, did not return from his night mission. He was never recovered.

I have often described this campaign as similar to taking an Alabama cricket, pulling off his hind legs, and placing him on top of a fire ant bed after stirring them up. I have no idea how many South Vietnamese soldiers were killed, but I have seen numbers that say close to 9,000. I do know that there were more than 800 U.S. and SVN helicopters shot down in less than two months. I have thought about that many times since. There were actually over 800 helicopters shot down in less than one-third of the ground area that I had been responsible for the past several months. That told me that the threat in my area was real, intense, and well beyond my estimation. One of my missions during Lam Son 719 was helicopter escort, and let me tell you, 18 and 19 year-old U.S. Army helicopter pilots were nuts – extraordinarily brave, but nuts. Many had been shot down four or five times but were ready and eager to go again the next day. An Air Force pilot, if shot down twice, got the option to go home, and most did.

In an area of Laos where the AAA density demanded that we fly no lower than 6,000 feet AGL as a normal course of business, during Lam Son 719, in that same area, there were no altitude restrictions at all. I flew every day and sometimes twice a day for over 30 consecutive days. Our runway was 3,000 feet long and constructed of perforated steel planking (PSP) with no overruns. Even the OV-10 didn't like this little runway with our munitions load and center line fuel tank.

I chose two stories from this period of my tour to share, although there were many, many more worth telling. It seems I had a tendency to get into trouble at sunset. I was on the last daytime mission. A fire support base came under heavy attack, and I was the FAC on station to support it. This was a troops in contact (TIC) situation and the fire ants out numbered the crickets badly. I was directing fighters as fast as I could get them on target safely. At one point, I had six sets of fighters stacked above me all telling me they needed to be next due to fuel. All pilots are trained that "bingo fuel" means "go home now!" That day, I had set my bingo fuel as usual, but because my replacement was late, and soldiers were dying, I decreased it to a "no shit bingo" and stayed.

I left with much less fuel than I should have. The weather was good at Quang Tri which set me up for what was to come. I arrived in a holding pattern with multiple airplanes after dark. At night, we had to recover with the assistance of a remote Army radar site set about 10 miles from the runway. That was usually no problem because you could see the field from far enough away to just transition to a VFR landing. Real weather remote GCA approaches weren't all that sterling. As it was just about my turn to start down and about five minutes *after* I should have declared emergency fuel, or as some pilots say, emergency fool, the field came under rocket attack. The controller started asking each pilot where he wanted to divert. Then it was my turn. I stated what was blatantly obvious by now – "This is Hammer 271. I am emergency fuel and must land at Quang Tri. I do not have divert fuel." The controller advised me that the field was completely blacked out due to a generator being hit – no runway lights, no time for pots, and no time to assess for possible runway damage. On one side of this 3,000 feet long, maybe 60 feet wide PSP runway were multiple revetments with OV-10s and O-2s inside. On the other, were maybe 500 U.S. Army helicopters.

After I made it *crystal* clear to the controller on duty that I had enough fuel for one short approach and landing, and if I missed, maybe enough to maintain VFR, keep sight of the runway and land, or last, to head east and eject over the water, the voice on the other end abruptly changed. A deep, confident voice said, "Hammer 271, turn left, descend and maintain 2,000 feet." This awesome controller's final words to me were, "on course, on glide path, over landing threshold, take over visually, if possible," to which I replied, "Negative," to which he replied, "on course, on glide path, on course…" I suddenly saw the centerline runway stripe illuminated beneath my landing light, but I had no depth perception, no idea how far down this short runway I actually was. I pulled the throttles back and promptly dropped in from eight to ten feet versus the normal six inches. I bounced several times, put the throttles in full reverse, pressed the brakes firmly and came to a stop somewhere on the PSP. I sat there for a minute to get my composure – you know that it is VERY IMPORTANT that pilots sound cool on the radio – then I thanked the controller with all I knew to say, which was certainly not enough. The next call was from my squadron commander demanding to know why the hell I had just landed at Quang Tri. The rest of this story must be reserved for another time.

The end of March was closing in. I took off on the first mission of the day. I arrived on scene to hear the desperate calls for help from a fire support base just inside Laos. This encampment was on top of a mountain maybe 1,000 feet above the valley floor. The mountain spread out a mile or so in each direction.

Now picture that wounded cricket on top of the fire ant bed. NVA regular soldiers were coming up the mountain on all sides. South Vietnamese soldiers had no place to go. We had tried to extract them, but could not get helicopters in due to intense and continuous ground fire. I told ABCCC to send all the fighters they could to my location. I would take snake and nape, Mk- 82s, CBU, actually any ordnance that was available. We were the priority mission for the theater that day. However, it took little time to realize that we were loosing this battle.

I called in another OV-10 FAC to work in concert with me. He took the west side of the mountain, and I took the east. I ran fighters north to south with a break to the east while he brought his in from south to north with a west break. One of us would occasionally hold our guys and the other would work both directly south and north of the fire support base. We dropped every ordnance type that any fighter had on board with lots of snakeye, CBU, and napalm. We actually held the fighters south of the target for 15 minutes twice in order to allow Arc Light strikes to drop about a mile north of the fire support base on an east to west run to try to stop the NVA from bringing in more troops.

I worked this target for nearly three and one-half hours non-stop, and turned it over to my replacement. Each subsequent FAC did the same. That night, we got the word that the fire support base had been overrun and all friendly soldiers were dead. We had used probably every type fighter in theater with every known combination of munitions as fast as we could employ. We had combined that with massive Arc Light strikes throughout the day. We had still lost.

My mission at first light the next day was to destroy everything that was left on the mountain. I believe that was probably the saddest mission I flew. NVA soldiers were scavenging. I could see them running with arm loads of whatever was left for the taking, their brown uniforms highlighted by the sun. I have no idea how many soldiers from South Vietnam died, nor do I know how many NVA our air strikes killed in the process of loosing. I do know that I estimated killing 150 to 200 NVA within an hour of arriving on station that last day. I had never then nor since seen anything like the determination of the North Vietnamese regular soldiers to win that battle – I never want to again.

Enough of Vietnam – it was time to go home – I had survived! I had been a Nail FAC at NKP, a Hammer FAC at Quang Tri, and the last few months, a Covey FAC at Da Nang. I now had a completely different perspective on the world that I still knew very little about, but I knew for sure that I had found myself a home as an Air Force pilot.

I had a plan. I stayed awake to make that dreaded 2am phone call back to the states, not just to anybody but to the person who was going to determine my future. I had all my priorities lined up and felt for sure that the officer on the other end of the phone would be amply impressed. He answered – "Assignments, Major Johnson." I said, "Major Johnson, this is Lieutenant Pitts calling from Vietnam. I know that you are working my next assignment soon, so I just wanted to make it easy for you. I am fully prepared today to volunteer to return to Vietnam as an F-4 pilot. I am single and can check out anywhere you want me to and return to the theater anytime you need." I sort of figured that my first option might not fly, so I was fully prepared to interject my next thoughts about how I would also be eager to go back to Hurlburt Field and instruct in the OV-10 which would probably have eventually guaranteed me a follow on to the A-7. Far back in my hip pocket was the idea of going to ATC and instructing in the T-38, but it was a very distant last choice. I now had 196 combat missions with nearly 800 combat hours. I had joined an elite group of always brave, sometimes crazy, but very competent pilots who could do anything that the Air Force wanted done. I knew that *Maj Johnson needed me.*

I didn't have time to say another word. The Major stopped me. He said, "Lieutenant, you are either going to fly a B-52, a KC-135, a T-37, or a T-38. What's your choice?" I realized immediately that he was very serious, and that *he didn't need me.* I figured that I could only make things worse by complaining at this point. I said, "T-38 <u>SIR</u>!" He laughed. "That's what everybody says when I give them those choices." Before he could say anything else, I interjected, "But, is everybody willing to go to Craig AFB to fly the T-38?" He paused and said, "Nope, you've got it." I had, without any assistance, sealed my fate to return to Selma, Alabama. How about that "join the Air Force to see the world" crap now?

I was back in Alabama for another four and one-half years. During that time, the war ended. The drawdown began. The Air Force was a smaller place to work, with many fewer airplanes. I was to be reassigned. I was the assistant chief of the T-38 Stan/Eval section, so I expected to compete well for a really good assignment. Not going to happen! Forty one pilots were leaving ATC in my same month, and there were a total of two T-39s available for all of us. There was a new thing called the "rated supplement." They called it "career broadening." I was definitely not going to fly this time.

I don't think it was Maj Johnson who called, but it might as well have been. This major said to me, "Captain Pitts, you have been selected to be one of 17 pilots to be part of a test program for the Officers' Open Mess Management career field." My first comment was, "Is that anything like being a club officer?" Of course, he said yes. I said, "Put me down as a non-volunteer," to which the major replied, "I'll put you on the same list with all of the rest of them." It was no longer a matter of if, but where I was going.

I had recently seen, on the cover of "Air Force Magazine," the airplane of my dreams. This great big ugly twin engine monster had 16,000 pounds of assorted munitions displayed in a triangle in front of it in the photo. The seven-barrel Gatling gun was the size of a Volkswagen and fired 30mm, not 20mm like the rest of our fighters. It was to be a tank killer. It was specifically designed for the air to ground and close air support missions. Most considered it ugly and mean and pilots appropriately nicknamed it the Warthog. It was built just for me. But I was going to be a club officer!

The next day, I called Maj Stinson at MPC. I said, "Since you are assigning me as a non-volunteer to the club field, could you at least give me my choice of bases?" It just so happened that he had already told me that I would either be going to Shaw, Gunter AFS, Myrtle Beach, or Pope. I knew that Myrtle Beach was getting the first wing of A-10s. I would at least be able to touch a new A-10 and maybe get to know the pilots. Who knows what could happen after that. Maj Stinson was impressed with my initiative and granted my wish. In September, 1976, I reported to Myrtle Beach AFB after having just graduated from a very challenging Open Mess Management School at Keesler.

If I were to tell stories about my tenure as the Club Officer at Myrtle Beach, I am confident that some old A-7 or A-10 pilot would put out a contract on me. I saw too much; I knew too much; I had career ending events, involving officers who eventually became very senior, embossed in my brain. Many of these Friday night escapades are simply memories that you occasionally remember, smile at, and then take to the grave. All I will say is that I was confident that the odds were stacked against my survival, and that my future as a pilot was totally dependent on the club doing well. I worked 60 and 70 hour weeks. The end result was that Myrtle Beach Officers' Open Mess became the best in TAC. My bosses liked me.

After over two years of making wives and lieutenants happy, (they were the ones that would get me fired quickest, especially wives), I had managed to be released from this career field to go back to the cockpit. The 354th Fighter Wing was still in the midst of its conversion. The Wing Commander, then Col Bob Reed, later a four-star general, went to bat for me. Through a series of events, I was selected to fly the A-10 at Myrtle Beach. It was 1978. I was going to get the airplane of my dreams. I was the happiest fighter/attack pilot in the Air Force.

Col Reed called me to his office one day. He told me he would be leaving soon but that he was pleased that I was on my way to A-10 training. He said, "Don't let me down; make me proud." I had my marching orders. He had just signed on to making a Club Officer an A-10 pilot.

There were only single seat A-10s and no simulators when I entered class 78 BCD. There were instructors with 50 hours more in the plane than me. I lucked out. My IP was Maj John Ralston, a pilot who I knew in Thailand. He flew both the OV-10 and the A-1 there – one of the good guys. I don't know if he had guidance from Col Reed or not, but he told me that it was his job to make me the class Top Gun, and that he had put money on it. This challenge came down to the last mission on the last day, but I did it – I had made Col Reed proud, and Maj Ralston richer.

I was now a fully qualified A-10 attack pilot in the 353rd Fighter Squadron, the third operational squadron to convert in the first A-10 wing. I spent the next two years learning as much as I could from a collection of the finest pilots I had ever flown with. During that time, I earned certification in every qualification category there was in the airplane. I loved the SAR role and was a certified Sandy 2. I was on the first Joint Air Attack Team Tactics (JAATT) deployment and learned to speak Army while working in harmony with Scouts, Cobras, and Apaches at 100 feet. I had mastered the 100 feet low altitude environment while employing my gun and the Maverick missile and now instructed while flying there. I had flown against F-4s, Aggressors, F-15s, and even F-16s in the dissimilar training world.

I was "Pigpen," my very first A-10 call sign, until "Pigrat" inadvertently shot a live M-1 tank during an exercise at Fort Stewart, Georgia. The 9th AF Commander, after reading the incident report, said no more "Pig" call signs in the A-10 community. I was pretty sure that taking away our "Pig" call signs would undoubtedly solve the problem of shooting stray, lost tanks in a tactical range target array. By the way, 13 30mm TP rounds will completely disable an M-1 tank – no right tread and a busted oil pan – way to go Pigrat!

I had jumped into the training world as my additional duty. AFM 51-50 was our bible. I studied it, I learned it, and I interpreted it for the Commander and Ops Officer. If I screwed it up, we were all in trouble. I worked with great schedulers to ensure that all of our pilots achieved and maintained mission ready status and didn't lose currencies. I tell this part because it led to a surprising and awesome assignment. The wing Chief of Training was selected to head the conversion from A-7s to A-10s at England AFB. He picked three pilots from Myrtle Beach to go with him, and I was chosen to be his training expert. Back to back fighter assignments as an operational fighter pilot – hard to get, but I was there and thrilled.

I stepped into the lair of the last holdouts in the A-7 community. Their airplane was going away, and the A-10 would replace it. These guys were very unhappy, and many did not want to learn how to fly the A-10. They just wanted to convince me that flying the A-10 with the same employment techniques as the A-7 was a better option – sorry, it didn't work that way. It was a challenging and rewarding experience. We had accumulated the finest A-10 pilots from Myrtle Beach, Bentwaters/Woodbridge, and even Nellis for this conversion – lots of talent, lots of experience, lots of opinions, and lots of hard work.

I jump forward to one of my favorite times with some of my favorite people. It was 1981, and the Air Force had just budgeted for the first worldwide air to ground gunnery competition since 1964. Gunsmoke '81 was on the horizon. In order to get there, we had to compete. Our only A-10 competition in 9th Air Force was with the Myrtle Beach wing – many old friends and great pilots. Maj Wally Moorhead, later to be Lt Gen Moorhead, was our wing weapons officer. He was tasked by Col Jimmie Adams, later to be Gen Adams, to gather the names of the top 10 A-10 pilots from more than 100 in the 23rd Wing, based on our one year of range data. After that list was verified, these 10 pilots would have a week of range missions to compete to be selected for the England AFB team. Boy, it was a lot of fun to fly twice a day for five straight days with 12 BDUs and 100 rounds of 30mm to fire. The competition was intense. At the end of the week, five pilots stood out, and the results were not surprising at all. The top five pilots from the original list of 10 were now the 23rd

Wing's team members and amazingly, we ended in the same order that we started on the list of 10.

We were all instructors with lots of A-10 time. We gathered to discuss how we would align our team. Since numbers one through four had been numbers one through four on all previous lists, we elected to stop the competition among us. Maj Lloyd Duncan was selected to be our leader because he was the oldest (just kidding, Dunc), but we did select him because he outranked us all, and he would make a great spokesperson for the team. I was number two, Maj Wally Moorhead was number three, Capt Tom Spada, number four, and Capt Mike Gill would be our spare.

We managed to piss off the entire wing of A-10 pilots since Col Jim Record, our DO, later to be Lt Gen Record, dedicated two sorties per day, 12 BDUs per sortie, 100 rounds of 30mm, sometimes 200, to our training spin up program. These all came out of our annual flying hour allotment; therefore, the resentment from the rest of the wing. I don't blame them.

It all paid off though. In August, we deployed to Myrtle Beach for the 9th Air Force gunnery meet, Gunpowder '81, to find out who would represent 9th AF at Gunsmoke '81. We would compete against Moody and Seymore-Johnson F-4s, MacDill F-16s, and A-10s from the Beach. We knew all the Myrtle Beach team pilots – friends from the past, but only one of our two teams would be at Nellis representing 9th AF when this was over.

For all you fighter jocks who flew fancy jets with neat, state of the art computers, in 1981, the A-10 pilot had a stick, two throttles, a map (always in his left hand), a HUD with an adjustable pipper, and mental calculations beyond that point. The winds on Dare County Range, on the coast of North Carolina, were out of the west at 35 knots every day of the competition. After day two, MacDill pulled out. There were "official" reasons given, but we all knew it was because they were too far behind both A-10 teams to catch up. One F-16 pilot had lost his computer and had to bomb and strafe in manual mode – I actually felt sorry for him – he had probably never done that before. His scores were absolutely AWFUL.

There were five events therefore six awards, which included 9th AF Top Gun. There were five teams with four pilots each who began this competition competing for those awards. I had the best weapons delivery week of my life. I won the low angle bomb, low angle strafe, and nav attack events. An A-10 pilot from the Beach won dive bomb, and an F-4 pilot from Moody won the low angle low drag event. I had strafed an average of 96 percent in 35 mph crosswinds – 92% on the first day and 100% on the second. That tells you two things and one of them is that the A-10 gun is awesome. My teammates also started harassing me about being the best navigator in 9th AF. However, in August, 1981, I had just become the 9th AF Top Gun, and our team was off to Nellis. I had made now Brig Gen Reed proud again. I was pretty happy myself.

If I am not mistaken, there were 15 teams from around the world competing in Gunsmoke '81 – F-4s, A-7s, and A-10s. There were four A-10 teams – ours from the 23rd Wing, Bentwaters, Barksdale (Reserves), and Hancock Field (Guard). This was the olympics of bomb dropping and gun shooting. After a couple of days of intense, nerve racking competition, two teams had moved away from the pack – ours and the 140th Wing flying A-7s out of Buckley Field. The A-7 had one of the best weapons delivery computers in the inventory. But, we were neck and neck.

It was now the last day, and we were very optimistic because we knew we could hold our own in bombing and certainly out shoot these guys. Every single bomb counted for team score. We were on the tactical range dropping dive bombs, low angle low drag (LALD) bombs from a pop up pattern, low angle bombs from a pop pattern, and low angle strafe pops. Things were going really well, and we were getting good scores.

The range was manned by Nellis pilots who had been selected to help judge. In the range tower that day was an F-4 pilot as the safety observer. The A-10 was relatively new to the fighter business. This particular F-4 pilot, therefore, hadn't seen many A-10s drop bombs. Because of our speed, or lack there of, and our tremendous maneuverability, the A-10 foul altitude for the low angle low drag event was 200 feet lower than for all other fighters at the time, by TAC Regulation, and as published in the Gunsmoke Rules. We all later assumed that confusion over this different standard is what created the problem which was about to occur.

I rolled-in from my pop for the first LALD, I rolled-out, aligned the pipper, waited very briefly and pickled. The instant after hitting the pickle button on this event, I completed what we had named the Gunsmoke pull, an instantaneous six and one-half to seven-G recovery. Within the rules, we were using up to a 25 degree dive angle to aid us with accuracy, but that meant we had to pull fast and hard in order to avoid fouling. I had done it a thousand times and never fouled, and the A-10 was quite capable of reversing course. Before my bomb impacted, I heard, "Foul 2!" and once he had said it he couldn't take it back. I was shocked because nothing in that pass was unusual to me. I keyed my FM radio, our inter flight comm, and said, "Oh shit!"

We were very quiet on the way home. We went into debrief with my gun camera film in hand to review what had actually taken place. The film showed exactly what I expected it to. I had a good pass. The altimeter in the HUD had stopped unwinding and started back up *200* feet *above* foul altitude. My bomb impact, as estimated by me and the other flight members, was about seven or eight meters from the target. That, by rules, would have counted somewhere between 100 and 115 points. But with the foul, it counted zero, nothing, nada. We were excited and ready to go to the rules committee and appeal the foul when Wally pulled out the rule book and read from it directly. "Fouls can not be appealed." By the way, the rules were changed for Gunsmoke '83 and fouls could be appealed for subsequent competitions.

We ended up loosing to the Buckley Guard unit by 39 ½ points out of 10,000 possible. That equates to 16 bullets at 2 ½ points each – (or one low angle low drag bomb score.) My bomb would have counted over 100 points, and we would have been the top team in the world at Gunsmoke '81 – it was just not meant to be.

For all these years, I have felt bad for our team. No one remembers number two in the Olympics, but if our A-10 team, with no computers augmenting our weapons delivery systems, had taken Top Gunnery Team in 1981, which I thought we deserved, no one would have forgotten. Sorry Dunc, Wally, and Tom.

Our team did come home proudly. We had won the following between Gunpowder and Gunsmoke: Top Gunnery Team, Gunpowder; Top Gun, Gunpowder; Top Maintenance Team, Gunpowder; Las Vegas Arrival Award, 0 seconds (a story worth telling); A-10 Top Gun (Tom Spada); A-10 Top Gunnery Team; A-10 Top Maintenance

Team; A-10 Top Weapons Load Team; World Champion Maintenance Team; and World Champion Weapons Load Team. My foul cost us World Champion Gunnery Team, the only other award we could have brought home.

Gunsmoke was a significant highlight in my A-10 career. I flew with the best of the best, and we are still friends today. We occasionally Email, talk, or see each other. I loved these guys as if they were my family.

When I arrived at England AFB in 1980, I became a member of a wing with unprecedented heritage dating back to Burma during WW II. The 23rd Wing had moved many times since its formation as the 23rd Pursuit Group in 1942. At that time, it was part of the China Air Task Force and was made up of volunteer pilots better know as the AVG, or American Volunteer Group, led by Brig Gen Claire Chennault. An interesting fact that I learned by talking with many of the original Flying Tigers at reunions was how the Flying Tiger name came about.

The Americans learned that the Japanese had an innate fear of sharks. Several of the unit's personnel got together and designed the shark teeth that were then painted on the noses of the P-40s. The Chinese knew little about sharks but much about tigers. After watching the planes fly day after day, the Chinese started calling these amazing pilots the "Flying Tigers." The only aircraft allowed to be painted with nose art in Air Combat Command today are the 23rd Fighter Wing Flying Tiger aircraft because of the heritage of the unit. Those are shark's teeth, not tiger teeth.

I was a Flying Tiger from 1980 to 1982 when I was reassigned to Alaskan Air Command, where I was on the planning staff for half my tour then Chief of Stan Eval and in charge of the FAC programs for AAC for the remainder. I returned to the Flying Tigers in 1985 and stayed until the end of 1990. I was a member of all three squadrons during my more than seven years there. I was a Flight Commander and Assistant Ops Officer in the 74th Fighter Squadron Flying Tigers, the Operations Officer of the 75th Fighter Squadron Sharks, the Commander of the 76th Fighter Squadron Vanguards, and the Assistant Director for Operations for the 23rd Fighter Wing. There is truly something special about being a Flying Tiger, and I was then and am still today very proud to have been part of that extraordinary organization.

In the summer of 1990, I was preparing for my next assignment. I had been reassigned to the 355th Fighter Wing at Davis-Monthan AFB. I had four more days until the moving vans were to show up at my doorstep. I received a call to report to an unscheduled staff meeting. At that meeting, all the senior staff were present. The Wing Commander advised us that the 23rd Fighter Wing had just received tasking to deploy to Saudi Arabia in support of Desert Shield. After the meeting ended, I followed the Wing Commander out and asked for a minute of his time. I told him that I was one of maybe four or five pilots in the wing that had combat time, and I didn't believe that he should go to war without me. After questioning my intelligence, he agreed – my household goods shipment was immediately put on hold. I was later tasked to be the senior member of the advanced party. I departed on a C-5 in late August for a long flight to King Fahd International Airport, Saudi Arabia.

At the time, this airport, designed to be among the world's largest, was still under construction. Most facilities were not started by then, much less complete. However, there were two 13,500 feet runways, one mile apart, painted and ready to go. The C-5 landed at about 2am. When I departed the airplane as the first Flying Tiger on the ground, the outside temp was something close to 120 degrees with 25 mile per hour winds. I actually thought there was another jet engine running somewhere behind us. It got hotter when the sun came up.

There are many stories that will go untold, but how we trained for Desert Storm was something for which I will always be proud. First, when we arrived, there were 150,000 Iraqi soldiers on the Saudi border with 1,500 tanks ready for the word to take the Saudi oil fields. Few knew that we only had enough fuel, bullets, and missiles for maybe two days of wartime ops. I believe that exaggerated media reports of our presence kept them from advancing.

I was now the DO for two squadrons of A-10s. Since the A-10 began operational flying in 1977, Warthog pilots had trained intensely in the low altitude environment in order to stop Soviet tanks in the Fulda Gap and other attack routes in Europe. We all eventually certified at 100 feet AGL and fine tuned our skills there. We assumed that killing Iraqi tanks in the desert would be no different; however, when we arrived, Lt Gen Chuck Horner had limited us to no lower than 500 feet because of multiple low altitude accidents already. The day that restriction was lifted, I flew our wing's first low altitude mission with one of the squadron commanders in order to personally discover how difficult it would be to employ in this desert environment. The short version is that neither of us could accurately determine our altitude once we descended below 500 feet. The A-10 did not have a radar altimeter at the time. Successful employment at low altitude would depend on pilot skill alone, and two of the most experienced pilots in the wing could not safely fly below 500 feet with nothing but sand as far as the eye could see and different shades of brown between the desert floor and the horizon.

No other 23rd Fighter Wing airplanes flew low after that mission. We began that day designing the tactics that would be so successful when the war began. We started training above 5,000 feet. On a mission with an Army unit where I was talking with an ALO and using U.S. tanks as simulated targets, I asked the ALO to let me know when he could no longer hear my aircraft. I climbed slowly, and he finally said that he could not hear us. I had just past 8,000 feet. It was a clear day with unlimited visibility, so I asked him to tell me when he could no longer see us. Passing 11,000 feet, we became too small for his eyes. We made multiple simulated gun passes on his location, and he only reported seeing us when we pulled off target. We had just learned that the A-10 was silent and virtually invisible to the human ear and eye above 11,000 feet. All we had to do now was to take out Iraqi radar units on the first days of the war. And that is exactly what happened.

A note of interest in our training is that we quickly learned that the A-10 IIR Maverick missile could lock up a camel in the desert at a range of close to seven miles. You can imagine how far out it could lock up a running tank.

The A-10 was reported to be one of the two airplanes that the Iraqi soldiers feared the most. They said the B-52s dropped many, many bombs and the A-10s seemed to never go away. Warthog pilots and their airplanes were tremendously successful during Desert Storm, and the Flying Tigers made another historic mark in their amazing legacy. I was truly proud to be a small part. From Burma to Baghdad, the Flying Tigers were awesome.

Within the first several weeks of being in theater, Capt Becky Colaw, the Myrtle Beach Public Affairs Officer, asked if I would help her with an article about the Flying Tigers. I enthusiastically agreed but asked that she contact and get comments from some of the original Flying Tigers from Burma – she did. Tex Hill, Ed Rector, and Donald Lopez all shared experiences and commentary.

While at King Fahd and during a media day, I was questioned by a "Newsweek" reporter. She said that she had been to two other bases and saw A-10s parked on the flight line. She commented that people around her kept talking about "that ugly A-10." Her question to me was, "As an A-10 pilot, how do you respond to all of those negative comments about your airplane?" My answer, which, unfortunately was published in "Newsweek" for my Mother to read was, "It's like being an ugly girl at an all boys' school – not so pretty to look at, but everybody sure is happy you're there."

In my nearly 14 total years in the A-10, I accumulated over 2,500 hours. I was part of the 353rd's first A-10 deployment in 1979 from Myrtle Beach to Su Won, South Korea – 10 days and 13 air refuelings. For all of you fast movers out there, the A-10 really doesn't have a clock – it just has a calendar. I deployed to Europe twice, and flew in England, Germany, and Denmark. I flew the second airplane from the factory at Hagerstown, Maryland to England AFB, and along with two lieutenants, delivered the first three A-10s from the factory to Eielson AFB, Alaska in 1982. I helped with the conversion from F-4s to A-10s at Eielson, flying for nearly three months as a guest help IP – what a way to start a non-flying staff job. In my first month as the Squadron Commander of the 76th Fighter Squadron, I was given my favorite call sign of all time. In July 1987, during my first roof stomp as the Commander, I was labeled *"BOSSHAWG,"* and I love it even today! Over the years, I have had the opportunity to fly against some awesome fighter pilots in other planes from around the world. I learned a lot, but they always learned that you shouldn't wrestle with a hog – you both get dirty but the hog loves it, and if you run, you will only die tired.

My Air Force career ended in 1994 after serving my last assignment as the Air Force Reserve Inspector General. I spent two or three months trying to figure out who I was going to be next until UPS hired me to fly 727s. I had just married a beautiful and wonderful lady from Arizona one year before I retired. She is an absolutely amazing person and entrepreneur. She started a business the same year I left the Air Force. Ruthanne began selling commercial office furniture and associated interior products to mostly DoD clients. During my days off from UPS, I helped with the paperwork, scheduling of installations, and what I called, "dialing for dollars."

When we met, Ruthanne was working with her brother selling office supplies and small amounts of commercial office furniture. One day, a client at Williams AFB asked her if she could sell office furniture on GSA contract. He wanted furniture for his new squadron building and had a $50,000 budget. Ruthanne said, "Absolutely!" She then went home and tried to find out what the hell GSA spelled.

She made several phone calls the next day and found a manufacturer who agreed to let her sell from their GSA contract. They were one of the country's "Top 5" office furniture producers. They had no other dealers in Arizona who were interested in government sales. After one year in business, her company, Simmons Contract Furnishings, had become their largest volume dealership in Arizona. Within three years, we had three sales staff in Arizona, two support staff, and had just expanded into the Las Vegas market, as well. Sales volume by now had more than tripled. A few more years passed and other territory became available. With the manufacturer's encouragement, we now had hired sales people in San Antonio, Norfolk, and Seattle, all key government locations. Sales volume skyrocketed. After seven years, Simmons Contract Furnishings, under Ruthanne's leadership, was the leading GSA dealership in the country for our primary manufacturer. She mastered GSA sales and had grown her once one person company into 25 people in five states at its peak. I left UPS at that point to work FOR Ruthanne. She was the Sales Manager and CEO, and I managed operations and finance.

One prideful event in our company's history will forever be emblazoned in our memories. The horrific terrorist attack of September 11, 2001 displaced many of the Pentagon's personnel. An Army four-star and his staff needed to relocate to temporary facilities. They needed furniture specified, designed, built, delivered, and installed in the next 21 days, a process that normally took eight to 10 weeks. Their last experience with office furniture with a local DC/Maryland dealership was a bad one. The regional Army contracting officer had done business with our sales and service team in the Virginia market and had nothing but positive memories. He sent an Army helicopter to Virginia, picked up our team, and took them to the site. Ruthanne focused all of our company on this one job. Our designers in Tucson worked nearly 48 straight hours to design the project. Our manufacturer made this their number one priority and pulled product from production orders from customers around the country. We shipped the product quickly, installed right away, and made the three-week deadline without a hitch. We don't know for sure that we were the first to help with relocating Pentagon staff, but we were among the first. We could not have been any prouder of our people, our manufacturing support, and the total dedication and professionalism of everybody involved. Even in furniture, there are patriotic memories.

Ruthanne and I decided to retire together after 15 years of life in the business world. We simply closed the doors to our company one day and walked away.

From fighter pilot, to airline pilot, to business executive, I have had an interesting, fun, and diverse life. Since Ruthanne loves to travel, as do I, I look forward to all the rest, especially our annual fishing trips to Alaska. She has the record so far – a 43 pound king salmon. Who else has a wife that would go to Kodiak Island, hike a mile and a half on a bear trail, and fish in a river filled with red salmon along side 15 Kodiak brown bears? I do, and we did just that.

I recently met a retired Raytheon executive at a political fundraiser. She asked me if I had children. My answer was that I have three very successful young men – all college graduates, no body piercings, and only one tattoo. We both agreed that was success by anybody's definition.

In actuality, my oldest son Michael is the Vice President of a national healthcare corporation; my middle son, Jeremy, built and owns his own successful commercial interiors project management company in New Mexico; and my youngest son, Andy, is now a fully-qualified F-35 pilot. I am a very happy husband and immensely proud father.

I mentioned Lt Gen Jim Record earlier. When he retired in Tucson, he and I became the best of friends and what I have labeled honorary brothers. Jim belonged to a group of pilots that called themselves the

Luncho Buncho. On several occasions, he invited me to join them for lunch. I found each man to be an amazing individual, proud, proven, and unwavering patriot, hero in his own right, with flying history that was essential glue for this group. Every Friday, different stories are told and different friends or leaders from the past show up in casual conversation. This group of amazing men range in retired rank from four-star general to the short time Air Force guys who went to the airlines early and retired as captains. We have three who were POWs in Vietnam. We even have one from the original two groups of astronauts. On Friday at noon, although there are plenty of stars to go around, there is no rank at the table. I look forward to hearing new stories every Friday – some old ones too.

When my great friend, Jim Record, died a few years back, the group asked me to keep on coming to The Friday Pilots' lunch – it was an honor for me to oblige. I have attended regularly now for several years and have found myself at home with a group of men that I absolutely admire for who they are today, and who they were back in the day when they actually considered themselves *handsome, virile, and the worlds best pilots.*

By now, you will have read many of the other chapters and will already have met most of these fabulous heroes. In combination, we are a lot of fun to be around – at least legends in our own minds. Join us for lunch sometime.

This story ends on a sad note: Ruthanne, the beautiful wife of Bill Pitts, passed away on 22 October 2014 during the publication of this book. She died of severe brain trauma as the result of a cycling accident. May a good and gracious God hold her and hers in the palm of His hand - Editor

After retirement from the USAF, Boris Baird became
team manager of the U.S. aerobatic team in 1996

Second only to flying, Boris Baird loved hunting, fishing
and the outdoors. He hunted big game in Africa and
pheasant and quail in the Midwest U.S. here he is with a
catch of Steelheads on the Snake River in Idaho

Bob Barnett by his F-105 Thud at Korat RTAB, Thailand, 1967

Bob Barnett and Nancy Reagan 1973, March
AFB Hospital, after his POW release

Pete Carpenter by his F-100, assigned to 417th TFS, Ramstein
AB, Germany TDY to Wheelus AB, Tripoli, Libya, 1962

Pete Carpenter's one and only P-47 flight,
Amarillo AFB, TX, December, 1952

Lew Daugherty and his A-1 Spad, 602d TFS,
Bien Hoa AB, South Vietnam, 1965

Lew Daughtery and his A-1 Spad, circa 2000, Tucson AZ

Bob Dundas and his beloved F-105, Tucson AZ, DMAFB

Bob Dundas and his beloved adult beverage – beer

Bill Hosmer and his F-105 Thud, Kadena AB, Okinawa, 1963

Bill Hosmer, first "un-chased" F-86 flight, Nellis AFB, 1954

Young, steely-eyed fighter pilot, Terry Johnson
in his F-101, Duluth MN ANG, 1970

Terry and Claudia Johnson as adventuresome
adults outside of Telluride, CO, 2003

Jim McDivitt, second group of U.S. Astronauts,
flew Gemini and Apollo spacecraft

L-R: Astronaut Ed White, Vice President, Hubert Humphrey,
and Jim McDivitt on steps of U.S. Capitol, 1965

Andy Muscarello in his T-33, 1959, Laredo AFB, TX

Andy Muscarello, retirement flight from American Airlines, 1994

Marty Neuens, F-105 pilot, Takhli RTAB, 1966

Marty and Cindy Neuens, Tucson AZ, 1999

Earl O'Loughlin in pilot training with his T-6,
Spence AFB, Moultrie, GA, 1951

Four-star General Earl O'Loughlin, Commander,
Air Force Logistics Command, 1984

Bill Pitts, "Bosshawg" in the cockpit of his beloved A-10 Warthog

Bill Pitts second from left as part of Gunsmoke
'81 A-10 team from England AFB

GAR Rose and his F-4, Ubon RTAB, 1972, shortly before his shootdown

GAR, Becky and Glenn Rose, family reunion at Andrews
AFB 31 Mar 1973, after his POW release

1st Lt. Gene Santarelli with his F-4, Ubon
RTAB, Thailand, Vietnam War

Lt. General Gene Santarelli, Vice Commander,
Pacific Air Forces, Hickam AFB, HI

Capt. Don Shepperd, 247th and last F-100 combat mission, Vietnam 1968

Colonel Don Shepperd, last F-15 flight, Otis ANGB Cape Cod MA 1989

Moose Skowron returns injured after shootdown
on his 99th F-105 mission, 1966

Moose Skowron far left, dressed for combat, Thailand, 1966

Rob Van Sice, F-4 at Phu Cat AB RVN, 1970, first combat tour

Rob Van Sice, F-16 Desert Storm, Al Dhafra UAE, 1991, last combat tour

Russ Violett. F-100, Misawa AB, Japan, 1961

Major General Russ Violett, retirement, 1987

Gordy Williams, West Point cadet, class of 1957
and grandmother, Ethelynn Smith

Major General Gordy Williams, Commander
13th Air Force, Pacific Air Forces

Doc Zoerb and his WWII "Ace" father getting early flight lessons

Doc Zoerb with his father in a "Kolb Ultrastar" ultralight
aircraft they built – their flying adventures never cease

Bob McMahon, owner of McMahon's Prime Steakhouse, where the
Friday Pilots lunch, far left, Ed McMahon from the Johnny Carson Show

Carrie Convertino our GREAT server and friend
at McMahon's Prime Steakhouse

Terri Lundgren our past server and GREAT friend at Ric's Café, Tucson

Bob Barnett and Carrie Convertino during
lunch at McMahon's Steakhouse

Another Boris Baird fishing expedition on the Snake River

Pete Carpenter, wife Honeyjean, daughter, Cricket, and
their Beechcraft Debonair, Duncan, OK 1965

Lew Daugherty, 57mm hit on his A-1 in
vicinity of Sam Neua, Laos, 1966

Bill Hosmer, second from left at top of ladder,
on the '61-63 USAF Thunderbird team

Jim McDivitt as test pilot alongside F-104, Edwards AFB, CA

Andy Muscarello, Chicago ANG KC-97, in Azores 1976

Earl O'Loughlin moose hunt, Alberta, Canada

GAR Rose and his F-4 at MacDill AFB, FL, for
RTU,1966 before his first combat tour

Major General Gene Santarelli in his F-16, Incirlik AB, Turkey, 1994

Don and Rose Shepperd, engaged at Air Force
Academy, 1961, by Pegasus statue

Four-ship fly-by for Oklahoma State Homecoming game, 1964.
The group then went to Tahkli RTAB, Thailand together L-R: Sam
Woodworth (KIA,) Russ Violett, Ken Johnston (rescued), Al Logan

Major General Gordy Williams escorting President Fredinand Marcos
of the Philippines into exile, Imelda Marcos in black dress, 1986

Doc Zoerb in front of his 48th FIS F-106, Langley AFB, VA, 1979

Earl O'Loughlin on his Appaloosa

Bill Pitts retirement, 1994
L-R: Lt. General Jim Record, Ruthanne Pitts

The group at the old Ric's Café
L-R: Terry Johnson, Andy Muscarello, Earl O'Loughlin, Bill Pitts,
Moose Skowron, Bob Dundas, Pete Carpenter, Bill Hosmer,
Gordy Williams, Lew Daugherty, Bob Barnett

Another view at the old Ric's Café
L-R: Bob Dundas, Pete Carpenter, Bill Hosmer, Gordy
Williams, Lew Daugherty, Jim McDivitt, Bob Barnett, Terry
Johnson, Andy Muscarello, Earl O'Loughlin, Bill Pitts

The Group at McMahon's Prime Steakhouse
L-R: Russ Violett, Bill Hosmer, Tunis Parsons, Andy Muscarello,
Terry Johnson, Gordy Williams, Lew Daugherty, Bob Barnett, Pete
Carpenter, GAR Rose, Don Shepperd, Rob Van Sice, Bill Pitts

CHAPTER THIRTEEN

They Called Me "GAR"

by George A. "GAR" Rose

The early years (1942-1960): Friday, November 13, 1942 was my birthday. Born Norbert Mishler in Kansas City, MO, I was placed with Kansas City Cradle, an adoption agency. My parents selected me at the age of six weeks to join them and create a family. I was given the name George Alan Rose; George after my maternal grandfather, and Alan after the actor Alan Ladd, a favorite of my mom and an Arkansas native.

Glen and Lois Rose were raised in Arkansas, attended the University of Arkansas in Fayetteville where they met, wed and began a lifelong allegiance to their alma mater. Dad was the first All-American in basketball for Arkansas in 1928. He would later go on to be head coach of the Razorback basketball team for 23 seasons in two separate stints.

When we departed Kansas City, we went to Brownwood, TX, where Dad was in training to be a company commander of a tank destroyer unit slated for duty in the European Theater of Operations. During maneuvers at Fort Hood, TX he injured his back and was relegated to non-combat duty for the duration of WWII. That duty was coaching football teams at Army camps in Illinois and Indiana. He was medically retired in 1945, and the family returned to Fayetteville where he resumed his coaching duties in all sports, but primarily basketball.

In 1948 dad received an offer to relocate the family to Nacogdoches, TX, and be head basketball coach at Stephen F. Austin State Teachers College. That fall I began school at West End Elementary. A significant event occurred while we lived in TX. On Air Force Day in 1951 the SAC B-36 bomber wing based at Carswell AFB, TX, put on a display of our aerial might for the public. Several flights of B-36s launched and flew along the major U.S. highways fanning out of the Fort Worth area to cover the state of TX, east along

U.S. Hwy 67 to Texarkana, then south along U.S. Hwy 59 to Houston, etc. The TOT for their arrival over Nacogdoches was well-publicized, so the populous turned out to line Main Street which was Hwy 59. The deep drone of those aircraft engines is still embedded in my memory. Mom told the story for years that as those huge machines passed over, I pointed at them and said something to the effect that my goal was be a pilot someday. A glimmer of hope in my dad's eye as he thought I had no motivation to do much other than ride my bike and play ball!

We remained in Texas until 1952, when Dad was asked by the Director of Athletics at Arkansas to return to Fayetteville and take over the sole duty of head basketball coach and rebuild the program to one of respect, which he did very successfully. The family traipsed along and in the fall I entered the Fayetteville Public School System in the fifth grade and began to make lifelong friends with whom I am still in close contact.

I never set the academic world afire but did enjoy the social side of the education process. Additionally, I was quite active in the Boy Scouts and the Presbyterian Youth Fellowship. When I realized I was too small to be competitive in varsity sports, I lobbied to be the intramural manager in junior high. Coach Benny Winborn was one of the coaches I worked for, and was probably my first mentor outside of the family. He worked with me to develop better study skills, to achieve better grades, then hired me to be the student manger for the Fayetteville High School Bulldogs basketball team. In high school I took the easy road and did not take many difficult science or math courses but concentrated on business prep. The Student Council seemed like a good thing with which to get involved. I was Student Council and Student Body Treasurer my junior year, then President my senior year. My dad became concerned about my proclivity to "flit in all directions and fly in none," so he encouraged me to do some testing at the university career guidance office. My aptitude scores were such that my strong points were a draw between forest ranger, accountant and PILOT! So, unbeknownst to me, the course of life was taking a direction but where to remained to be seen.

Charting the course (1960 – 1964): The fall of 1960 found me with the mass of newbies on campus at Arkansas. I'd been readily accepted because anyone could attend the university if they were an Arkansas resident. My grades were decent enough that I didn't have to take any of the 101.X classes! ROTC was compulsory at all land grant colleges, so I signed up for AFROTC. Dad had always said if you have a choice, flying is better than crawling, and if you're going to be in the service, be an officer. So there I was in Air Force BLUE.

I adapted well to the ROTC regimen and enjoyed the program. The instructors were mostly fighter pilots and regaled us with stories of adventure and combat. To keep their currency and flight pay, the instructors had to fly four hours per month. The instructors went to Fort Smith to fly the Air National Guard's F-84s or T-33s. We were frequently subject to "attack," when they made passes on our marching formations on the drill field. On more than one occasion, I was admonished for not having "eyes front." I was watching the fighters instead.

My first semester came to an end, and I found that one of my professors had a different interpretation of a piece of world literature than me. I bombed the final exam and was suddenly on academic probation. I consulted one of the ROTC instructors for guidance. My recovery from probation was successful. I was asked to join a fraternity, Sigma Alpha Epsilon, my sophomore year, and college was now fun. I entered the advanced ROTC program. Along with two other fraternity brothers, I spent hours at the Student Union drinking coffee and being brainwashed by Captain Ewald Glenn Kruggel about flying the F-84 and F-100 in Europe and New Mexico. A few stories of Friday night happy hours and weekend cross-country trips also crept in. Glenn Kruggel was the most significant individual in my decision to enter advanced AFROTC. As a cadet lieutenant I enjoyed the leadership roles. The summer of 1963 meant ROTC summer camp. England AFB, LA, was the place for four charming weeks in July and August. We cadets were treated to a T-33 orientation flight; loops and rolls and maneuvers from basic flight training all in a 30-minute sortie. I thoroughly enjoyed the whole ride! One more flight in a C-119 put the cap on our flight experience. Then, came the all important flight physical to determine our medical fitness for flight training. The afternoon prior to my physical there was an officer with wings at the bar who inquired how the training was going and what was next. We told him we were up for our flight physical tomorrow. He asked if we anticipated any problems. I was naïve and said I'd had a mild inconsequential concussion as a kid but had not lost consciousness and did not intend to divulge this information. Do you see it coming? The guy was a flight surgeon and he nailed me. I failed the flight physical! A few days later we completed camp and returned to Fayetteville. When I walked in the door at home, Mom said Colonel Hardin, the PAS, wanted me to report to him ASAP. Yes Sir! After a serious butt chewing he laid out what had to be done to get back on track for the flight program; a letter from the attending physician in TX; an x-ray skull series at my expense; an EEG at my expense; another complete physical by a USAF flight surgeon. The stars aligned and in October I began the Flight Intro Program, soloed in the Cessna 150 after 10.2 hours and in March passed my FAA private pilots license written and flying exams!

The highlight of my aviation career up to then was my first non-student flight when I took my dad, all 6'5" of him, up for a short flight around the area to include a fly past our home where my mom had waited patiently in the backyard for us to arrive. Mom never did fly with me. My senior year of college was FUN. Hey, go bug smash around one day a week, maybe two – most of the classes were seminar type, and I was going to USAF UPT. Not so fast Rose! Your active duty report date is 16 Jan 1965 at Laredo AFB, TX. Now what to do in the meantime, no job, no money. Remember the aptitude test and forest ranger? A call to my previous boss landed a minimum wage job as a laborer. I wrangled a job with the Bureau of Land Management in Colorado building fences and fighting fires. My base of operations was a small town in north central Colorado, Kremmling. As I rolled into town past the small airport I spotted a Cessna 150 in a T-hanger. Wow! The owner of the Esso station told me it was his but he had a heart condition and could no longer fly. "But if you buy the gas you can fly it." And so, I did, several times a month. I learned a couple of important aviation lessons that summer. Kremmling is at slightly more than 7,000' MSL. One warm afternoon I consulted the owner's manual for takeoff performance. The numbers appeared OK. Have you ever seen a 4,000 ft. + takeoff roll in a Cessna 150? I did and I don't want to do it again. Aviation lesson #1 – just because the book says you can, does not mean you should. Lesson #2 – What goes up will come down.

I transitioned from the BLM to the U.S. Forest Service near the end of the summer. Tramping through the forest marking off vast tracts of timber that would be sold to the logging industry was my primary task. Ah, the great outdoors and I had finally become a forest ranger, albeit only temporarily. Happiness was when my supervisor offered me time off in exchange for "flying the district" every other day or so. I'd takeoff shortly after sunrise and fly south towards Dillon, then north along the Gore and Rabbit Ears Range to Muddy Pass, then southeast toward Byers Canyon on the Colorado River and return to Kremmling. I was airborne about 1:30 looking for fires, any smoke other than from a campfire. I made three such flights and then it was back into the field. The first good snowstorm blanketed the area negating the need for a fire patrol. My forest ranger flying career came to an end. The next big storm put an end to the field work for the season, and the funds for temporary help were exhausted. It was back to Arkansas to await the next phase of my flying career.

Off we go into the wild blue yonder with UPT Class 66-E (1965-1966): 16 January 1965 and off to Laredo AFB, TX. Like a lot of UPT guys, I'd requested Williams AFB, AZ. Active duty lesson #1: rarely expect to get what you ask for from the USAF. I was sure the end of the earth was just over the horizon as I rolled south down I-35 beyond San Antonio. Well, it wasn't, but darn close to it! I located my "sponsor," a member of Class 65-E. He and some of his classmates took several of us for dinner at Golding's Steak House for margaritas, say what? nachos w/jalapenos; more jalapenos, great beef steak and a lot of "this is what you can expect" conversation. My love of the cuisine of Mexico has never waned!

Orientation Day was led by our TAC Officer. He gave us the official version of "this is what you can expect!" - aviation physiology, altitude chamber, boom bucket and the first academic test that would be part of our all-important final class standing that helped determine aircraft assignment upon graduation. Oh yeah, the concussion that I thought was behind me, reared it's ugly head. It seems the Air Force medics did not agree on the waiver (I never knew I was waived) for me to attend UPT - off to Wilford Hall Hospital at Lackland AFB for an ATC-approved exam - same song, second verse - skull series,

EEG, flight physical! You pass Lt and no waiver required! Sierra Hotel!

Class 66-E at Laredo began the journey to silver wings with 32 or 33 aspiring aeronauts. Before we ever went to the flight line, two guys SIE'd (Self Initiated Elimination) noting they had never really wanted to be pilots anyway and would rather be a motor pool officer and band director instead! YGBSM!

We began to bond as a class and really work together. Our IPs entered the room, introduced themselves with a couple of background items about their career, then they proceeded to THEIR table.

Capt Carroll B. Arnold, F-86, GCI Controller, second tour in ATC came towards the table where I was seated. My tablemate and I snapped to attention and rendered a hand salute. In the "get to know you" session that followed, my fellow 66-E'r, James S. "Stu" Mosbey answered the question, "If you graduate, what is your choice of aircraft, Lt Mosbey?" He said an F-4. "And, what about you Rose?"

"A C-135 with an airline career in mind, Sir."

Capt Arnold peered over the top of his "readers," fingered his mustache and said, "We'll see about that!" I got the impression it was not the preferred answer.

T-37 flying seemed to pass quickly and without problems. We 17 "survivors" were really bonded now in flying, academics, PT and socializing. One of the married gents asked me one day if I would be interested in taking out his wife's sorority sister, Rebecca Gaines Bearden, while she was in town visiting. "Sight unseen? An anglo lady in Laredo? You betchum Red Ryder!" One of the key decisions I've made in my life and unarguably the best as we are pushing 48 years of wedded bliss and turmoil together.

We had a great relationship with most of our IPs. Since we had to "initial" all our gradeslips, I was given the moniker, "GAR," and so it has been for almost 50 years. Our class was pretty evenly split between married and bachelors, and almost every weekend there was a party. Stu Mosbey, Tal Hass and I bought a ski boat to use on Lake Casa Blanca that bordered the base. Life was good. UPT was not a snap but if one of us needed assistance, the assistance was there. We adopted the class title of "66-E, The Laredo Escadrille" as a display of unity. We had been informed in our "this is what to expect" presentation that our class would be the FIRST T-38 CLASS

AT LAREDO! We were issued our flight manuals, checklists and academic materials for the T-38 and began to study the systems of the "Talon." Capt David Burney knocked on my door one evening with the word the Director of Operations, Colonel Frank Gailer, had ordered the class to his office the next morning at O-dark thirty! Active duty lesson #2 – even when it's for sure, it may not be.

Colonel Gailer gave us the good news that we would be flying the venerable T-33 for the duration of our training and the bad news that we would NOT be the first class in the T-38! And so it was in August, we began T-33 flights. This actually was a good deal, well, kind of a good deal. The ramp was loaded with a lot of T-33s with a decreasing number of IPs and students to fly them. We were able to fly almost every day, weather permitting!

We finished T-33s in fine fettle and it was ASSIGNMENT TIME! Our block of aircraft assignments was delivered and due back the Monday before Thanksgiving. Our IP had given Stu and I strict orders to not turn in our aircraft assignment requests before he had the opportunity to review our desires and talk to us. On that Monday Stu and I trudged down to Standardization in the cold drizzle and fog, reported in a military manner to the man we've come to admire so much as a teacher, pilot, mentor and especially a friend. Arnie looks at Stu's list and true to form from day one, F-4 USAFE, F-4 TAC, F-4 PACAF and on with the multi engine aircraft deep into the list. I handed Arnie my list and he reviews it, looks over the top of his readers and asks, "When did you decide you wanted a fighter GAR?"

"On my Dollar ride, Sir!"

"You little shithead!" he laughed. We broke for the holiday season and all headed north, the only direction to what we referred as "civilization." Two weeks later we returned, and as I walked the hallway to my room, Gary Anderson called to me, "Hey you F-4 driver!" Assignment, 12th TFW, Cam Ranh Bay, Republic of Vietnam!

1965 at Laredo AFB with the men of The Laredo Escadrille was one of the most formative of my life. The bonds we formed as a class are still unbroken. We've been very fortunate to have lost only one member of The Escadrille. Almost all of us were in SEA at one point or another and one made it to Desert Storm! The list of combat decorations is staggering – Silver Stars, DFCs, Air Medals and fortunately, only one Purple Heart. We have in our membership one four-star general, Walter Kross, several Colonels and Lt Cols, airline captains, business entrepreneurs; all-in-all, the finest group of men with whom I've been privileged to associate. The gentlemen who taught us, Carroll B. Arnold, Rocco deFelice, Ray Healy, Dave Pennington, Mike Goold and the list goes on - we are forever grateful to you.

On the way to Cam Ranh Bay (1966): The journey to Cam Ranh Bay began the morning of 7 Feb 1966 when my silver wings were pinned to my Class A blues by Mom and Becky who had journeyed to Laredo for the occasion. A couple of days later we began the trek west. We had a mini-convoy with three cars initially, but Dick Jaeger pushed it up in his Corvette and waited for us in El Paso. Walt Kross was driving his old Ford convertible, with no heater, and I in my trusty Chevy with heat. Stu Mosbey alternated between Walt's car and mine for survival purposes. It was two days to Tucson to drop off Walt's car at Davis-Monthan AFB to which we would return for initial F-4 training. We departed for Reno and Stead AFB, the USAF Survival School. Two weeks of classroom instruction on how to survive in a hostile environment, a simulated POW camp (little did I suspect how relevant this would later become) with all the trappings and a trip into the Sierra's for hands-on instruction and practice of what we'd learned by camping in the snow, lots of snow. My Boy Scout experience came in handy and I was able to assist some of the troops, who had never camped in their life, adapt to the unique situation. The last exercise in the training is commonly referred to as, "The Trek." It is putting it mildly to say our "Trek" was snow-filled. It was deep winter in the Sierras, but we survived and it was "time for a beer!"

Next, it was back down the road to Tucson and the F-4 Pilot Systems Operator (PSO) radar training course. This was a three-week course crammed into two months. We were trained in the fine art of air-to-air intercepts in the classroom and the flight simulator. To continue to receive flight pay we logged four hours flight time each month in a T-33. As I was T-bird qualified I was allowed to fly the frontseat while the T-38 guys had to ride in the back seat! Payback! I have great memories of the Friday afternoon pilot meetings followed by beer call in the Polynesian Room of the DM O-Club where the likes of Col Daniel "Chappie" James would hold court. And then, there were the parties at the infamous Escalante Gardens, an apartment complex leased by the USAF as TDY quarters for the many pilots in training. Nuff said!

After completing radar training at DMAFB, came a long road trip to MacDill AFB, FL, outside Tampa and the meat of the training, flying training in the F-4C Phantom II. My RTU (Replacement Training Unit) class was composed of an all fighter-experienced group of pilots in the frontseat and brand new UPT graduates (me) in the backseat. Now we're talking! My first flight in the Phantom on June 1 was with my assigned nose gunner, Capt Jack Arnold, a former F-100 pilot. As we were taking the runway, the control tower asked us to make an immediate turn after takeoff to fly over Davis Island and see if we saw an aircraft down. No need, as we could see towering black smoke from that area and another F-4 was already over the crash site. Both pilots ejected safely, but of course the Phantom was destroyed as were a couple of houses in the impact area. So, Jack advanced the throttles, selected the afterburners and we shot down the runway at a speed I could not even have imagined in my wildest dreams. My gosh, the power of those twin jet engines was amazing compared to the T-33. Rotate, nose high to 20 degrees, 300 knots, out of burner and we're still climbing several thousand feet a minute! Yee Hah! This is how it should be! Over the next two and one-half months we trained in air-to-air combat over the Gulf of Mexico, air-to-ground munitions delivery day and night, air intercepts and refueling from a KC-135 tanker. I recall the program called for us to receive about 75 hours of flight time and at least that amount in ground school.

About halfway through training, I proposed to Becky, and she accepted. We were married on June 25, 1966 at the MacDill base chapel. Our immediate families were in attendance but the big majority of the attendees were my classmates, each and every one of them, 54 people, signed our guest book. When my O-Club bill came due at the end of the month, I discovered why we had a great party. 54 bottles of the bubbly had been consumed!

As the training wrapped up we were notified of our departure date from Travis AFB, CA, westbound for Vietnam. Becky and I parted at Tampa International for what we assumed would be only a one-year tour with a Hawaii R&R mid-tour. One of our class was able to decipher the code for the type of transportation we would ride westbound. Our class met in a bar next to the terminal and Capt Hollis Wilkerson announced broke the news we would enjoy the hospitality of Saturn Airways in one of their DC-7s, 10 hours to Hawaii; eight hours to Wake Island; eight more into Clark AB! Nothing but the best for our troops going to take on the Commie Pinko bastards, huh?

We survived and once at Clark were taken to an off base hotel to spend three days lounging by the pool before the five-day Jungle Survival School, aka "Snake School." A captain on his way to Bien Hoa to fly the F-100 introduced us to the famous "San Miguel sandwich" while poolside, claiming there was a pork chop in every bottle! We had to leave the hotel for the tents of snake school and found the rest of our RTU class had arrived that afternoon by Saturn Airways and were they ever po'd – no pool time – no San Miguels! Snake school was much more interesting than the Stead experience perhaps because of the relativity. Two days of classroom, then off to the jungle for two nights in an elevated sleeping bed to avoid things that crawled on the jungle floor, then one night with a partner hiding from the indigenous Negrito's who were able to find anything, even with their eyes closed. The last day in the PI was back at the off base hotel. At 10 PM, the class went their separate ways – Cam Ranh Bay – Da Nang – Ubon via C-130.

My first war (1966-1967): As we deplaned from the C-130 at CRB, a jeep wheeled-up with a full colonel at the wheel. "Welcome to Cam Ranh Bay, gentlemen. I am James Allen the 12th TFW DO. Throw your gear in the back of that deuce-and-a-half and follow me to the wing headquarters building." As we entered his office area, two squadron commanders also arrived. "How many do you need Gerry?" he inquired of Lt Col Gerald Bisner, 558th TFS commander?

"At least six Sir!" was the response. So, Col Allen counted off six of us then said to the other squadron commander he could have the other two for the 357th TFS. Col Bisner led us next door to the oversized quonset hut that was home to the four squadrons assigned to the wing, the 557th, 558th, 559th and 391st TFSs. When we entered

Whiskey Ops, (the squadron call sign was Whiskey), a Lt took one look at us and said, "Thank You Lord," dropped his flight gear on the floor and told Col Bisner that he was done! Col Bisner agreed and then told us that the Lt was one of the initial cadre that had deployed to CRB from MacDill a year ago and was due to depart within the next few days for the USA with his Vietnam tour completed. We were the first replacement pilots to arrive in several weeks and the Lt was not alone in flying right up to his DEROS. Manpower was in short supply since the personnel "pipeline" was not yet full. One of our group flew his first combat sortie within about six hours of arrival on base. My first sortie was on 8 October with Major Jim Gammon. We were sitting "Boxer Alert" at the south end of the runway, when we were scrambled for a TIC (troops in contact). We were loaded with four cans of napalm and a SUU-16 gatling gun to use in the close air support mission for U.S. troops in combat with VC insurgents. Jim laid the napalm at the base of a hill where the FAC said a machine gun was positioned, pinning down a U.S. patrol. Our wingman dropped four 500 lb. snakeye bombs on the napalm smoke and the machine gun was silenced. Our troops lived to fight another day. Welcome to combat, GAR!

The 12th Wing did not fly many missions deep into North Vietnam but routinely flew in the southern part of the country interdicting the supply routes used to move arms into SVN. These missions were not as treacherous as those into the Hanoi-Haiphong area, but we took plenty of ground fire and several planes from the wing were shot down or badly damaged in this area called Tally-Ho. Some missions were questionable in our mind as we would go north with two 250 lb. bombs when there WAS a bomb shortage regardless of what the Washington whiz kids told the public. But, in true political games, the sortie counts became the measure of successes to conceal the shortage of ordnance.

My first war ended with 176 missions, 64 into NVN and 337 hours of combat time. Several of us departed Cam Ranh for Seattle on a chartered DC-8; Seattle to Chicago on a Northwest Orient Airline B-727, complimentary upgrade to first class; then, a Delta Air Lines flight to Knoxville on a DC-7, complimentary upgrade to first class; a heck of a way to return compared to the way I went to war. Becky met me in Knoxville with her dad and stepmother.

I had 30 days leave before reporting to McGuire AFB, NJ, for a flight to Frankfurt, Germany and an assignment to the 49ᵗʰ TFW, Spangdahlem AB! Against a lot of odds, Becky and I spent our first wedding anniversary together while on the way to Fayetteville to see my folks.

Fighting the Cold War: The flight to Germany was an all-nighter. If you think the TSA are a hassle, you should have had to deal with the MAC aerial port bureaucrats at McGuire, then the U.S. Army MPs at Rhein-Main AB, GE. We ran the gauntlet and boarded a Greyhound type of bus, The 49er, for the trip to Spangdahlem. Along the way we stopped by a gasthaus for a rest break and our first German beer. Then, we stopped at Hahn AB. Then, we stopped at Bitburg AB. And finally, Spang. One long-assed day!

I went to the personnel office because I'd been unable to reach my sponsor who had rotated back to the CONUS. The 49ᵗʰ was in the midst of transitioning from the F-105 to the F-4D. A few of the F-105 pilots were trained in the F-4 and remained as the main cadre. Capt Bo Odle (an American original) showed me around and told me I was the only Pilot Systems Operator (PSO) in the squadron, but others were inbound. He took me to meet Lt Col Felix C. Fowler, 9ᵗʰ Sq. Commander. Col Fowler was a hulk of a man. He'd commanded the 389ᵗʰ TFS at Da Nang AB, RVN, and had earned a great reputation as a combat leader as far back as WWII. Everyone loved and respected him. I don't think he was overly impressed with my experience in NVN since most of my missions had been in the less treacherous area of the country.

As the squadron began to reform and flesh out with pilots, I learned that as the junior guy in the unit, I was THE snack bar officer, until a less senior Lt showed up. Becky and I stayed in the BOQ while looking for a place to reside. My buddy from UPT, Stu Mosbey was at Bitburg AB, a short 15-minute drive. He and Judy treated Becky and I to our first real German meal. Stu said not to worry about the menu that he'd order for us. We went to the Post Hotel for dinner. For openers, escargot, and it just got better from there, all accompanied by great Mosel wine! How can you beat snails and a wine that's not Thunderbird?

The first few months at Spang were spent building-up to a combat ready status to pass an ORI from the USAFE IG. Most of the training for this inspection was accomplished flying out of Aviano AB and Wheelus AB, Libya where the weather conditions were more favorable than in Germany. The ORI was passed successfully and we began the cold war routine of sitting Victor (nuclear) Alert, some flying and a lot of practice exercises. We were prepared for an immediate takeoff with nuclear weapons if the Warsaw Pact launched a surprise attack. The Cold War was real and we practiced for war continually. Apparently Major Tom Wilson was impressed by my snack bar operation too. Years later he wrote a book based on his F-105 Wild Weasel experiences, *Termite Hill*. I saw Tom at an event before I'd seen the book, and he asked me if I'd read it. I hadn't. "Well, you better read it, because you're in it." And sure enough as I read the book there was Tom's mention of the best snack bar and snack bar officer he had known.

All good things come to an end. Early in 1968 the reassignment of the 49th TFW from USAFE to TAC was announced. The aircraft would be ferried back to Holloman AFB, NM, non-stop. There would be one final TDY to Wheelus so the PSOs could get some "frontseat" gunnery training before the long haul to NM.

About this time Becky and I were blessed by the birth of our son, Glen Rose II, on 12 June 1968. He was prepped for his first PCS ASAP because we were to transfer to Hahn AB, after we delivered the airplanes to Holloman.

On July 11 we launched 18 Phantoms from the 9th TFS in three cells of six for Holloman. I returned to Spang, gathered up my family and traveled across the Mosel River to Hahn AB and an assignment to the 10th TFS Singing Swords. Hahn meant the same drill as Spang with Victor Alert and incessant target study, exercises and TDYs to Wheelus and Aviano. Great friends were made that we still see occasionally. I was selected to attend the USAF Fighter Weapons School at Nellis AFB, NV, for an experimental class that included four of us who were PSOs.

FINALLY, the day arrived when I could advance to the frontseat of the F-4 after almost three and one-half years in the pit. A local upgrade at Hahn was carried out with the same intensity of an RTU program in the States, all while still performing as a PSO due to our low manning; harried days they were for sure, but well worth the sweat. Hahn was notorious for the crappy winter weather.

As the time came to look at my next assignment, I contacted a friend at TAC assignments, Capt Jim Thornton, to plead my case. Jim was able to wrangle an assignment for me to Seymour Johnson AFB, NC, FRONTSEAT in the F-4E Phantom II with the 4th TFW, 334th TFS Fighting Eagles. I reported in March 1971. The 4th TFW was the prime mobility wing for TAC, subject to deployment anywhere in the world, any time. We trained for multiple scenarios from the USAFE/NATO model to PACAF for the defense of South Korea. I was upgraded to IP status shortly after my arrival.

During a TAC ORI at 0400 in the wing briefing room all of the 334th crews selected for an air defense exercise were gathered. But, not one Lt Col or above, nor any IG guy was in sight. Hmmm? After about an hour, our squadron commander, Lt Col Crawford O. Shockley, entered the room, released non-essential personnel and told us, "No phone calls, no one leaves the building, and that's an order!" About 0700 Shock came back and announced we were to execute a mobility plan for deployment and we should go to the mobility section, collect our bags, go home and pack them for real! "Be back by 1000 and don't tell your wives anything!" By 1000 we were all in our seats awaiting word on the next event. Shock selected three guys and told them to go to Base Ops where they would be assigned to a C-130 or C-141 as OICs of the en route support teams for where ever we were deploying. Not much doubt in our mind that we were responding to the invasion of South Vietnam by the Communist army of NVN. Of course, we couldn't be told for security reasons. "Report to the mobility processing center, then you are released to your quarters until 1800 tonight if your name is on the flight schedule!" were our orders. My name was on the schedule as number five in the lead six aircraft

The next morning we had a low residue breakfast at the base chow hall, then to 334th Ops for a quick brief of the trip. Each cell of six F-4s would be with four KC-135s once we refueled over Tennessee, then again over the Grand Canyon, and joined the tankers just outside the Golden Gate. We were 18 334th Fighting Eagles westbound and technically clueless of our destination.

Ten hours and 15 minutes after departing NC we arrived at Hickam. The next day was eight hours and 25 minutes to Andersen AB, Guam. From Guam it was five and one-half hours to Ubon RTAFB, Thailand, which we were finally told, was our destination.

War #2: My first sortie was on 15 April 1972, a pre planned mission to attack a storage area in the Mu Gia Pass area of NVN. Our missions covered almost all aspects of fighter ops in the theater from Close Air Support in the An Loc region of SVN, armed road recee along the Ho Chi Minh Trail and of course the worst mission in theater, chaff dispensing. This mission involved eight to 12 aircraft loaded with M-129 leaflet bomb dispensers that were filled with chaff strips to confuse or negate the SAM radar threat.

Two missions stand out in my memory: The 8ᵗʰ TFW, formerly known as the Wolf Pack, had adopted the nickname, the "Bridge Busters." Most of the targets attacked by the wing were key bridges on supply routes. In mid May a mission was designed to destroy as many bridges as possible along the northeast railway from Hanoi to the Chinese border. As a decoy move, the 334ᵗʰ was tasked to make a chaff run into the Hanoi area with 12 aircraft. I was in line for the next "heavy" as we referred to the missions into the highly defended area around Hanoi and was on the flight schedule for the bridge mission as a chaff bird. The words from on high were to make this happen regardless of weather conditions. The planned route was up to NE Laos with refueling along the way, turn easterly toward Hanoi and set up the chaff corridor as we'd done several times before. As we turned towards Hanoi, we were met by a wall of clouds. Each flight dropped into a loose maneuvering formation while seeking to find a hole in the wall.

Suddenly, the flight lead called he had a relatively clear area directly in front of him and directed us to follow him. He initiated a split-s to about 45-degrees nose low, then rolled out pointed toward the Thanh Hoa area. Each of the remaining 11 aircraft followed and at the base of the clouds, about 15,000 feet, we began a turn towards the target area and somehow all of us got into position, 12 aircraft somewhat line-a-breast just as lead called to initiate the chaff delivery. We were hauling ass and pushing the mach thanks to our descent through the hole. About the time we hit the outskirts of Hanoi, the last bomb was released and the fleet made an in-place 180-degree turn to exit whence we'd come.

The defenses came alive with AAA bursting at all altitudes and quadrants but fortunately inaccurate and not one plane was hit. The bridge busters were highly successful and shut down the northeast railroad for a long time with multiple bridges destroyed.

The next memorable mission was on 2 June, the rescue of Capt Roger Locher. Locher was the WSO with Capt Bob Lodge, a MiG-killer crew from Udorn RTAB. Their plane had been shot down on May 10 without any evidence of ejections. Locher evaded detection and capture for 23 days before he was able to make contact using his survival radio with a flight of F-4s passing near his position.

The rescue was going to be dicey, at best! I was selected as one of our eight best bombers for this special mission. Our target was Yen Bai Airfield, a MiG base located in the vicinity of Locher's position and a very important cog in the NVN air defense network. U.S. forces had not been able to attack NVN airfields in years under the rules of engagement set down by the foolish civilian war planners in Washington for fear of upsetting the Soviets or Chinese. Each flight member was assigned a specific aimpoint on the airfield to stop the MiGs from getting airborne and disrupting the rescue.

Departure, refueling and ingress to the target were "standard." As we began our ingress to Yen Bai, we could hear the rescue group begin to make contact with Locher. The lead Sandy, an A1-E, asked Roger a couple of "personal identifier" questions to which only he would know the answers. The radio chatter during most missions into this area of NVN was normally chaotic. On this day, very little was heard on the radio other than transmissions from the Sandys and Jolly Green helicopters as they made their way across the Red River and into the pick-up area. We had armed our ordnance shortly after departing the tanker, and with a wing dip lead signaled us to go into our briefed attack formation. Not one word was spoken as we approached Yen Bai. All ordnance was delivered on the designated impact points, and the MiGs were grounded for several days. As the strike force headed westerly to refuel for the trip home the lead Jolly transmitted, "WE'VE GOT HIM!" Capt Roger Locher had been rescued.

June 21 – the longest day, or the day I thought I was dead four times: The next heavy mission was scheduled for around the 7th of June. An eight-ship formation was tasked to lay a chaff corridor into an area north of Hanoi so the bridge busters could take out some key bridges in the Thai Nguyen area. The DO then announced there would be a hold on missions to the Hanoi area for several days imposed by the Pentagon while a high-ranking member of the USSR Politburo was in Hanoi. On June 21st the mission was back on. I was number three with Capt Med Bowman on my wing. Lt Pete Callaghan was in my backseat. The flight was uneventful through the refueling. A call from Red Crown, a radar warning operation onboard a Navy ship, called MiGs inbound to our vicinity. A lone Mig-21 was seen at our one o'clock position, then turned hard to pass in front of the formation about a mile out. I moved the aircraft around to look aft of the flight but saw nothing. As I started to check Med's six o'clock, I felt a tap on the aircraft followed by all hell breaking loose.

The aircraft nose pitched down violently, and the tail section separated from the aircraft. I tried to fly the plane to no avail. We were tumbling through space with positive "Gs" then negative "Gs" tearing at our bodies, first pushing our butts into the seat and then causing us to hit against the canopy. I saw all of the warning and fire lights in the cockpit illuminated and made the decision to pull the handle between my legs to initiate the ejection sequence for both of us. The ejection seemed to occur in slow motion like a movie. The seat started up the rail, then a horrendous blast of wind hit me along with debris from the cockpit or the disintegrating aircraft. My helmet was torn off, and I could not open my eyes. I heard the seat stabilization drogue chute fluttering above me and knew I'd escaped dying, at least for now. The last altitude I recall seeing on the altimeter was around 18,500' and I was at an airspeed of 450 knots.

Suddenly, I was hanging in space beneath a fully-opened parachute, and it was a long way to the ground. I saw one other parachute above me. I called out Pete's name, then Med's name on my survival radio. I attempted to steer my chute into the wind to slow the rate at which I was moving easterly towards Hanoi. I lost sight of the other parachute and touched down hard, but did not bash against any of the rocks in the area. Just prior to hitting the ground, I spotted a lone individual running in my direction and crossing what appeared to be a cultivated field. So, someone knew my approximate position, and it was paramount I relocate.

I rolled-up my chute and took off uphill. I threw my parachute harness into a ravine and continued to move. After a few minutes, I heard voices, so I slipped into a thick bush, pushed the branches and grasses back into place and tried to conceal my entry point. The searchers went up and down the hill past me several times, then left when they discovered my harness. One individual sat on a rocky outcrop just above me for a smoke break and discarded the match into the grass a few inches from my face. I was able to pat the small flames out with my gloved hand. About an hour after I'd crawled into my hiding place, I could see a crowd gathering nearby. Then, a rifle was pushed into the bush stopping just short of my chest. The holder began waving the barrel about and jabbering very excitedly. Jigs Up!

I moved part way out of the bush and was grabbed by what seemed like a hundred hands. Almost instantly my garments were removed, and I was standing in NVN in my shorts, t-shirt and socks. A noose was placed around my neck with a long rope while my arms were trussed-up until my elbows touched behind my back. We began to move downhill while the group abused me with long bamboo poles and spittle. I have no idea how long we walked, but the size of the crowd kept growing and the screaming and whacking of my body was intense. The guy with the rope jerked me off the trail and forced me to my knees. The crowd cleared and became subdued. A sound very similar to that of my .22 cal. rifle bolt closing occurred behind me. This was it! I looked up to the sky, silently, said a prayer for Becky and Glen and closed my eyes. A clamor arose from off in the distance and the tension on the rope seemed to relax. A guy yanked me by my bound wrists upward to a standing position.

I turned to see a pith helmet with a red star on it. I never thought I'd be glad to see a red-starred uniform, but I guess it wasn't my day to die. This militia guy took charge and the walk continued. We came to a small village where I was led into a pig pen and made to sit on a stool while the locals gathered, stared and spoke among themselves. An older guy spoke to me in French, and I kept saying, "Water, water, water, please!" Something clicked and he came back with some lukewarm tea that did slake my thirst temporarily.

As dusk approached, I heard a vehicle off in the distance. I was paraded out of the village, and as the truck slowed to a stop, another crowd came over a slight rise in the road. Pete's head showed over the rise. It appeared he was uninjured. I was elated.

A NVN officer stepped out of the truck and with a purposeful stride came up to me and laid a haymaker to my cheek that caused me to see stars. He was showing the locals who's who with his cowardly move. I got it! He pops a shot to Pete too, then ripped our shirts off and made a blindfold of sorts that he tied around our heads. The soldiers threw us into the bed of the truck, and we left the scene to great cheering and more taunts. At every little hamlet we came upon, the driver began honking so that by the time we arrived, the villagers were ready as we lay helpless in the truck bed. Several such hamlets were on the route and the same treatment was meted out at each one.

The Red River had to be crossed by ferry at one point in the journey. My guess is the crossing took place near Viet Tri. Our truck was the sole vehicle on the ferry. A noisy throng could be heard on the far side of the river and the frenzy seemed to intensify as the ferry drew closer. The truck was allowed by the crowd to exit the ferry but was then surrounded by the mass and stopped any forward movement. We were forced to sit-up by one of our guards, presumably so the madding crowd could get a good look at the Yankee Air Pirates. The crowd began to beat on the truck with their bare hands and bamboo poles adding to the din. The driver attempted to move forward several times with limited success. I sensed the crowd was out for blood. The truck began to rock side-to-side. The guards became unnerved. I saw their rifles, with bayonets, move from holding Pete and I at bay to a position pointing outward toward the rowdies. Some of the crazies backed off and the truck began to advance as we proceeded toward the next stop. My life was spared once again, but my adrenalin level was running low! I actually went to sleep, or passed out from exhaustion, for a bit. The truck took us to a building somewhere out in the wilds. Pete and I were pulled from the truck and separated. When my blindfold was removed, I was looking at a panel of three or four military officers, or enlisted, or impostors seated on an elevated platform.

I was addressed by name, presumably from my dog tags, and rank and told I was now a prisoner of the Democratic Republic of

Vietnam (DRV) and would be considered as a war criminal. "What were you flying?" And when I didn't respond, they responded for me. "An F4 Phantom!" Where was your target?

"I don't remember," was met with a rifle butt to the back. And the questioning continued, at one point with the cold steel of a pistol to my head seeking some insignificant piece of information. They seemed to know a lot about me and the mission we were on. "Name, Rank & Serial Number," it rapidly became apparent, wasn't going to cut it, and I would now have to abide the best I could to the Code of Conduct.

Pete and I were eventually taken back to the truck, sans blindfold. We got to watch a Keystone Cops episode of untrained and clueless soldiers trying to change a truck tire. Pete and I were left alone while this show went on and I was able to slightly loosen his wrist bindings and he mine for some minor relief. We quietly talked of disappearing into the night but then quickly decided two white guys in under shorts and socks who were bound-up like livestock would be slightly "out of place." We were blindfolded again and began to move to the next stop. About daybreak I sensed we were nearing the end of the road when the stench of POL permeated the air as we passed the infamous and oft-targeted Hanoi POL dump. The truck stopped, reversed track and we heard the unmistakable sound of a heavy gate swinging. Pete and I were ushered into the confines of Hoa La prison, the Hanoi Hilton.

Nine months and eight days: Someone led me into a cell, made it readily apparent I was to sit on a stool, then left the cell. Every time I made any kind of move a grunt would be uttered from behind. I was not in this cell alone, and the other occupant was not a friendly. Many writings are available from GREAT MEN who survived far worse conditions and treatment than me. I cannot begin to express my admiration for the attitude these MEN ABOVE MEN displayed to our captors causing them to, in my opinion, ultimately abandon the torture for the sake of torture and "break the will of this man just for the hell of it" methods of interrogation and punishment. Yes, I got knocked around, but was not beaten within an inch of losing my life. I've recounted being trussed-up to where my elbows touched, but I wasn't hung from the ceiling until my shoulders were dislocated. What I did encounter was extreme sleep deprivation, long hours of questioning about topics of which I was clueless, all while trying to figure out what the interrogators were after. I was held in almost total isolation in a small space with a continuously illuminated light bulb. I received meager rations of food barely fit for human consumption from people for whom the bicycle was a modern invention. I saw the result of Communism up close and gained a deep appreciation for the FREEDOM so many of us take for granted.

During the numerous interrogations I began to come out of the fog of "what the hell happened" to "this is your status, deal with it" and could kind of figure out what the interrogators had been told to find out from me. The "V" knew by this time that captains really didn't know much of anything of importance, so asking about future targets or plans did not reveal any useful information. Every time the cell door rattled and opened, a new pair of guys would come to "interview" me about topics of which I was clueless. Early one morning, two guys entered after the guard rousted me off my bed board and asked their first question. "How many B-52s are stationed at U-Tapao RTAB in Thailand?" I had no idea and this led to an all-day, or all-night interrogation, bantering back and forth. They kept throwing out numbers to which I would agree, like 12, then 16, and on and on. Ultimately they told me, "There are 52 B-52s at U-Tapao," the number they had been sent to extract from me. They wrote the answer down in their book and departed. I crawled on to my bed board, curled up into a prenatal position and actually got some sleep before being rousted and moved to what is known as the Heartbreak section of the Hanoi Hilton.

The long wait for freedom: On the short walk from the interrogation cell to Heartbreak, the guard leading me stopped at a cistern and indicated I should remove my clothing and take a bath! I can only imagine what I smelled like after the many days from ejection through numerous interrogations. In the dead of that quiet night each bucket of cool water I dumped over my body was a welcome relief. All too quickly it was over, and the door to my cell clanged shut. The Heartbreak cell was maybe 6' x 6' with only a bed board on which to roll out my straw mat and a relief bucket. It was HOT! HOT! and HUMID! I stripped in a failed attempt to get some relief from the heat. I drifted off into sleep but was rudely awakened by the rustling of keys and chains. A guard grunted for me to hand my metal cup to him through a small door. He poured a liquid into the cup, handed the cup back to me, then gave me a small 5" baguette of bread. This was to be the morning rations for the duration of my incarceration. The liquid was a very thin reconstituted milk drink. The guard made checks of me through the small door several times daily and occasionally grunted for my cup to fill it with water, thank goodness. I seemed to be constantly on the verge of dehydration.

Several times during my interrogations and now in solitary confinement, an air raid would occur. The incredible blast and pressure of the AAA guns firing was almost unbearable. The guns were placed close because the enemy knew the guns would not be attacked for fear of hitting the prison. An ever present bright light bulb dangled from the ceiling 24/7, except during air raids. The air raid break from the glaring light bulb was welcomed but the cacophony of the AAA guns was not. I kept alert for sounds to indicate another POW was nearby. I talked aloud to myself, when I thought the guard was not around in case another POW might hear. No contact.

After about a week in these mind-boggling conditions, I was moved to a type of holding cell where I could actually see the sky. From there I was taken to a larger cell where I was rejoined with Pete. Two other POWs, Lt Gregg Hansen and Lt Dick Fulton, were also in the cell. Late one evening a guard unlocked the cell door and told us, "Prepare to move!" We were led to a truck and through the semi-blacked out streets of Hanoi to the prison we POWs called the "Zoo." At the Zoo we were led to a building called "The Barn" that consisted of four cells. Not a breath of air stirred in the cells. Our guard was named "Felau." He was not particularly harsh but we quickly understood he was not a pushover either. We could hear other groups of POWs on the other side of the walls surrounding our cellblock and attempted to let them know who we were by talking loudly using our names in every sentence. Felau caught on to our attempts to communicate.

The rations were whatever was in season, some pumpkin soup, some cabbage soup, rice noodles, very little meat and no fruits. Rice? Not a chance. That was the people's food and not for war criminals. Fish heads? I could only wish. Our daily baguette was made from flour that was rife with weevils. Of course they did not survive the baking process but were in evidence when the bread was torn open. We gave the baguette the name, "Bug Bread." I urged my cellmates to eat the bugs and think of them as "protein."

The days passed very slowly. Routinely each of us would be told to put on "long clothes," meaning the long sleeve shirt and pant POW uniform, and be marched across the quadrangle courtyard for an interview with the camp political dude. This guy was known to us as, "Plato," because of his "I'm smarter than you" attitude. He was also known in other circles as "The Rabbit" for his big ears and buck teeth. He was a notorious interrogator! A group of five POWs were moved into the cell adjacent to ours. We were able to establish some limited contact and learn about them over the weeks before Felau opened the cell door and announced, "Prepare to move!"

We walked across the quadrangle to a building we called the "Pig Sty." The Sty had larger cells and a larger courtyard. In the courtyard was a basketball court that had been seen in a *Life Magazine* story titled "Pilots in Pajamas" in the late 60s. I was the SRO (Senior Ranking Officer) and soon became known as "the Old Man," all 29 years of me. Our routine was less rigid in the Pig Sty. Felau unlocked the cells in the morning for us to get our rations, then we would kill time exercising, playing basketball when the court was dry enough, until after the mid-day rations, and we would be returned to our cells for the afternoon quiet time the "V" observed. After quiet time, we were let out again until the PM rations came and clean up had been completed. Then, it was back into our cells until the same thing happened the next day. BORING! Once a week one of us would be summoned to visit with Plato for one of his BS "quizzes." One afternoon during quiet time two older POWs we had not seen appeared at our window. They introduced themselves and no rank was provided. Who were these guys out walking around during quiet time unescorted? When asked their ranks, they said, "That doesn't matter now. We are senior to you." When the guard came to open the cell doors he greeted these two guys like old friends. Suspicious? You bet! We didn't want to get involved with these guys. They were collaborating with the enemy and receiving special favors such as real beds and not bed boards, better rations etc. They were held at the Zoo away from the other pre-1972 POWs, presumably for their own protection and their exploitation by the "V." Upon return of the

POWs to U.S. control in early 1973, disciplinary action against these two was recommended by the POW leadership. For whatever reason, politics held the trump card and they were both allowed to leave the service unscathed but are despised by their comrades!

Linebacker II: On December 18th at about 8 PM, Mel Matsui, Gregg Hansen and I were playing "no peekie" gin rummy with cards made out of toilet paper. Out of the east, an F-111 with 18 MK-82 HD 500lb. bombs seemingly came in our cell door, passed through the cell and exited through the rear wall. A few seconds later we counted 18 explosions as the first bombs of Operation Linebacker II hit their targets! Later, we heard the sound of BIG aircraft overhead, then the detonations of strings of bombs that went on for what seemed endlessly! The B-52s were in the shooting war. Gregg was tall enough that he could see out a small 4" diameter ventilation port. He saw one B-52 in pieces as it fell through the overcast. By the end of the second night of bombing and AAA blasts, the tile roof of our building was caving-in, one piece of tile at a time. Mel, Gregg and I fashioned a makeshift bomb shelter from extra bed boards.

By Christmas Eve night the roof over our cell was non-existent and we had serious reservations of how we could survive a bombing. Shortly after dark and before the first wave of Buffs arrived for the night run, our cell doors were unlocked, "Prepare to move, quickly!" We sped through the Hanoi streets back to Hoa Lo.

At the Hilton the whole group, about 30 in all, were put into large room without any lights. Christmas morning Capt Keith Lewis led us in a simple but poignant Christmas service. Also in this cell were four guys very recently shot down who were able to give us some really good updates on the world outside the walls. I found out that the day I was hammered, Yen Bai launched 14 MiGs against our flight alone, a very big push for the NVNAF. Apparently the "V" didn't like us exchanging news because they moved us into the area of Hoa Lo we called "Little Vegas" and we were segregated once again with the guys we'd been with prior to the move.

Bud Breckner, our SRO, convened nightly staff meetings of the cell SROs and we BSed at will. One of the Zoo Crew had a quiz session with Plato and was informed the U.S. had agreed to return to the Paris peace talks and the bombing of Hanoi had ceased. Yeah, right! Who

Agreed? Was this just another false peace? Winter had really set in and for what seemed like weeks we spent our days wearing every article of clothing we had to ward off the cold – MISERY!

We were moved back to the Zoo and were pleasantly surprised when my Pig Sty group was combined with one of the other groups to make a large group of about 12-15 POWs. Then, other trucks arrived, and guys we'd never seen were taken into cell blocks that had been unoccupied previously. Lt Col Joe Kittinger became the Zoo POW SRO. The "V" set up a volleyball net in the quadrangle courtyard and games between cellblocks ensued. A C-130 Hercules flew over the prison one day, but with strange markings on it? WTF? Col Kittinger had a quiz with Plato and then went to each cellblock to tell us to don our long clothes and await further direction. As Joe came back from the last cellblock we walked to a type of auditorium where we sat down as though in a movie theatre. Plato stood behind a podium and proceeded to read us the mandatory notification set forth in the Paris Peace Accords concerning our release.

The order of release was to be the sick and wounded first followed in shoot down order by the remaining POWs. The releases would commence in two weeks and follow at two-week intervals until all POWs were released. The "V" had expected a robust response but Col "K" put out the word to be cool and we would return to our cellblocks for quiet celebration. Plato was beside himself, to say the least, at our cool reaction.

During quiet time on Feb 12th one of our guys said, "Hey, listen. I hear a C-141!" We all leapt to the eastward facing windows and sure enough over a small grove of banana trees arose this BEAUTIFUL white and gray C-141 with a Red Cross emblazoned on the tail as it climbed out of Gia Lam International Airport. As the plane made a slight turn to the southeast and climbed higher the Zoo erupted in an almost ear-splitting crescendo of Shit Hots! – Yee Hahs! And Go! Go! Gos! Every two weeks saw a repeat performance as we waited for our turn.

To say the rations had improved is an understatement. The diet prior to the Accords was subsistence at best. My weight dropped to what I'd weighed as a mid-teen. Now we had rice at least once a day, gummy stick to your bones, rice. And, a little more meat was also on the menu. But, the bug bread never became un-buggy. One by one we were processed by giving us our "go home" clothes and any personal items that had been taken from us during the capture process. I had no personal items, but one fella was given back the two $100 bills he had in his flight suit. Another received the USAFA class ring of his classmate and frontseater who was killed.

We were all wired big time for our release date. At first light we were all up and ready to don our ill-fitting go home attire, when the transportation arrived to take us to Gia Lam. But, nothing happened. Oh, Shi..! Col "K" crossed the quadrangle in long clothes being escorted by a guard. A few moments after he entered Plato's office, he emerged and headed for our cellblock. "Bad news guys. There is some type of diplomatic problem and releases have been put on hold." The adrenalin just evaporated from our bodies with those words. The diplomatic problem was the "V" refused to release the POWs captured in Laos they were "safe-keeping" for the Pathet Lao, claiming that was a separate issue from the Paris Accords. YGBSM! A few terse exchanges and the "V" rapidly understood their B-52 journey back to the stone age could resume immediately if they balked any further. The issue was resolved.

Finally, at the podium at Gia Lam to read off our names was none other than the pain in the ass, Plato. Then, I heard my name, George Alan Rose, Captain, USAF read, and I stepped forward, reported in a military manner to the General who took my hand and said, "Welcome home, Captain Rose!" After takeoff, we heard the PA announcement, "Gentlemen, we are now in international airspace. Welcome home!" And, the celebration began!

Operation Homecoming: As we began to settle down and truly comprehend our FREEDOM a public affairs officer made the rounds and asked for our attention as he explained the procedures we would go through at Clark. "Expect three or four THOUSAND people to be at the arrival ceremony." What? "The 7th AF Commander will be greeting you after you are introduced and walk down the ramp to him. Then, proceed to the bus waiting to transport you to the hospital. You will spend three nights at Clark for physical exams and some initial intell debriefing, then on to the CONUS."

At Clark, my escort officer asked if I was ready to call home – a silly question - Becky and I had our first live conversation in 11 months, then I spoke with my mom and dad.

Day 4 at 8 AM was the departure time for my flight. Sixteen of us boarded a bus and headed to the Clark flight line for the next leg of our FREEDOM journey. Once again a very large crowd wished us bon voyage. The C-141 I was on was the "East Coast Express" and would deliver us now EX-POWs to Scott AB, IL, and Andrews AFB, MD. As we approached the U.S. the California coast loomed out of the morning haze and we could see the Golden Gate Bridge. The A/C asked if I'd like to make the initial radio call to Oakland Center? Sure! "Oakland Center, MAC Flight XXX, Homecoming 03, FL 290."

"Radar Contact 03, Welcome home! Cleared Direct Scott AFB, heading 090." At Scott AFB several of the guys left and boarded waiting C-9s for their final destinations. Our arrival time at Andrews was late afternoon and the weather was miserable, but in my heart the sun was shining! I was the SRO of this group, so after meeting the welcoming party at the foot of the ramp I was expected to make a few short remarks. As I walked the few feet to the microphone I saw Becky, Glen, Mom, Dad, and Lee and Terri Alton waiting for me. My remarks were few and short as I thanked the hundreds of people who had turned out in this miserable weather to welcome us at the final stop on our FLIGHT TO FREEDOM. Turning in the direction of my family I was grabbed by Becky who had raced through the rain puddles, coat tails flying followed shortly by Glen. My dad had been holding Glen, but when Becky headed my way he demanded, "Put me down Oopa!" So we all embraced laughing, crying, emotions exploding. Then, it was Mom and Dad's turn. Then, Lee and Terri joined the hug-a-thon! Lee had been my roommate at Ubon, my Summary Court Officer, after I went down, and now the escort officer for my family from NC to Andrews. A friend who was checking our mail called to tell us a letter from The White House had arrived and he was sending it on to us in Arkansas. President and Mrs. Nixon invited all of the returnees to what was essentially a state dinner at the White House on Thursday, 24 May. The war was finally over for me!

Returning to the air: The USAF had set up a program at Randolph AFB, TX, for the returnees who wanted to return to flight duty to get re-acclimated and re-current in the T-38. Shortly after Labor Day I reported for temporary duty at Randolph. During the summer I had been in consult with several people about "where to go" for my next assignment. One option was to separate from the USAF and go with Delta Airlines and another was an assignment to Eglin AFB, FL, at the Tactical Air Warfare Center (TAWC). I needed a FAA Commercial License and current instrument rating for the Delta job. I had the commercial ticket but not the instrument rating. My first flight at Randolph was a VFR "go have fun flight" with a former IP from Laredo, Lt Col Rocco DeFelice. Using my new call sign, "Freedom Flyer 60," I had my first flight in the T-38.

When my T-38 checkride was complete, I contacted the pilot hiring office of Delta and scheduled an interview. The interview at Delta went well, and the indication was to expect a hire date in January. The Yom Kippur War erupted on Oct. 6 and then came the Arab oil embargo, and the airline hiring came to a screeching halt. Eglin AFB it would be for my next assignment flying the F-4 again but in a testing environment.

In 1975 I was selected for promotion to major. A Sgt. from base outbound assignments called me with the news I was on my way to Moehringen, GE. What? Where? The Direct Air Support Center for the U.S. Army VII Corps needed a Director (Operations Officer) and I was next up in the pot of bodies. General McMullen tried to keep me at TAWC and Lee Alton, who was now at AFMPC, tried but his advice was, "This is the best of a bunch of crap jobs coming and it is accompanied. Several of the others are remote, unaccompanied." I accepted Lee's advice and went to spend three years with the Army. Moehringen is a suburb of Stuttgart. This turned out to be the crappiest job I had in my career but the best assignment given the superb location of Stuttgart and access to southern Europe. Becky and I became involved with the American Youth Activities (AYA) ski group. We made frequent trips to Austria, Italy and Switzerland. Three months prior to my scheduled return to the CONUS the assignment Sgt. called and told me I was going to an RTU assignment at Davis-Monthan AFB, AZ. Wait! There are not any F-4s at DM.

Nope, just the tank-busting A-10 Thunderbolt II. Active duty lesson #3: don't worry, be happy!

Hog driving time: After I checked in at the 355th Training Squadron for A-10 upgrade, Becky and I went house and school hunting; what a shock. IBM had moved into Tucson with a large workforce transferring from CA and CO, sending house prices through the roof.

The A-10 training program was heavy on academics. There was no simulator, but we had cardboard boxes with wooden knobs for switches where we could sit and pretend. The first flight for an A-10 student was solo with the IP in a chase position, but the student was "on his own" should an emergency develop. What a neat feeling the next morning to run the checklist, start the engines, taxi to the runway, then lineup on the runway with no other body in the plane, a big change from my F-4 days. As the aircraft rolled down the runway gaining speed, I glanced over my right shoulder and Maj Dave Sawyer, my IP, was in a formation takeoff position. I think I broke into a big grin at some point after liftoff with the thought, "This is the way it should be!"

I was selected for promotion to Lt Col in the fall of 1980. In May of 1982 Col Rod Beckman, the Wing Commander, called me to his office and asked if I would be interested in assuming command of the 355th TTS, the squadron responsible for the academic training and administration of the students attending RTU. "YES SIR!" Later, the squadron was recognized by the TAC/IG during a Management Effectiveness Inspection as, "The Best TTS in the Command," probably the crowning event of my career.

Brig Gen Ron Fogelman, the air division commander, asked me to change platforms and move to the 602nd Tac Air Control Wing and the position of Assistant DO for Operations. "YES SIR!" With this job came another aircraft. The OA-37 Dragonfly was used as a forward air control aircraft, a T-37 with T-38 engines. My checkout was in the dead of winter at Battle Creek ANGB, MI. Two weeks and six flights later after arriving at Battle Creek, I was ready to return to Tucson. I can't endorse Battle Creek as a vacation spot. Supervising the operations of the 23rd and 27th TASS was a full time job for sure. Each unit had over 80 pilots and 30 aircraft and the units almost always had aircraft and crews TDY to support exercises, both Army and Air Force. I did not fly the OA-37 very often, just enough to stay current and be in touch with the young pilots. I took the option to retire effective January 31, 1986. My final USAF flight was on January 16, 1986 closing my career at 3418 hours that encompassed 215 months of operational flying.

Grounded: Post retirement I was offered a job as a tech rep by what was then Hughes Aircraft, now a component of Raytheon Corp. Specifically, the job required an extensive working knowledge of the AGM-65 Maverick Missile. Or, as my new boss, Mr. "PK" Kimminau, described the job, translate what the engineers have written into language the fighter pilots can understand so the Maverick can be effectively employed in combat. Once I had mastered the intricate wiring diagrams of the missile and how it interfaced with the delivery aircraft, the F-4, F-16, and A-10, I went on the road to USAF units all across the country and Europe to support aircrews training with the Maverick. In 1987 a new model of the Maverick was introduced using Infrared (IR) technology. As the new missile reached the fighter units a tech rep spent several weeks with the aircrews helping bring them up to speed with the new weapon. One trip was to Morocco and Spain accompanying an international marketing team. A family matter led me to depart Hughes in early 1989. Becky accepted an executive position with a large property management firm in Sacramento. I became the "trailing spouse."

Flying again: I'd not turned a wheel since retirement but got antsy to fly again. A long time friend, Ed Maxson, ran a flight training operation in Sedona, AZ. He offered to let me fly his aircraft to regain currency, so I spent a few days with him doing just that.

Back in Sacramento I joined a flying club and bug-smashed around once a week or so in Cessna 150s and 172s. A United Express pilot took my info to the chief pilot at UE in Fresno and I received a job application shortly thereafter. Just for good measure my new buddy also sent me an application for a small airline dba American Eagle Airlines, Wings West Airlines. I interviewed with UE first but was told I needed an Airline Transport Pilot (ATP) rating to be competitive. A what? So, I went to Long Beach and shelled out $750 for three flights in a Piper Seminole, then another $150 to the flight examiner and received my ATP. Wings West hadn't mentioned an ATP, but I think it helped get an interview at the American Airlines flight academy. After a very long day at the academy to include a physical, followed by a simulator exercise, then a face-to-face interview with a Wings West captain, I was on the "list."

Side note: The interviewer was a cocky guy based in Los Angeles. He wasn't very impressed by my USAF experience, "You got your training for free!" He really had an attitude and my fuse was getting shorter by the minute when he stated, "We have several female captains who will be senior to you. Do you think you can handle that? I don't think the Air Force has female fighter pilots!"

I leaned across the desk and told him, "I know several women who fly and I will have no problem, AND I won't have any problem flying with young bucks with less experience than me either!" End of interview. I was sure that was it, but a few weeks later I was notified of a class date with Wings West Airlines in San Luis Obispo, CA. This also coincided with Becky's pronouncement that I had flunked Cooking and Housekeeping 101 and needed to get a real job.

Airline Time: The first day of class I knew I was in for a real learning experience. Wings West operated the Fairchild Swearingen Metroliner, a 19-seat turboprop. Propellers? FARs? Call outs? With the aid of a good roomie, I made it through the academics and actually did well enough to earn one of the higher seniority numbers in the class. Flight training was another whole new experience with V1 cuts and more single engine time than I care to experience again. My choice of base was San Francisco International.

The airline was expanding so I did not have to be on the reserve list long. After 11 months I was able to bid for a captain's seat and went back for more training to learn the left seat tricks. The Metroliner gave way to a BAE turboprop, the Jetstream, another 19-seat puddle jumper. In 1993 an economic downturn led to furloughs and downgrades. I was moved back to the first officer seat but was able to now bid-up to the Saab 340, a 34-passenger turboprop, with a flight attendant added to the crew. In the meantime Becky had been hired by a firm in the Bay area. The commute certainly got easier to San Fran or San Jose. Wings West was moved out of the Bay area when American closed the San Jose operation and opened a base at DFW.

I was very senior in the first officer seat and could bid number three at DFW which meant plum trips with decent report times plus the downgraded captains were still being paid at the captain scale, so off to DFW. Life was good! Oops, upper management discovered the aforementioned pay rate and put the kibosh on that deal. Fortunately, about this time I was able to bid back to the left seat at DFW. The commute was an unpleasant fact of life but workable.

Becky received another move to Denver and I considered bailing out of the airline business. In 1995, AMR Corp extended some benefits to the American Eagle employees. If you were over 55 and had 10 years of good service with the company, you qualified for lifetime travel benefits on American Airlines and American Eagle. I could stand on my head for that benefit. It meant one more relocation, this time to Houston. The Saab years were a repeat cycle of four days on, then three off, or as many of us said, "One day off to recover from the crappy schedule we had just flown; one day to get stuff done at home; one day dreading going back to work." In early 2000 I was driving to Houston Intercontinental to go to DFW for another four-day tour of Texas and Louisiana airports. The traffic was stop-and-go on I-10 and time was growing tight to make the flight. I muttered, "I hate this commute crap!" And, a voice answered back, "You don't have to do this you know."

I lunched with the chief pilot on the occasion of my 10th year with the company in September. He asked how long I planned to stay with Eagle and I responded I'd like to fly the new jets that were starting to come on line. He did some quick calculations and noted I probably wouldn't get to that point before my 60th birthday. The wheels began to turn. So, on that January day I went to work, flew my trip, then told the chief pilot I would be taking sick time to cope with some family matters involving my mother in Arkansas. He wished me well, noted in my employee file I was clear to travel while on sick leave and that was that.

My airline career ended on January 20, 2000, with 7,324 hours over 10 years and five months. I remained on the payroll until early June and received my travel card shortly thereafter. I flew with some very competent pilots at Eagle. The people, overall, were the best part of the experience. But when the flying wasn't fun and it had become just a job, it was time to move on. So, I did. Was it worth the pain of 0330 wake-up calls, the 16-hour days, the nit-picking check airmen and the, at times, inept management and not to mention the selfish union leaders? Every time Becky and I travel, domestic or international, and are seated in First Class the answer is a resounding, "Yes Sir!"

Except for nine months and eight days in North Vietnam, aviation was very good to me.

Chapter Fourteen

One Small Step for Man...One Giant Leap for Mankind

by Eugene D. "Gene" Santarelli

It was July 22nd, 1969, and I awoke from a fitful sleep in a totally dark room. This was home and had been for the last 11 months. I had been at Ubon Royal Thai Air Force Base on my first Southeast Asia combat tour of duty. I knew it must be mid to late morning, and I probably had logged about six hours of sleep, because that had been my routine. My roommate, Kenny Boone, aka Dr. Boone, aka KB, was still asleep in his bed about five feet to my left. I did not want to wake him, so I had to slip out of the room as quietly as possible.

I knew I could do it as I had many times before, having memorized every obstacle. We had the routine down, because we never knew who would wake first to this totally black world. The room was about 10 by 15 feet. There were two single beds, with a desk and chair fitted between them. A lamp was on each side of the desk that was both for the desk and a reading light for the respective bed. At the foot of each bed was a standard metal clothes locker about seven feet high by three feet wide. It held all our clothes and sundry items. We had a floor to ceiling blackout curtain running wall-to-wall, between the lockers and the beds. The one window, above the desk, with the panes painted black, was also covered with a blackout curtain. You see, we were, "Nite Owls," members of the 497th Tactical Fighter Squadron. We flew and fought at night, relaxed and/or partied until near sunrise, then slept as best we could until late morning or afternoon, on a good day/night. Then, it was repeat the routine. I'll get to the "routine" a little later, but back to the moment.

Now that I was awake, I slipped out of the "bedroom," (area behind the blackout curtains), as quietly as possible, slipped into swim trunks and T-shirt, grabbed a small transistor radio and sun glasses, both of which were always placed in an easy to feel spot of the dark room for these morning departures. I then opened the door just enough to slip out onto our luxurious front porch, which we shared with the six other rooms in our "hooch." The glare of the Thai morning sun almost drove me back into the dark room. I quickly closed the door behind me so as to not make my roommate think he was approaching the bright light of the "pearly gates" in his dreams. After a quick trip to the bathroom to relieve myself, I plopped into a rusted but comfortable easy chair that was on the porch. This was the morning ritual when an "Owl" awakened early enough to relax some before needing to get ready for work. On this day I had that luxury, so I sat in the lounge chair to listen to our favorite and only radio station at Ubon, the Armed Forces Network (AFN). This was the brief time to let the awakening process proceed and ease into the day. Behind the sunglasses, I would just stare into the bright sky of another tropical morning, sometimes thinking about the future, but most of the time wondering what tonight's combat mission would bring. Before I go on, let me tell you about our luxury living quarters, the "Hooch."

The "Hooch," our home for a year, housed 12 officers from our squadron. The squadron had six or seven of these buildings. The one in which I lived was a one-story, wooden structure with six separate rooms. A pair of fliers shared each room. The center of the building was a small day room with two common area bathrooms in the rear. To each side of this common area were three of the separate living quarters. Along the front, a six foot wide porch ran the length of the building. A three to four foot railing was on the outside of the porch, and the rooms opened onto this porch. The porch ran into the day room into the middle of the building. Three buildings were arranged in a horseshoe, facing inward to our common front yard, sunbathing area, and all around playground. The buildings on the side of the horseshoe back up to another "hooch," which was the side of another horseshoe of living quarters. The horseshoes opened onto a paved street.

Each room was approximately 10 by 15 feet. As explained above the rooms contained a pair of built-in wood frame single beds, a desk between the beds, two full-sized lockers, or shrunks, for clothes, and a sink. There was a single door into the room, that opened onto the porch. In the back wall, two holes had been cut; one was a window, which in our room was painted black and covered with a blackout curtain, and one hole large enough for a window-sized air conditioner. This was deemed essential for the combat aircrew, and much appreciated.

The "Hooch" also came with a "houseboy," who cleaned the rooms, shined our combat boots and any other shoes left for him, and did our laundry, or I should say his wife did our laundry. Our dirty clothes went into a laundry bag, and every few days, the laundry bag would disappear, and the next day our clothes were returned clean, but a little tattered. I suspect the laundry was done in the river that ran through the nearby town. Our houseboy was Somsoc, a kind gentleman, old enough to be my father, and always with a grin imprinted on his face. Each of the residents paid him 100 Thai Baht per month ($5.00 US) for his services. Communication was usually in English, and mostly one way. We would use our best American English, Somsoc would grin and nod in the affirmative, then walk off to continue with his duties. When communication was important, the "pointee-talkee" method with pictures was the most successful.

Now, more about our neighborhood: The street on which we lived had a sidewalk that paralleled a four to five foot deep ravine between it and the roadway. This was the "Klong," a part of our open rainwater run-off network. During the monsoon season, it was usually full of water. For the dumb/brave, it could be used for swimming laps, if you did not mind the creatures who might share it with you. Since many of these creatures could be deadly venomous, "swimming the Klong" was discouraged. During the dry season, it was a valley of grass and rock, into which you could stumble, in the dark, when en route home from the Officer's club, in less than a sober state. Some have ended up in it, even when sober. During monsoon season, a stumble at this point put you in the class of "swimming the Klong." The desired route from the Club to the Hooch took you across a sidewalk bridge over a large sewer pipe, which provided a walkway across the road.

Across the road, there were two-story open bay barracks for the enlisted men of our squadron and others. They housed 25-30 troops on each floor. Their HVAC system was wire mesh screens totally surrounding the building on each floor, to permit airflow, and overhead fans to attempt to move the air and generate some cooling effect. The open-air window system was covered with eaves to keep the rain out, but during monsoons, when the rain would blow sideways, these offered limited protection. We admired the enlisted force for accepting these living conditions, while continuing to do their jobs at such a high level. This could explain why many of them could be found at work, even during their off time. The work area offices, and break areas were usually air-conditioned.

Now back to the story: I am still in the easy chair on the porch. After a few of our favorite tunes of 1969 that put me into a mild slumber, or day-dreaming state, I noticed that AFN news was talking of a historic event occurring on this day. The US had landed a manned space capsule on the moon, and AFN was playing a recording of the live message from astronaut Neil Armstrong, who was on the moon! I have been in Southeast Asia, engrossed with flying combat, and could not tell you one thing about the Apollo 11 mission, that had been ongoing for a few days. Launched from half way around the world, Apollo 11 may have had the attention of millions, but to this combat night fighter, it was new news, the morning of July 20th, 1969, Ubon Thailand time.

For me, professionally, the road to July 22nd, 1969 began 6 September, 1966, the day Second Lieutenant Santarelli entered Air Force Undergraduate Pilot Training. I was there due to two earlier influences on my life. They were the threat of Universal Conscription, being drafted to be an infantry soldier, to hike and camp out in Vietnam, and my older brother, Frank. He was the aviation buff in our family. He built the model airplanes, as a young boy. I was the one that usually broke them, when I was not supposed to touch them. I was more into cowboys and Indians, playing ball in the streets, or other activities that did not require a deep understanding of mechanical or engineering skills.

Frank, who was three years older than I, left college and a great social life after two years, to enter the Air Force through the Aviation Cadet Program for pilots and navigators. He spent his first year as an Airman Basic, going through boot camp, officer training and Navigator training, simultaneously. He relayed to me that being an Airman, he was confined to the base and the barracks. However, the officers, going through the same Navigator training were free to do whatever they wanted after duty! This fact convinced him there was a better way to serve your country while learning to become a flier. His advice to me was simple and straight forward. It was almost inevitable that I would end up in the military, following college, because of the draft. The odds were heavily in favor of ending up in Southeast Asia, very shortly after graduation, since we had 500,000 Americans in uniform there, and they were turning over every year. His advice: If you must serve your country, do it as an officer, rather than as a grunt.

To become a military officer, there were three roads available to me: I could enter ROTC while at the university, and upon graduation be commissioned a second lieutenant; I could wait until graduation, volunteer for Officer Training School, and possibly be selected; or, I could try to get into the Air Force Aviation Cadet Program, like my brother, spend my first year as an Airman Basic, while going through officer training as well as flying training to be a pilot or navigator. My brother also had sound advice for these choices: To become an officer, you can go through officer training as a grunt for an intensive 90 days, if you are lucky enough to be selected. Through the Air Force Aviation Cadet Training Program, you could be an enlisted grunt for a year, while you learned to be an officer as well as learn to fly. Lastly, you could become an officer through ROTC, spending two days a week in military training classes as a student, and six weeks, one summer, in boot camp. The logic for selection of a flying career was also simple. My brother was a navigator, who always had to take orders from a pilot, in the air. He told me this also inferred a social class relationship that carried over to activities on the ground. Given the option, become a pilot! They are the important aviators in the Air Force.

As for Vietnam, his advice was that you can work in a foxhole, or in the air. Make a choice. Through the power of deduction, the lesser of evils was the Air Force ROTC route to become an officer, and if physically qualified, to become a pilot. I volunteered to enter the Air Force ROTC program while attending Notre Dame, and was lucky enough to be selected. More importantly, although I did not have the aviation passion at a young age, I was healthy enough to be selected to attend pilot training. Thus, on September 6th, 1966, I entered pilot training at Laughlin AFB, a small training base on the Rio Grande, in Southwest Texas.

Undergraduate Pilot Training was a one-year program that included learning to fly three different aircraft. The initial screening of the class was done in a Cessna 172, which in the military vernacular was a T-41. The "T" represented it was a trainer aircraft, the "41," I do not have a clue. During this phase, my instructor was a World War II, Army Air Corps pilot, old enough to be my grandfather, but a very good pilot. I was an average student, which followed my academic prowess in school. The one exciting day of this phase occurred one afternoon when we were airborne learning the basic skills of slow flight, stalls and falls and recoveries. The southwest Texas thunderstorms were rapidly building, and as expected, we received a radio message for a weather recall, which was an order to immediately return to base, land, and secure the aircraft. We started back toward the airport, when my instructor asked, "Have you ever flown backwards?" I did not know how to answer, even though we were expected to answer all flying questions asked. He took control of the airplane, "Then just watch." We maneuvered toward a couple of huge, rapidly building thunder bumpers, while slowing the aircraft to just on the edge of a stall. After some small turns left and right, back and forth, he said look down at the ground. We were flying at 65-70 kts. airspeed, and moving back over the ground. When he saw the surprised look on my face, he did an immediate steep turn back toward the airport, accelerated to normal flying speed, and said, "Your aircraft." He then proceeded with a lecture on the dangers of thunderstorms, not doing stupid things around them, watching your headwinds when flying cross-country, and the value of flying airspeed, not just how fast you were going over the ground. "You can always land short of your destination, should weather or headwinds force you. If you don't maintain flying speed, even if you think you are going backwards, you are going to crash." My grandpa T-41 instructor had many stories with a moral, when it came to flying.

After proving we were not prone to air sickness and could master basic flying skills, most of my classmates and myself moved onto phase 2, our primary jet trainer, another Cessna product, the T-37 "Tweety Bird." It was a straight-winged, jet aircraft, with two side-by-side seats. We dressed-out in full flight gear, to include a parachute, as it was an ejection seat aircraft. The aircraft was named "Tweety Bird" due to the high pitch shrill sound of the jet engines. It was not comfortable to stand near, with the engines running, but it was a fun airplane to fly. It was fully acrobatic and spin certified. During this phase of training, we had to prove we could master acrobatics, spins, take-offs, landing with both engines (normal) or if necessary in an emergency, with just one engine, instrument flight, and cross-country navigation. I started to really get into flying at this point, and began to excel, mostly due to my instructors.

My IP, Capt Clint, came from the Check Section and was a friendly but demanding teacher. He had a bet with his IP buddies on who would be the first student to solo in this class. Capt Clint was intent on that student being me. Thus, during this initial T-37 training, the race was on, throughout the entire class. As we approached time to solo, the race was down to two, Capt Clint and myself, versus a friend, Lt Gary with his IP, who was also from the Check Section. On solo day, we were both in the air at the same time, having taken-off within minutes of each other. After our area work, we raced back to the traffic pattern to demonstrate to our instructors we could safely land. After a couple of landings, we both landed with our instructors, stopped the aircraft near the end of the runway, shut down the right engine, let our instructors get out and walk to the mobile control tower, restart the right engine, complete the pre-take-off checks, then take-off, to be a solo jet pilot. We stayed in the pattern, required to complete three landings. I was the first off, so it appeared Capt Clint had the bet in the bag. Gary was right behind, following me around the pattern. After two touch-and-go landings, the plan was for both of us to request a closed traffic pattern for immediate full stop landings. We both did this, with the lead still in my possession. Just as I lowered my gear and called for landing clearance, another student called for clearance to land from a straight-in approach. Tower directed me to break out of the closed traffic pattern, and re-enter the traffic flow for a normal landing. Nearly heart broken, I complied, and my friend Gary became the first to complete solo flight in our T-37 class. After I landed, we both celebrated the honored tradition of being dropped by our classmates into a small, plastic wading pool that was kept behind the squadron for just this occasion.

T-37 training continued normally after that, taking up the next four months. I discovered a love and a knack for acrobatics and spins. Instrument flying was a bit more challenging, living under a hood to show we did not need outside references to fly and could navigate and accomplish approaches to landing in the weather. At the end, we were introduced to formation flying. Successfully completing two check-rides, one in contact and the second in navigation and instrument flight, we moved on to the final phase of pilot training, learning to fly the supersonic, twin-engined, T-38 jet trainer.

The T-38 phase involved checkrides in contact or visual flight, instrument and navigation flight, and formation flying. I found the T-38 to be more demanding, requiring quicker thinking due to the increased speed with which things happened, and the need to develop a better feel for flying, due to the sensitivity of this high performance aircraft. I held my own through this phase, graduating seventh of over sixty pilot graduates in my class. Follow-on assignments were based on aircraft assignments available, our requests, our class standing, and IP recommendations. I ended up with my second choice, a fighter aircraft, the F-4 Phantom. However, rather than being a "Pilot Aircraft Commander," I would be a "Pilot Systems Operator," a backseater, commonly referred to as a GIB (Guy in Back). At that time, there were no frontseat F-4 assignments being offered to pilot training graduates.

The next leg of my journey to Ubon, Thailand and July 20th, 1969, was through MacDill AFB, FL for combat crew training in the F-4. At the time, the 46th Tactical Fighter Squadron, my assignment for this training, flew both the F-4C and F-4D models. For the Pilot Systems Operator, this meant learning the different avionics, navigation, and weapons systems in the two models. The differences were not major, but required one to stay up with which model you flew on any given day. As for flying characteristics, both models handled the same.

The F-4 course trained you to be qualified as a combat ready crew, in the basic mission areas, aerial combat and air-to-ground weapons delivery, both visual day and night deliveries, and all-weather radar bombing. It was a six-seven month program, and due to my assignment to Ubon, I was selected toward the end, to complete follow-on special weapons training, learning how to employ the "precision, electro-optically-guided" TV bomb, "the Wall-eye." This extended my combat crew training an additional six weeks, and put me as part of a group of three select crews, "Wall-eye-qualified," en route to Ubon RTAFB.

However, I must take you back to the basic F-4 course to relate a story that occurred during one of the final phases of this program, night gunnery: I should have realized it was "foreshadowing" for me.

In this program, I was paired with a front-seat pilot, Jim, who had just returned from an eight-month assignment at Ubon as a GIB, having completed 100 missions over North Vietnam. We got along well, and spoke frequently about follow-on assignments. Jim felt assured that his next assignment would be somewhere other than Southeast Asia, because Air Force policy was that everyone should go once, before anyone had to go back a second time, involuntarily. To upgrade to the frontseat, Jim had to volunteer to return to Southeast Asia, but the Air Force did all it could to avoid this. Jim encouraged me to volunteer for a Southeast assignment because it was the quickest way to the frontseat. Southeast Asia was a maximum of one year as a GIB, and with the "100 mission over North Vietnam" policy, you could likely be back to the States to upgrade to the frontseat in six-seven months. That had been the norm.

During more than one of our conversations, Jim explained to me how much he hated flying at night, particularly night combat. He said as a GIB, he was never comfortable at night, so when we got into the night phases of our training, he emphasized good crew coordination, and open talk if I did not feel comfortable with what was going on. Everything was OK until our first scheduled night bombing mission in the course. I could tell Jim was uncomfortable during the preparation and briefing. As we stepped to the airplane, he again emphasized that I should not be afraid to say anything if I was not comfortable with what we were doing.

Take-off and departure were normal. The join-up into a four-ship formation was a little rough, but no problems. In our flight, we had an Instructor Pilot flying in the frontseat of the lead aircraft. He was the boss of the mission. In the backseat of the #3 aircraft was another Instructor Pilot. He was second in command of the mission, and should the Flight leader abort, #3 would take the lead so the mission could proceed. At least one instructor was required in the flight to go onto the gunnery range. Jim and I were in the #4 aircraft, and like #2, were an all student crew, both front-seat and rear-seat. All was normal en route to the gunnery range, and with the entry into the bombing pattern, a rectangle with each aircraft at one of the turning points of rectangle. As a flight we flew around the pattern at altitude getting into the rhythm of positioning ourselves and making the appropriate radio calls to help keep each other in sight.

It was a black, moonless night, but the range was well marked with fires or lights on the ground highlighting the pattern turn points, the bombing run in line, and the target circle. After the second trip around the pattern, at 8,000 ft., the flight lead directed we arm up our aircraft, and called in on his first dive bomb attack. I sensed the atmosphere in our cockpit tense-up a bit, but this was normal, right? It was our first night bombing ride, together, and my first ever. Number 1 called off target, number 4 in sight, and Number 2 called in on his bomb run. The breathing in our cockpit picked up. Then it was the same sequence for number 3's bomb run, as we turned base leg to set up for our attack. At the appropriate time, Jim started a diving left turn toward the target, and called in; however, we continued to roll and get steep. I called "Jim," and heard, "Ooooh, you've got the aircraft!" I must say, I about peed my pants! I grabbed the stick, rolled the wings level, and pulled with all my strength. The grunting and groaning from the G forces came next. Going on just the instruments, I pulled the airplane into a climb, and asked, "Jim are you OK?" No response. So, I asked again, and got a weak, "I think so." I climbed back to our pattern altitude and kept talking to Jim until he said he was all right, and ready for control of the aircraft. He took control, but by this time it was too late to think about our next bombing pass, so Jim said we would stay at altitude and fly in our position around the pattern; a good plan from my vantage point. He made the radio call, but it did not sound right. Something was wrong with our radios; there was dead silence; no reception, no feedback, and no normal background noise. Since I had control of the radios, I started feeling around, turned up my cockpits lights, and then started looking around to try to determine what could be wrong. It took about a minute for me to realize the radio on/off button, which was spring loaded in the on position, had popped out to the off position. I told Jim and punched the radio back on. The first thing we heard was the flight leader transmit, "Has anyone seen a fireball yet?" Those words have been indelibly imprinted into my memory, and I will likely take them to my grave.

We came up voice and checked-in with the flight leader. Stunned silence for what seemed to be the longest five seconds of my life. Since we had been radio-out and the flight lead could not contact us, he assumed we had crashed. He directed us to orbit at 10,000 ft., above everyone else. The flight lead then got the flight reorganized to continue the training mission without us, but before restarting, told us to immediately go home on our own and we would meet at the debrief. What happened after that was incidental. Jim and I were grounded until the squadron completed a quick review of the events. I was immediately re-instated into the class, while Jim went through a series of evaluations. He completed the course, but with a different class, and I never flew with him again. We stayed friends, until assignments separated us. As Jim suggested, I volunteered and was assigned to Ubon RTAFB, following the special weapon "Wall-eye" training. His assignment took him elsewhere in the F-4 community, I am not sure where.

The last two vignettes are to set up my arrival, in August of 1968, to Ubon, following appropriate survival training in the States and Jungle Survival training in the Philippines. During in-processing, at Ubon, I was met by this guy in a black flight suit and black baseball hat, with an insignia, a white emblem of an owl and a sliver of moon. Arcing over the top was "497th TFS." His words were, "Welcome to the Nite Owls, Owl. My name is Tim, and I am your frontseater."

I stood there stunned for a moment. "What about the special Wall-eye training? Do the Nite Owls use the weapon?" I got a stunned look back. He told me that since bombing above the 20th parallel in North Vietnam had been "postponed," none of the squadrons used the weapon, and if the wing needed Wall-eye crews, in the future, they would likely come after me. He was a good man, understanding, and told me I had joined the best squadron for a GIB. GIBs were a necessity in night combat. My thoughts jumped back to that first night gunnery mission, at MacDill. He was definitely right about that. Thus, the beginning of a career as a combat night fighter that would last for two years. Let's now return to year one of that relationship.

Back on the porch of the hooch, I became somewhat alert, turned up the volume on the radio and listened to this crackling voice from 241,013 miles away in outer space saying, "That is one small step for man, one giant leap for mankind." Neil Armstrong had just stepped onto the surface of the moon, and he was talking to the world. Lieutenant Gene Santarelli was sitting on the porch of his "hooch" in Ubon, Thailand, listening to the words of this U.S. astronaut, standing on the moon. After the rest of the AFN coverage of the Apollo 11 mission, I mouthed, out loud, "I wonder what this all means?" There is a real man on the moon, and he is making a radio transmission, that I can hear on earth. Some nights my radios would not even transmit clearly to my wingman, just a couple of miles away. I pondered the significance of this event for a few minutes, then, reality set in.

It was time to get ready for my world; clean up, put on my flight suit and boots, head off to the squadron and begin the planning for tonight's mission. I would again be part of a flight tasked to interdict the flow of supplies that moved down the "Ho Chi Minh Trail" from North Vietnam, through Laos and into South Vietnam. Like me, there was someone on the other side, starting his day, getting ready to drive his loaded truck down the trail, hoping to avoid the "Yankee Air Pirates," or someone cleaning his anti-aircraft weapon to be ready to shoot down the "Yankee Air Pirates" that ventured into his area. No doubt someone would try to kill me tonight. That was the way it was.

Man on the Moon; one small step for man, one giant leap for mankind; all this would have to wait. I had work to do and I had to be sure I would stay alive. This would take my full attention. I had less than 30 days left on my combat tour, and I wanted to get home to the U. S. of A, and get on with my life. I had a slot in an upcoming F-4 upgrade class, this time as an Aircraft Commander, the FUF (Fellow up Front). But, I had several more nights of combat as a GIB, before going home, and I would continue to try to be the best I could be and make my contribution to stopping the Communist Domino game in Southeast Asia.

Let me tell you a little about this work, flying night combat, in the F-4D Phantom, circa 1969. There were a variety of missions for which we could be tasked, with the most common being Air Interdiction (attacking a geographically specific target); Armed Reconnaissance, or patrolling sections of the Ho Chi Minh trail in search of targets of opportunity (usually trucks, or supply concentrations); escort of AC-130 Gunships; or working with an airborne Forward Air Controller. On this first Southeast Asia tour of duty, Lieutenant Santarelli was an F-4 Weapon System Operator, a GIB. Our area of operation was usually the southern sector of North Vietnam, Route Package I, or Southern Laos, an area called Steel Tiger. Our missions were usually Armed Recce.

However, during the latter part of this tour, the AC-130 Gunship arrived, with low-light TV and Infrared video targeting systems, and the Nite Owls began working with them as an escort to counter anti-aircraft artillery (AAA) fire. The Gunships had the advanced technology to be much more effective in the Armed Recce role in Laos; however, they needed escort to suppress the enemy AAA defenses that would come up and drive them out of the area. By this time, the North Vietnamese had deployed AAA guns throughout the entire network of the Ho Chi Minh Trail. If there were truck convoys, or war supply caches in the area, there were AAA guns that would light up the skies to fend off the "Yankee Air Pirates."

I digress, so I must return to our most common Nite Owl mission of the time, Armed Recce of Route Pack I and Steel Tiger. We were looking to find and attack rolling stock: trucks, trains, human caravans, animal-drawn carts, motor bikes and/or bicycles pulling trailers; anything that could be moving war supplies from North to South Vietnam. We did it at night, because that is when 90% of the supplies moved. If the NVA tried to move supplies in daylight, it was almost assuredly susceptible to air attack. American airpower owned the day but we did not own the night. This did not stop the Nite Owls, We were determined to disrupt NVA night activity as best we could.

Our airplane, the F-4D, Phantom, was the Air Force's primary, frontline fighter-bomber, by far in numbers, and overall capability. It was multi-role, which made it good at many things, but probably not the best in specific missions. This presented challenges doing Armed Recce at night. Our primary means of navigation was an onboard inertial navigation system, which was advertised to consistently get us within five nautical miles of a designated geographic point. Sometimes it was more accurate, and sometimes less. With target area study, on moonlit nights, and with no cloud cover, we could see well enough to find the roads, and prominent features to get closer to the target areas. We carried flares, and dispensed them when over a specific target area, or when we thought we saw movement on the roads. This hopefully gave us the illumination needed to identify the targets, and deliver our ordnance.

The moon was our friend, and the North Vietnamese truck drivers and gunners knew it. The truckers seldom-to-never drove with lights on. Like us, the moonlight let them easily drive the roads "blacked out" at higher speeds. They avoided the open roads on moonlit nights, or would move from cover-to-cover, when they were notified by traffic directors that aircraft were in their area. Radars alerted the traffic directors to post signs/signals to let the drivers know the areas to which it appeared we were headed. Jet noise was often their warning, and this activated the warning networks. Even on the best of nights for us, this was a cat–and-mouse game. The truckers, "movers," tried to stay out of sight, while we patrolled the assigned road networks on our mission. With experience, we learned where many of the suspected "hide sights" were located, and these became our targets, if we did not find any "movers."

On the dark nights, which were more than half of the month, the cat-and-mouse game shifted to the mouse's ("movers") favor. On these nights our flares were the only source of light for refined navigation and attacks. We would navigate via our inertial navigation system to a specific geographic point, (five NM accuracy), "pop a flare" to enable us to visually fix our position, then use our more precise bombing computer to give us the direction and distance to fly the suspected roads, or navigate to the suspected truck parks; however, this was only good for about five-seven NM, so we would need to repeat the process. You can imagine the tactics of the mice. Flare light was the final warning to go into their hide mode, or to change roads and stay away from us.

We tried a variety of tactics using different ordnance. Most all our missions were scheduled two-ship flights. Because of the weapons loads, and for safety, take-offs were single-ship with 20 sec. separation between aircraft. We would join-up after take-off, then inspect each other to insure the munitions and aircraft were OK. To and from the combat area, we usually flew close enough to keep each other in sight. Depending on the weather, this was close formation (wing tip separation only), or a route formation (wider separation). Prior to entering the combat area, we separated into a radar-trail formation, turning off all lights and electronic emitters. We patrolled in this trail formation working as a team, to be able to identify and attack targets quickly. The lead aircraft was the finder, and usually the first shooter, depending on ordnance load. For these Armed Recce missions, the lead was always loaded with flares, and additionally had rockets or 500lb. bombs, or cluster bomb units (CBUs) for area coverage. The second aircraft had more firepower, because he did not carry flares. Usually #2 had a mix of 500lb. bombs, rockets or cluster bombs. His role was to ID targets under the flare light, and if lucky, make the first attack. When carrying a special cluster bomb, CBU-2, that dispensed out the backend of a 19-tube canister carried on the wing, #2 would be the first attacker covering an area with a rain of bomblets, in about a 1000 by 300 foot pattern. The timing was intended to be dispensing bomblets just after the flares lit. On those bright moonlit nights, the preferred tactic would often be to make this run before the flares lit. Flying under flare light was inviting every gunner in the area to zero in on your pink rear, and shower your aircraft with lead (Not a good thing!). We were always changing tactics, so as to keep the gunners guessing.

The Nite Owls informally rated the gunners in the areas we patrolled, on a scale of 1-10, from "very scary" to "relatively ineffective." I use this latter reference cautiously, because every gunner, even the #10 guy, could get lucky. The gunners in the 1-3 category could be frightening. They figured out how to pull lead on jet noise and put up a string of tracers that stayed in one spot on your canopy, which meant you were flying into that string of lead. This required an immediate break turn to avoid getting hit, followed by swearing and heavy breathing. If we were able to pinpoint the location of the gun on the ground, a 500lb. bomb or CBU was saved to attack that position. Even if we could not pinpoint the position, the gunner's general area got a deserving CBU. We often called this, "showing that gunner f-----g respect."

Another tactic was to "fly to the sight of the guns." The NVN gunners did not often waste ammunition. When working an area, if the guns started shooting when the flares lit, or even before, the odds were that a valued target, something worth them protecting, was down there close. Frequently, working over a protected area produced secondary explosions and fires. This was a pretty good indicator we had found a truck park or supply storage area. Getting shot at was no fun, but it usually indicated an area we needed to work.

Armed Recce, at night, was not an easy mission, circa 1969 in the trusty F-4D, but we worked at it, and being totally dedicated to night fighting, the Owls were reasonably effective, given the technology available. At times, I referred to our efforts as scientifically and thoughtfully floundering around in the dark, stumbling onto lucrative targets, then laying waste to them. The Nite Owls were just a small part of the sum total of American airpower dedicated to interdicting the flow of supplies from the North to the South. It was a massive effort, both ours and theirs.

It is time to move to part II of the story: Fast forward 25 years. Major General Santarelli is assigned to Sembach, Germany, the 17th Air Force Commander. I was the operational commander of all the U.S. Air Force units, north of the Alps and south of the English Channel. At the time, 17th Air Force included six major flying wings, a variety of detachment locations and munitions storage areas. One of my primary responsibilities was to insure the combat ready status of my subordinate units. This involved flying with them, and I maintained a combat ready status in the F-16. Maintaining this combat ready status required that I fly regularly with my two F-16 wings, Ramstein Airbase, Germany and Spangdahlem Airbase, Germany. I also was required to pass a combat ready checkride in the airplane on an annual basis.

Part II of this story revolves around a training mission that I flew with one of the Spangdahlem F-16 squadrons, in the summer of 1993: The mission was a two-ship simulated air interdiction mission tasked to destroy a small bridge deep behind enemy lines. We were to fly a 30-minute, visual low level, at 500 ft.; navigate our way to the target at 500 miles-per-hour; avoid enemy defenses represented by German villages; conduct a pop-up bombing attack; then, immediately descend to low level to egress the area, safely returning to friendly territory, another 15 minutes at 500 ft. and 500 knots.

The briefing took place two hours before takeoff, but was preceded by an hour or more of preparation, route and target study. The briefing covered all aspects of the flight, to include formations to be flown, a thorough review of the low level route, and the tactics to be used by each of us for the simulated attack on the bridge. Avoiding the German villages was a priority, since jet noise was a sensitive issue. Having the villages represent enemy AAA concentrations, was an attempt to bring realism to a training requirement to minimize jet noise over populated areas. The mission briefing lasted about one hour. We then gathered our flight gear, suited-up and boarded a van that would take us to our aircraft. The aircraft were parked in reinforced concrete-hardened aircraft shelters, a carryover from the Cold War.

Our planes were the F-16C, Block 50s. The avionics systems were the most modern versions. The plane had an inertial navigation system (INS) that by itself frequently demonstrated accuracy to less than a mile. The Block 50 had an integrated Satellite Global Positioning System (INS/GPS) that would bring position accuracy to less than 300 feet. The bombing computers were continuously computing, giving delivery accuracy in the 10s of feet. Using 500lb. or 2,000lb. bombs, we would be well within the blast and frag envelope to destroy the bridge we were going after.

Take-off and the flight to the low-level entry point were uneventful. We completed our pre-combat checks, descended to 500 ft. and accelerated to 500 knots. Flying a spread formation about 3000 to 6000 ft. apart, we could keep each other in sight, and maneuver to avoid overflight of the numerous German villages along the route (If you have ever flown in Germany, there was usually a German village over every other hill). This required us to maneuver the aircraft continuously, thus depending on our INS/GPS to keep us on course to the target.

As we approached the final run to the target, about three or four minutes away, I transitioned to an attack formation offset to be able to visually cover my leader's attack, and far enough behind him to be able to independently pop-up and conduct my attack outside the leader's fragmentation pattern for the simulated weapons he delivered. This enabled him to arc the target at low level, after his attack, and visually cover mine. As we raced toward the target, I watched the leader pop-up to his roll-in altitude, complete his diving attack and call off target, which was my clearance to conduct mine. The attack formation I flew was at a distance to set up the timing so that at his "off target" call, I would be at the right distance from the target for me to start my pop-up attack from 500 ft. to 4000, roll-in towards the target, pick up the aiming cues in the heads-up-display (HUD), adjust to put the pipper on target, simulate the release, and pull off the target outside the fragmentation pattern of my own bombs, descend back to 500 ft., pick up the egress heading and look for my leader who was maneuvering to get us back into formation and get my eyes back on him.

On our first attack, everything was going as planned for the final run-in; however, all the hills looked the same, with no prominent features, so I was following the navigation needles of my INS/GPS. When the distance clicked down to my pop-up range, I pulled up, holding my heading, and allowed the nav needles to swing to the left about 45-60 degrees, then I pulled down into a diving attack to center the needles on my nose, simultaneously picking up the aiming cues in my HUD. To my pleasant surprise, as I rolled-out wings level in a 20-degree dive, the target aiming cue was settled on the south approach end of a small bridge, our target. I completed my attack as briefed, and in less than 30 seconds from the time I started the climb from 500 ft., I was back down at 500 ft. racing away from the target on egress. On my leaders radio call, I was able to get a visual on him and maneuvered back into our low level formation to provide mutual support. We raced out about three minutes, and the leader called reset, and we maneuvered to run another attack on the bridge. We did three separate attacks that day, using a few different attack plans, and on each, the green aiming cue of the HUD was setting on the bridge when I rolled-out to complete the bomb pass.

After the third attack a low level egress back to friendly territory, and during the 30-minute flight back to Spangdahlem, for some unbeknownst reason, my mind drifted back to July 20th, 1969, and Lieutenant Santarelli sitting on the porch of his Hooch, wondering what it all meant, "That is one small step for man, one giant leap for mankind." So, on that summer afternoon in the skies over the western Germany countryside, flying back to Spangdahlem, it hit me. In just my world of air warfare, this is what it was all about: 25 years of research and development brought me from scientifically floundering around at night in the skies over Southeast Asia, to pinpoint accuracy, whether it be during the day, or at night. On this day, I flew a daytime pinpoint bombing mission in the F-16C Block 50. Its sister, the F-16C Block 40 had the specialized systems to do the same thing at night. In Southeast Asia, American airpower easily owned the day. In 1993, what I had done during the day, a modern day "Nite Owl" could have done in the dark of night. On that day in 1993, we had the capability in our Air Force to own both the day and the night. Thank you Neil Armstrong for setting up this story, and more importantly, a big thanks to all the American ingenuity that has brought our Air Force to the position it is today.

In a 32-year military career, much of it in the cockpits of U.S. Air Force frontline fighters, I remember many fascinating experiences. This is but one of them, and pays tribute to American ingenuity, talent and dedication to providing our warfighters with the best capabilities our nation can provide. Much of it was derived from our space exploration programs. This personal story is what connected me to Neil Armstrong, on that historic day in his life. I did not realize it at the time, but we did have a connection. It just took me 25 years to realize what it was.

CHAPTER FIFTEEN

War Seemed Wonderful

by Donald W. "Shep" Shepperd

It started long before WWII, 1916 in Alvin, Texas: an Army Signal Corps Jenny JN-3 aircraft returning from operations against Pancho Villa in Mexico, crashed upside down in the field behind my father's house. The pilot crawled from beneath the wreckage, dusted himself off, wiped the dirt from his goggles and Dad was hooked on aviation. My father saved a piece of the aircraft strut and gave it to me. I kept it for thirty years and lost it when household goods disappeared during one of our many Air Force moves. I wish I still had them both, the strut and my dad.

Dad graduated from high school in 1928, tough timing. His father had passed away when he was six-years old and the family of four boys and three girls lived a subsistence life, hunting, fishing, raising chickens, taking in laundry, odd jobs. This was long before Social Security, unemployment insurance, safety nets and Obamacare. Dad didn't have the money for college, so he washed dishes at a local restaurant until he found a job, a dirty job, with Shell Oil Company, doing geophysical work, exploring for oil in the swamps of Louisiana and Mississippi, living on camp boats.

When the Depression hit in 1929, Dad was furloughed by Shell and enlisted in the Army Air Corps as a crew chief in the open cockpit days at Randolph Field in San Antonio. He always dreamed of being a pilot, but, "...no college, no wings," he was told. He said he came close to being a pilot. On weekends the instructor pilots would throw a crew chief and their toolbox in the backseat of their BT-1s and land in Mexico. The pilots went to the bars and left the crew chiefs in the sun to keep the cows from eating fabric from the airframes. Dad longed for the more glamorous life of a pilot. Shell called him back in 1932. He got out of the Air Corps and married my mother. I came along in 1940 and our first house was a camp boat.

The Japanese struck Pearl Harbor and our whole family was involved in WWII. Dad was a Civil Service worker modifying aircraft; Cousin Alec was a belly turret gunner on B-17s in England; Uncle Al was in the Army in North Africa and Sicily and Italy; and Cousin David was in B-29s in the Pacific. I lived during the week with my grandparents, Big Mama and Daddy Zach. My cousin, "Snooks" (Uncle Al's daughter), and I worked in Big Mama's "Victory Garden." Everything was rationed, gasoline, meat, sugar, and we were issued coupon books. Everything excess went to the soldiers and the war effort. We grew vegetables, rolled bandages and saved metal and tin foil, raised chickens, had hives of bees. I kept a long stick and sharpened the end just in case. I am happy to report not one German or Japanese soldier made it past Terrell Avenue.

It was a wonderful war, easy to understand. Half the enemy didn't look like us and the Nazis and Japanese were easy to hate. There were newspaper maps showing distant continents containing countries with front lines. There were battles with names like D-Day and St. Lo and The Bulge and there were victory parades. It was a wonderful war at least until cousin Alec lost a leg to triple-A over Regensburg; and until contact was lost with Uncle Al's unit on the Rapido River in northern Italy during the assault on Monte Cassino Abbey; and until Cousin David's B-29 went down in the Pacific. Then, even at five-years old, war didn't seem quite so wonderful.

Events were held to promote the sales of "War Bonds," and Dad took me to my first air show at Randolph in 1944. After the show, Dad asked if I would like to go for an airplane ride. Oh, you betcha! We proceeded to a small building near the taxiway. Pilots were allowed to keep their private airplanes on base. The ramp was filled with Piper Cubs. I picked one out and Dad stuck his head into the building from which smoke was pouring, cigarette and barbeque. Inside people were wall-to-wall, laughing, dancing and yelling over loud cowboy music. "Hey, Bob! Someone wants to ride in your airplane." Bob came out of the building with a bottle of beer in one hand and his arm around a gorgeous, tanned blonde with two great big, beautiful...b...b...b...blue eyes and right then I decided, "This is the life for me!" My aviation career had begun.

I remember when we dropped the "A-bomb" on Hiroshima. I rushed in and asked my dad if the Japanese would drop one on us.

He said, no, because no Japanese was as smart as Harry Truman or any other Democrat for that matter (Dad would later become a Republican).

I woke up in the Nix Hospital in downtown San Antonio on 14 August 1945, groggy from anesthesia after having my tonsils removed. Bells were ringing and people were dancing in the streets. It was VJ-Day. "The war is over!" said my mother, wiping tears from her eyes. It was especially joyous for us because although Cousin Alec lost a leg, he came home with a new artificial one and a disability pension for life. They found Uncle Al after losing contact with his unit at Monte Cassino, and Cousin David was rescued by a PBY after ditching west of Iwo Jima. Some of his crew weren't so lucky. We had won and war seemed wonderful again.

When the war was over, many assume the troops came home, used the G.I Bill for college, got their degrees, the economy took off and life got better. It did, but not for a long, long time. Wartime euphoria dissipated quickly. The troops came home all right and were discharged, but there were no jobs, no houses to buy and no consumer goods. Industry had to adjust from wartime production to consumer demand. Suddenly, there was unemployment and despair almost like the Great Depression.

Dad's wartime Civil Service job vanished and he was laid-off once again. He sold his half interest in the bee business to my grandfather for $500 and bought an old Model-T Ford. He called it "Old Seldom;" it seldom ran before he fixed it and seldom broke after. We sold our house on South Cross Boulevard and Mother and I moved in with Big Mama and Daddy Zach. Dad headed north and said he would call for us when he found a job. He did, two years later.

Mother and I headed north to join Dad in our "old" '39 Chevy that had been little used due to wartime gas rationing. It was the "polio scare" years and kids were not allowed in restaurants and all the swimming pools were closed. Travelers were looked at askance if accompanied by children lest we spread the dreaded disease. We arrived in Pueblo, Colorado in 1947 and used all our savings to buy one of the very few available houses. We paid $9,000, a fortune, for a one-bedroom house near the CF&I steel mill. I had my own private bed, a pull-out couch in the front room. Dad had a job as a lineman with the Atcheson, Topeka and Santa Fe Railroad and our new, more prosperous life was about to begin. Every Wednesday morning the steel mill blew out its furnaces and ugly black soot rained down on our neighborhood. I asked Dad what it was. "It's jobs, son." was his reply.

Two years later we moved to Denver. Dad found a job as a civil engineer with the Colorado State Highway Department and we bought a house in something new called "the suburbs." I was a 10 year-old boy on the floor, reading the Denver Post, watching the lines move south towards the "Pusan Perimeter."

"How can this happen?" I asked Dad. "We just beat the Japanese and Germans and these crummy little North Koreans are pushing us into the ocean." Dad told me not to worry. President Truman was sending General MacArthur and MacArthur would figure out something. And, he did, the Inchon landing. The lines began to move north and when they reached the Yalu River. I jumped up and down shouting, "WE WON! WE WON!" and once again war seemed wonderful.

A week later, seven Chinese armies invaded south across the Yalu, bugles blaring, and drove a wedge between the 8th Army in the west and the 10th Marine Corps in the east and by Christmas Eve of 1950, 205,000 American fighting men were withdrawing in full retreat from the port of Hungnam in eastern Korea, and war didn't seem quite so wonderful. We're still there almost 65 years later.

During my senior year of high school, Dad asked me what I had in mind for college? In those days, college was up to us, no SAT prep classes, no college visits, no school counselors hovering and helping with catalogs, information and advice. I said I planned to go to medical school at the University of Colorado. He asked me how I planned to pay for it, "Uh...uh...uh..." and thus began my search for a "free" college education.

I didn't know much about the military, but leafing through a Life Magazine in the local barbershop, I came across pictures of an aircraft carrier with some cool-looking Navy pilots in leather helmets alongside blue airplanes. My barber said he was in the Navy in WWII and thought they even had a Naval Academy, kind of like a college. I wrote to my Congressman and asked if I could apply for admission. He said, sure, sent me the forms and soon I had an appointment to

Annapolis. The glamorous career of a naval aviator and a "free" college education were within reach.

Christmas season 1957 I caught a bus to downtown Denver and picked up a discarded Denver Post with some pictures of cadets at a new Air Force Academy being built in Colorado Springs. When I got off the bus, I saw an actual Air Force Academy cadet, in uniform, just like the pictures in the paper. It was obviously an apparition, a vision, a message from God. I was meant to be an Air Force pilot, not a "Swabee." What to do?

I rushed home and wrote Congressman Hill. "I made a terrible mistake. I finally realize what I want to do in life. I don't even like to swim. Could I please switch to the Air Force Academy?" No problem, but there was a small catch: From my status as a "Principle Appointee" to Navy, I would now be one of ten competing for USAFA. Gulp! My dad thought I was a dummy, giving up a bird in the hand. Somehow it all worked and I received news of my USAFA acceptance during the state high school track meet. They even announced it over the loudspeaker to thunderous applause from the spectators (nine) and back-slapping by my harrier teammates (four). It was late in the day and no trophies were in the offing.

My four years at USAFA seemed interminably long, but in retrospect, passed in a flash. The first cadet classmate I met was Don Watson. He was the relative of a neighbor and we gave him a ride to Induction Day. Little did we know, six years later, Don would be the first classmate name on the USAFA war memorial, an F-100 lost in Vietnam, and there would be many more.

Graduation Day at USAFA was a memorable occasion. Lyndon Johnson was Vice president and the graduation speaker. He presented our diplomas. My turn came. I saluted and said, "Thank you Mr. Vice President. It is an honor." He looked me in the eye and presented my first lesson in high level, executive leadership and mentoring with these inspiring words, "Keep the line moving, boy," and I did.

During my third-class, sophomore, year at USAFA, I called an old high school acquaintance, Rose Driskill. It turned into serious courtship, the Ring Dance and engagement. My father told me marriage was a serious matter and not to rush into it; we didn't. Rose and I waited two whole hours after graduation, jumped into our new 1962 Chevy Impala convertible, top down and headed south for a honeymoon in Mexico. Our Air Force life was about to begin. One of my fondest memories was the view of the Academy in the rearview mirror. At our class reunion 50 years later it finally looked better.

Pilot training was as good as life gets: flying the new supersonic T-38 and getting paid to do it. F-100s at Luke followed and then a dream come true: assignment to Europe flying the Hun at Hahn Air Base; the Hunsrück wine country in the Eifel area along the Mosel River of West Germany; a Deutschmark at 4:1; deposit on beer bottles more than the cost of the beer and wild parties at the O-Club every Friday. There was a God!

The base apartments we lived in wouldn't be suitable for welfare families today, but Germany was just recovering from WW II, we were young, and life was just plain fun. Rose and I traveled all over Europe, even driving to Paris on weekends and skiing in Austria and Switzerland. The squadron flew to Wheelus AFB in Libya every three months for gunnery training. We sat alert at home station and in Italy and Turkey with nuclear weapons. I don't think I bothered the Russians much, but it would sure have scared hell out of my old neighbors in Colorado: "THAT KID WITH A NUKE??? You gotta' be shittin' me!"

I was checked out in F-100s but was just a kid fighter pilot. I really learned to fly in Germany. I learned to stick hard on the wing in really bad weather and fly off 8000 ft. NATO-standard runways that were always wet. I learned "fighting wing" and "fluid four" both of which were useless, but fun. I learned how to hold over an NDB and penetrate to an ADF approach. Old heads like Rollo Elam, Ned King, Art Bergman, Charlie Goodwin, Ray Hanson, Jim Fox, Jack Powers, Dave McGilvary, Troy Dobbins, Joe Mecsiji, Art Bergman, Frank Miller, Jim Dailey, Chuck Cunningham, Dick Clark, Lynn Officer and Mal Dickey were my mentors. They sat me down and said, "Son, you either become a really good pilot here, or you'll be dead very soon." I took it to heart and loved it, every minute of it. There were cross-countries to England and Denmark and France and Italy and Turkey and Greece and Spain and faux emergencies to pick up cases of gin, vodka and bourbon at rock-bottom prices in Malta, and Walter the bartender and Bruna the barmaid at Aviano, and aircraft deliveries and pickups at Getafe. Names like Las Cuevas de Luis Candelas, the Plaza Major, Botin's, the Columbia House, Gorgazzo's,

Pordenone, the Casablanca, were part of our regular lexicon and cross-country planning. We bought Danish furniture in Copenhagen, wrought iron screens and silver wine and punch sets in Madrid, camel saddles in Tripoli, fine china in London, bird cages in Tunisia, and brass samovars and rugs in Turkey. We went to bullfights, Swiss Ski School and cruised the canals of Venice. We drank the best German beers from decorative steins, Mosel and Rhine wines, Greek Ouzo, Danish Acquavit, Italian grappa, nikolashkas and afterburners, AND WE GOT PAID FOR IT! It was the greatest of all times in the lives of young fighter pilots.

"The F-4s ARE COMING!" was the announcement at the daily pilots meeting. But, not so fast, Shepperd. I needed a full year of retainability on my USAFE tour after returning from a stateside F-4 checkout. I didn't have it, so I went kicking and screaming as a first lieutenant to an Air Liaison Officer (ALO) tour with the 24th Infantry Division in Augsburg. It turned out to be a great experience. The Army brigade commander didn't care about airstrikes because he was short of officers due to Vietnam. He wanted me to be a tank company commander. We enjoyed Bavaria and I learned a lot about the Army and grunt leadership. And then, there was war!

We left bases in the U.S. and Europe, deposited our wives and kids all over America and headed for combat in the steamy jungles of southeast Asia, a place called Vietnam, part of the old French Indochina, Graham Greene's Orient. I walked to the airplane at Stapleton Field in Denver and looked back at Rose. She was crying. I was excited. It was everything I ever dreamed of. I would be a fighter pilot in a real war, a jungle war for men with hair on their chests. There were missiles and MiGs and AAA and flak and our bases were attacked at night with rockets and mortars. What was not to like?

I stopped through the P.I. (the Philippine Islands, Clark Air Base) for Jungle Survival School and then headed for war. I stepped off the airplane at Tan Son Nhut in Saigon. The oppressive heat hit me in the face, and the country smelled like a fart. I jumped on a bus, the windows of which were covered with screens to prevent in-coming hand grenades and headed for Bien Hoa, a two-hour bus ride. I joined the 90th TFS, "the Dice," had two orientation rides and a USAFA classmate, Pete Robinson, later a major general, checked me out for night bombing missions under flares in the F-100. I think I hit South

Vietnam. Pete signed me off. He wasn't about to risk another ride. I was a combat pilot, a full-up round and ready for the Communist hordes. War was once again wonderful.

By the time I got to Bien Hoa, 12 of my Academy classmates had perished in aircraft, eight in combat. By the time I left, four more would be added to the list including one who was killed by a VC rocket, his tour complete, waiting to board the flight home to America. We learned early, life is not fair.

About three weeks into war, I contracted dengue fever. I was out of commission for almost a month with extremely high fevers, chills, cold, soaking sweats and the draftee doctors didn't even know enough to give me IVs. I wanted to die; almost did. Out of the hospital I went to Phu Cat to fly F-100 Misty FAST FAC missions over North Vietnam. We found and marked targets for bomb-laden fighters: truck parks, POL, supply depots, SAM sites. It was miserable flying and a shitty, dangerous job. In Misty I learned about heavy AAA. I didn't like it. Bud Day, our first Misty commander, had been shot down and was missing. He would later be awarded the Medal of Honor for his actions while a POW.

I reported into Misty shortly before Christmas 1967 and said hello to Guy Gruters and Bob Craner as they departed for their airplane and an afternoon mission. I had known Guy at USAFA. I said I would see them at the O-Club when they returned. It would be many years before I saw them again at a Misty reunion. They were shot down and captured late in the afternoon. It was the second time Guy had been shot down in three missions.

Several USAFA classmates and old USAFE friends were at Misty. I was checked out by some and checked out others. All the pilots were experienced and topnotch. The tour was limited to 60 missions over the North due to the high exposure and loss rates. Twenty eight percent of Mistys were shot down, some twice. We flew the two-seat "F-100F," the family model and alternated seats every other mission. The pilot in back handled the radios, maps and a handheld 35mm camera. The flights were extremely fatiguing. Each mission lasted four–six hours with two-three mid-air refuelings from KC-135 tankers over the Mekong in Thailand or the South China Sea. We tried to maintain 400 knots and stay above 4,000 ft. while constantly jinking. We were shot at constantly while searching for targets, sometimes not realizing it, just a hole found on post flight inspection.

Although there were a few bigger guns around major river crossings, 57mm and up and an occasional SAM in the area, we did not have to contend with MiGs which stayed north in the Hanoi-Haiphong area. We had no RHAW gear, no ECM, no chaff and flare (MANPADS did not come until later in the war) and one UHF radio that often died if we fired our 20mm guns. By any measure we were ill-equipped.

Our greatest danger by far was 37mm AAA. Six-position 37mm gun sites were ubiquitous. You could hear rounds passing close, thump, thump, thump and see tracers as they whisked past the aircraft like dots coming out of the middle of a computer screen. When you were hit by 37mm, there was no doubt. It most often resulted in aircraft loss. Our responsibility was Route Pack One, the southern panhandle of North Vietnam, north of the DMZ and south of Vinh, the final funnel through which war materials passed en route to the Vietcong in South Vietnam. Our mission – stop the flow – GOOD LUCK. Those were the days before precision weapons and night vision equipment. We could find targets, but it was hard to hit them. Lucrative targets were hard to come by. Truck convoys moved during bad weather or at night. POL and equipment storage areas were widely dispersed. It was a losing effort to stop the flow once it left the ships up north, and the ports were off limits. It was easy to lose a multi-million dollar aircraft attacking a $20,000 truck. It seemed every third or fourth mission turned in to a RESCAP as we located downed pilots and capped until the Sandys and Jollys arrived. It was satisfying to recover aircrews but the repeated loses became discouraging.

I got shot up on one mission and made an emergency landing at Da Nang. I visited a USAFA classmate, Dick Klass, who was in the hospital hooked to IVs after taking a shot in the throat on an O-2 FAC mission over the Ho Chi Minh Trail in Laos. I laughed at him and said that shooting a Rhodes Scholar in the throat was a message from God. Dick thought the war was useless and we were losing. I disagreed. He was smarter earlier than me.

After returning from another long, sweaty mission over the North, I shut down the engine. The crew chief came up the ladder and handed me a note: "The Command Post called. Your friend, Capt James Brinkman, was killed today on a mission out of Bien Hoa." Throat lump, one of too many in the flying business. Jimmy B, the irrepressible Jimmy B, the funniest man I ever knew was dead. I remembered Jimmy B at the Academy, on wing staff, in F-100 training at Luke, sitting nuclear alert at Hahn. I remembered the day he accidently shot his crew survival weapon, a .45, at a nuclear weapon on his aircraft from the alert shack. "Jim, this is not funny." I remembered he was given one week for R&R in Hawaii from Vietnam where he intended to become engaged and how he showed up a month later and didn't understand why his squadron commander was mad. "Well, Jim, you see there was this little thing called, TET, while you were gone…" And now he was gone, dead gone, in a shitty war. It wasn't fair and war didn't seem wonderful any more.

I decided to get off active duty after Vietnam but I was selectively retained for a year. My terminal assignment was F-104s at Luke, but while our household goods were en route we were informed that we would be going to England AFB, Alexandria, LA to instruct Vietnamese students in the A-37. It was an interesting year and I gained great respect for the young Vietnamese kids, some just off the backs of water buffaloes, drafted into what would become a hopeless cause. We taught them the best we could. They learned the best they could. Language was always a problem. Some were good. In the end Congress pulled the plug and we abandoned them.

My decision to leave active duty was the second worst decision I ever made. The first worst was joining Trans World Airlines (TWA). During my first furlough, which lasted six and one-half years, I joined the Air National Guard. We lived on the East coast. We had no income, meager savings, and I got a job as the east coast regional sales manager selling light airplanes for American Aviation Corporation out of Cleveland. I sold a lot of airplanes and learned to love light aircraft. I learned a lot about flying in the bad weather, poor visibility and icing conditions on the east coast. I later became national sales manager for the company and we moved to Cleveland.

I went back to TWA, but after my third furlough, we decided poverty was highly overrated. Rose asked me to get serious about life, and I joined the Air National Guard fulltime in Tucson, AZ. While in the Guard I flew U-3s, O-2s, F-100s, A-7s, F-106s and finished in the F-15. I commanded squadrons, groups and wings. I went to the Pentagon in 1989 and was promoted to Brigadier General as Deputy Director of the Air National Guard. Later that year the Berlin Wall came down and the bells of peace rang all over eastern Europe. The Soviet Union was no more, and the U.S. was the world's only superpower. War seemed a distant possibility.

On 2 August 1990 I was sleeping soundly in Washington D.C. when at 2:00am Rose hit me on the side of the head and asked, "Did you hear that?"

"Did I hear what? I'm asleep."

"Iraq invaded Kuwait," (she sleeps with a radio in her ear).

I replied, "Well that figures," because I had been sitting through repeated briefs in the Pentagon: CIA, DIA, Army, Air Force and Navy Intelligence saying, "Saddam is not going to invade. He is simply posturing to take back the oil Kuwait stole from him." Of course they were wrong and we began to move forces. On 7 August the first F-15s arrived in Saudi Arabia. There was a devastating 39-day air campaign followed by a 100-hour ground war, the magnificent "Left Hook" employed by General Norman Schwarzkopf. Colin Powell decided it was "piling on" to destroy Iraq's retreating forces and a ceasefire took effect. Despite widely circulated photos of "the highway of death," most of Saddam's men and equipment fled north unimpeded. In a hastily-arranged and ill thought-out ceasefire agreement, the terms of which were accepted by the Iraqis on 8 April, Saddam was prevented from flying his jets but allowed to continue flying his military helicopters over southern Iraq. He used them to punish, kill and control the southern Iraqi Shiites leaving a population far less than grateful to the U.S. We would pay for this 12 years later.

George Herbert Walker Bush, the 41st President of the United States, declared a coalition victory. There were parades, even flyovers in Washington D.C. reminiscent of WWII and war temporarily seemed slightly wonderful again.

In 1994 I was promoted to Major General and head of the Air National Guard. I had 89 flying units, 1900 aircraft and 119,000 people under me. I retired in 1998 after almost 40 years in uniform. I finished with 5500 flying hours, mostly in fighters and had lived my dreams. I was a happy, fulfilled man. I started my own defense consulting firm, The Shepperd Group, Inc. (innovative, huh?).

On the morning of September 11, 2001 I was leading the dream life – a retired general with a working spouse. Rose worked the U-2 program at Raytheon. I came downstairs to use our computer, bathrobe on, coffee in hand and the phone rang. It was Rose calling from work. "Do you have the TV on? An airplane just hit the World Trade Center in New York."

I snapped on the TV and saw what everyone else saw: clear weather, smoke. It had to be some kind of freak accident. Then, I saw the second airplane hit and I knew immediately, THIS was TERRORISM! I picked up the phone to call my old office in the Pentagon to say, "Do you think they could be coming here?" I couldn't get through. They were already in motion. Later that morning I felt the third airplane hit the Pentagon. We only lived a mile and one-half away.

The next day the phone rang and it was CNN asking if I would like to do some on screen analysis of the attacks. I told them, "NO! I have avoided you liberal bastards all my life and have no intention of getting involved with you now." I gave them names of several others I thought would be better. CNN called back in two days and I agreed to try a session or two. That started my five years with CNN covering the wars in Iraq and Afghanistan. It was interesting, but not fun. I compare it to being on nuclear alert 24 hours a day, never knowing what or when something will happen and feeling slightly threatened and ill-prepared for each event

One must admit that war seemed once again wonderful when U.S. forces moved rapidly north from Kuwait, made the "thunder run" into Baghdad and the world watched as Saddam's statute was toppled in Firdos Square by jubilant Iraqis. While with CNN I traveled the Mid-East and made three trips to Iraq. The first trip was 30 days after combat ceased and the euphoria and optimism still surrounded the chain of command, our troops and even the Baghdadis. I visited with Dave Petraeus in Mosul and Ray Odierno in Tikrit. I asked Odierno if he thought Saddam was still alive and if we would find him. He replied he thought Saddam was alive, somewhere near us and we would get him, and we did. Once again war seemed wonderful as an American soldier drug Saddam Hussein by the back of the collar from his spider hole. The war was surely over, a victory, right?

President George W. Bush declared, "Mission complete." Well, not quite.

When combat ceased, Tommy Franks turned the reins over to Ambassador Bremer who promptly disbanded the Iraqi Army, a giant mistake. On my second trip to the AOR the insurgency was beginning and it was apparent we had created, or inherited a mess. No Iraqi nuclear weapons had been discovered because there weren't any. Sunnis, Shias and Kurds whose relations had been controlled and dictated by the brutal tactics of Saddam's Ba'ath party were blowing up our troops and each other with IEDs and car bombs. Chaos was beginning.

On my third trip I visited the Iraqi 9th Mechanized Infantry Division HQ in Taji, north of Baghdad. The 9th was being "reconstituted" with tanks and APCs, a combination of old Iraqi and newer U.S. equipment, plus American advisors. An Iraqi officer tried to give a Power Point briefing and it suddenly occurred to me that we had lost the war. We were attempting to impose U.S. culture, standards and values on a nation and military neither capable nor desirous of absorbing same. I left depressed.

We are out of Iraq now after the loss of 4487 Americans who tried their best. Iraqi losses, military and civilian, were estimated in the multiple hundreds of thousands; we probably don't want to know for sure. Did we accomplish our mission? Certainly not, but historians will write the final outcome, for it is now up to the Iraqis. A new air war has just begun against ISIL – so many bad guys, so little time.

Almost the same can be said for Afghanistan: we routed the Taliban; failed to get Osama bin Laden at Tora Bora; finally killed him in Pakistan and did it make a difference with over 2300 U.S. KIA? Probably not. When we finally strike the U.S. flag, Afghanistan will return to what it has always been, a tribal society ruled by warlords, riven with corruption and violence and peopled by illiterate, ungovernable masses.

As I look at major wars in my lifetime: WWII, Korea, Vietnam, Desert Storm, Iraq, Afghanistan, it appears we won one, lost one and tied four. Such a record would get an NFL coach fired.

The lessons I learned from watching and participating in wars are not complicated: when the U.S. interests are wrongfully attacked, the American people are incensed. Patriotism runs strong, the President deploys forces and Congress acts (or at least are supposed to). "Cry havoc! Unleash the dogs of war!" becomes our national mantra and war seems justified and even wonderful. Revenge and justice seem appropriate goals. Then, reality and imperfect endings ensue. Caskets full of our kids and grandkids return, and war hardly seems wonderful. Every time I visit the Vietnam Memorial in Washington D.C. with 58,000 American names including classmates, wingmen, close friends and comrades I am reminded once again – WAR IS NOT WONDERFUL!

The conclusions I draw from lessons learned are equally uncomplicated: there are things worth fighting for, but we need to be sure what they are. When we go to war, we must have the American public behind us and we need to get in with overwhelming force, win and get out. Nation-building and changing the cultures of other societies are not American core competencies.

I am in my mid-70s, the age when we begin to reflect seriously on our lives. I think of the Air Force Academy often. I smile. I'm glad I went there. It wasn't fun, but it gave me the foundation for a good life, better than I deserved. Three of my six great roommates are gone. Our class was successful. We had 17 generals including one four-star, but that was not the measure of our success. Our success was: we were good lieutenants and captains. We flew when the airplanes were dangerous, but flying was fun and life was simple. I'm glad I served.

CHAPTER SIXTEEN

"Hi, I'm Moose, and I would like to be rescued"... or...Steep In, Steep Out, One Pass, Haul Ass!

by Edward R. "Moose" Skowron

"Pintail lead's got a truck in the road up here," Leon Garner called out as he led us on a road recce south of Vinh on Route 1 in North Vietnam. We were working the route at 3-4,000 ft., keeping the speed 350-400 indicated and about a half mile apart, S-turning to cover each other's tail. I replied, "Let it go, lead, I'll check it out, could be a flak trap."

I'm on my 99th mission this early a.m. of September 3rd, 1966, and I'm giving Leon a flight lead checkout. He's more than ready and has proven himself on many tougher missions. I've got one more to fly to finish my 100 (we get to go home after 100 missions North). "My bags are packed, I'm ready to go, taxi is waiting and he's blowing his horn." Just like Peter, Paul and Mary put it, and I'm ready.

I've been at this off and on now for two years. I had begun flying clandestine escort missions in Laos in 1964 and then on the first organized strike on January 13th, 1965. Little did I know that I'd also be flying later on the last day of air operations in Cambodia on August 15th, 1973.

In the event it was a flak trap, I didn't want to fly directly over the truck, so I eased east a bit and swung south in a right turn. I could see it was a burned-out truck hulk and at the same time I looked below into the muzzles of a mixed battery of 37 and 57mm AAA guns, all pumping tracers coming straight at me. So much for the "I'll check it out" call.

I felt the first WHUMP! and called, "I'm hit!" and started heading toward the South China Sea 10 or 12 miles east. Leon said he had me in sight and I was smoking, and with that, another WHAP! and the flight controls went crazy and a rapid JC-maneuver porpoise started so badly that my 35mm Canon camera on the glare shield was crashing between the canopy bow and the glare shield and showing all of its working parts, levers, gears, lens elements, loose film and other junk, followed by thick white smoke filling the cockpit so thick I couldn't see anything but the ball of the sun showing through the left quarter panel of the windscreen.

It was just after sunrise, and I was looking in the direction of the water. The porpoising stopped, but there were no flight controls. I punched the tanks and five napalm cans off and felt I had an upward vector in the right direction. The bottom of the sun began to slide towards and under the nose. I felt I was going inverted and nose down at about 1,500 ft. I wasn't sure I'd made the coast, but no matter what, I had to go NOW!

I called, "I got to go!" and assumed the ejection position and tried to raise my armrests to blow the canopy and expose the ejection seat triggers. Not so fast, Yankee Air Pirate. All I got was the metal click of the armrest striking the seat safety pin. That seat pin is a T push-to-release type pin located along the narrow and tight area between the seat and right cockpit sidewall, difficult to reach and pull even under normal conditions. My thought was, I'll never get out in time.

In aviation, problems often start with a break in the flow of the normal sequence of steps, and this was one of those times. It started as a very early 4:00 a.m. preflight and before daylight takeoff. On check in, Leon said he had no exterior lights. I told him I would take the lead until it got light and then we would revert back to the briefed mission, him leading, and me observing as his wingman.

While that conversation was going on, the steps of the pre-taxi procedures were occurring: the crew chief pulls the gear pins, walks to the front of the aircraft and shows them to the pilot. In return, you show him your seat pins. In the dark, all I saw was his figure with arm raised taking for granted he had the pins in hand. I'm sure he felt the same way, because he couldn't positively see that I wasn't showing mine. I gave him the "pull chocks" signal.

At that instant, when I felt there was no way I could get the pin (the one I had failed to pull out and show the crew chief) out in time to eject, I felt no panic. In fact, I felt I had had a great life, and as the saying goes, this was it. Little did I realize there was a lot more life to live. Later, I understood why they send young men to do this job: young men just don't understand what they might be missing.

With that I thought, "Yeah, but you better give it a try." I slid my hand down to the pin, barely touched it, and it fell into my hand. Stunned, (somebody must have decided it wasn't my time?) I raised the armrest and heard and felt the canopy go, reached and squeezed the trigger, and "WHAM!" I was blown out into space.

I felt the chute grab the air, and I was jerked into an upright position facing west. My first sight after the smoke was the coastline of North Vietnam under my boots, left to right, much too close to the shoreline. I looked up and checked the canopy, looked good, but so small. I looked down, and my raft and seat pack were deployed and swinging freely beneath me. I also noticed looking down that I was not low at all. In fact I was quite high. Not sure how high I was, I pulled my oxygen mask off my helmet and dropped it, and it went out of sight.

I could see Leon in a wide turn and heard a lot of weak but heavy ground fire. I felt they were shooting at him. I thought I should try to slip the chute out to sea a bit. I didn't do the "four-line cut" to give the chute some forward speed because my drift was in the wrong direction. I grabbed a handful of back risers and pulled them down, hoping to tilt the canopy and slip seaward. I did that for a bit, not sure if it did any good. Then, I pulled one of the two radios out of my vest and called Leon.

Leon responded, and I told him I was okay. He said an HU-16 "Duckbutt" was 15-20 minutes out. The Duckbutt was on his way north to the orbit point in the Northern Gulf where he held for the morning to perform emergency pickups. The HU-16 was an amphibious aircraft of an Air Force Reserve squadron out of Luke Air Force Base on the first mission of their tour. It would be a hell of a first day for them and I wasn't so thrilled with it right now either. I observed another flight of Thuds entering the arena. They responded when Leon called for support.

It was time for me to concentrate on my water landing. Either the slip or an offshore breeze had pushed me a few hundred yards out to sea, as best I could tell. As I got closer to the surface, I began to notice splashing under and around me. The gunners weren't shooting at Leon, they were shooting at me – BASTARDS!.

I wanted to get as low in the water as I could (shoot low, they're riding shetlands!) without drowning, so I only opened one side of my underarm life preserver, (LPU). BIG mistake! When I hit the water, I was drifting to sea. My chute stayed inflated and was dragging me east. "Good."

Well, not so good. That one side LPU had rolled me sideways and under water. I tried all the tricks they taught us in water survival: Go spread eagle, arch your back. No help! I was drowning. "I'm not going to drown after all this bullshit," was my thought.

On the next cycle with my head above water, I grabbed a big gulp of air and canned the school solution. I grabbed the left riser strap with my right hand and pulled some slack into that side and reached up with my left hand and found the canopy release and squeezed it free. Everything stopped, and I was okay. I pulled my raft to me but decided not to get in, but to stay low. I got on my radio and told Leon I was down safe. He said the Duckbutt was on the way. Then, the Duckbutt came on frequency and said they thought they saw my plane hit the water while they were inbound.

I was down in some mild swells and hadn't seen anything hit around me, so I got into the raft just about the time the HU-16 arrived. He came by at about 50-100 ft., and I looked directly into the pilot's eyes. He said he couldn't land as there were too many boats around me. I didn't see any, so I asked Leon to take care of the boats. He made a low pass over them, and they got the idea and turned away.

On the next pass, I didn't think the HU-16 was going to land as he was about 150-200 ft. away from me at about 30-40 ft. and moving fast. He pulled the power off and with that fell into the water like a big duck with little or no forward movement. Holy shit!

To be free to get in the raft, I had taken my parachute harness off and hung it over the edge of the raft; another not so bright idea. All my floatation gear was connected to that harness. I was still wet and heavy with nothing on to help me stay afloat. I was about 50 ft. from the left aircraft float and paddling towards them with the pilot looking at me and the crew chief and para-rescue man (PJ) in the open hatch on the left side behind the wing.

Then, things changed very fast. Large explosions and geysers started erupting all around us. The pilot's eyes went VERY wide along with mine. I motioned to the rescue guy to dive in and swim to me. We had been briefed PJs would do that, and with a lanyard attached, we both would be pulled in.

It went just that way. We grabbed hands, and the crew chief pulled us to the hatch. I arrived backwards, and the crew chief tried to lift me by the shoulders. He was a slight kid, and I was wet and heavy. I kept yelling, "Let me turn around! Let me turn around!" That way I could chin myself on the sill. Before I turned, I saw a Thud flight lay a long splash of napalm along the beach.

I turned, and with the crew chief pulling me and raising myself, I crashed into the cabin. He and I turned and grabbed the PJ by the top of his upper wetsuit and pulled him in so hard his fins hit the overhead and ripped off. I looked forward, and the pilot and copilot were looking at us wide-eyed with explosions erupting around us and showing through the windscreen.

I waived my arm and yelled, "GO! GO!" They firewalled the left engine, and we spun around to face out to sea and started bouncing off the swells. When the bouncing stopped, the three of us in the cabin gave out a loud cheer.

When things settled and I tried to get up, I found I was fortunate to have landed in the water. I couldn't walk or stand. Both legs were traumatized from my butt to my ankles. They were swelling like balloons. I was bleeding from wounds in my upper left arm and the left side of my neck. The PJ patched me up, and we headed for Da Nang.

How did I end up here, beat up and having spent the morning acting as a target for a bunch of NVA anti-aircraft gunners? Well, I'll tell you. It went something like this:

In the beginning: I was born in Adams, Massachusetts in 1934. I had a great childhood playing in the woods, lakes and streams of the Berkshire Hills of Western Massachusetts. The small village of Cheshire was home to my two sisters and my mom and dad in a little two-bedroom, single-bath house. I never thought anything about the fact that when my number two sister arrived, the girls would get the bedroom and I would go to the couch in the living room and eventually to a bunk in the basement. The few "go to church" clothes I had hung in a closet. My day-to-day things hung from a couple of pegs behind a bedroom door. I had a bike, a Red Rider, a ball and glove and a fishing pole. I had a sled and skis in the winter. Oh, yeah, I also had an AM radio, wonderful thing.

Like just about all of the "Friday pilots," our values and attitudes that shaped the rest of our lives were formed by World War II. The war was happening all around us. Our parents and other family friends were the Greatest Generation, although we didn't know it at the time. They came from the Great Depression, which I heard about daily. You would get the lecture about the Depression if you left a light on in an empty room or didn't shut the door in the winter or maybe didn't clean your plate.

My dad worked as a routeman for a baking and wholesale grocery company out of Schenectady, New York. He worked at the outer edge of the route structure of the Northern Berkshires. Being out there, no one ever bothered him. He was his own boss and loved it. He drove a big, two-ton truck, a Jimmy or Chevy. It was not user friendly: sat high with a large cargo box with heavy doors and latches; split in the middle with bakery stuff in the rear and groceries forward; everything from 100-pound bags of sugar to light boxes of ground pepper. I asked him once how he got paid: Nine cents an item, large or small.

Over time, I would work with him in the summers, and he taught me to drive that monster in traffic and on narrow streets. He taught me to plan ahead. If I got stuck in traffic, or something I could have avoided, he would remind me that he got paid to deliver, not drive. That would stick with me and define my feelings about fighter pilots who couldn't hit the target. I always felt it's what we got paid for. Flying was so much fun, but it was all about delivering the goods.

My dad was on-the-job for 39 years, winter, summer, sick or well. It was his job, and he was proud of it and the responsibility it carried. There was no retirement plan or big parting gifts or a gold watch at the end of the ride, just the last paycheck and, "So long."

My mom was a classic mother of the day: Nurturing, a teacher of manners and a wonderful homemaker. She could do more with leftovers than a TV chef can do with a full pantry. Friends or family would drop in, "Stay for dinner," was the call, and the magic would begin; always room for one more. During the war she took a job with Sprague Electric Company soldering the ends of condensers. Until she figured it out, there were a lot of burns and blisters.

Sometimes Dad would help Mom out with the cooking. He had been a cook in the Army in the '20s. His favorite dish was Army

SOS, shit on a shingle. If we complained, he would remind us he cooked for 600 men, and in unison we would reply, "Yeah, but only 200 lived."

From the very beginning, I had a love of airplanes. Lindbergh was still a big hero, and in the living room we had a picture of him in front of the Spirit of St. Louis and a picture of FDR at his desk.

In the late '30s and early '40s, my entertainment consisted of comic strips and about half a dozen 15-minute AM radio shows that ran from about 4:00 to 5:30 in the afternoon. I think they were designed to keep kids busy while their moms prepared dinner. Captain Midnight, Don Wilson of the Navy, "CX4, CX4, Calling Control Tower. This is Hop Harrigan coming in," And my favorite, Terry and the Pirates, a clang of Oriental cymbals and some Asian gibberish, and I was there with Terry and his macho guardian, Pat Ryan.

As the war progressed, so did these strips. Pat would become an Air Corp colonel and would pin Terry's wings on when he graduated as a cadet from a Chinese flying school. I still have a copy of that script. He tells Terry that as hot as he might be, he wouldn't turn a wheel without the entire force behind him.

It would stick. These scripts were also reinforced by the Saturday afternoon double features in the Adams Theater, 10 cents that went up to 11 with the war tax. The movies were great: 30 Seconds Over Tokyo, a Yank in the RAF, Flying Tigers, Captains of the Clouds, all with the theme of the excitement of flying, fighting, winning and getting the girl. Who wouldn't want to be a fighter pilot?

One problem: I hated school. My mother took me to the first grade, and at the very first recess I walked home. She marched me right back to Miss Nina King. And so started years of daydreaming about flying and drawing airplanes and dogfight scenes on my project papers.

During these days we had a lot of air activity over our heads. Thunderbolts were coming off Long Island and Grummans from Beth Page. Squadrons were being put together at Bradley and Westover. TBMs would make mock attacks across the lake. I could still see us hanging out of the school windows as Hellcats chased P-47s so close we could see the pilots.

On one spring day with patchy snow still on the ground, a neighbor friend and I were walking across fields from school to home. We looked up, and an olive drab P-47 with an orange nose passed over heading east at what I would now say was about 1,500-2,000 ft. We sat on the hillside and watched him cruise across the valley. As he reached the other side, without warning, he rolled left and went down. We looked at each other and blared out, "I think it crashed!" We ran home and told my friend's mother. No big response there. I caught my dad shoveling snow off the walk, and he gave me the old, "Sure, sure."

About that time, the rural school bus was heading up the other side of the valley with my classmates, and as they passed a field, there was the Thunderbolt. There was one apple tree in that field, and the P-47 pilot caught it. The bus driver and the kids ran to the wreckage. The pilot was alive but badly injured, and as they tried to get him out, he expired.

That was traumatic for 10 and 12-year-olds who only saw the war on film and in Life Magazine. On the weekend, a flatbed came and picked up the hulk, and there was a lot of .50 caliber ammunition around town as remembrances of that day. This crash didn't dampen my love of airplanes, fighter planes.

With the war over and in high school, I did a little better. I had a math teacher who had been a gunner on a B-17 who spent most of the war at a ski lodge in Switzerland. He took a liking to me, unlike the principal, and helped me catch up on some basics and a touch of algebra. At this time, I was part-time working in "trailer sales" in town. The owner's son, Norm Dean, was a Navy vet who went to Embry Riddle in Florida on the GI Bill. He got an aircraft A&E ticket and suggested I attend and add a commercial pilot rating. I liked the idea of both. He also had a black '49 Mercury that he would let me use on dates -- wonderful.

In addition to my trailer work, the Deans had goats and chickens, and so a lot of my weekends and after school work was directed at that, milking a dozen goats in the cold, dark early a.m. of winter and collecting eggs from half a dozen coops. That wasn't my idea of the good life, and all this for 50 cents an hour. Time for a career change.

Everett Lamb, my godfather, owned and ran an auto garage just up the street. Tools and engines looked better to me than all that goat and chicken manure. He gave me an after-school and Saturday job pumping gas, cleaning parts, running stock, and changing a lot of tires.

Fred, a Navy Vet, and Bob, his younger brother, were great to be around as were another three or four mechanics working there. Still 50 cents an hour, but I bought a '38 Ford convertible with a rumble seat for $200. Because I worked at the garage I got gas for 15 cents a gallon and parts at cost and a lot of free fixes. I was dating a great girl, who I would marry in the years to come. I was in a great place.

I was also building and flying a lot of model airplanes. Another vet, Tony Biagini, took an interest in this with me. He had also used the G.I. bill to get a private pilot ticket at Harriman Airport in North Adams, Massachusetts. He asked if I wanted to learn to fly. I was 16, and he said I could take lessons and get my private when I turned 17. "You 'betcha!" The next Sunday, we went to Harriman, and he introduced me to George West, the FBO owner and a well-known name in New England aviation. He said it would cost me about $300. It cost $11.50 for an hour of dual. The instructor got $5.00, and the airplane got $6.50. I was making about $18 a week. No sweat. I had money left over for gas, burgers and a date. It was a different America.

My first ride was not an auspicious start. After a short demo of what the controls did, he had me point the airplane at Mt. Graylock and hold that heading. I was nervous and sweating and worked so hard in trying to keep it straight I made myself sick and filled a burp bag with breakfast. Had I just pointed at the mountain and let go, it would have done much better on its own. I never chucked in an airplane again for the next 52 years of active flying.

My senior year and graduating from Adams High School in Adams, Massachusetts in 1953 could have been the pilot script for Happy Days, right down to painted whitewalls on old cars, white shirts, jeans, ducktails and girls in poodle skirts. For a guy who started off hating school, I was a bit sad to have to give up that part. I was living the life of "the Fonz."

About that time, I made the "acquaintance" of a state police officer. The details we won't go into now. The officer had come to our house to question me and I was in the basement working on a model airplane engine. It turned out he had been a pilot in World War II and we got to talking airplanes. The Korean War was over and a lot of World War II pilots who had been called up were getting out. He asked what my plans were. I told him I wanted to be a fighter pilot but had no college and it required at least two years. I told him my fallback position was attending Embry Riddle. He said, "Let's take a crack at the Air Force and Navy recruiters and see if there's a way of getting around this." He would go with me and ask the right questions.

The Navy stonewalled. No two years, no chance. Captain Crookshanks, the Air Force recruiter, an F-86 pilot from Korea, was a lot more promising. He said if I passed the entry test, I could go through Aviation Cadets as a navigator, do one year as a navigator, and then request pilot training. It sounded good to me. He had a deal. In November, I went to Samson Air Force Base in New York for three days of physical and mental testing.

Fate truly is the hunter. While testing was going on, an airman went down the line of the 33 in my group and said there was a need for more pilot assignments in the next few classes and anyone who qualified and wanted to change to pilot training, speak up. "Wow!" Can you imagine? The right place at the right time.

During testing, we had to pee in a bottle. I just couldn't. All the bottles were placed on a lab table, and I hung back as the group started to move on. I picked up a bottle that "looked good" and poured some in mine. I guess the guy was okay. When we finished, we sat in a briefing room surrounded by aviation cadet posters. I wanted to be in one of those pictures.

A sergeant came in and went to the podium. He thanked us all for our interest and effort and then called out a list of names, but not mine. He excused those to leave, and I expected the 13 of us remaining would get the thanks for coming, we'll call you speech. Not so. We were the chosen ones. What a wonderful feeling, yet not realizing that the best times and some of the toughest times of my life were about to begin:

For once you have tasted flight,
You will walk the earth with your eyes turned skyward;
For there you have been.
And there you long to return.

...Leonardo Da Vinci

Aviation Cadets: I just turned 18, and the minimum age for the program was 18 and a half. I would be eligible after December 9th of '53. In a matter of days I received a formal letter from the Air Force of acceptance and a start class date for preflight at Lackland in January of '54; orders and travel to follow.

It came by the numbers, and my mother drove me to the Pittsfield, Massachusetts rail station on January 14th. The morning was 22 below, and I remember the snow crunching as I walked to the train. I'd had a few supportive words from my dad the night before. He wasn't much for deep talk, and I was glad. Mom was a bit choked up but put on a big smile even with frozen tears on her cheeks.

My girl was already attending a junior college in Boston, and we had agreed to see how we felt about each other after a year apart. I think we both knew things wouldn't change as we had "dated" the first time as kids at a birthday party when we were about nine, but then we started seriously dating as sophomores in high school.

The train to Springfield, Massachusetts, a short physical, a swearing-in and a plane trip to San Antonio were just a blur. Then, the first two weeks or so under the "in your face" harassing by upper classmen, made it even more unreal. We started out with two floors of double bunks in an old World War II barracks, and in 12 weeks, we were down to one floor and nobody on a top bunk.

Once I had gotten used to the routine, it just became a game to outwit the upper class. After we, Class 55 L, became "that" upperclass, the load lightened, and I began to really enjoy my classmates and the cooperate-to-graduate attitude. We became the first of many "bands of brothers" I would find great comfort and satisfaction with, the Friday pilots lunch group being the latest.

In the spring, I was assigned to Primary training at Columbus Air Force Base, Mississippi, a contract flying school operated by California Eastern. A short check out and solo in the Piper Cub and then to what looked like the biggest airplane in the world, the fire belching T-6 Texan. It got small fast, and I could hardly wait to solo and spend some time just enjoying the roar of its engine and being free and on my own. "Alone in the air" was intoxicating for me. I knew I had to get a fighter assignment out of there. After six months, my class standings were high enough to get an early pick, and I chose the single engine jet fighter course at Bryan, Texas, the T-28 and the T-33.

My Primary instructor was an easygoing, patient man who was calm and forgiving. Nice, but probably didn't get the best I could have given. It was work but fun. On the other hand, my Basic instructor was just the opposite. He was an F-86 first lieutenant from Korea who rolled everything an instructor was not supposed to be into one person: screaming, swearing, jerking the airplane out of my hands and banging my head against the canopy, disorienting me and then handing the controls back to me and saying, "Now, Goddammit, do it right, or I'll have you on a bus to the navigator's school tonight." Oh, no, the picnic was over!

Fear and failure were now my constant companions. I would wake up at night and swear they were standing at the end of my bed scowling at me. This is not a joke. When I finally went solo in the T-28 in formation, I would be on the wing, he, in the backseat of the lead ship glaring at me, me flying wing with that big prop just feet away from his seat. I wanted to kill that sombitch so much! The good part of this: it's what I needed. Did he know? I don't think so, but the result had me second in my class.

My roommate, Al Bulhman, (no kidding), ex-crop duster, was first. With fighter slots slim in '55, we only got three fighter assignments in the class, one F-86 and 2 F-84s (sorry, Bob, we didn't count the two F-86D spots). We had a helicopter, a B-29, an HU-16, a C-119 and other odds and ends. Al took the F-86, and I, second choice, got a supersonic F-84F slot at Luke Air Force Base, Arizona, one of the first classes in the F.

The "real" Air Force: Graduation was very special. My folks, one sister and my girl, Margie, came to Bryan for the event. I had written a letter to Margie's parents asking for their approval to ask Marg to marry me. I'm sure my mother-in-law to be had many reservations. In any case, I got their blessing and bought a ring and popped the question at graduation. Acceptance added the frosting to receiving my wings and commission as a Second Lieutenant in the United States Air Force. Off to Laughlin Air Force Base on the Rio Grande at Del Rio, Texas, for three months of lead-in gunnery training in the armed T-33. Then, on to Luke for the F-84F.

"You love a lot of things if you live around them,
but there isn't any woman and there isn't any
horse, not any before, nor any after that is as
lovely as an airplane. And men who love them
are faithful to them, even though they leave
them for others. A man has only one virginity
to lose in fighters, and if it is a lovely plane he
loses it to, there his heart will ever be."

...Ernest Hemmingway, circa 1944.

I checked into Luke and found my F-84F class didn't start for a couple of weeks. My training squadron commander said, "Go out to mobile and watch some landings." I grabbed a folding chair and hitched a ride to mobile sitting facing the approach end of the runway. There was a speaker on the outside of mobile. A student checked-in with a rough engine and then a flameout. His IP on the wing talked him to a low key and had him set up for a high base, and it looked good until the gear came down.

The F-84F flew on little lift and a lot of lower wing surface ram. With the gear down, there wasn't much lower surface, and the nose came up as he tried to stretch it to the runway. A few short yaw movements left and right and then a roll to inverted and an impact and explosion. I observed enough landings and returned to the swimming pool, a bit shaken but okay.

At the pool, aircraft in the break to the downwind passed over the pool. A flight of Fs pitched out and individually passed overhead. The first three looked normal. The fourth was low, and as he passed, turned slightly right and ejected. Just another day at Luke.

The early split tail 84-Fs were accidents waiting to happen. My checkout reflected that, and I ended up flying the E, F and G while there and finished in the G. Luke was a very exciting place. I would be back there for F-100 and A-7 checkout later in my career, and it wouldn't have changed much.

First Assignment: Prior to leaving Luke, I received an assignment to the Far East, Misawa, Japan. I called Margie and passed on that news. For a bit, she was stunned until I explained it was an accompanied tour and after we were married, she would join me there. With that, we confirmed our plans. We were married on December 18th, 1955. After a 17-day honeymoon, I shipped out, and she joined me seven months later.

By then, I was established in the 8th Fighter Bomber Squadron of the 49th Fighter Bomber Group, still flying the straight wing F-84G but now with the added responsibility of delivering the MK-7, 47-kiloton nuclear bomb: a 21 year-old juvenile delinquent with a nuke. It was a great first assignment with a special squadron commander, Paul Imig. We called him 1 MIG. If ever I became a squadron commander, I would remember his teachings.

We were mostly young, newly married couples. Our social time as a group was wonderful, and following the great flying, parties were next on our list. Experience may be the best teacher, but expensive, and I almost made the full payment a number of times while learning the fighter trade. We lost seven pilots from the squadron during my stay, and I got my first taste of being a Summary Courts Officer, caring for the effects and the family of a lost mate. It wouldn't be the last.

In the late '50s, a large reduction in force was reducing fighter assignments. Many pilots were being assigned to motor pools, air police, GCI and other non-flying support positions. In 1959, I was very fortunate to be assigned to Westover Air Force Base, Massachusetts, 40 miles from my hometown, as a T-33 IP in SAC's Jet Upgrade Program, JUG.

JUG was a program designed to transition support prop pilots to jets. It appeared the underlying reason for the program was to reduce the number of support pilots who were flying solely for pay. Many were not at all comfortable wearing a crash helmet in a tandem seated single engine jet after years of side-by-side relaxed multiengine flying. I called it a Flying Evaluation Board, FEB, in a bread truck, as many just gave up their wings in the van returning to OPS.

At Misawa, Margie and I added a son, Steven, to our family, and at Westover, a daughter, Liseann. Life was good there, but I didn't realize it. I wanted back to TAC and fighters. I had gone to Instrument Pilot Instructor School, IPIS, while there and then became the Officer In Charge (OIC) of the 8th Air Force Instrument Refresher School, a week of annual boredom required by all Air Force pilots of the day.

I took the challenge of turning that week into something of value for those forced to attend. It worked, and pilots began sending glowing letters of enthusiasm rather than hate mail. The school got an outstanding from SAC inspectors. General Hunter Harris, the 8th commander, had attended and asked if there was anything I needed.

I told him I had been trying to get an assignment to combat crew training, but I couldn't get the request off the base. He said run it through again and note that it would be for his endorsement. I did, and it flew through, but with no results. The general's aide finally told me that he couldn't endorse a command change for an up and coming young officer, but that the 8th Air Force DO, General Walter Sweeney, would.

When I reported in a military manner to General Sweeney, he returned my salute and glared at me with red-faced anger. He rose and came to me face-to-face and began cursing and ranting about how fighter pilots thought the sun rose and set on their asses and they didn't have the big picture. He approved my request with a, "I better not see you again," statement, and I left in shock and awe. The strange part: I would meet him again when he became the commander of TAC and the leader of all those idiot fighter pilots who "thought the sun rose and set on their asses and didn't have the big picture."

So, after an 18-month SAC tour, I was back at Luke Air Force Base for a full six-month F-100 checkout followed by three months at Nellis for the HUN(D) top off program. A close friend, Monty Montgomery, and I were assigned to the 18th TAC fighter wing in Okinawa. The wing was to shortly start F-105 transition at Nellis, so the plan had Monty and I staying at Nellis, towing "dart" targets twice a day until our squadron, the 44th TAC fighter squadron, showed up. It didn't!

Multiple groundings of the newly-gained THUDs delayed all plans. We ended up checking into the 44th at Kadena and flew the HUN for the next six months. Of course, just after we got our families situated on Okinawa, we were back to Nellis for two or three months in F-105 training.

We lost two pilots during training, one to a mid-air with a civilian light plane, and the other badly injured by the prop of another light plane. We ended our checkout and went to the Republic plant on Long Island, picked up new 105s and "high flighted" them to Okinawa. We spent the next year getting combat ready, and sometime in '64, we deployed to Korat, Thailand on a training exercise.

Little did we know it was the prep phase for the large scale air effort that was about to begin in Laos and North Vietnam. I did a couple of two-month tours flying "non-counters" in Laos.

I never thought the guys who were shot down in Laos and were never heard from felt they were non-counters. After we acknowledged we were active in Laos, they became counters, and I ended up with a 117 combat missions. The 44th ended up being permanently assigned to Korat as the 13th TAC Fighter Squadron, and I would fly my last 50 missions under that banner.

About that time, my family was still on base at Kadena, and we added another son to our mix, Richard. I flew a lot of great missions with many great leaders and wingmen. War is not fun, but I can never say I didn't enjoy flying combat. It was the one time in my life I felt I knew what I was doing, except maybe the last day...when I had to bailout.

And that's how I ended up in the back of an HU16 on the 3rd of September '66. After a short recuperation, I returned to my hometown and the family for a month or two of leave before starting another dozen active flying and staff jobs in the Air Force.

In 1970, following a tour at TAC headquarters, I was the OPS officer and then commander of the Operational Test and Evaluation Team for the newly acquired A-7D. During that time, I demo-d the A-7D to MAC as a replacement for the A-1E prop-driven search and rescue aircraft in Southeast Asia, "the Sandys." My demo took, and before long, I was back at Korat as the OPS officer and then commander of the 3d TAC Fighter Squadron, now the "A-7D" Sandys.

Just before I arrived, the 3d had participated in Linebacker missions in North Vietnam and the end of the air war in the North. Now all combat flying was in Cambodia, a far cry from the MiGs, missiles and guns of the North; a lot of close air support and interdiction in support of the then Cambodian government against the Communist backed insurgents up until the last day on August 15th, 1973.

I had received orders to the Fighter Weapons School at Nellis; however, there was a fly in the ointment. I received a phone call one night from a major at TAC personnel. He said I would be receiving orders shortly. I told him I had them in hand. "You can forget those," he said. "You're going to Shaw Air Force Base, South Carolina."

"What fighters do they fly there?" was my reply.

"They don't," he said. "You are going to a staff job at 9th Air Force.

I said, "Let me guess. The director of TAC assignments, that brigadier general, got wind of it?"

"Yup, and his guidance was, send that 'sumbitch so deep in a staff he'll never smell JP-4 again."

I was stunned but not surprised. I had a history of ill-timed buzz jobs and illegal flybys that I had tap-danced out of over my career. Remember, I was a student of the World War II Class B movies and comic strips. Often, I was Van Johnson in a Guy Named Joe, or Charles C. Charles, Hot Shot Charlie, a character in Terry and the Pirates. They were always beating up somebody's airport and getting away with it; great in the comics, not so good in what was now a peacetime Air Force.

So, I did find myself in the 9th Air Force training shop, scheduling flare ships, Air National Guard man-days and even the DO's retirement party while flying the T-Bird as much as possible.

Then, after finding out that I had both A-7 and F-100 time, the director of 9th Air Force, Stan Eval branch, asked me if I would like to work with them, "dual currency." I think I'll smell JP-4 again, a lot of it! I did and began flying evaluations of all the A-7 and F-100 active and Guard units east of the Mississippi, also with the option of regularly borrowing one of their planes for currency flying.

I was out-briefing the 9th Air Force commander regularly and was receiving glowing efficiency reports with great endorsements from the 9th Air Force commander. About then, the director of TAC personnel got wind of what I was doing and informed the 9th commander of my past indiscretions. My next OER was Outstanding, however the endorsement simply read, "Do not concur." That pretty well established the end of my career progression. It had become obvious: I was my own worst enemy.

As my tour at Shaw was coming to an end, I wrangled an assignment as the Air Force Advisor to the South Carolina Air National Guard unit, a wing that had just converted from F-102s and the air defense mission to the A-7D and to a tactical strike mission. They were current in the airplane but not wildly enthusiastic at throwing their bodies at the ground from a low level dash to a pop-up to dive-bombing, not at all like flying straight and level under a GCI controller's direction.

I did get the commander to move a few pilots to positions more suited to the mission and began making some headway. My goal was getting them prepared for attending Red Flag, a combat exercise at Nellis, often tougher than actual combat. They attended and did well, and I felt great satisfaction.

When we got back to our home base, McEntire ANGB, South Carolina, I asked the commander how he liked attending Red Flag. His reply was, "Wonderful, but we'll never do that again." Well, they would as they eventually converted to the F-16 and were the first Guard unit to deploy to the first Gulf War in 1991. They excelled.

In 1978, on an A7 cross-country flight, I over-nighted in Tucson and visited an old friend and future Friday pilot, Jack Francisco, who was a production pilot with Learjet in Tucson. A visit to Learjet with a flight line of new, shiny planes the size of a fighter and a flight room of ex-fighter pilots all of whom had flown the F-100 looked like a great way to transition to a civilian life without pulling my mental throttle to cutoff. They offered me a job, and I took it.

Life after: After 24 years in the Air Force, I felt I would put in another 10 with Lear. In two weeks, I was out of the Air Force and starting on a completely new career that would last for 26 years. I became a utility infielder at Learjet, production tests, experimental, demo pilot and as an FAA-designated engineering representative, DER test pilot, completing the certification of many supplemental aircraft modifications. I was doing this worldwide and in some not-so-comfortable locations: Yugoslavia just as the Communist block was dissolving, South Africa during apartheid when Americans were not appreciated, and I was damned near sent to jail on both of those trips.

We did a lot of military demos towing various airborne targets. In Germany I got to fly with Condor, historically the company that had German pilots fly as volunteers in the Spanish Civil War.

In 2004 while I was working in Oklahoma on the certification of new fan jet engines for older Lears, I discovered a small lump in the corner of my eye. The short of it: cancer, radiation, retina detachment in both eyes, followed by a number of eye operations. I spent three years working or fighting with the FAA to get my commercial medical back. After flying a single vision flight check with an FAA examiner, I did. All I needed was one eye, 20/20, and to demonstrate being safe and capable.

Learjet got wind and called me to go back to work. I gave it some thought, but felt I couldn't give an honest evaluation to the customer. Throughout my career with Lear, I never felt I worked for the company but for the next pilot to fly that airplane. So that was that: 52 years of active flying came to an end.

Was there life after jets? I missed it desperately for some time but found other endeavors with family and friends. When I look back, I can't believe what I see in the rear view mirror: a kid who had been walking in the woods with his trusty Daisy air rifle, to sitting at lunch on a Friday with a group of aviators so diverse and so skilled as these.

Fate, luck, effort? When we visit, I don't at all see us as we are now, be-speckled, hard of hearing, slow-moving, but as we were: aggressive, competitive, and with an amazing attitude of getting a job done, no matter how hard it was or what fright might go with it.

Like Lou Gehrig said: "I'm the luckiest man on the face of the earth."

June 9, 2014 (My 80th birthday!)

CHAPTER SEVENTEEN

Vietnam and Desert Storm, Bookends to My Career
by Robert B. "Rob" Van Sice, Jr.

Youth: I was born in Helena, Montana in 1945, to Rob and Mary Van Sice. Dad had been a very young WWII P-38 pilot, flying in North Africa and Italy with two confirmed kills and three probables, and was in College at Montana State when I was born. I was the oldest of four, three boys and a girl. Peggy, the youngest, and I are the surviving siblings.

Growing up, mostly in Idaho and Montana, was good...lots of outdoor time, camping, hunting, fishing and generally horsing around. Mom and Dad were demanding, so we were all good students graduating high school and college with honors. I attended Montana State University, graduating as an Electrical Engineer. I thrived in college, getting good grades while belonging to a fraternity, being a member of several honoraries and participating in four years of ROTC.

During the transition from my sophomore to junior year of college in 1965, ROTC first offered scholarships. Up to that point I really had no intention of going "advanced" ROTC, but when I realized that with a scholarship came enough free money to buy my first car ('56 Chevy -- $350.00), I applied for and got the grant. Little did I know that by choosing a car, I chose my life's future, the best choice I could possibly have made.

As a senior, I was President of my fraternity, taking flight lessons in FIP, and dating Lynne, my future wife. As our relationship got more serious, we decided we would get married, but only after she did one more year of college to graduate, and I went to Vietnam, something I wanted to do. I quickly came to the realization it would be at least three years before we married, and wisely convinced her we should marry prior to pilot training, then she could do her senior year while I was in Vietnam....and that's the way it happened.

Vietnam, F-4, 1ˢᵗ Lt in front: I did well in pilot training. Having a fighter pilot for a father, there was no question in my mind but that I would be one too.

In those days ('67-'68) pilot training was loaded to fill the pipeline. My class consisted of ROTC and OTS Lts many of whose objectives were: to avoid being a ground pounder draftee, or to get wings and become an airline pilot. Many of them washed out. About 60% of our initial cadre actually got their wings.

Our instructors at that time (Vance AFB, 1967-68), in both my T-37 and T-38 flights, were either FAIPs (First Assignment IPs, always in Training Command) or transport pilots; so, while being great guys and good instructors, their emphasis (and knowledge) was not from the fighter world....in fact, I don't recall having a single training flight with a fighter guy. That didn't deter me, nor did the fact that almost all of the class assignments for those graduating before us were trainers, bombers, heavies, or backseat F-4s. I didn't want those, so I busted my tail to graduate high enough to get my choice. My goal was to get an F-105 or F-100, with an F-106, 102, 101, or A-1E being the backup choice.

I was not number one, and the guy ahead of me was gifted as a pilot, but because "his wife didn't want him to go to Vietnam" he chickened out at the last minute and chose FAIP. That made it clear I was going to get what I wanted, "if" any fighters were in our assignment block.

At graduation, the unthinkable happened: our block was loaded with fighters, such that even the number 12 guy got an F-105. The other thing we got in our block was the first "frontseat pilot F-4" choice. I recall there being four frontseat F-4 choices spread among the several ATC base classes graduating with us. You can't imagine the confliction I felt, having decided on Thud or Hun, yet realizing the Phantom represented the future of fighter aviation. I chose the F-4. I regret not having flown the Century Series but am confident I made the right choice.

F-4 RTU was at George AFB, CA, and it was one heck of a challenge, not only because I was new to fighters, but because I and one other, were the first "lieutenant" (green bean) Aircraft Commanders. Additionally, most of the class frontseaters were upgrading GIBs with a tour in Vietnam behind them and a second tour in Vietnam facing them. They were not happy campers to see us in the frontseat without having "paid our dues!"

My instructor at George was a great guy, a major just out of Fighter Weapons School with a Navy exchange tour in SEA prior to that. He'd never been a backseater and had never instructed from the backseat until he got me. Initially, he was thrilled to have me, expecting he could create a skilled fighter pilot out of the skinny Second Lt he'd been assigned. I became a good fighter pilot, but nearly at the cost of "his" career. We got to meet the Wing Commander more than once, with the big event being, when on my first ever inflight refueling (him in the back), I managed to get into a "dutch roll" and break the boom off the tanker while tearing out the receptacle on our airplane. We had to make a cable arrestment on landing, followed by meeting Col Harry Trimble. That wasn't the only event, and I'm sure my IP still curses his memories of flying with me.

En route to Phu Cat and the 480th Tactical Fighter Squadron (F-4Ds) I had some surgery and a resulting delay in departing the USA, causing a loss of landing currency. When I arrived at Phu Cat, the squadron was at a loss how to handle me. I was only their second first lieutenant with my predecessor (and sponsor) having just been put in the backseat as punishment for something he'd done. They didn't even have an IP qualified to get my landing currency back..... plus that would be a wasted sortie! It all worked out and I started flying combat about three sorties later.

I clearly remember, on my eighth combat mission being part of a close air support (CAS) two-ship assigned to a "troops-in-contact" mission in the Mekong Delta region of RVN, flying under a 600-800 ft. ceiling - talk about a steep learning curve! Just staying geographically oriented, achieving the correct "restricted run-in" and not dropping ("Snake and Nape") on the friendlies, was all I could handle. I have no idea how my backseater survived that flight, but I think I "earned my spurs" and became an accepted member of the gang at that point.

The 480th was typical of "in-country" fighter squadrons at the time. "In country" meant stationed in Vietnam under MACV (Military Assistance Command, Vietnam) as opposed to the 13th Air Force squadrons stationed in Thailand. The differences were astounding: the MACV folks (me) got R&R (usually Hawaii or Australia) and a possible C-47 flight for a weekend in Hong Kong. The 13th AF crews had the same R&R, plus multiple weekends in Bangkok or similar "garden spots," and 30 days leave in the USA. I met up with one of my college fraternity brothers "on the tanker" one evening (voice recognition) where he proceeded to tell me about just returning from Bangkok and his pending leave in the USA. We, on the other hand, got lots of combat flying! Our missions were highly diverse, normally as two-ships. We flew day and night CAS throughout the country to include some extraordinary missions protecting fire support bases from Vietcong and NVA, whom we sometimes had to "strafe off the fences."

We flew about 50% of our missions bombing "the Trail" (Ho Chi Minh Trail) in Laos at night, working with FACs as we dive-bombed trucks, convoys, holding yards, and a lot of trees. Ours was always an interesting mission because we flew as two-ships, but worked the targets singly. We would "black out" our lights as we worked the target, so the gunners could only shoot at our sound… seldom accurately. They employed 37mm anti-aircraft guns, that fired a tracer every fifth round. The tracers were very visible, easily defeated, and in a strange way "beautiful" to watch. I was happy if I saw them and scared if I didn't, because I knew they were always shooting.

There were also some day-missions on the Trail that were very sporty and very high risk. We were "seeding" the Trail, usually with mines, but sometimes sensors, which required very low altitude, non-maneuvering and somewhat slow-speed delivery passes…in the road passes between Laos and North Vietnam. In two-ship flights, one aircraft would hold high observing the other make his delivery, then we traded places….the second aircraft was sure to get a warm welcome. We minimized the "level, non-maneuvering, and slow" delivery passes, and hence, never lost anyone on those missions.

We also flew "Combat Skyspot" missions on which we were guided by a radar site and told when to release our bombs. We viewed this as the ultimate waste of flying time and bombs, but someone deemed it important and appropriate.

We played a big role in the Cambodia invasion, which was then, "Top Secret." Lots of crazy stuff went on as we flew what were essentially CAS missions without a FAC. There were few defenses, so the missions were not high threat, but still demanding because of the proximity of "friendlies" to the targets.

Phu Cat occasionally got rocketed by the Vietcong, seldom with any serious effect other than waking us up. Usually, the sirens went off after the first rocket hit, so the wakeup was a bit jarring. The "standard" was to immediately roll-off your bed and under it. Normally, the concussion would knock the overhead fluorescent light covers off the fixtures which landed in the space between our beds. Amazingly, the light covers always seemed to land on top of me as I hit the floor for my roll. We had helmets and flak vests to don during attacks. The first attack during my tour was the first in a long time for Phu Cat, so the reactions were hysterical. Our "hooch" doorknobs would not unlock when you opened them, so closing them resulted in being locked out. You have to imagine seeing almost 100% of the pilots in their underwear with flak vests and helmets on, standing outside their closed and locked doors waiting for the CE locksmith to come let them back inside.

We had lots of morale problems at Phu Cat, particularly late in my tour. I attribute them to many things, but among them were: GIBS were leaving, replaced by navigators, many of whom were not really WSOs and not at all happy; also, many older pilots were coming from ATC, MAC and occasionally SAC (majors and lieutenant colonel "retreads" who had no business being in fighters or in the war) who were also not happy. The retreads were afraid, they were not skilled pilots, and the navigators had to fly with them....and, we junior fighter pilots had to be their wingmen because they were senior to us. Several unnecessary "combat losses" occurred because the wrong guy was up front. It got to the point where some navigators refused to fly. It was an ugly situation.

I flew 150 combat missions at Phu Cat, staying for an entire year. I look back on that as one of the best years of my career, because I learned so much. I only wish that McNamara and his ilk had been in the thick of it to see what they were doing to our people and the nation, rather than bragging about it long after the fact!

One last Lieutenant story; My assignment after Phu Cat was Misawa, Japan. As orders came, so did notification that I could not take Lynne with me due to housing problems. Having spent a full year apart (she did finish her degree per our plan), I was not interested in more separation, so I concocted a "plan." We had friends from RTU at Misawa who agreed we could stay with them until housing opened up, but I had to go to Misawa to get all the paperwork prepared, signed, etc. Sooo, I got leave orders signed to go to Japan, independent of my PCS orders back to the States via Japan (and then returning to Japan). Here's how it worked:

- I left Phu Cat on leave orders, space available on a C-141 to Kadena, with the intent of getting another C-141 to Japan; however, when I got there, Kadena was in the middle of a Typhoon evac, and no aircraft were leaving.
- Nearby, Naha was evacuating all of their C-130s, and one was heading for Misawa—perfect! I caught a cab to Naha, got there in time and boarded the C-130 as their only PAX.
- En route, the C-130 lost an engine and landed at Itazuki airport, formerly a U.S. Air Base.
- From Itazuki, I flew commercially to Tokyo Airport, then found my way to Yokota Air Base.
- At Yokota, I switched to my PCS orders so that I could catch the Air America C-54 that serviced Misawa.
- I got to Misawa, had my orders amended, flew back to Yokota via the C-54, and made my portcall at Yokota, returning to the States just as planned.
- No one ever questioned me on my travels, and Lynne and I got to spend six months in Misawa prior to PCSing with the Wing to Kadena.

Life as a Lieutenant was pretty darned good!

Desert Storm, F-16 Colonel, D.O.: Many years later (1989), after teaching at Nellis in both the Wild Weasel School (F-4C) and the Fighter Weapons School (F-4E), serving as a Flight Commander and Wing Chief of Weapons and Tactics at Torrejon, having a TAC Staff job in Operational Requirements (DR), taking an F-16 unaccompanied assignment to Kunsan, serving as an F-16 Squadron Commander at MacDill AFB, and moving to the Pentagon to serve in RD/AQ as a

Colonel Select, I was chosen to go to Shaw AFB to be the 363rd Wing DO, working for Col Ed Eberhart. The best job I ever had.

Ed was the ideal boss. He was the Wing Commander, and I was his DO. Once he knew he could trust my judgment, I had pretty much complete purview over the flying operation, so long as I kept him aware of what I was doing. He never interfered.

We had three F-16C/D (block 25) squadrons (17th TFS, 19th TFS, and 33rd TFS), along with the last active duty RF-4C Squadron, the 16th TRS; what a dream job, with four superb squadron commanders, a great friend as Chief of Maintenance, Col Bud Templin, and very strong 0-6s at every position. Additionally, the pilots were phenomenal. These were the cream of the crop by any measure, and the younger they were, the more impressive; smart, physically fit, fun loving, and skilled fighter pilots....but only the Wing Commander, myself, and one of our Squadron Commanders had been in combat; hard to imagine in today's world, but not back then.

Shaw was a two-year assignment (if I did well), with six years of excitement crammed in. We had an ORI (Excellent), a Hurricane (Hugo) and a war. What more could a fighter pilot ask for?

Then it came time for the war: Saddam invaded Kuwait on 2 August, 1990, the 1st Wing (F-15s) began to deploy, and we followed immediately after. We took two squadrons, the 17th and the 33rd, with the 17th first, deploying 24 airplanes non-stop in groups of six. I was number three in the lead six leaving Shaw at 1700 on the 9th of August and arriving at Al Dhafra, UAE at 1700, 16 hours later. The flight was twice as long as an F-16 had flown non-stop, so there were questions about oil consumption, oxygen depletion, and a myriad of other "unknowns." Amazingly, we launched 24 with no air spares and landed all 24 at Al Dhafra the next day.

Flying over was quite an event. There were an incredible number of air refuelings, not all as planned. At the last minute during our deployment preparations, we decided to load two additional air-to-air Sidewinder missiles (making four total per airplane), thus changing our weight and drag profile. These were block 25 F-16s, among the real pigs of the Air Force, underpowered and overweight, so those missiles changed our service ceiling. Some of us had to tap burner to stay hooked-up on the tanker, and there were a couple of engine compressor stalls as a result (impressive at night). We didn't report them because we were intent on getting to the war! Also, the flight lead, Lt Col Billy Diehl (Squadron Commander of the 17th,) and I each had our air conditioning systems go "full cold," causing us a great deal of discomfort. I had numb fingers by the time we landed, despite all my attempts to "unfreeze" the system.

When we took off from Shaw, we had three possible destinations with the decision to be made at TAC Headquarters, but still TBD at departure time. Entering Saudi airspace, we were with our fifth tanker, a KC-10, which fortuitously had hot intercom through the boom into my cockpit. I hooked-up, asked them to HF me to Langley, and requested our destination. I think they'd forgotten about us, but the answer came quickly, "Al Dhafra!"

Al Dahfra meant another two + hours of flying without the tanker, meaning we had to get into the Air Traffic Control system to file a flight plan and fly down the Gulf that was full of USN ships and planes with whom we couldn't communicate and who didn't know we were coming. There was a storm of maps in the cockpits as we route planned, talked with the British expat controllers, and settled into our route.

In the meantime, our RWR and radars were working overtime with lots of false SAM warnings changing the pitch of a couple young pilots' voices (no prior combat). As we approached Qatar, we tracked a flight of four unknowns running a split intercept on us. We weren't talking with them, and ATC was not aware of them. Being prudent, we "spread" ourselves, armed chaff and flares, and thought about arming our sidewinders, but worked to appear "non-threatening" since the planes coming at us were flying from the south. We later learned they were USN F-18s and had been <u>cleared to shoot</u>. A very good Navy flight lead had gone for the visual ID and avoided an unpleasant first engagement of the Gulf Air War!

The total info we had on Abu Dhabi and Al Dhafra was a sketchy overhead photo of the runway and a TACAN frequency. We briefed that the smart thing to do if we ended up with Al Dhafra as our destination, was to not overfly Abu Dhabi, but to swing northwest of the airfield to avoid their HAWK missile defenses. All worked well and we landed with exactly 16.0 hours of flight time, as we had planned.

It was HOT, it was HUMID, and we didn't have our support element there! The C-141 with all our advance element and equipment had broken in Ramstein, so we were essentially alone. We taxied to park, parked ourselves without marshallers, safed our many missiles and devices and went to meet our hosts.

The UAE Defense Minister, our U.S. Ambassador and a multitude of dignitaries were there to meet and greet us. I was senior, and so had the privilege, frozen, dehydrated, exhausted and disinterested, to meet each individual, let them know how proud we were to be there, and tell them how much we appreciated the single pickup truck and school bus they were lending us. In two weeks we had 2500 plus USAF folks, a tent city, and 325 vehicles in place. What a ball!

Our support element arrived a day later, along with the 20 of 24 aircraft from the 33rd Squadron. Among the diverts, the 33rd Squadron Commander and his wingman had to land at Rota, Spain with an engine problem and were delayed almost two weeks in joining us.

Once in-place, we were dealing with **one** phone line for the entire wing to use to coordinate with TAC, Shaw, Riyadh and everyone else. Communications were resolved in a few days as we spun-up into a fully operational entity, but in the early days, it was a hoot!

Al Dhafra was a beautifully configured base with brand new German-built aircraft shelters for the UAE Mirages, but no space to set up our large operation or house our people. The Emirates Air Force were great hosts, but very uncertain that they wanted us there for any length of time....they weren't sure we weren't invading. The relationships warmed with time, and by the end of our seven-month stay we'd become good friends with many of them.

We were quickly given Al Dhafra's "Academy" building to house our wing and nearly all its functions. The DO functions to include the squadrons, intelligence, command post, mission planning, flight briefing rooms, etc. were crammed into the space which became, over time, our home.

It was August in the Gulf, with temperatures exceeding 115 F every day, with humidity in the 50-60% range, and nights cooling to 95 F. As a wing, our greatest immediate focus had to be in figuring out how to gain and maintain an alert status, safely function, run a full training schedule, build a tent city, create an enormous bomb storage area, and plan the coming war...all without letting the heat kill our folks.

The MA and I decided we would not fly during the middle of the day... it was simply too brutal, particularly with limited SAR capability. Initially, our logistics pipeline was tenuous as MAC tried to get their processes and tracking methods up-to-speed. While they were learning, we resorted to FEDEX. For the first several weeks, much of our spares and equipment came to us directly from Shaw via FEDEX...without them, it would have been pretty shaky.

For the first several weeks, we had an "alert" commitment to have planes and pilots armed, "cocked" and ready to head north if required. We also did a light "two-go" day, flying early and late sorties, getting our pilots some flying time while developing a feel for the environment. That environment drove us to quickly evolve our tactics.

We initially found intelligence to be a challenge. The whole system was designed to push information up to the generals, not to disseminate it quickly to the wings and aircrews where it was needed most. After a good deal of feedback to Riyadh, and replacement of an individual 0-6, the problem was largely resolved. I sent one of my more tenacious 0-5s to visit the planning "Jedi's" at Riyadh on a weekly basis. He always returned, after influencing the planning, in possession of thousands of pieces of overhead photography for our target planning.

Tactics evolved quickly. The mantra, when we deployed, was to avoid defenses by using very high speeds and low altitudes, then to "pop-up" and quickly deliver weapons. In short order, we discovered that low altitude visibility was universally terrible over the Gulf countries, making it nearly impossible to effectively fly formations in the numbers we required. We quickly morphed into medium altitude "large force employment" packages involving up to a hundred aircraft ingressing together (F-16, F-15, F-4G, EA-6B, and others). We rehearsed endlessly with multiple fullscale packages during Desert Shield...and we became very proficient at what we were doing. We even did 44-48 ship comm-out rejoins and refuelings with multi-tanker (up to six) cells...planned, rehearsed and exquisitely executed, time-after-time. Our ingress formations were built on multiple "line abreast" four-ships in 30-second trail at 20,000 ft. making a package quite long. Roll-ins were four-ship "echelon-to-trail" with absolute minimal spacing, planned for 45-degree dive bombing and near supersonic release of two 2000 pound "dumb" Mk-84s, using our CCIP aiming system (smart planes, dumb bombs). Bomb release was at about 14,000 ft. and recovery at 6-7 Gs, bottoming about 10,000 ft. When it became evident the defenses were not as effective as we expected, the altitudes were lowered, but not by much.

Al Dhafra, being in the UAE rather than Saudi Arabia, had gained an exemption from "General Order Number One" that banned alcohol…as a consequence we were a popular location to host most of the planning conferences that built our "game books" for working with the other aircraft and services while flying with minimal radio chatter.

Our tent city was extraordinary: a German construction firm had built the shelters shortly before our arrival. They left their construction camp, consisting of multiple "trailer-like buildings," abandoned in the on-base desert. We reconstituted their camp and built our tent city adjacent to it, so there were some actual structures among the tents. We eventually had a small hospital, a commissary, BX, gymnasium, beer hall, movie tent, chapel and "clubs" for people to use and enjoy in their off duty time.

The first three days of the war had been planned in extraordinary detail by our whole group working in coordination with the Riyadh Jedi's as well as the other wings. The plan was to transition to a daily Frag Order following the first days…and there is a story to be told later about that!

On 1 January 1991, we added a third squadron, the 10th TFS from Hahn AB, to our group; so now, we had 72+ F-16s and just over 100 pilots in the wing. The Wing Commander, Col Ray Huot, and I immediately decided two things…first, no 0-6s from Hahn would join us, and second, the 10th would be immediately and fully integrated into our wing and plans. They were an incredible squadron and very quickly spun-up to fly the new tactics and work for and with their new wing. We maintained squadron integrity flying in our four-ships, seldom mixing pilots, but early-on we decided to centrally schedule our aircraft ignoring squadron integrity. The result was nearly 100% daily maintenance availability enabling us to always "fill the Frag."

We had one real issue with mixing ECM pod-types in our formations. Hahn had ALQ-131 pods, while Shaw had ALQ-119s, and we had no confidence those could successfully function when mixed together. It turned out to be a non-issue, but was initially a real concern. In the early days headed for targets in and near Baghdad, the pods were a "big deal" and an absolute "go/no-go" criteria for crossing the border into IRAQ (as were the presence of our Eagle, Weasel, and USN EA-6B escorts).

Missions into the Baghdad area were six-seven hours in duration, with pre-strike refueling mandatory, and post-strike sometimes required. As rehearsed, the pre-strikes were all "comm-out" rejoins and refuelings involving up to 48 F-16s (usually eight jets per tanker) cycling on and off the boom in sequence and "pushing" at the right time to join all the support assets prior to border crossing.

It worked flawlessly for the first several days, but then broke down because the **tankers were not there**! The daily Frag Order coordination between SAC and TAC" broke down badly, and the weather was rotten for the first time in the deployment. We ended up with aircraft recovering on Riyadh taxiways, jettisoning fuel tanks while searching for divert airfields, and an endless list of near disasters (jettisoned fuel tanks falling through the overcast and landing in an Army mess tent w/o injuring anyone!). Clear-headed, professional and flexible flight leads performed magnificently in chaotic conditions, averting disasters and aircraft losses.

The tanker planning/scheduling was finally properly integrated and we reverted to Vietnam style "anchors." The tankers were individually and universally great in their support, to include making border crossings to rendezvous with "low fuel" jets coming home out of the northern parts of Iraq and even allowing 16 jets to fly on one KC-10, refueling in the weather, so we could make our "push" time.

Our initial missions were into the heart of the "defended" airspace around Baghdad, and we planned for high threat, using pods, Weasels, F-15s and other assets to dilute the defenses, while employing medium altitude, high speed, and rapid attacks to reduce exposure. We put 48 aircraft, each with two Mk-84s, and each with a unique aimpoint/target, on and off target in less than three minutes total time. It was awesome! And, we did it without loss or damage in those early days of the war.

One "funny" (not at the time) incident that happened was the unintended firing of Sidewinders: Our guys were highly-trained and followed the Fighter Weapons School techniques for coming off target. We used CCIP aiming, so the computer was involved in determining when the actual release pulse was sent to the bomb. Once we pushed the pickle button, we started pulling off target, wings level until we felt bomb release, then we started maneuvering. The technique upon bomb release, was to immediately switch to "dogfight" mode by flipping the switch on the throttle handle. This changed the aircraft configuration into an "air-to-air" mode from "air-to-ground." Electrical and software "interlocks" were supposed to prevent a Sidewinder missile release pulse during that process, even if the pickle button was not released from having dropped the bomb. No such luck, as over a period of days, we had multiple inadvertent missile firings during pull-off. Fortunately, the system was designed to launch the missile "dumb," so that it did not inadvertently lock-on to anything and destroy a friendly aircraft.

In trying to resolve the absolutely ingrained habit pattern problem, I began by, "Don't do that!" then, changed to, "You'll be grounded for a day!" then, to, "I'll send you to Riyadh," all of which I did, and none of which solved the problem. We finally solved it by changing our mission software "loads" so that the first station the fire control computer saw was a "dummy" with nothing loaded on it. The pilot would have to physically/consciously "step" to a loaded station in order to get a "live" missile to shoot. Problem solved and never repeated.

Ray Huot and I were the flying 0-6s in the Wing, and also the ones in charge. One of us would fly while the other ran the outfit through its daily events and planning. As the Wing Commander, Ray flew the first day. I flew the second, and we alternated from there. We were "religious" about getting eight hours of "crew rest" prior to flying, which generally took about 10 hours to brief, fly and debrief. Upon landing from a mission, we swapped responsibilities and the "landed" guy would begin his "ground" duties. So it was rest, fly, don't rest, rest, fly, with every other night allowing about three hours of sleep. By the end of combat (42 days), we were both exhausted....a longer war would have required a change, but we each were eager to fly as much as possible, and each of us got 21 combat sorties.

As the war progressed, we went through several phases such as "Scud-hunting" with 24 aircraft formations flying in northwest Iraq, on missions that exceeded eight hours duration and were an utter waste of time, but were politically and diplomatically necessary.

We also did "bridge-busting" on the Euphrates River south of Baghdad, using four-ship formations and finding our own targets. There was no mission ROE provided, so I created them in an effort to limit collateral damage and keep the guys from "hanging it out." Bridges required flight leads to use good judgment selecting the run-in headings, as well as the number of passes. We were also tasked for "road recce" against "movers." The ROE I dictated, since none was provided, was to hit only the larger vehicles and only those headed south...lousy ROE, but provided in a vacuum....

On one of those "armed recce" missions, I had one of my more challenging missions of the war: There were no provisions for in-flight tasking to work troops in contact (TIC) particularly where it was required in Iraq and north of the Euphrates. On this particular day, a Hill AFB F-16 with a LANTIRN IR Pod, was serving as a FAC, independent of anything we were tasked to do. The LANTIRN bird received a "Guard" (emergency frequency) radio transmission from people claiming to be a SOF roadwatch team in trouble. They used the callsign "Guard". So, it was, "This is Guard on Guard, we need help!" The LANTIRN bird found us on the radio, and requested we head his way while he worked to sort out the problem. We arrived to a very confusing situation. We had to determine the validity of the request, the absence of a "flak trap," and most importantly, the location of the "good guys" who were supposedly hiding in a ditch vs. the "bad guys." We were loaded with CBUs, certainly not an ideal weapon to use in proximity of the good guys.

After several minutes of talking on Guard channel, since the "good guys" had no other compatible radio equipment, and making lots of "dry" orientation passes, our number four pilot, a 1st Lt, was confident that he had them spotted. The SOF guys were desperate and, understanding the hazard, cleared us to drop the CBUs because they were being over-run by a "couple of thousand" enemy troops. Our number four made his passes followed by the rest of us. Then, we made multiple passes, all to the applause of the SOF guys. As we ran out of ordnance and fuel, another Shaw flight replaced us on-scene, and the final result was all of the team was safely extracted by helos a couple hours later. The early chaos ended up with a miraculous ending.

Early on, prior to combat, I established some wing ROE, among which was…"Unless it's Troops-in-Contact or SAR (rescue of a downed pilot), you will not descend below 8000 ft. in a defended area, because there is great risk of getting shot down." That was OK for most of the war. We suffered no combat losses, but late in the war, it happened. As the "Highway of Death" was being worked, the weather was somewhat iffy with overcast or partly overcast in the target area. "Psycho," one of my flight leads and a great guy from Hahn, decided he would penetrate the ceiling to check things out while his flight stayed "high." He was quickly hit and had to eject. He was shot at while descending in the chute, somehow broke his leg, and was captured soon after landing. His story is a good one and is on the net. He initially escaped, broken leg and all, hid in a bunker, was recaptured and ended up in jail in Baghdad. He was eventually released, had a successful career, made 0-6 and is now an NDU Professor. If he had obeyed my ROE, he would not have been shot down; however, the rest of his story might not have happened either.

Psycho being shot down was devastating to our pilots, particularly those from Hahn. I immediately held a very intense and emotional "pilot meeting" with all the guys, reminding them to keep their focus and intensity, and to not get complacent, and assuring them Psycho would be OK.

Unlike Vietnam, Desert Shield/Storm morale was universally very high, with our greatest problems occurring early in our seven-month deployment. None of the "young guys" had ever experienced an "open-ended" deployment with no defined end-point, so it took a bit of time to get them adjusted to the fact we were really going to war "for the duration!" We got through it just fine, and by the time we began combat, we were a highly-tuned team.

The end of the war came a few days later, actually being announced on "Guard" while some of my pilots were in the midst of attacking targets. With the exception of the fact "Psycho" was still unaccounted for, it was a happy time accompanied by some impressive parties; however, with the end came a "stand down" during which there was hardly any flying; hence bored people and new leadership challenges.

Fortunately, the two Shaw Squadrons, being "first-in," were among the very first to redeploy back to the USA, via Zaragoza AB in Spain. A college friend was the Zaragoza wing commander, and met us in fine style with fire-trucks spraying and the whole shooting match giving us a preview of what was in store back home.

After a couple days in Zaragoza, we were off to the US of A, crossing the Atlantic and into Shaw. As we crossed the ADIZ and spoke with "Center," we were greeted by the Center Manager who welcomed us each by name...a bit more emotional than I would have thought. Back at Shaw, the Sumter community was absolutely amazing in their enthusiastic welcome. Even President Bush came in Air Force One to personally welcome us back. The enthusiasm was so intense, I eventually had to ask the Sumter mayor to "back-off" a bit to allow our folks time to "de-tune" and be with their families.

That welcome really said it all. When I returned from Vietnam, I was told to not wear my uniform for fear of the "Hippies" (I still despise them). When we returned from Desert Storm, it was to an entirely different reception and really, a different nation. I feel immensely fortunate to have been able to experience and influence the two "bookends" of my Air Force career.

CHAPTER EIGHTEEN

Adventures in the Saudi Desert
by Russell L. "Russ" Violett

My Grandparents had homesteaded in 1908 in northern Montana with a common misconception that verged on a lie: "Free land, enough to feed your family!" But, the land wasn't quite free, and it was far from enough. In exchange for building a house on a chosen site, planting a crop, and maintaining five years of residence, you could "prove up" on 160 acres. That is, you would be granted a title. That had occurred, and my dad was farming and ranching on those original acres and several hundred more that had been added as other neighbors went broke and gave their land to my grandfather. My dad had stuck it out. He bought more. The land was mostly short grass, prairie and sagebrush. They plowed it and seeded it to wheat. As I grew up, we were still plowing land and seeding it to wheat and barley and oats.

The farm was located about 17 miles from the town where I went to high school. In the 6th grade, my dad had me driving my brother to school, and also driving a tractor and truck to assist with haying, cultivating and harvesting operations. My wife to be and I met in the third grade and went through school together, we were two of 17 students graduating from high school in 1954.

I was five years-old in 1940. I had not started to school and the Japanese attack on Pearl Harbor had not yet occurred. Mom and Dad married in 1934 and moved into what had been a granary made from a homesteader's shack for a home in northern Montana. They attached a second shack to that house providing space for a living room, bedroom and kitchen and added an upstairs with three bedrooms. An oil-burning stove was in the living room and a small register was cut into the ceiling of the kitchen that led into the center bedroom upstairs which provided a source of heat. For light, we used a gas lantern that hung from the ceiling and was moved from

295

room-to-room. Also, table lamps with wicks and glass chimneys were used. We did not have electricity in those early days.

The toilet was located outside the house. We walked about 100 feet on a wooden sidewalk to get to it. We had a porcelain chamber pot in the bedroom to use at night if Mother Nature called and it was too cold or dark to walk outside to the toilet. First. you had to strike a match and light the lamp so you could see. But, having access to a match was not something you were allowed to use in the dark so that resulted in getting Mom or Dad to come to the room with a lamp. This experience led to all kinds of encounters with the dark, broken lamp chimneys, and then of course, cleaning the pot the next morning.

For cooking, an old "Majestic" coal-burning stove was in the kitchen. It had a flat boilerplate for a cooking surface, a water reservoir and an oven. The requirement to keep the heating stove oil tank filled and the coal brought into the kitchen to keep the water in the Majestic water tank warm became part of the chores that my brother and I learned early in our lives.

Mom would get the stove fire going and prepare the meals. It was hard work for them and the struggle to keep warm and have light at night was overwhelming.

They purchased and installed a 32-volt electric system in the house about 1943. The system consisted of a wind charger and 16 two-volt batteries and also a gas motor driving a generator that would charge the batteries when the wind was not blowing. To install the system, they first dug a basement under the house. That was done with shovels and horses pulling a thing called a "slip." They dug a hole beside the house by hand, then opened that up under the house by pulling the slip into the hole, loading it with dirt, and then the horses pulled it out of the hole and up to the surface using ropes and light chains. The basement became a bedroom for me, also a washing area for the Maytag gas-powered washing machine, the water pressure system for running water in the kitchen (replaced a hand-operated handle pump hooked up to cistern beside the house) and the space for a floor-mounted furnace replacing the oil-burning stove. Then, the rural electrification program began, and we had "real" electricity beginning in about my seventh grade living on the farm.

Dad and Mom rented a house in the little town of Chester during the winter months to avoid the storms and winter conditions associated with driving on unimproved roads and blowing snow. Every day in the winter, the cattle had to be fed. Dad made that trip in a four-wheel drive Jeep. He had a tractor in a heated machine shop that he hooked up to a sled. Hay was pitch-forked onto the sled, and then, pulled to a sheltered area for the cattle where it was pitched off the sled. All this took a good portion of the day. When the temperatures were in the minus numbers, and the wind was blowing, it was hard work and dangerous. My brother and I got to help on the weekends. All this began the process of me deciding that there must be a better way of life out there somewhere. But, I loved the farm then, and still do.

When I graduated from high school and headed for college, I was making decisions on whether or not I should stay on the farm. Dee and I had married in our sophomore year of college and were recognizing that it is not easy to decide how to break up a farm between the kids. I had two brothers. Dee had one. Size is crucial to success in farming. Ranches and farms that have been patched together by tenacious parents and grandparents can't be easily broken into pieces for every brother with a spouse and kids of their own, and maintain a viable operation. There simply isn't enough income to support multiple generations of an extended family.

When I went to college, I signed-up for Air Force ROTC. I thought maybe I could do the Air Force and the brothers could stay home and farm.

I was commissioned a 2nd Lt in the summer of 1958, went to pilot training, got my wings in January 1960. I requested fighters and got an F-100 with training at Luke. After three years at Misawa, I was reassigned to McConnell AFB where I checked out in the F-105 in 1964.

In "Thor's Hammer, A Requiem" by Thomas R. Carlson, the author describes the Thud much better than I and says everything I want to say about the aircraft and my experience with it:

The Thunderchief was a giant of an airplane. I viewed it with suspicion and admittedly some trepidation. For such a machine to be powered by a single engine and operated by a single pilot seemed optimistic at best. Twenty- five tons of machine when fully loaded gave weight to the term "Fighter,

Heavy." The Thunderchief name would give way to the universally adopted term "Thud" and would be a badge of honor and respect that would be worn with pride.

The Thud had an explosive canister much like an oversized, slow-burning shotgun shell. Pilots and ground crews became accustomed to the acrid smell of burning cordite as the coffee can sized powder cartridge spun the big turbine engine to life. To the Thud driver and his crew chief it usually meant a successful engine start. In many ways, it was a hint of things to come. An almost imperceptible movement of the machine could be felt as compressors and turbines came up to speed, pumps and generators came on line and the start sequence was completed.

There was the thrill of advancing the throttle to full power for take-off. The landing gear struts which stretched nearly eight feet from their mounting point in the wing to the surface, bent slightly aft as the power was advanced and sprung forward as the brakes were released. Feeling the gear "walk" was a uniquely Thud experience.

Each pilot has his own indelible list of remembered names. The Plain of Jars, Vinh, Than Hoa, Sam Neua, Mu Gia Pass, Dong Hoi and Route 1 were the locations of early targets and were on my list. Those pilots who were there as the war intensified would be exposed to a far more dangerous and foreboding environment of air defenses and a new set of names. Thud Ridge, Downtown, Haiphong, the Paul Doumer Bridge, Kep, Phuc Yen, the Red River, most of these in what was known as Route Pack Six, would be imprinted in their memories and many in mine. One engine, one seat, one pilot, one set of thoughts. Dryness in the mouth and the hint of the taste of bile were the signs of trepidation, however slight or well concealed from the others.

Last flight return to base. Of course, a good solid 4 G pitch-out to downwind from a 500 knot initial approach would be in order for the last overhead traffic pattern. To hell with it, make it 650! In for a penny, in for a pound! Stay just under the mach so I wouldn't end up in jail for destroying the place with a sonic boom. The massive speedbrakes, idle power and

6Gs would combine to slow to the 275 knot gear down speed. The voids in the outer wing panels where the cover plates had been removed would shriek their high-pitched wail. Dogs for miles around would howl and the ground-bound folk would look up and take notice. Some of them would have known immediately without even seeing it that this wasn't just another aircraft in the pattern, this was a Thud!

Attack on a Surface- to-Air (SAM) missile site - 27 July 1965 - Background: The 563rd Tactical Fighter Squadron, a unit of the 23rd Tactical Fighter Wing, McConnell AFB, KS, was a typical fighter unit in 1965. Days were filled with training flights in the F-105 aircraft with most of the pilots recently converting from other fighters (F-100s, F-102s, F-101s, etc.). The aircraft arrived from the factory with only a few hours of flight time in the records. The older heads kept the inexperienced types "between the lines" so the squadron could maintain mission readiness. The squadron pilots were extremely tight. They liked being together and with other pilots and their families and friends. We only skipped a few nights stopping by the "stag bar" on the way home for a drink with buddies. The camaraderie was invigorating, and motivational. We wanted to become the best of the best. Nothing was impossible. We thought we could do anything, and also thought the F-105 an incredible aircraft, especially for high-speed flight and interdiction missions, although much of our training was spent training for the use of special weapons (NUKES!).

The wing deployed for war games on several occasions and pilots returned with stories of encounters with members of the "Blue or Red forces." These were confidence-building exercises and got us all rapidly on the same page with teamwork.

On several occasions, the base siren "blew" requiring a response from the wing and its members (or a telephone recall would be implemented). On most occasions, everyone recognized it as another practice for an operational readiness inspection, so we stuffed a pillow in our A-3 bag and headed for the squadron. in the squadron we went through the mobility assembly line and recognized we had to update our personal data. But, something different happened on an April morning in 1965. I rolled over in bed that morning to the sound of the siren, and said, "Jesus, this one is for real!" and told Dee to pack a real bag, I would be back and get it later. Sure enough, after arriving at the squadron, we were told we were to deploy to a "classified destination" and no one was to know where we were heading. Departure was set for the next morning. After getting our packed bags in order and saying our goodbyes, we took off as a squadron from McConnell and landed at Hickam AFB, HI. We flew as two-ship flights on KC-135 refueling aircraft from over California to Hawaii, an eight-hour flight in a single place fighter. It was an uneventful trip, except the radio chatter was excessive. We were told in no uncertain terms that the next leg to Guam (Anderson AFB) would be radio silent! And, it was, until we were about to land. We noticed that one guy was having a lot of trouble getting a contact for the refueling. Fuel was constantly vaporizing at the point of contact and it took him a long time to complete his refueling. He broke radio silence when he asked lead for a straight-in landing approach. Lead asked why and he said, "Well, I have a hydraulic failure and need to put my wheels down using the emergency system." He landed uneventfully, after another eight-hour flight. We left the next day for Takhli RTAFB, Thailand where we landed after a seven-hour mission. The following morning found us scheduled to bomb targets in "LAOS and NORTH VIETNAM!" only two days after arriving from the States! Our body clocks hadn't yet adjusted from flying half way around the world.

The transition had taken place; we were now in combat for real. We were in screened-in buildings, with tin roofs, built on stilts in 100-degree plus temperatures with high humidity and thunderstorms. And, lots of bugs; And Rats; And Snakes. We slept on cots covered by a mosquito tent. We had briefings starting at 0230 with takeoffs beginning at 0430. Our typical configuration was six 750-lb. bombs on the centerline and a single on each outboard pylon for a total of eight bombs (and there were several other variations). With two 450-gal. external tanks, our takeoff weight was near 54,000 lbs. which generated takeoff rolls of about 7000 ft. with water injection. These were always exciting; then to the tanker, refueling then to the target at about 20,000 ft., with a recovery direct to home base at 35-40,000 ft. cruising at .92 mach. We planned to land with 2000 lbs. of fuel, but it didn't always work that way. Sometimes we stretched our stay in the target area and found ourselves making idle throttle letdowns to get on the ground with 1000 lbs. or less, which was even more exciting.

The squadron was flying combat in the initial "Rolling Thunder" air campaign as well as other Southeast Asia campaigns such as "Barrel Roll, Steel Tiger," etc. Daily missions into Laos and North Vietnam became routine, and after a few missions, the reality of combat became very clear. We lost one, then two of our mates. We reported them as "Missing in action" (MIA), but both turned out to be killed in action (KIA). We lost more aircraft, and witnessed a pilot taken prisoner in Laos. Other pilots were recovered. The war became very real and very hard. It was becoming evident that the odds of being shot down were going up and the odds of being rescued were going down. So, we attacked each mission with a vengeance. We rapidly learned that revenge is an emotional state, and reacting in that manner is very dangerous. We learned to remain cool, stay deliberate and stay with the planned and briefed actions as the order of the day.

We had many types of leaders: some always had things planned out and were in constant control; others didn't. When things became complicated and confused and not going as planned, the ability to rapidly adjust and adapt to the emerging situation was essential to survival. Most of the time, leaders could cope, but not always. I remember one "leader" who repeatedly called on the radio about 200 miles from a navigation aid and asked the number three man to take over the flight. Only later did we realize that he had broken lock on the Tacan at 197 miles, the maximum range, and was immediately lost, so he handed over the flight to the element lead. On one hand that was good, but why was such a pilot put there as lead in the first place?

Some began to emerge as outstanding combat leaders. One in particular became a legend in my book. People in the squadron wanted to fly with him. He could be counted on to get you in and get you out, and he always told it the way it was, no sugar coating, just right in your face with the facts; absolutely great! Later on, I worked for him in a non-combat environment and he operated the same way. Still a close friend to this day, he made things happen, or made you make them happen. Some of us called him "Charlie, the xxx...." (censored). He was Paul Craw. I was not assigned to his flight, but I knew his reputation, and he lived up to it every day.

The Mission: On 24 July 1965, a flight of F-4s were escorting a flight of eight Thuds that were to attack an ammo factory north of Hanoi. They were in the clouds at about 25,000 ft. The F-4s were hit by a SAM missile and down goes one F-4. We stood down on the 25th and 26th. In the meantime, the North Vietnamese moved more guns around the missile sites.

For the past several weeks, as we had bombed different targets in North Vietnam (bridges, railyards, roads, storage facilities, gun sites, etc.), we observed surface to air missile sites being constructed in different areas of North Vietnam that had been designated as "no-fly" zones. Our government had put the missiles off limits. Later, we were told that Russians were on the ground at those sites and the U.S. did not want to create a political incident. The missiles that shot down the F-4 had been fired from one of the sites in a no-fly zone west of Phuc Yen; however, the "no-fly" was suspended and those sites became our target for the day. Korat was fragged on the eastern site and was attacking from south to north. We (Takhli) were to attack the other site heading north to south.

On 27 July, we got up for our standard 0230 briefing and after forming at the squadron, were told our target was the missile site and our time over target was now 1300. In the meantime, plan the attack, then go back and get some sleep, right. We drew our lines on the map for ingress and egress and planned the specific attacks for six flights of four. Each flight was to carry un-finned napalm (a new weapon for us) or CBU-1s (a cluster weapon of bomblets that were dispensed out the back of a wing-mounted canister). Both these weapons required us to fly directly over the target at low altitude, GULP! The immediate problem for the weapons planners was that we only had preliminary weapons data for the napalm. We did know that the recommended delivery speed was slow compared to our normal delivery speeds for other ordnance. We decided to release it at our normal speed which was about 560 KCAS.

We planned to refuel after takeoff on the western and northern-most refueling tracks, then proceed over Laos at medium altitude, let down in western North Vietnam, and go to the deck about 100 miles out and fly down the Red River to the target. Our attack run-in was planned for 100 ft. and 560 KCAS. Our planned egress was to turn to the right off the target, fly down the Black River, then climb out on a southwesterly heading, reform and recover to Takhli.

In the planning room, two missile sites were identified about two miles apart with one of them being our assigned target. Our egress after hitting the target put us in close proximity to the other site causing us to plan to remain at very low altitudes until well clear of the target area.

Flight Line Up - 27 July 1965 compiled by H.W. Plunkett - 10 Feb 2010 (abbreviated)

SAM Site 6	SAM Site 7
NVN 64th Missile Battalion	NVN 63rd Missile Battalion
21-09-04N 105-22-18E	21-10-30N 105-21-40E

Korat

"Pepper"	357 TFS
(12:50 Take Off]	1. Farr (KIA Mid-Air)
SAM Site	2. Bartholomew (KIA Mid-Air)
BLU-27s	3. Saffel
	4. Weeks

"Willow"	357 TFS
(12:50 Take Off)	1. Rademacher (Aborted)
SAM Site	2 Gordon
BLU-27s	3. May
	4. Ferguson

"Redwood"	357 TFS
(12:50 Take Off)	1. Myhrum
SAM Site	2. Horner
BLU-27s	3. Koenitzer
	4. Culen

"Cedar"	12 TFS
(13:20 Take Off)	1. Reed
Barracks	2. Purcell (POW) 14:40
BLU-27s	3. <Aborted>
	4. Joyce

Takhli

"Healy"	563 TFS
(12:50 Take Off)	1. Brown
SAM Site	2. Kosko (KIA) 14:03
CBU-2s	3. Violett
	4. Pazel (80 TFS Spare)

"Austin"	563 TFS
SAM Site	1. Harris
CBU-2s	2. Carson
	3. Rhodes
	4. Fowler

"Hudson"	563 TFS
(12:57 Take Off)	1. Craw
SAM Site	2. Berg (POW) 14:07
BLU-27s	3. Sparks (61-0169)
	4. Case

"Valiant"	80 TFS
Barracks	1. Coll
CBU-2s	2. Atkinson
(Hit SAM Site)	3. Reichart
Spare: Pielin (No go)	4. Redmond

"Dogwood"	12 TFS	"Rambler"	80 TFS
SAM Site Cleanup	1. Hosmer	Support Facility	1. Mearns
LAU-3	2. Tullo (Resc) 15:13	BLU-27s	2. Vizcarra (62-4301)
	3. Anderson		3. Hayes
	4. Daughtrey		4. Gainer

"Chestnut"	12 TFS	"Corvette"	80 TFS
SAM Site Cleanup	1. Copin	Support Facility	1. Detwiler
Guns only	2. Fronk	BLU-27s	2. Boswell
	3. Kelch		3. Smith
	4. Bogen		4. Walcott

We went back to the "hooch" and went to bed. We got back up about 0900, had some more breakfast, and went to the squadron. We briefed again on the mission, started our aircraft and taxied to the arming area. There were 24 aircraft lined-up, with arming crews working each flight. I was number four in a flight with the Squadron Commander, Jack Brown, as leader. When the number three aircraft was armed, all his ordnance and fuel tanks jettisoned on the taxiway, and fuel was running everywhere. The pilot, Al Logan, shut down and made an emergency egress from his aircraft. He was adjacent to me. I taxied away rapidly and continued arming at a safe distance. A spare, Pazel, would fill-in my position as number four, and I moved into the number three position in the flight. The Wing Commander and Chaplain were beside the runway and saluted everyone as we started our takeoff rolls.

After takeoff, en route to the tanker, the spare joined the flight on my wing. He had never flown a combat mission. He arrived the day before with aircraft replacements from Yokota AB in Japan and wanted to fly, so they scheduled him as a spare. The F-105 rarely aborted, so no one thought the spare would really fly, but here he was, on my wing and needed to be given some advice, poor bastard. I held my fist up at the top of the canopy, which told him to go to the squadron UHF common radio frequency. On squadron common, I told him three things: on the target run, I wanted him on the left side of my aircraft; never fly below me; and stay slightly back of line abreast so I could see his pitot tube on the nose of his aircraft without looking back. He "rogered" those instructions and we went back to the refueling frequency. No other conversations took place.

The Takhli group flew north across Laos and then to Yen Bai and proceeded on the deck. The refueling operation and letdown were normal, then after hitting the deck at about 420 KCAS, we accelerated to 500 about 30 miles from the target. It was at this point we began to see flak and tracer rounds, growing in intensity as we approached the target. I picked out the target. The lead element had already hit it and there was lots of smoke and dust in the air.

Walt Kosko was Jack Brown's number two man and he took a hit at the target. We lost the number two man in several flights and figured they were shooting at the lead aircraft, under-leading him and thus hitting number two. In all cases, both for the Korat group and the Takhli group, the guns were shooting from the number two man's side of the flight. Korat lost three number two men, Frank Tullo, Bob Purcell, and Black Bart Bartholomew. Frank Tullo was the only rescue that day. Black Bart got safely across the river but was losing fluids rapidly and Jack Farr, the flight leader, made the mistake of moving in close to check him over when Black Bart's aircraft suddenly went out of control and the resultant mid-air collision killed them both. The total loss for the day was six aircraft.

We were fighting tracer rounds, flak, and the ground. As I egressed, I realized the 85 mm guns were in revetments directly in front of me with their guns depressed to level and firing as we went by. The explosions of those guns firing, the fire, smoke and shockwave donut of those bursts were awesome and scary as hell. I rolled a little bit to the right, and went down a little lower, my wingman was right there beside me on the left when I "touched" the top of a revetment as well as some banana trees in the area and then met another flight of F-105s going in the opposite direction. It must have been a Korat flight. At the target, I heard number three (Billy Sparks) in another flight tell his leader that two (Kyle Berg) was on fire, and then immediately said, "Too late, he crashed." We then decided to egress the area, but that was not in the cards.

The command and control aircraft requested that I go to a tanker with my wingman and return to the target area to assist in aircrew recovery efforts. On our post-strike battle damage check my wingman didn't see any damage from my "touching" the revetment and banana trees, and I didn't have any cockpit indications, nor changes in flight characteristics, so we proceeded to the tanker. We alternated with

Jack Brown. Jack had been trying to encourage Walt Kosko to stay with the airplane just a little longer so he would cross the river prior to ejection. I was telling Jack to get his nose down. I thought he was too high in a missile threat area. Walt didn't quite make it over the river. In fact he went down "in" the river. The Jolly confirmed that Walt was in the river, but was unable to pull him out of the water with his chute attached. At that point, my wingman and I were no longer of assistance. The rescue forces were occupied with another pickup in the same general area and in contact with Frank Tullo from Korat. The Jolly Greens had never been this far North, so it was a major effort to work the rescues. Since there were no other rescue forces in the area, no additional effort was made to locate number two from my flight because we had no radio contact with him. We cleared the area, having operated at very low altitude for most of this operation, being continuously aware of tracers and flak.

My wingman and I made another refueling and headed for Takhli, but after attempting to land with thunderstorms in the area, we diverted to Korat. It had been six hours of hell, and with one thermos of water, I was so thirsty, I swear my mouth didn't want to form sounds. I climbed down the ladder. My flight suit was soaking wet and white streaked with sweat. I drank water and more water, then went to my wingman's (Pazel's) aircraft where I helped him down the ladder. He said, "My God, are they all like this?" "No, thank God, they are not," was my reply. We checked my aircraft and the center fin on the bottom of the fuselage was scrapped as was the fin on the right outboard 450-gal. tank. Neither required immediate repair. I had successfully tied the record for flying low. After some debriefing, we received word to return to Takhli. We arrived about 9 PM and upon arrival, some squadron mates climbed the ladder and handed me a bottle of Chivas Regal. It tasted really good! Eventually, I made it to bed feeling no pain, but it had been a hell of a 27 July 1965.

Aircraft/Pilot losses for the 563rd in 1965 (April/July):

Date	Location	Cause	Other action	Name	Status
4/17/1965	Mu Gia Pass	Ground	Didn't pull out	Samuel Alex. Woodworth	KIA
5/9/1965	AAA Mu Gia Pass	Guns	No Ejection at Target	Robert Carl Wistrand	KIA
5/15/1965	Strike Mission	Eng Fail	Off end of runway	Robert Greskowiak	KIA
5/18/1965	Road E of Sam Neua	Ejected in Laos	Captured	David Louis Hrdlicka	POW Died
5/31/1965	Thanh Hoa Bridge	Just S of Target	Captured	Robert D Peel	POW
6/5/1965	SAR Escort Laos	Guns	Ejected in Laos	Walter B Kosko	Rescued
7/3/1965	Plain de Jars, Laos	Fuel Exhaustion	A/C fuel problem	Ken Johnston	Rescued
7/27/1965	SAM Site Hanoi	At target	Captured	Kyle Dag Berg	POW
7/27/1965	SAM Site Hanoi	At target	Drowned in River	Walter B Kosko	KIA

I returned to Takhli in 1969, after my TDY tour in 1965. I flew a total of 126 Thud missions, with 56 missions in North Vietnam in the '65 time period, and the remainder primarily in Barrel Roll with a few in the Steel Tiger areas.

Four years later, I would have tears in my eyes as I watched the POWs step off the freedom flights to the Philippines from Hanoi. It was a great day! 27 July 1965 remains a crystal clear memory.

Ejection from F-100, 18 Nov 1960, 1343 Hours: I was a student in F-100 training at Nellis. I was added to the afternoon flying schedule when four pilots came out of a briefing room for an afternoon Dart mission and one of them ran and threw up in the waste paper basket at the duty counter Dutch Horras, a bachelor had stayed out all night and come in late. The flight lead, an exchange Canadian (Carothers) with a call sign of "Maple" said to me, "Get out from behind that counter. You are now number two, same briefing as your flight this morning. Suit-up. We are heading to the aircraft now, any questions?"

"None Sir," and I found myself on the left wing of lead taking off on Runway 02 at Nellis (now 03). Carothers used his hands and head a lot as an IP. It seemed his hands and head were moving all the time.

After we released brakes, and rolled a couple thousand feet, Nellis tower called, "Maple Lead, Nellis Tower."

Maple responded with, "Standby, Tower" and we continued, everything still normal with me glued on his left wing. His hand appeared with the palm up moving upwards indicating he was going to raise the nose for takeoff and then immediately after that a big head nod for gear. As the gear came up, Maple said, "Nellis Tower, go ahead," and that's when things got exciting.

Tower then said, "Roger Maple lead, be advised your number two man has fire coming out of the left side of his fuselage," and I said to myself, Jesus, that's me. Maple yawed his aircraft for me to spread it out. I did and looked at the instruments, all appeared normal except one which read, "FIRE WARNING!"

At the very least I probably said something to myself like, "WOW!" The aircraft shuddered from an explosion, and was rolling to the right into lead. I was pulling up a little and lead was slightly below me and to my right. I saw Carothers looking back at me and heard him say, "Jesus Christ, get out of it!" We were about 3-400 ft. above the runway. I stomped on the left rudder, the aileron did not seem to be responding, the aircraft rolled left slightly and the nose kept coming up a little.

As I went through 6-700 ft. over the end of the runway, I could not hold a wings level position and the airplane continued to roll slightly to the right. I blew the canopy by pulling up the ejection levers in this "C" model (811) with my right hand. I had my left hand on the throttle and still in afterburner and was pushing the throttle through the instrument panel as I tried to get more altitude. I reached for the trigger on the left handle but could not find it. I looked down at the handle, the airplane was rolling a little faster, so I fired the seat with the right trigger. There was lots of noise. I reached for the lap belt. It was gone. I pushed away from the seat, and it became very quiet. My helmet had rotated 90-degrees, covering my eyes, in the process. I straightened it and determined my parachute canopy was okay. The seat and other bits and pieces came flying by and I could see smoke from the aircraft crash between Nellis and the Nuclear Storage site southeast of the runway. Then, I hit the ground, really hard! The wind was blowing about 25 knots. I landed across the highway a little right of a 02 centerline extension. The parachute had one quick release on the left riser. It had a cover on it to prevent inadvertent activation. I was squeezing it to release the riser instead of pulling it down to expose the release. The wind was dragging me, so I decided the release wasn't working, and pulled on one riser until the chute collapsed. I took the harness off and sat down on the ground. My body was shaking, so I laid back on the rocky ground and hit my head on a piece of shale. I started bleeding from the back of my head. The chopper arrived, the tech jumped out, asked if I was okay. I said, "Sure," waving my bloody hand at him after I had rubbed the back of my head.. He was not convinced, so into the chopper we went and landed near the base hospital. I was fine except for the head cut and a "zipper burn" on my left chin where my head went into my chest on ejection while I was looking at the left handle. They put me on the schedule the next day and then sent me on leave for a week.

Years later, while talking about ejections with Ralph "Hoot" Gibson, former Thunderbird Leader, I learned from him he had been the Airdrome Officer at Nellis the day I ejected. He was on the ramp in a vehicle watching activities. He told me what the aircraft looked like (fire and smoke) when we went by the tower. He had watched the canopy come off and the ejection seat trajectory, he didn't think the chute was going to open in time. He saw it fill, make a couple of swings, and I hit the ground. Lucky.

EID AL-FITR holidays in Saudi Arabia: I was Chief, United States Military Training Mission (USMTM) to Saudi Arabia. I lived in the city of Al Khobar. My house had four security patrols (a jeep with a driver and a .50 cal. machine gun with operator) located at each corner of my compound). The commander of the military forces in the Eastern province was my next door neighbor. He also had similar security forces around his home. This was an experience within itself.

Significant experiences seemed to occur rapidly. One of them came at the end of Ramadan in Saudi Arabia in the fall of 1985.

This centered around a series of holidays known as Eid Al-Fitr. This holiday lasts five-seven days. It is brought about by the beginning of a new moon after the 28-30 days of Ramadan. For Ramadan to be declared over and the Eid Al-Fitr to begin, two honest Muslim men must verify that they have seen the "silver sliver" of the crescent of the new moon. I and Azum (my Arabian Affairs Advisor in USMTM) proceeded to pay our respects to the officialdom of the local area. The day was clear and hot, probably around 110 degrees.

We left Dhahran Air Base and arrived at the home of the Governor of the Eastern Province, Muhammad Fahd. He was approximately 40 years-old. We were directed through the expansive halls by armed men dressed in thobe robes and gutra headdress (traditional Saudi dress), diamond daggers and scimitars at their sides. After a two or three minute walk through the halls (I was sure I was the only individual that appeared in the *"Tales of Arabian Nights"* in a Class A blue Air Force uniform), we arrived in a huge reception room and were very quietly seated near the Governor's seat. Dick Lord, the Director of Operations for Arabian-American Oil Company (ARAMCO) was there ahead of us. Many others started to arrive – a large crowd of Americans, Saudi Military, Saudis in thobe and gutra by the dozens and many young boys. The Governor came into the hall. He received we special guests first, then throngs of people came up to greet him. A group of Saudis had incense burners that were lit, and the burners were smoking robustly. The burner carriers would approach, and you were expected to fan the smoke into your face. "More precious than gold" is the sandalwood *oud* (incense) that Saudis burn in their hand-crafted mabakhirs (incense burners) as a gesture of hospitality and respect for guests in their home. Like the cardamom-flavored coffee served in small cups, or the sweet dates offered to guests, incense has long been part of the art of hospitality practiced in Saudi homes. This group moved around the room and we had several opportunities to participate.

I had stumbled through my first of many "Eidkum Mubaraks" (the Saudi phrase for "have a happy holiday"). We proceeded to a huge room where approximately 25-30 round tables were set. "Being set" means eight lambs were on each table and a small mountain of rice was loaded as centerpiece. After getting on my knees and placing half of the huge floor mat over my Class As we commenced eating. A

Saudi Colonel was the table server. He tore the lamb apart and threw chunks with perfect aim right in front of you. The food was excellent. At the Governor's table they also had the delicacy of baby camel, yum. The rice was gummy with all kinds of nuts and spices whereby one could roll it into little balls, pop it in and it was a delicacy by itself. We ate rapidly, maybe four minutes at most, then washed our right hands in the center of the room where water boys with soap, water and towels were stationed. Then, we headed back to the huge reception room to have gowa (coffee) and tea. The gowa was not too bad but a little stronger than American coffee. The gowa server came to me and he only had 10 little cups and there were 350 people in the room. I was in the first 10 to get coffee and suddenly realized that everyone was going to drink from those same 10 cups. Tea was then served the same way. Then, the Governor stood, some of us close to him wished him "Eidkum Mubarak" and we were shown out.

Off we went to the Eastern Providence Chief of Police's office. We were greeted by the Police band, decked out in red coats and black pants. While there, we ran into the American Chief of Consulate and the Consulate Staff. Again, we had coffee and tea, and candies and dates. We chatted with the Police Chief for 15 minutes while being serenaded and then went to the Commander of the Military Forces in the Eastern Province. The same protocols were exercised again.

We next pressed on to the Director of Naval Training's office, half-way between Dammam and Al Khobar. After being taken into a huge room, and Eidkum Mubaraks were exchanged, we were led to a huge table, probably 200 feet long and 10 feet wide. It was overloaded with every kind of sandwich and dessert known to man. I managed half a sandwich, lots of nuts to cover the plate and a small piece of gelatin cake. I was seated next to a Navy Captain who was going back to Monterey, California soon, and we discussed our professional military education system. Suddenly, it was suggested that we go meet some new Saudi Navy recruits and off we went. We met 10 of them. Forty Eidkum Mubaraks, and one giant table decorated with every kind of food imaginable, got us back on the road again. This time we were headed to visit Mr. Al Gosaibi, a very prominent billionaire in the city of Al Khobar. He was a gentleman, extremely talkative, and I thoroughly enjoyed his stories of living in Khobar in the 1930s when there was absolutely nothing there. In 1933, King Abdul Aziz gave a concession to the Standard Oil Company of California to search for oil. That concession became ARAMCO over time. Al Gosaibi walked one and a half hours to work each morning where he learned to drive a truck, and then, after learning to drive, he worked for ARAMCO during the day and drove pipe in his leased truck into the oil fields at night. More trucks, more pipe, the purchase of land in the area, and now Mr. Al Gosaibi not only owns the hotel but owns enough in the Kingdom to make him a billionaire.

From there it was off to the Emir of Al Khobar's office. He spoke absolutely no English but Azum my advisor (a Palestinian by birth) did a great job. The main subject of conversation centered on hospitality in Saudi Arabia and how we were all sure that Saudis in America received the same hospitality.

We had a one-hour break and I raced home. My clothes reeked of the incense smoke, and Dee said to leave my blouse hanging outside (note: women are not included in official festivities in Saudi Arabia). In one hour, I was expected at the RSAF Officers Club for a "holiday feast." It was to be my second "goat grab" of the day. Oh! God! Tummy, just stay with me for two more hours.

I arrived as the Emir of Dammam was also coming for this dinner, and he was to be there at 1230. We entered the club reception room and were served orange juice and then directed to a large hall in the rear of the club. We were there a good 10 minutes and it was very quiet. Suddenly, we were directed into a huge hall. This time the places were set in a western motif but there was one huge lamb and one server for every four people. After shrimp cocktail, salad, more lamb and more rice, we plunged into dessert. I knew my belt was going to pop but I hung in there. As abruptly as we went into the hall, we left, took up the same seating arrangement and had more coffee. Within the Royal Saudi Air Force there are a few Princes and they had come dressed in thobe and gutra to pay their respects, All in all it was quite a "culinary" day. The experience certainly falls into the "once in a lifetime" category.

From a Montana farm, to a steamy jungle war, through an aircraft ejection that almost cost my life, to the deserts of the Middle East, the Air Force offered Dee and me a life about which others can only dream.

CHAPTER NINETEEN

From the Army to the Air Force to the Navy

by Gordon E. "Gordy" Williams

There I was…six-hundred feet above the Pacific Ocean, 200 knots, gear and flaps down, 30 or 40 miles from land, pitch-black, off the northern California coast, strapped into my Navy F-4B. And, I was having a crisis of confidence, an unusual state of affairs for the average Air Force fighter pilot. To "carrier qual" (be qualified to fly off Navy carriers) one needed 10 day landings and six at night. If all went as programmed, I would get through this in one night. But wait! Let's step back and see how I got myself into this scary mess:

"Live Free or Die!" - that is the motto for the State of New Hampshire, where I was born in the city of Nashua. I lived mostly in Hudson, a small town of perhaps 3000 people. My family were long-time New Englanders. They didn't come over on the Mayflower, but it wasn't too many decades later. I lived with my grandparents full-time from about the sixth grade. My Mom, Doris Williams Smith, who when she married my dad became Doris "Williams Williams," really "got around." She and my father were divorced right after WWII. As my Grandma said, "Uh, Gordy, your mother has had a lot of boyfriends."

My grandfather was quite the guy. He was born at a time that found him ineligible for the WWI draft but he was quite the politician. He was a Town Selectman for 24 years and a force to be reckoned with in the town's business. He also held a town position that now makes me chuckle when I think how politically incorrect it would be today. He was the: "Overseer of the Poor. " Folks came to the house to plead their case. He gave them what he thought they needed, and it could only be spent in a few small stores where he was plugged-in (graft anyone? – hey, just New England politics). And, woe to they who tried to buy a little whiskey. He died of cancer at the then advanced age of 66. I was a plebe at West Point at the time, and it was one of the few reasons one could escape the place for a few days. My

Grandma died when I was on the USS Ranger in the Gulf of Tonkin during Vietnam. Both of those are other stories. I wept unabashedly. She outlived him by more than a decade.

I don't know who brought up the idea of West Point. I knew it was essentially a "free college" if one could qualify. Normally, an applicant must have a congressional appointment; however, I found I was eligible by virtue of my father's circumstance of death. He had died when I was sophomore in high school. We had only lived together until I was five or six years-old, but he was my ticket to West Point.

After divorcing my mother, my dad married a southern belle from South Carolina. I stayed one summer with them in Sumter where she had pioneered a school teaching airmen at Shaw AFB clerical skills. She eventually remarried a "good ole boy" and lived in the thriving metropolis of Hagood SC (pop. 600). She was a wonderful lady, and one of my proudest life moments was dropping into Shaw in an F-15. I was a brigadier general at the time. She asked, "Should you really be flying that plane all by yourself?" She bragged on me a lot.

I entered West Point in 1953. For a kid who knew very little about the military it was a rude awakening. "Live Free or Die!" had been my state motto, but I found very little freedom at the United States Military Academy. In fact I found myself pretty much only free to study. It was a long four years. I graduated with the Class of 1957 and a general engineering degree. As Gen Douglas MacArthur said in his farewell speech to the cadet corps, "My days of old have vanished - tone and tints." Yes, my memories of West Point have faded, some intentionally, but I do remember one high point and it had to do with athletics.

I was a baseball player at West Point, outfield and occasionally pitcher. A yearly tradition was for the New York Giants professional baseball team to come to West Point pre-season and play an exhibition game. Game day I came to bat against a pitcher, Mike McCormick, who was a much-ballyhooed rookie hired in 1956. In fact he had thrown a no-hitter the previous year. McCormick wound-up and on my first at bat, I slugged the ball out of the park for a homerun. He was visibly pissed. During my remaining at bats, I don't think I ever saw the ball. So, my cadet claim to fame is - I am probably the only

West Pointer that ever hit a homerun against an eventual Cy Young Award winner.

My class of 1957 included some well-known four-star generals including Carl Vuono, later Army Chief of Staff and Don Kutyna, later head of Air Force Space Command. The famous football player and "Lonesome End," Pete Dawkins, was two classes behind me.

After graduation I took my commission in the Air Force. That could be done in those days because the Air Force Academy had not yet been established; remember, in 1957, the Air Force was only 10 years-old. About 15 percent of every West Point graduating class opted for Air Force. I traded-in my Army green for Air Force blue (actually "silver tans," a handsome uniform we should bring back) and headed for pilot training at Laredo AFB, TX. At Laredo we flew the T-34 and T-28 in Primary and the T-33 in Basic.

Pilot training was a blast and I even learned to enjoy the heat and "Tex-Mex" Mexican food, a big change for a New England boy. Weekend forays into Nuevo Laredo were a definite side benefit and I never spent a night in a Mexican jail. The biggest blast was receiving a graduation assignment to the F-100 Super Sabre in Tactical Air Command (TAC). The F-100 was the USAF's first truly supersonic fighter.

The "Hun," as we called it, was meant to replace the F-86 as the frontline air superiority fighter. The first F-100As had significant stability problems and a very high accident rate. Modifications were made and by the time I finished F-100 training at Luke and Top-off at Nellis AFBs in 1959, I was assigned to my first unit, the 510th Tactical Fighter Squadron at Clark Air Base in the Philippines flying F-100Ds. The aircraft had been further modified to assume the role of a fighter-bomber, capable of conventional and nuclear weapons delivery - bombs, rockets, missiles and guns. This was an exciting time for me – how good could life be? – a young, single fighter pilot flying a supersonic aircraft in the Orient and getting paid to do it!

After a year and one-half in the Philippines flying the F-100, I moved to Louisiana and England AFB. Having grown up in southern New Hampshire, just 50 miles north of Boston, I had an accent like Jack Kennedy. The Cajuns had an accent all their own. I was living in a foreign country. An outsider overhearing a conversation between me and a Cajun would need a translator. Our fighter wing had four squadrons, each equipped with 24 F-100s, at least on paper. A drastic shortage of spare parts led us to perhaps being 50 percent in-commission on any given day. One of our squadrons was deployed overseas at all times. Those were the days of heavy TAC rotations that took a toll on careers, families and marriages.

Our squadron commanders were often of WWII or Korean War vintage. They and we young fighter pilots were from different planets. We were in a training rut. This was the Cold War and most USAF fighters of the day were capable of delivering nuclear weapons. So, we sat nuclear alert all over the world ready to turn parts of the planet and its occupants into "crispy critters."

Midway through my time at Alex, I was selected to attend the USAF Fighter Weapons School (FWS) at Nellis AFB, NV. This is where you went to get your PhD in the fighter business. The USAF FWS "long" preceded the Navy Top Gun school. It was also far more disciplined and realistic. We spent the weekend in downtown Vegas, but Monday we were back at it "full throttle." I managed to come away with awards for Academics, Flying, and overall Top Gun. Over time, the plaques and trophies have migrated from living room to den, to office, to garage. Such is life; past glories fade into memories.

I did have a very minor advantage. The year before I attended FWS, the Air Force sponsored, "The World Congress of Flight." One pilot from each fighter wing in the Air Force competed. I won the shoot-off at Alex and represented the 401st TFW. Although I was a mere 1st Lt, I finished 5th in the world; not bad by almost any standard, but for a fighter pilot, not very fulfilling. My backup pilot for this event was Capt Jim Ryan. After I had won the competition at Alex, the Wing Commander, likely a little nervous about the junior lieutenant brought Jim back from temporary duty in Turkey to go head-to-head with me in one more shoot-out. I was more than a little pissed at having to win twice, but didn't get a vote. I beat Jim by a whisker, validating the previous competition. We've been good friends ever since – one helluva' guy.

One late spring morning, my squadron commander called me in to tell me I had a new assignment. I was going to fly with the U.S. Navy on exchange duty – what a hardship - Miramar Naval Air Station in San Diego CA. I was soon off to the first of four assignments in the

Golden State, where I was to spend nearly a third of my Air Force career.

The first four or five months were spent in the F-4 Replacement Air Group, or "RAG," VF-121. A like squadron trained naval aviators on the east coast. The F-4B was an early version of the nearly 5,000 Phantoms produced by McDonnell Douglas Corp. and flown by dozens of countries. Between our Navy and Air Force, "the Phantom," was in service for nearly 50 years; still is in some foreign countries. There were a few F-4As at Miramar when I first arrived, and I took my first F-4 flight in the backseat of one on the long journey (15 miles as the crow flies) from Miramar to North Island where it wound up on a pole, displayed at the main gate. Over time I checked-out in the F-4C, D, E and G. The aircraft got heavier every passing year. In the tropical atmosphere of the Philippines in the 1980s an F-4G simply would not climb above 25,000 ft. without stroking the afterburner.

A bachelor in San Diego has lots of distractions - think back to the songs of the '60s, California Dreamin'. My first pad was bayside on Mission Beach. I could fall off my second floor patio and land in the sand at $110 a month. Later, I moved into the "Poonderosa," appropriately named and another "bachelor shack" more inland but with the ocean in sight. Remember Lorne Greene and the Ponderosa? - pool, palms - no telling who you might run across or in what state when the sun came up. It was an eclectic group who lived there over time: a "conventional" submariner who had been in some verrrrry interesting places (these guys did risky things you would not believe); a rookie naval aviator, later to be a rear admiral; and many more. I was only five years out of West Point and my eyes were being opened – WIDE!

When I arrived at Miramar, I was already a combat veteran. I had flown a few F-100 missions from my Alex rotation days into the Plain of Jars and other interesting spots in Southeast Asia (SEA) that would soon become part of the American lexicon. Our USAF squadron had rotated to the Philippines and from there forward deployed into Da Nang. On one mission we were personally briefed by the senior Air Force general in-country. The mission was led by Maj Dave Ward, the 615th TFS Squadron Commander and was in many ways a comedy of errors. The bad guys had shot down a USAF recce bird, an F-101 in the Plain of Jars. Someone in Washington thought that was a bit much, and the perpetrators needed to be punished.

The Wing Commander at Clark, to whom we had ceded operational control, was a WWII veteran with a few kills under his belt, but the intervening years had invalidated the tactics of two decades prior. The Wing King was flamboyant. At George AFB, his personal F-104 was specially painted and had white sidewall tires! He insisted he be on the mission.

We got through the mission without hurting anyone, but I give Lady Luck most of the credit. We made multiple passes on a gun site like we were on a gunnery training range in the U.S. Good grief! Lots of orange tracers came whizzing past. The Colonel's flight of four hit the wrong target. They also mismanaged their fuel, and had to recover in Thailand. My flight got back to Da Nang OK, although my wingman and I had less than 1000 lbs. of JP-4 left between us; within the range of instrument error in the F-100.

Lessons learned? If you go over five years between combat excursions, your tactics are probably amiss. Red Flag and advanced unit training at Nellis and overseas has improved this dilemma, but it is not solved. This was just one of many examples of early "goat rope" tactics in a screwed-up war.

Oh, yes, back to the Navy and the "carrier quals" that elevated my heart rate at the beginning of this story: I made it that night, successfully "qualed" and shortly after, I transferred to my regular Navy squadron that had just returned from a Pacific cruise. After a few weeks of light duty, they began the training cycle work-up for their next trip to the western Pacific and Southeast Asia. This would become my second combat tour, the first being out of Da Nang with the Air Force.

Navy F-4 pilots were trained as interceptor pilots with the primary mission of fleet air defense. The Air Force had operated the F-4 for a few years in both air-to-air and air-to–ground roles. For their mission in Vietnam, the Navy F-4 community needed to learn how to "bomb." To say the F-4 pilots were less than enthusiastic is an understatement. They viewed themselves as "MiG killers" and dropping bombs was beneath the dignity of an air-to-air fighter pilot with silk scarf and carrier qual.

Since I was an "old head" in the bombing business I decided to try to help with the introduction to "pointing your nose at the ground." With the assistance of my friends at Nellis I got my hands on some invaluable training material. Then, I persuaded the somewhat reluctant (a gross understatement) squadron commander, he needed to get in the game. He wasn't all in, but agreed to give it a go, and his enthusiasm brightened as time passed.

Ground school came first: dive angle; bomb fall line; ballistics - the very basics. As I stood at the blackboard, I too often saw "Xs" or maybe blanks for eyes. Persistence, an important principle in warfare, began to pay off in the training world. We deployed to Yuma to take advantage of nearby training ranges and the pilots began to find out air-to-ground could be fun.

One morning, we were to drop some live ordnance, Mk-82 500 lb. "Snakeye" retarded bombs. I took a stroll through the jets on the ramp and was glad I did. The retarded bombs were grossly miss-wired. They would have dropped from the jets armed, but not retarded, and may have gone off right under the airplane and blown up a jet or two. I got the Squadron Commander to call a halt to flying. Somehow we got through our work-up without hurting anyone, and were off to the war on the aircraft carrier, USS Ranger.

The Navy decided we needed a little "warmup" before heading for North Vietnam and copped some missions with FACs down in the Delta area of South Vietnam. It wasn't pretty, and I'm sure the FACs were in wonderment, less than impressed, but we survived and headed north.

One morning my Skipper (the Squadron Commander) said I needed to take a wingman and go see the Admiral. I knew there was an admiral aboard someplace, but he lived in a world of which I knew not. I took a young LT JG and we finally found where the Admiral spent his time. Only the Admiral and a Captain were there. What happened next sounded like one of those sixties TV shows: "I have a special mission for you, should you choose to accept." I was probably picked because I was the "mad bomber" from the Air Force.

Intelligence reported a large Vietnamese PT boat regularly left the vicinity of Haiphong and sprinted east to a small harbor perhaps 100 miles distant. On board was reportedly a North Vietnamese Admiral. My "wingy" and I plotted it out. We depended on dead-reckoning because the F-4B didn't have an inertial navigation set. It was simply "time and distance" on a very big lake.

Occasionally in war, the gods are with you. We flew low to stay off the radar, and the weather was "clear and a million." As we closed with our predicted target, we drifted-up to a thousand feet, and lo and behold, perhaps 45 degrees left, at a perfect distance, there she was: the PT boat with a roiling wake behind her. Earlier, I had chosen to load out with wall-to-wall Zuni 5-inch rockets. My wingman and I each carried 24.

I let the ripple go, probably a little close, but I had fangs out and these dudes were going to die! My first rocket hit right on the bow and sequenced aft. Bodies flew everywhere. We didn't stay around to look but beat feet back to the boat (only naval aviators can call a ship "a boat"). To tell the truth, I was shaking like a leaf; what a rush. Post strike photos, probably from a sub, confirmed our claims.

On return to the States, I had anticipated an assignment to the Air Force Fighter Weapons School, but not so fast, Williams. The Air Force had another idea. Since I already knew how to land on a boat, they would like me to deploy with the Navy's first A-7 squadron. I wasn't very interested, but what was a Captain to say? I guess I could have checked out of the Air Force like my good friend John Anderson, and gone on to other things. But I acquiesced.

The A-7A was grossly underpowered and had a primitive bombing-navigation system. The Air Force eventually saved the airplane by insisting on a whole new digital avionics suite that paved the way in tactical aviation for years to come.

There was no way out of another long boat ride, so off I went to NAS Lemoore, an Air Force officer preparing for another trip with the Navy to the Gulf of Tonkin for a third combat tour, two off carrier Ranger. This put me in combat parts of five consecutive years and near the end of the tour, we scrambled to Korea where the North Koreans had captured a US intelligence ship, the Pueblo, and imprisoned its crew. Korea and surrounding waters were cold, and we had to fly with "Poopy suits" in case of over-water ejection. Climbing into the jet one very cold morning, I strained my back so badly I could neither get up nor down the aircraft ladder. I had back spasms that were no fun at all. Of course I sought medical help and a prescient Navy Flight Surgeon, a friend to this day, decided I had had enough. He grounded me, and for a while thought it was his duty to notify the Air Force. I told him if he did he was a dead man walking. He relented but that back bites me to this day.

I am often asked how it was flying off a carrier? Well, the rooms were small, but air-conditioned; the food pretty good; every officer had a safe that also served as a liquor cabinet because liquor was prohibited on board; and the 12-hour work shifts tiring. We flew once or twice a day and the flying was exciting, challenging, rewarding. In our off time we slept, read or played poker. We were "on-station" for a cruise about six-seven months. We pulled back into Subic Bay in the P.I. for resupply every 30 days. I am a member of the "Triple Centurion" – 300 hundred arrested carrier landings (called "traps") on the Ranger. The Navy offered me great experiences. I thank them. They are a professional service with a tough life in a demanding business; however, I must admit I have reached the age there are things I would rather do in life than trap on a small pitching deck at night in the weather.

Unlike many of my cohorts, I escaped my combat tours unscathed. I departed the Navy with mixed emotions and headed for Edwards Flight Test Center as TAC's project officer for A-7 testing, then to the Pentagon in the Tactical Fighter Division, Ops Requirements. National War College came next followed by Izmir, Turkey where I was Base Commander, then a tour as Director of Operations at Zaragosa, Spain. When the A-10 arrived at the 81st TFW at Royal Air Force Station Bentwaters in the U.K. I was sent first as Vice Commander and later became Wing Commander. It was another great flying assignment in a long list. From Bentwaters I went to Ramstein, Air Base Germany to be the Inspector General for USAFE and completed seven concurrent years in Europe.

I assume, to renew my English, I was sent from Europe to be Director of Aerospace Safety at Norton AFB, CA. I was promoted to two-star and became Center Commander. My stateside tour didn't last long. A year after becoming Safety Center Commander, I was ordered to Clark Air Base in the Philippines to become Commander, 13th Air Force, Pacific Air Forces.

I've always had an appreciation for the Philippines since my first assignment there as a buck fighter pilot, and even before that. In Military History class at West Point the tales of our involvement in the P.I. particularly after the Spanish-American War in the very late nineteenth century had been of great interest to me. My first Fight Commander at Clark was Capt Fred Funston III. He was the grandson of Col Fred Funston who captured President/General Emilio Aguinaldo back in 1902 during the Philippine Insurrection. Aquinaldo defeated the Spanish but was no match for the Americans.

My Philippine tour was interesting, not from an operational standpoint, but from a geopolitical perspective. The political landscape in the P.I. had been dominated by Ferdinand Marcos for a long time, but the natives were restless. His administrations were corrupt by any standard to a point they were almost laughable. This led to what was called, "the People Power Revolution." Corazon Aquino became the right lady at the right time. Aquino spent years in the States in quasi-exile, but was now ensconced on Hacienda Luisita, a semi-fiefdom not far from Clark Air Base. Her husband had been assassinated on the tarmac at Manila International upon his return from exile a few years earlier. No one of importance was ever brought to justice over that crime, but it was commonly accepted that the Marcos's were behind it. The revolution was a story unto itself, too long to be detailed here. But, suffice it to say that Aquino courageously toppled the 20-year Marcos regime and saved Philippine democracy. She was Time's "Woman of the Year" in 1986.

Unrest in Manila burgeoned day-by-day. A key player in the drama was Gen Fidel Ramos, West Point class of 1950. Gen Ramos and I had gotten along very well since my arrival at Clark as West Point "ring knockers" were wont to do. From time-to-time he came to Clark, and we played golf. In many ways it was an intelligence dump. I needed to be careful about what I passed on to the Ambassador. I was torn between good friendship and duty.

I had developed a good relationship with U.S. Ambassador to the Philippines, Steve Bosworth who was a "risen" star in the Diplomatic Corps. Bosworth was on his third ambassadorship and younger than me. We met often at the weekly country team meeting at the Embassy on Manila Bay. Steve liked golf, and the Air Force managed a conference center, resort and golf course in Baguio, a delightful small town in the mountains 120 miles north of Clark. It was a great place to escape. One of the perks of command was access to a beautiful villa, with seven bedrooms, and built-in maids and cooks. One could stand on the veranda in the morning and look down on a brilliant white undercast as far as the eye could see. The elevation was 5500 feet. (Mile High Club anyone?)

The Ambassador also had a magnificent residence in Baguio. General Jonathan Wainright, who was cruelly imprisoned by the Japanese during WWII, accepted their surrender in that residence in 1945. When appropriate, we scheduled joint conferences there. That allowed me to use my small twin-turbo support aircraft to pick up the Ambassador in Manila, and avoid the long drive. He sometimes seemed a little nervous when I was flying the plane.

The streets of Manila were full of protesters, but the protests were rarely violent. The revolution was in full swing. To all but the blind this would end soon. President Reagan didn't want an assassination of Ferdinand and Imelda Marcos to end this popular people's movement. Reagan was persuaded by Secretary of State George Schultz to approve the Marcos's exile to asylum in Hawaii.

There were three very large U.S. Air Force helicopters at Clark, not under my direct command, but always supportive of our needs. We planned to land just outside the moat surrounding the Philippine Presidential Palace, pickup Marcos and make our way back to Clark, no small feat to pull-off safely in view of the unrest.

I was at the U.S. Embassy. The choppers stopped and picked me up along with Brigadier General Teddy Allen, Chief of JUSMAAG, the assistance group. We then picked up Marcos and his entire entourage just after dark and made our way to Clark. An adventurous six hours later, the Marcos's were on their way to Guam and thence to Hawaii.

The end of my Philippine tour was filled with medical drama. I met a "bad mosquito" and contracted encephalitis, a viral brain infection that can be life-threatening and mine certainly was. I lost my memory and was really down for the count. It was a horrible experience. I was assigned as Deputy for Programs and Resources in the Pentagon but spent most of the year in medical rehab at John Hopkins. I am not sure I ever totally recovered. When I returned to duty, I went to Stuttgart, Germany as J-5 for European Command. From there I retired with just over 35 years in the military.

Looking back on my career, I am grateful to the Air Force for all the opportunities and challenges they pushed my way. I never had a bad assignment. I met wonderful people, made good friends and held great commands. I got a view of the world few get to see. What a ride!

Chapter Twenty

Always The Hard Way

by Daniel R. "Doc" Zoerb

Early Years: I was born at a very young age (yep, that's what my mother told me) in Kingsport, Tennessee, the oldest of three brothers, and the son of an East Tennessee State music major turned fighter ace with seven kills and a South Carolina farmer's daughter. The year was 1947.

After WWII, my father, with his father as a silent partner, bought enough land for a small airport, graded the runway on top of a hill, bought several airplanes and began to provide flight training in Johnson City, TN near Kingsport. My grandfather worked at Eastman Chemical Company in Kingsport and had hired a young lady, a recent graduate of Winthrop College from Britons Neck, SC, to work in his personnel department. My father recognized his father's superb judgment and married her, then set about trying to make a go of the airport business and raising kids. My earliest memories in life are of utter fascination at the sight of the houses getting smaller as my father and I took off in his Gullwing Stinson Reliant or one of the Ercoupes.

The airport business broke even in 1950 and, still a Reservist, my father was recalled when the Korean War began. Despite his pleading, the closest he got to Korea was McChord AFB, WA in the F-94. Remaining on active duty, he and my mother introduced us boys to some of the world's garden spots...like Rabat Morocco (camels spit), Wheelus AB in Tripoli, Libya where my youngest brother was born (try using Libya as "place of birth" on your next application) and where we lived in base housing (more about that particular base housing later), and Turner AFB in Albany, GA (F-84F SAC fighters). The trip to North Africa was made aboard a C-54 and I can still remember spending hours in the jump seat transfixed with the gazillion dials, levers and switches, and thinking how cool it would be to fly. Tours in Arlington, VA (Fort Fumble), Cheyenne,

WY (F.E. Warren AFB) and Riverside, CA (March AFB) rounded out my time as an Air Force brat.

About the time I finished high school in Riverside, I began to think of myself as brilliant...a genius without need of parental guidance. As a matter of fact, if my parents suggested a course of action, I'd pursue the opposite. "You could go to the Air Force Academy since you have an appointment from Tennessee Senator Howard Baker," says they..."no", says I, "believe I'll go to the University of Tennessee majoring in football and track with a very-minor in engineering...and I'll get married to further assert myself." It only took a few years of being on my own to realize the errors of my ways (slow learner) and that I was going nowhere at a great rate. Wait! I've got an idea...let's join the Air Force. Always the hard way.

Enlisted Years: In 1968, the recruiters were happy to see volunteers and shortly after being sworn into the Air Force, the Army, just to be sure, sent me their "greetings" forwarded to Lackland AFB where I was mid-way through basic training. I finished basic as the #1 graduate and got to pick my technical school, as long as it was Aircraft Mechanic, Reciprocating Engine Aircraft at Sheppard AFB. I also finished that course as the #1 graduate, a safety wiring expert, and was off to my first assignment at Seymour Johnson AFB, NC, which, in 1969, had no McDonald's and one restaurant which allowed brown-bag liquor. Pay in those days was interesting...apparently, AF didn't trust airmen to bring home their paychecks. So, the wife received a monthly check for $100, which included the monthly $60 housing allowance and $40 from her husband's pay. I was assigned to Base Flight and learned the glorious inner-workings of Gooney Birds and T-29s, while watching F-4s fly and getting plenty of cockpit time in them when they were hangared.

I also found out that, with a little time and experience under my belt, I could upgrade to flight engineer and at least get off the ground after working to fix those tired old airplanes...and draw flight pay! Flying (cheating death) with old, not-so-current Lt Cols from the wing staff also motivated me to start the night-school thing in hopes of finishing a degree and doing the flying myself. Flying all day and going to school or fixing broke airplanes at night was a challenge, but arrival of the first-born certainly upped the ante...the first daughter in the Zoerb Clan for five generations. Speaking of clans...recent generations of Zoerbs take a lot of flak for large celebrations of St. Patrick's Day by folks with a German name. Both my parents were pure-blooded Irish, and we have the Zoerb name because my father was adopted as an infant by Archie Zoerb.

Back to the saga...as a qualified recip flight engineer with a new car, a new baby and still no college degree...I received orders to Vietnam in 1971. After a C-123K checkout at Lockbourne AFB, now Rickenbacker, and snake school in the P.I., Buck Sergeant Zoerb found himself on the flight schedule with the 311th TAS at Phan Rang AB, RVN. Flying 125-knot trash haulers around people that enjoyed easy target practice, carrying loads of people/paratroopers/chickens and pigs/fuel bladders/food and medicine/etc. and landing on short, red-dirt strips, where the mighty Hercules dare not tread, made for about a million stories...an abbreviated sample of which follows:

On an assault takeoff from a special forces camp, small arms ground fire started a fire in the right oil cooler just ahead of the nacelle, which was a fuel tank. I jumped down off the flight deck, confirmed the fire, jumped back up and recommended to the pilots that we jettison the nacelle...vigorous head nods from both, a large "ka-thunk" and much wing rocking, and we diverted into Da Nang. Two weeks later back at Phan Rang, some Army recce types brought in a small piece of charred aluminum with a serial number on it and asked if we knew what it was. It turned out to be a piece of our jettisoned nacelle which had been found amongst some dead enemy troops and a machine gun. Somewhere, I have a picture of a **B**C-123K with the silhouette of a machine gun stenciled on the side of the airplane below the pilot's window.

Carrying chickens and pigs...sometimes steers...was almost always the source of some dark humor. Invariably, a few of the flimsy crates would break and we'd have farm animals racing around the cargo deck. Some loadmasters felt compelled to try and catch them, but TSgt. Luther Byrd Farmer from Little Rock, AR, my hard-crew loadmaster, had an easier solution...he'd open one of the aft troop doors, and as soon as farm animals saw daylight, out the door they'd go, little legs/wings flailing all the way down. Steers were mostly air dropped to remote sites and after parachuting a couple thousand feet stiff legged, were partially butchered when the troops recovered them...steaks were excellent, I was told. A final animal story involves a huge, bull water buffalo being transported by my C-123K as a gift from one provincial chief to another. Luther, with much help, secured the beast to a tie-down ring in the floor of the cargo deck via one tie-down strap though the bull's nose ring and several other nets/straps. The beast stood surprisingly quietly through taxi and takeoff, but about half way to the arrival ceremony at about 5000 ft., he decided he'd had enough. With much bellowing and thrashing, he managed to rip the tie-down ring out of the floor (a corrosion issue), escape the nets and began to do considerable damage to the inside of the airplane...the wheel well area contained hydraulic lines and equipment and various "nice-to-have" electrical components. Fearing we'd become a laughing stock at the bar if it turned out a water buffalo had brought down our airplane, I voted to shoot the thing. Luther, hiding in the smallest portion of the tail cone safe from the marauding beast, agreed. But, the pilots felt a need to have a discussion with themselves and with HHQ since this was a "high-vis" political mission. As more "nice-to-have" systems began to fail, the pilot finally granted permission to fire at will, and two shots later, the bull went down. Taxiing in with blood pouring out of the airplane, we were met by a very unhappy political wonk and told to park in the boonies. A forklift hauled the beast away and I understand chow was good that night.

Other memorable C-123 missions, like being escorted by fast fighters while spraying ugly stuff and flying Candlestick FAC out of NKP, generated some great stories for a Friday night at the bar. The challenge of escorting a 100-knot spray bird at low altitude with a 400-knot fighter can't be overstated...fighters strafe a little early – bad guys are irritated and shoot the slow mover...fighters strafe a little late – bad guys are irritated and shoot the slow mover...no win. FAC'ing with a C-123 was also a challenge...paint the undersides black, install flame arrestors on the exhaust stacks, turn out all lights, troll "the Trail" with a navigator staring through a starlight scope in the forward troop door and when you find something, kick out a flare which clearly illuminates the large, slow airplane making a fine target. We flew with two navigators because after 15 minutes or so staring through the starlight scope, the first nav would hurl and the second was needed to replace him...and so on for hours.

As flight engineers and loadmasters, dripping wet with rain/sweat each time we landed and refueled/loaded cargo...then shivering in frosty flight suits at altitude...we were ok...we were enlisted troops and that's what we signed up for? The C-7 Caribou crews were a different story...they had only one enlisted crewmember with two hats...flight engineer from engine start to shutdown, and loadmaster after shutdown. That meant the co-pilot, usually a lieutenant, had to pump gas and pour oil. This usually required two or three five-gallon cans per engine while standing on a greasy wing in the rain/wind, many feet off the ground. We engineers just grinned and enjoyed the show. Our crews were usually led by a SAC Lt Col with thousands of hours in KC-135s, in the left seat, and a brand new Lt in the right seat who was probably not first in his UPT class. The good news was that we engineers made LOTS of money from pilots not proficient in starting a hot R-2800, and most of the time, they had the engineers start engines. But, the bad news was the need to constantly play defense, to the point of slapping hands, and to master the art of the tactful suggestion – "Sir, would you like me to put the gear down before we land? How 'bout some flaps?" - as a result, I became totally committed to becoming a fighter pilot. If I was going to die in an airplane, I'd rather do it to myself...by myself! Always the hard way.

Commissioned Years: After Vietnam, I was assigned to Kincheloe AFB, MI as a Staff Sergeant crew chief on the B-52H (a recip flight engineer assigned to multi-multi-engine jets...makes sense?). We maintained the airplanes on an open ramp and learned how miserable maintenance can be in a winter with over 200 inches of snow (having just returned from the jungle). Even more determined than ever to be commissioned and fly, I stumbled across the AF Bootstrap Commissioning Program, a one-year TDY to college followed by OTS and UPT, which required that you be within one year of degree completion and, less than 27 years-old. CBPO at Kincheloe AFB forwarded my application and low and behold, I was accepted...off to the U of Nebraska! A year later with my degree in hand, I reported to OTS at Lackland AFB where those of us on the pilot-track also did a mid-OTS tour at Hondo for pre-flight qualification training in T-41s. I dropped back to the following OTS class after Hondo and became the OT Wing Commander, graduating #1. December 21, 1973, my father pinned his old gold bars on me...a proud moment for both of us.

After the ceremony, it was off to Webb AFB in Big Spring, TX for a UPT class that started two weeks after OTS graduation. No McDonald's in Big Spring either...neighbors going shopping in Midland would take orders and bring back soggy, cold Big Macs...a real treat! What Big Spring did have was lots of crosswinds and dust storms which probably made us all better aviators, but created lots of excitement/anxiety in solo cockpits. I wasn't too sure of myself until my IP, Maj Al Smith, hung himself by his oxygen hose when he stepped over the side of the T-37 trying to deplane on my solo sortie...I figured if a dude that performed embarrassing stunts like that was qualified to fly – I was too. I graduated with a new son, a few awards and a #3 ranking, entitling me to one of the three fighter assignments our class of 34 received...the two ahead of me took the F-4 and RF-4 leaving me the F-106. Brig Gen Chuck Yeager was the guest speaker at graduation. My father, the ace, pinned his shiny silver wings on my puffed-out chest and neither one of us can remember a prouder moment...go fly single-seat, century series fighters and make all your landings single-engine no flaps...just doesn't get much better!

But it can get a little worse: Towards the end of the T-33 qualification course at Tyndall AFB, a precursor to the F-106 course, the commander called me in and told me he had gotten my assignment changed. Now, instead of the F-106 course and a move to Castle AFB, I was going to be an IP in T-33s and remain at Tyndall for a year to help alleviate the IP shortage...then, I could have a Six to anywhere I wanted. The time spent teaching, in aircraft tail numbers found in my father's logbook, was probably well spent and generated some classic flying stories.

The F-106 course happened as promised, and I got an assignment to the 48th FIS at Langley AFB, VA. Air defense alert at most ADC bases was time to nap, watch bad movies and study, but at Langley and with the Alert Detachment at Charleston, it was unusual <u>not</u> to get scrambled...TU-95 Bears trolling up and down the East Coast (usually at 0-dark thirty) and general aviation aircraft not talking to FAA or lost (many coming from Bermuda). Often the targets were identified and the scramble cancelled, but not until we were already airborne. Our response times were well less than the allotted five minutes.

Early morning scrambles also generated one of the funniest, but descriptive write-ups in the maintenance discrepancy book: "Airplane makes night, overwater noises in the daytime, over land" (attributed to Maj Dick Stultz).

One scramble stands out as being unusual. In January 1980, Bo Rein, the LSU head football coach, and Louis Benscotter, the pilot, took off from Shreveport, LA in a Cessna 441 and were given clearance to deviate for weather en route to Baton Rouge. When I intercepted the airplane, it was still on the heading used to avoid the weather and flying at over 40,000 ft. directly above Norfolk, VA. The second F-106 aborted the scramble takeoff with his nose off the ground just below 190kt flying speed because one of his gear indicators went out (go figure!). So, I was by my lonesome on a clear moonlit night about 0100. Guard F-4s had tracked the Cessna on radar, but I was the first to rendezvous with it. Because of the slow speed, I was only able to stagger past as slow as I could go and continue doing orbits trying to signal or see some signs of life. About 100 nm out over the Atlantic, the Cessna began a slow, descending right turn (possibly one engine quit?) from an easterly heading around to a northerly heading, then rolled out (other engine quit?) and continued the descent until it departed controlled flight at about 28,000 ft. and spun/tumbled into the water. Some debris was found, but that was it. Hypoxia was believed to have been the cause. The only bright spot in the whole thing was Walter Cronkite actually pronouncing my name correctly on the nightly news.

Flying a snap-up intercept and shooting an inert AIR-2A (850lb. nuclear rocket) at a Bomarc target at 60,000 ft. (spectacular!); graduating from Interceptor Weapons School (learning to teach enough chaff and jamming to make a grown man cry; lots of DACT; shooting missiles/guns; a final checkride under the bag in the backseat at 500 ft. over land at night as a two-ship vs. multiple unkowns; and testing the M-61 gun following integration on the Six (finally, a useful weapon for air-to-air vs. other fighters) round out the many memories of the four years spent in that beautiful airplane.

The 48th FIS was selected to be the first air defense squadron to convert to the F-15, in part because the 1st TFW at Langley had

331

transitioned a few years before and was getting rid of their old, tired jets in favor of newer machines. The transition was an eye-watering example of how far technology had come in the 20+ years between the Six and the Eagle...performance/maneuverability, radar, visibility, number of missiles and a cockpit big enough to get lost in, and more than a few old habits to break. The Six had a mike button on the right-hand stick grip so when you were operating the radar with the left-hand side of the split stick grip, you could talk on the radio...in most other fighters, including the Eagle, what had been a mike button in the Six is the "pickle" button...which didn't make a great excuse when the IP graded my film and charged me with many bad shots. One drawback to the new airplane was the time it took to launch from alert when the klaxton sounded. After engine start, while waiting on the INS to time-in, very often the scramble would be cancelled...much less flying from alert. With the transition to TAC, we were also faced with many more regulations than in ADCOM (hard for some of us cowboys to swallow)...like weather minimums for various categories of pilots (we thought published minimums were good enough?); being at 300 ft. at a mile on final in the VFR pattern (wings level in the overrun had always been expected); having to put on poopy suits during scrambles in the winter (no way to make a five-minute scramble); limits on the number of sorties that could be flown in a 24-hour period (fly til' you ran out of extended crew rest on exercises?), etc. In the end, I'm sure we were all better off.

As part of my transition to the F-15, and because of time on station, I was selected to establish and command the first F-15 Alert Detachment at Tyndall AFB, FL. The Tyndall alert facility had no permanent occupants since the Coon Ass Militia, Louisiana ANG, had been banished by Maj Gen Reed for poor judgment at the bar (another story for another time). I successfully lobbied for the best Chief I knew, Chief Allison Jacobs, and between the two of us, we were able to hand-pick 45 of the finest Eagle maintainers in the USAF, along with 12 other support types. The existing facilities were refurbished and the facility became a showplace...best facilities awards...best personnel awards...best airplanes, and an almost constant stream of visiting dignitaries. With the only Eagles at a base full of F-106s, F-101s, QF-102s and T-33s we were a proud organization. We kept two F-15s on alert and two-four more outside the alert hangars to fly daily training and to spare the alert mission…a real flying club. Early on, when I successfully proposed a change to the scramble departure procedure requiring a near-vertical afterburner climb/Immelmann off the northwest runway to a heading out over the Gulf, base leadership had questioned the need. I maintained it was a necessity since it ensured the quickest possible intercept of unknowns. That worked, and we had a great time showing off the F-15 climb performance every time we flew daily active air scrambles or "practice scrambles," until General John Jaquish took command of the Wing. "Doc," he said, "Why do you guys always do burner climbs on takeoff?"

"Well, sir, because we have to," said I.

"No, you don't," said the general in a gnarly tone, and that was the end of the fun at Tyndall.

As the end of the command tour approached, I applied for the pilot exchange program in an effort to head-off a staff assignment. In a call from MPC, it sounded like I would be doing the AF a favor if I would take this brand new exchange billet to a place called NAS Lemoore, CA flying an F/A-something or other, strange place, strange airplane, or so said the MPC dude. Without hesitation, I took it and in so doing, became the first USAF pilot to fly operational F/A-18s with the Navy. The initial assignment was to the Hornet Replacement Air Group (RAG), VFA-125, where I became an IP after qualifying in the airplane. Having never dropped <u>anything</u> off an airplane, except a C-123 nacelle, the air to ground phase was a real eye opener! Coaching by IPs would invariably include the phrase, "Doc, just roll-in and establish the normal sight picture"…to which I invariably replied… "What's that look like?" Once I finally got the hang of manual deliveries, the auto and CCIP modes were a piece of cake, mostly because the airplane was a bullseye bomber. In the air-to-air role, the combination of great slow-speed maneuverability and the director gun sight made the Hornet a knife-fighter's dream, but going fast, or the ability to extend out of a fight, was <u>not</u> a strength.

Flying a brand-new airplane, a first for me, resulted in some exciting experiences…like discovering that at low altitude and high speeds, rapid aileron input caused rolls in the opposite direction (unhandy) because of wing twisting. The McDonnell Douglas tech reps were unperturbed and had the 4-channel fly-by-wire flight control program software revised to reduce aileron response at low altitude/

high speed and increase inboard flap and rudder response to roll commands (magic!). Flying instruments using the HUD symbology, a no-no in F-15, probe and drogue refueling and learning to speak a new language were a few of the adaptations I managed to make. In the midst of it all, I was promoted to Major and the Skipper called me into his office to ask me why I was still wearing Captain's bars. I explained AF promotion lists and promotion sequence numbers and that I wouldn't be able to wear the new rank for many months. He shoved the paperwork across his desk for me to sign, frocking me to Major, and said, "You're in the Navy right now and this is how we do it." Thus, I became Doc Zoerb, "LtCdr, USAF."

Other than learning to speak "Navy," it became clear that if I was to discover what the operational Navy was all about, I needed to go sea. The first carrier with F/A-18s had just deployed from the West coast, and the next to deploy was an East coast carrier, USS Coral Sea. VFA-131 adopted me and with help from VFA-125, scheduled me for carrier qualification. The AF reluctantly, because I only had 18 months on station, agreed to a PCS to NAS Cecil Field in Jacksonville, FL. Carrier qualification training was intense, endless night field carrier landing practice, but unlike my Navy brothers who had been exposed to carrier ops in undergraduate pilot training, nothing prepared me for my first look at the ship. We flew out to USS Kitty Hawk at 20,000 ft. and the boat looked very small. No worries, said I, it will look bigger when we get lower. Not so! As an aside, the Navy does have a few two-seat Hornets, but carrier qualification is done in the single-seat airplane. No IP wants to ride with you and nobody needs to hear you whimper unless you key the mike. The memory of that first pattern and landing will remain burned into my brain forever...near-terror...together with the added pressure of making sure I didn't embarrass the AF. After two touch-and-goes, six day traps and four night traps the LSO, Lt Dan "Groper" Moore, signed-off on my qualification and they shot me to the beach where landing on a 12,000 ft. runway felt strangely comforting.

In October 1985, Coral Sea pushed-off from the pier in Norfolk and shortly after, Air Wing 13 flew aboard, headed for the Mediterranean. CVW-13 was the first "all-Hornet" air wing, meaning there were no F-14s or A-7s, only four squadrons of F/A-18s, two Navy and two Marine, to perform both fighter and attack roles; there was also a squadron of A-6/KA-6s (no EA-6s), E-2s and helos. The deployment was largely uneventful. We flew two-three weeks, then spent a week in port. In December, when the airports in Rome and Vienna were bombed, the air wing began a non-stop strike planning effort focused on Libya. The lack of EA-6s aboard Coral Sea created a thrash at Whidbey Island and interrupted the New Year's bash at the club with a "No Notice Deployment" by the Joint Chiefs of Staff to augment CVW-13 with Electronic Countermeasures/Jamming Support. Prowlers trapped aboard Coral Sea 2 Jan 1986 (amazing!). The USAF had not yet decided to what extent they would be able to participate (overflight issues and others) if an attack was ordered. So, CVW-13 strike planned all of the approved targets. As an air wing strike lead, I was able to pick the target I wanted to plan/attack, a training facility near Tripoli that had once been base housing at Wheelus AFB. Our family's old house was still there. The F-111 wing at Lakenheath sent an assistant ops officer to the ship to monitor planning and to feed the wing info needed to prepare for their potential participation, and of course, I was responsible for the AF Lt Col. He continued to whine about how much he had always wanted to fly off the boat, even after I told him the KA-6 would be his only option and suggested he really didn't want to do that. In the end, everyone signed off and VA-95 loaded a five-tank KA-6 (heaviest shot) and launched the Lt Col from the waist catapult (the shortest one). The cat shot crushed his face and caused him to admit he probably wouldn't need to do that again. February and March were more of the same, intercepting well-behaved MiGs, which was disappointing for those of us aspiring to become aces, conducting ops below Gadhafi's "Line of Death" in the Gulf of Sidra and strike planning.

Towards the end of March, Lt "Huey" Morrison and I were shadowing the Libyan IL-76 command and control airplane as it descended for landing at Misrata. Near-constant illumination of our radar warning receivers was a fact of life close to the Libyan coast, but on this day, as we broke off the IL-76 shadow, RWR displayed a flashing SA-5 indication and looking to the South, I saw two missiles launch from the vicinity of Sirte. Impressive smoke trails helped us keep track of the missiles as we did our "funky chicken" SAM break. One of the two SA-5s detonated as the missiles reached the top of their arc, and we lost sight of the other. No friendlies were hit.

The launch of strategic SAMs was reason enough to take action, we thought, but the bombing of a disco in Germany that killed a U.S. serviceman ended the dithering, and on 15 April 1986, we launched Operation Eldorado Canyon. The Lakenheath F-111s attacked the Tripoli targets and Coral Sea attacked the Eastern/Benghazi targets including the first-ever employment of HARM and the destruction of the SA-5 site at Sirte. Those of us that had lost our targets to the USAF flew air-to-air CAPs, but none of the Libyans chose to fly that night, nor the following days.

About mid-way through the eight-month deployment, in the midst of strike planning, AF MPC sent a message giving me a staff assignment with "early reporting authorized." The assignment was eventually turned off, but they remembered my name (not good). For the next year or so, as VFA-131 Ops O., I was responsible for executing the post-deployment turn-around training plan in preparation for the next deployment. The Navy in their wisdom, transfers many of the experienced aviators just returning from the deployment and fills gaps with mostly junior aviators (nuggets), a challenging training environment. After nearly four years with the Navy, the AF got serious about an assignment for me, but the rules had changed. If you had not been flying your primary airplane (F-15) for longer than two or three years, it was _required_ that you be re-assigned to a flying job at an operational wing (dammit...you mean I can't go to the staff?).

So, after a requal at Luke, off I went to the 33d FW at Eglin AFB, FL. The flying, along with new F-15C weapons integration, a promotion to lieutenant colonel, and living at the beach was hard to beat, but meeting and marrying a truly wonderful woman was the real highlight. In December 1989, the 33d FW got another chance to hunt MiGs with the initiation of Operation Just Cause, the invasion of Panama to capture Noriega. After sitting alert on the edge of the parking ramp for over a week, we launched our fully-armed, three tank F-15C buffarillos to establish MiG CAPs between Cuba and Panama, and to de-louse the heavies (and others) as they egressed their objectives in Panama. Once again, radar contacts, but no MiGs.

Finally, in the summer of 1990 with over 15 years of uninterrupted operational flying and over 20 years total time in service, I received the dreaded staff assignment. I tried, once again, to have the assignment deferred since the wing was standing by to deploy for

Desert Shield, but apparently, MPC remembered the last two or three times I had escaped a staff assignment and told me to cease whining, salute smartly and report to the TAC DO staff as assistant chief and later chief, of Advanced Programs (DOTZ). With brand new "staff uniforms" ready to wear, I watched the 33d FW Eagles shooting MiGs on TV in Langley AFB temporary family housing. To make matters worse, the DO, Brig Gen Mike Ryan (later CSAF), gave me the additional duty of compiling Desert Storm lessons learned... always the hard way!

After three years of "staffing" and a new son, I figured it was time to go back to flying...but MPC just laughed and handed me an assignment to NATO's Air South in Naples Italy working for Lt Gen Joe Ashy. A few months into that assignment, after I had figured out that there was no pleasing the Greeks and the Turks regarding air defense responsibilities, General Ashy made me chief of the Deny Flight operations center. Amongst other planning and targeting responsibilities, what that meant was, every morning I got to stand up in front of Joe Ashy and have my face ripped-off trying to explain what Lt Gen "Bear" Chambers at the CAOC in Vicenza had been doing overnight. There was no love lost between the two. The international rhetoric began to ramp-up in response to atrocities in Bosnia and potential responses, or lack thereof, began to stress the UN – NATO (and U.S.) relationship as Lt Gen Ryan, with a new dual hat, took command of both AIRSOUTH, the CAOC and U.S. forces (along with Maj Gen Mike Short as his chief of staff). I was tasked to develop a contingency plan we called Deliberate Force which detailed attacks on specific target sets and targets in response to likely "triggering" actions or violations of the UN resolutions by the belligerents. With a line number for Colonel (thanks to Gen Ashy), General Ryan decided to frock me to facilitate coordination with UN leadership in Zagreb and Sarajevo and with the CAOC execution staff in Vicenza. So, while my family and visitors from the States toured Italy, my hearty staff of planners and targeteers generated numerous iterations of the Deliberate Force plan and accompanied ADM Leighton "Snuffy" Smith (CINCSOUTH) and Lt Gen Ryan on trips to Zagreb, Sarajevo, Ramstein and Vicenza soliciting support from French, British and American leaders. On 10 Aug. 1995, CINCSOUTH and UNPROFOR signed a memorandum of understanding on the execution of airstrikes. On 30 Aug. after the Serbs shelled the market in Sarajevo again, we began execution of airstrikes on Deliberate Force targets which lasted until 14 Sep. when airstrikes were suspended (terminated on 20 Sep.).

Six months later, when time came for an assignment, General Ryan offered me a choice of two vice wing commander jobs...52nd FW, Spangdahlem AB Germany or 48th FW, Lakenheath AB UK... either way, another flying job (dammit!), and we picked the 52nd arriving there in June 1996. This time, my F-15 requal was at Tyndall in a two-man senior officer's course with Col "Buzz" Moseley...a gentlemanly approach to flying training. With the 52nd commander TDY most of the time at "charm schools" and other taskings, leading a wing with two Block 50 F-16CJ squadrons, an A-10 squadron and an F-15C squadron, and developing a close relationship with the local villagers and leaders, it's hard to imagine a more rewarding two years...even though it included my fini-fini-flight in the F-15.

Then, in mid-1998, back to the staff with an assignment to Air Combat Command at Langley AFB as chief of Advanced Programs Division (DRZ...my initials and the designation I chose in a reorganization...formerly DRB) in the Requirements Directorate. The division portfolio contained many emerging, leading-edge classified programs and was staffed by some of the Air Force's finest. Although much of my time was spent at the Pentagon (SAF/AQL), I was grateful not to have to live there. One late Friday evening in late March 1999, working in the vault instead of being at the bar, I received a phone call from Lt Gen Mike Short, now commander of Air South in Naples. The Allied Force bombing of Serbia had begun a few days earlier and apparently, SACEUR, Gen Wes Clark, had expected the Serbs to fold after two or three days...so there were only two or three days-worth of targets planned and they were already into re-attacks on that target set. Gen Short said he'd already cleared it with ACC and he needed me in Vicenza Italy by Sunday, two days later. I found out upon arrival that not only was there no Allied Force plan, but there were no Allied Force planners...so, in short order, we emptied the HQ USAFE staff of anyone with an ability to help and started to work. The result was similar to the planning and targeting done for Deliberate Force and for reasons we may never fully appreciate, the Serbs quit on 10 June. Always the hard way.

Retirement: The remaining time at Langley was challenging... sometimes, rewarding...and as is typical, bright, dedicated, hardworking colleagues made most of it a true pleasure. After 33 years, 6 months and 10 days I retired on 24 May 2002, the same day my father scored his first kill, a German Me109 in 1944. After some family time and travelling, I went to work for Raytheon in Tucson as Director of Strategic Planning...quite a change from the military organizations I had come to know...but, once again, my work-buddies were inspirational. I retired from Raytheon in 2009 and finally discovered the art of making long lists of things to do... and choosing to do none of them! Free time enabled a little flying in my Rutan-designed, Zoerb-built VariEze, one of several Zoerb-built airplanes my father and I built/flew, a little riding on my FatBoy Harley, catching up with old friends and making new ones, enjoying Arizona...and swapping war stories with my Luncho Buncho buddies.

About the Friday Pilots - What happened to them after the USAF

Boris Baird became a squadron commander and a Lieutenant Colonel after 24 years in the USAF. He retired in Tucson where he was surrounded by close friends. He continued his love of aviation by joining the U.S. Aerobatic Team and became team manager in 1996. He was a big game hunter in North America and Africa. He succumbed to cancer and was eulogized in a memorial service on 5 July 2014 attended by his family, friends and Friday Pilot buddies.

Bob Barnett retired as a colonel. He followed a POW dream of owning his own airplane business. He became a Rockwell Commander and Grumman American dealer and developed the business into a full service FBO. He sold the business and traveled extensively around Europe and the world. He was chief and only pilot for a silver/gold mine in Tombstone. He was hired by Flight Safety International as a simulator and ground school instructor and got his ATP and flew the Learjet. He then got a dream job living and flying out of Geneva, Switzerland. Bob was the Secretary Treasurer of NAM-POW for five years and Vice Flight Captain and Flight Captain of the Daedalian "Old Pueblo" Flight. He was a founding member of the Friday Pilots group. His wife of 60 years, Anita, passed away in 2012. He has since met beautiful, Suzanne, widow of a NAM-POW. They are enjoying life and traveling the world. He has a wonderful daughter, Lori, and four terrific grandchildren.

Pete Carpenter retired as a colonel and considered buying an east coast FBO until his sanity returned. He moved to Tucson and got into real estate as an agent, then as a broker. He made commercial real estate investments and got into the restaurant/deli/catering business. His wife, Honeyjean, passed away and he enjoys time with his grandson and lunch with his flying buddies on Fridays.

Bob Dundas retired after 20 years in the USAF and became an investment banker in Fredericksburg, VA with Anderson &

Strudwick. He then retired at age 55 and went to Bigfork, MT where he spent summers hiking Glacier National Park and winters in Tucson. He and wife, Jean, are now fully retired residents of Tucson and Bob enjoys Daedalians and Fridays with his old flying buddies.

Lew Daugherty retired as a colonel and moved to Tucson with his family. After checkout with the DMAFB Aero Club his instructor recommended him to Cochise Airlines and ten days later he was an airline captain. His fun meter pegged after a couple of years of commuter flying and he became a Piper Pawnee pilot spraying cotton in the Eloy, AZ vicinity. He stopped flying, got a Masters degree in Agricultural Economics at the University of Arizona and remained in the Ag Econ Department as research specialist. He also taught farm management to underclassmen. He and wife of 60 years, Caryl, enjoy their three daughters, 11 grandchildren and 10 great grandchildren.

Bill Hosmer retired as a colonel and joined Cessna Aircraft as a Citation demonstration pilot. He flew, delivered and demonstrated aircraft in South Africa, New Zealand, Japan, China, South America, Europe, India, Burma and Moscow. He flew for a Tokyo company until the Tokyo stock market bottomed out, then got serious about golf in North Dakota and Arizona. He finally realized that golf was not serious about him. He thrives on his social network in Tucson of military retiree friends that provide him the vitality that at one time came with flying fighters with good people that shared his same values. Life has been very good.

Terry Johnson finished flying fighters with the Air National Guard, became a production test pilot with Learjet, joined North Central Airlines which became Republic Airlines which became Northwest Airlines which became Delta Airlines. He raced sports cars for Mazda, Nissan and Chevrolet. Later, he and wife, Claudia, raced motorcycles. They are enthusiastic tennis players and enjoy their beautiful retirement home in the foothills of Tucson.

Jim McDivitt was in the second group of U.S. astronauts. He retired from the Air Force and NASA in 1972. He was a brigadier general and manager of the Apollo spacecraft program. He made the big step to private industry becoming Executive V.P. of Consumer Power Co. He later became President of Pullman Standard, a railcar builder. Then, he became Executive V.P. of Pullman overseeing three worldwide engineering and construction companies as well as the railcar company. After Pullman, he joined Rockwell International as Senior V.P. of Strategic Management, later becoming President of Autonetics and finally retired in 1995 as Senior V.P. of Government Operations and International for Rockwell. He and wife, Judy, split time between Tucson and life on a Michigan lake in the summer.

Andy Muscarello flew all over the world finishing 20 years in the Air National Guard and 29 years with American Airlines. After retirement, he purchased a Beechcraft V-35 Bonanza and flew it extensively. He has four children, a physician son and two other sons, who are United Airlines captains. His daughter owns her own business. He and his wife of 59 years, Ginny, are in good health, have 12 grandchildren and smile a lot.

Marty Neuens retired from the Air Force after 26 years and settled with his wife, Cindy, in Tucson. He was active in starting Christian Prison Ministries, a half-way house, called, "The Bridge," that helps men coming out of prison become productive citizens. He continues as a board member and Treasurer and leads a bible study at The Bridge. He also worked with two boys through Big Brothers for about five years each. He enjoys the cooler weather in Pinetop, AZ during the summer.

Earl O'Loughlin retired from the Air Force after 37 years and returned to his home, East Tawas, MI. He pursued membership on corporate boards. At one time he served on eight boards. His passion was to hunt and fish and enjoy life with his wife and family. His travel took him hunting in Russia, New Zealand, Alaska, Canada, South Dakota, Michigan, Kansas, Georgia, Colorado, Texas, New Mexico and Arizona. He lost his high school sweetheart, Shirley, to cancer in 2003. He remarried an old friend, Thelma, and they enjoy splitting the year between Tucson and East Tawas. His four married children and 10 grandchildren love Thelma and life is good. He enjoys his farm in Michigan feeding deer, turkeys, and rainbow trout and Fridays with his buddies when in Tucson.

Bill Pitts retired in 1994 as a colonel after 26 years with almost 14 as an A-10 pilot. He was hired as a pilot by UPS within three months. His wife, Ruthanne, started her own commercial office furniture dealership and proceeded to grow it to 25 people in five states. He left UPS after seven years to partner with Ruthanne in the business. After 15 very successful years in the small business world, Bill and Ruthanne closed the doors. Today, they enjoy retired life and the occasional business venture back into the furniture world. From fighter pilot, to airline pilot, to business executive, to retired - what a life! But Bill says, "Don't forget - Vietnam created who I was intended to be." Sadly, Bill's wife, Ruthanne, passed away as the result of a cycling accident during the publication of this book.

GAR Rose was hired by Hughes Aircraft Company in Tucson as an engineer and tech rep working in the AGM-65 Maverick missile program. He followed his wife, Becky, to several cities pursuing her career as a property manager. After flunking cooking and housekeeping 101.0, he returned to flying with American Eagle Airlines until retiring in 2000, when he became a kept man and played golf poorly. In 2007 he and Becky returned to their Tucson foothills home that they use as a base while traveling extensively. They have one child, Glen, and two adorable granddaughters.

Gene Santarelli retried as a Lieutenant General and Vice Commander of PACAF after 32 years having commanded a numbered air force, an air division and three wings in the U.S., Europe, and the Mid-East. He also served as Exec to the CSAF. He is one of five USAF Senior Mentors for general officers on command and control of air operations, a consultant to the defense industry, the State of Arizona and the cities of Tucson and Glendale, AZ. He has served as member and co-chair of the Arizona Governor's Task Force on Military Installations. He serves on several boards. He and wife, Kay, have been married 38 years and enjoy the Tucson climate from their beautiful foothills home.

Don Shepperd retired as a Major General and head of the Air National Guard. He formed his own consulting company, became a TV personality covering the wars in Iraq and Afghanistan for CNN, served on several corporate boards and retired near his three grandchildren in Tucson where he and wife of 52 years, Rose, are mad University of Arizona Wildcat basketball fans. He writes and edits books.

Moose Skowron retired from the Air Force after 24 years. He went to work for Learjet as an independent test pilot for 26 years. He was a utility infielder flying production and experimental tests and demo and as an FAA Designated Engineering Test Pilot flying worldwide. His childhood sweetheart and wife, Margie, passed away and he lost an eye to cancer, but was able to fight with the FAA and get his commercial renewed. He just celebrated his 80th birthday and still considers himself one of the "the luckiest men on the face of the earth."

Rob Van Sice retired from the USAF in 1994 and moved to northern Virginia to consult with Whitney, Bradley and Brown. In 1995 he was hired by Hughes Aircraft Company to work in Rosslyn, VA. Raytheon purchased Hughes and in 1998, Rob opened the Seattle Raytheon office to support the Boeing/Raytheon Joint Strike Fighter team. In 2002, he moved to Raytheon Missile Systems in Tucson where he was an Engineering Director until retiring in 2008. He serves on several non-profit boards in Tucson, travels extensively, and spends time with his grandchildren in Virginia. One of his weekly highlights is the "Friday Pilots" gathering.

Russ Violett went into the consulting business and worked with several major companies in marketing and management focusing on Saudi Arabia. He traveled monthly to the area. He spent several weeks at a time living in the Mid-East and filling positions temporarily when personnel were fired or others were not yet hired to take over their tasks. He stopped traveling to spend more time with his family, wife, four daughters, their husbands and 18 grand and great grandchildren and play golf. He is active with and a member of the Board of Trustees of the Pima Air and Space Museum in Tucson.

Gordy Williams retired as a Major General from the J-5 position in EUCOM. He moved back to his house in the D.C. area of Virginia and consulted for several major defense firms. With his military expertise and Mid-East contacts, he traveled to the Gulf, after Desert Storm, and spent time in Kuwait and the UAE. He soon tired of the Virginia winters and moved to Tucson in 1996 where he majored in golf. He is active in Daedalians and the Air Force Association.

Doc Zoerb retired from Langley after 33 years, 6 months and 10 days on 24 May 2002, the same day his father scored his first aerial kill of WW II, an Me109 in 1944. Doc went to work for Raytheon in Tucson as Director of Strategic Planning, retiring in 2009. He finally discovered the art of making long lists of things to do and choosing to do none of them. Free time enabled him to do a little flying in his Rutan-designed, Zoerb-built VariEze, one of several Zoerb-built airplanes he and his father built and flew. He enjoyed riding his FatBoy Harley, catching up with old friends, making new ones, traveling Arizona and swapping war stories with his Friday Pilot buddies.

EPILOGUE

Clouds are appearing. The sun cuts itself on the western horizon and bleeds into valleys below. The blasts of afterburners and jet engines can be heard in the distance. We are straining to hear the laughter of friends and remember their faces. They are calling. Rock your wings and we'll rejoin, just not too soon we hope.

The Friday pilots

GLOSSARY

This section contains a glossary of terms found in the stories and widely used by pilots:

AAA/Triple-A/Triple-A site - anti aircraft artillery/anti aircraft artillery site – enemy guns that shoot at aircraft

ABCCC/AB Triple-C - Aircraft that operated as Airborne Battlefield Command and Control Centers such as Hillsboro, Cricket, Crown, Panama, Waterboy et. al.

AB/Afterburner/burner - system of spraybars that inject jet fuel into the engine exhaust which is then re-ignited producing extra thrust

Abort/Aborting – to stop doing what you are doing immediately! i.e. "Abort your pass!"

AFSC - Air Force Specialty Code – personnel jargon for "job title"

AGL - above ground level. Refers to altitude above the ground, i.e. – 100 ft. AGL meant at 100 feet above the ground

ALO - Air Liaison officer - Air Force officer stationed with the Army to assist in coordinating air support

Ammo - ammunition

Alpha Strike Package - the package of fighters used to attack targets in the heavily defended Route Packages near Hanoi and/or Haiphong during the Vietnam War

Anchor - refueling orbit tracks flown by KC-135 aerial tankers, such as those over Thailand and the Gulf of Tonkin - Brown Anchor, Blue Anchor, etc.

Bailout - eject from the aircraft. In fighter aircraft the pilot ejects by pulling handles to fire the rocket-powered ejection seat

Barrier – arresting device installed at departure end of runway – cables to catch aircraft arresting hooks (now Bak-9/12s). In the old days nets and chains were used

BDA - bomb damage assessment - the results of a strike, what the bombs hit

Bingo - pre-designated fuel level that warns the pilot to leave for home base, or the tanker

Break - a hard, high-G turn usually made to avoid gunfire, or a missile from an attacking enemy fighter, such as, "Olds 4, BREAK RIGHT!"

Briefing/Brief - the pre-mission session during which the pilots meet to plan the mission and receive information on the weather, latest intelligence, route of flight, etc.

Buffs – "Big Ugly Fat Fellows" - affectionate term for B-52s

Canopy - the parachute canopy. Also refers to jungle tree cover. Also the glass that covers the cockpit on a fighter aircraft that is opened for aircraft entry/exit

CAP/Capping – Combat Air Patrol - orbiting a location such as a downed pilot

CBUs - cluster bomb units - bomblets carried in multi-tubed canisters on wing stations of fighter aircraft and delivered at low altitude requiring flight directly over a target

Chatter - talk on the aircraft radio, as in, "Hold down the chatter!"

Chopper - a helicopter

Chute - parachute

Cong - slang for Vietcong - enemy soldiers

Counter – a mission over North Vietnam. Due to the high risks, a Vietnam tour was defined as one-year OR 100 missions over North Vietnam

DCO - Deputy Commander for Operations - Colonel on wing or squadron staff in charge of operations

Debrief - after mission sessions reviewing mission performance and mission results

Delta - the agricultural rice paddy area forming the southern-most part of Vietnam, fed by the Mekong River, often called the "Mekong Delta" area south of Saigon, now called "Ho Chi Minh City"

Delta Points - numbered geographic points on the ground over prominent geographic features used to designate locations, to abbreviate radio chatter and prevent enemy from knowing location of aircraft, e.g. "We are just west of Delta 60"

Delta Sierra – vulgar term referring to "dog poop" used normally to describe bad weather as in, "The weather is Delta Sierra today"

DEROS - date of rotation stateside. A pilot's return home date.

Dragchute - a parachute deployed from under the aircraft after landing by pulling a cockpit handle to assist with slowing the aircraft down

DMZ - Demilitarized Zone dividing North from South Vietnam during the war. The DMZ followed the Ben Hai River

DOD – the Department of Defense located in the Pentagon in Washington D.C.

Duckbutt – aircraft used to monitor overwater flights or support water rescues. In Vietnam the HU16 Grumman Albatross amphibian aircraft was used when appropriate

ECM/ECM pods – electronic counter-measures/pods to provide electronic jamming against ground radars

EGT - engine exhaust gas temperature (measured on EGT gauge in cockpit)

Eject - bailing out by pulling the ejection seat handles, firing the rocket-powered ejection seat, which subsequently fires the pilot out of the aircraft

FAC - Forward Air Controller, finds and marks targets with smoke rockets for bomb-laden fighters

Fast FAC - FACs who flew jets. In Vietnam Fast FACs flew F-100s and later F-4s with radio callsigns such as "Misty, Laredo and Wolf"

FCF - functional check flight - a test flight

Feet-wet/Feet-dry - operating over water, or over land

Flak/Flakbursts - smoke and shrapnel caused by anti-aircraft artillery shells exploding at pre-set times after firing. 37mm bursts were gray, 57mm, 85mm and 100mm were dark black

Friendlies - the good guys. Used to explain the location of U.S. troops, i.e., "The friendlies are on the north side of the river"

FUBAR – Fouled-up beyond all recognition

G/Gs/G-forces/Pulling Gs - the force of gravity exerted on a pilot's body by turning the aircraft, or pulling on the control stick. "Pulling 4-Gs," means the pilot experiences feeling 4 X his body weight

GIB/GIBs - "guy in the backseat." The backseater in a two-place aircraft

Gomers - the bad guys - the VC and NVA

Groundpounder - a soldier, or non-pilot

Grunt - Army soldier

Guard or Guard freq - frequency 243.0 - the UHF radio frequency used for emergency radio transmissions and monitored by all UHF-equipped aircraft

Haiphong - the major port city of North Vietnam

Hanoi - the capital city of North Vietnam

Highdrags/Retards - 500 lb. finned/retarded bombs used to drop at low altitude

Hilton/the Hanoi Hilton - infamous prison used to hold American POWs in Hanoi

Ho Chi Minh - Ho Chi Minh Trail - named after the communist leader of North Vietnam who died 2 Sep 1969 - the series of roadways that led from the Hanoi/Haiphong area south through southern North Vietnam and Laos to Cambodia and South Vietnam to resupply Vietcong and NVA forces

Hook/Tailhook – large metal hook used during landing and takeoff emergencies to snag a steel cable that stretched across the runway to arrest the aircraft (like those used by Navy carrier aircraft)

Hootch – on base living quarters for pilots

HHQ - Higher headquarters

Hun - pilots favorite nickname for the F-100

I Corps/"Eye" Corps - South Vietnam was divided into four Corps areas. I Corps was the northern-most Corps area closest to North Vietnam and the DMZ; II Corps was the Central Highlands; III Corps was the Central Highlands to Saigon; IV Corps the Mekong Delta area south of Saigon

IFR - instrument flight rules - in the weather - flying on instruments in the weather

In-country – referring to inside South Vietnam such as an "in-country aircraft checkout" or "In-country missions" meaning inside South Vietnam, rather than over North Vietnam

Intel/Intel Officer - intelligence/Intelligence Officer

Jink/jinking – turn/turning the aircraft randomly and unpredictably to confuse ground gunners and defeat aimed AAA

Jolly or Jolly Green – Air Force HH-53 rescue helicopters

Karst - geographic features, jagged limestone protrusions forming mountains, common in North Vietnam, Laos and Thailand

KIA - killed in action

Klick - slang for kilometer - 1,000 meters - .6 of a mile

Knots - measurement for airspeed - a "knot" is one nautical mile/hr., i.e. - 400 knots = 400 nautical miles/hr. A nautical mile is 1.15 statute miles. Jet aircraft cockpit airspeed indicators are in knots

Life Support - section in a fighter squadron that maintains the pilot support equipment and survival gear (parachutes, life rafts, survival radios, etc.)

Linebacker/Linebacker II – 1972 renewed air campaigns designed to force the North Vietnamese to the Paris peace table to end the war

LOC - lines of communication - refers to roads, trails, rivers, etc. over which men and material are moved

LPUs - Life Preservers, Underarm - the inflatable life preservers worn under the pilot's armpits. Used in case of over-water ejection

Mach – the speed of sound, roughly 666 knots or 766 mph, a mile in five seconds. Mach two is twice the speed of sound. "Breaking the mach," means exceeding the speed of sound

MANPADs – man-portable air defense systems – shoulder-fired IR, heat-seeking missiles. The SA-7 was first employed in Vietnam, now increasingly sophisticated models proliferate throughout the world

Mark - the white smoke cloud caused by the explosion of a white phosphorous marking rocket head fired by a Forward Air Controller and used to visually mark targets for attacking fighters

MAYDAY! - emergency radio call made to alert others that an aircraft is in trouble. From the French, "Venez m'aider!" meaning, "Come help me!" e.g. "MAYDAY! MAYDAY! MAYDAY! Ejecting west of Delta 60!"

MIA - missing in action - pilots, whose status could not be confirmed, were listed by DOD as "MIA"

Mike/mic/mike button - the microphone in the pilot's mask. The button on the stick the pilot pushes to transmit on the radio

Mistys – Fast FACs that flew the twoseat F-100F aircraft over North Vietnam to locate and mark targets for bomb-laden fighters

Movers - any enemy vehicle that moved on the ground

MSL – altitude above mean sea level – the altitude shown on the cockpit altimeter

Nape/napalm – thick, jelled fuel that was dropped in tanks and ignited to burn ground targets

nm - nautical mile

NORDO - no radio - radio out

NOTAM - Notice to Airmen, an advisory message

NVA - North Vietnamese Army

O-Club - Officers Club

PACAF/PACOM – Pacific Air Forces was/is the Air Force component HQ for PACOM located at Hickam AFB, Honolulu, HI. PACOM (Pacific Command) was/is the unified command HQ in charge of Pacific military operations.

PCS - Permanent change of station - a military move from one base to another

PE - Personal Equipment - the flying and survival gear worn and carried by pilots and maintained by the squadron Life Support Section

Pickle/Pickle button/Pickling - to press the bomb button on the control stick, releasing a bomb or firing a rocket

PIO - pilot-induced oscillation - usually caused by over-controlling the aircraft at high airspeeds

Pipper - the center of the gunsight on the pilot's windscreen. Used for aiming to fire guns, rockets, missiles or to drop a bomb

Pit/the Pit - the backseat of a two-place aircraft, as in "riding in the pit"

PJs - para-rescue crews that rode on the Jolly Green helicopters to rescue downed pilots

Playtime - the amount of time fighters have to work with the FAC on a target - limited by fuel, i.e., "We have 30 minutes playtime"

POL/POL storage area - petroleum, oil and lubricants, gasoline and oil

POW - Prisoner of War

Punchout/Punch - to eject (bailout) from the aircraft

R&R - rest and recuperation - a vacation - all military members in Vietnam got a one-week R&R during their tour, usually to Hawaii, Australia, Thailand or Malaysia

Recce - reconnaissance

RESCAP - capping (flying over) a downed pilot while taking part in a rescue attempt

RHAW/RHAW-gear - Radar Homing and Warning gear - electronic system that warned of radar lock-on by SAM radars or gunsites with visual symbols and audio sounds displayed on a cockpit gauge and in a pilot's headset. Modern gear is called RWR (Radar Warning Receiver)

ROE - rules of engagement - the rules established by HQ to be followed by all pilots while attacking enemy targets

Rolling Thunder - the air campaign over North Vietnam

Route Pack/Route Package - North Vietnam was divided into six Route Packages - areas of operations. Route Pack 1 was the southern-most just above the DMZ. Route Pack 6 was divided into 6A (Hanoi) and 6B (Haiphong). The Air Force had primary responsibility for RPs 1, 5 and 6A, the Navy, 2, 3, 4 and 6B

RPM - revolutions per minute - engine speed - i.e. "operating at high RPM" meant operating at high engine power. RPM was shown on a cockpit gauge

RT - radio talk - the conversations on a radio, as "Let's hold down the RT"

RTB - return to base - go home

Sabre Jet - nickname for the F-100 (the Super Sabre)

Saigon - the capital city of South Vietnam, now "Ho Chi Minh City"

Sandys – USAF A-1 (also called "Spads") aircraft used to escort Jolly Green helicopters and perform location of, protection for and rescue of downed aircrews

SAM/SAM site - Surface to Air Missile/Missile site

SAR - Search and Rescue mission

SEA - Southeast Asia, generic term used to include the countries of Vietnam, Laos, Thailand, Cambodia, and the Philippines during the Vietnam War

Secondary - an explosion of something on the ground caused by dropping bombs on it, such as ammunition, or POL

Seventh Air Force/7th AF – the HQ in charge of the Vietnam air war, located in Saigon at Tan Son Nhut Air Base

Shack - a direct hit, as in - Lead "shacked" the truck.

Sierra Hotel - vulgar term used by fighter pilots to denote something is good (hot), such as, "That was a Sierra Hotel job of bombing today"

Slicks - refers to un-retarded bombs with tailfins, i.e. 500 lb./750 lb./1000lb. "slicks," vs. 500 lb. "retarded" or "Snakeye" bombs

Slow FAC – FACs in slow propeller-driven airplanes such as the O-1 and O-2

Snakeyes - 500 lb. retarded highdrag bombs dropped at low altitude by fighters

SOF - Supervisor of Flying - pilot stationed on ground in command post to supervise flying operations

SPADs - propeller-driven A-1 aircraft used to escort Jolly Green helicopters on rescues

Steel Tiger - the air campaign over Laos

Strafe/strafing - firing the 20mm aircraft guns (30mm in case of A-10)

Super Sabre – another nickname for the F-100

Supersonic - faster than the speed of sound

Tallyho/Tally - I have it/you in sight

Tango Uniform - vulgar term used by fighter pilots meaning "lying breasts up," or dead, such as "Our radio is tango uniform"

Tanker - airborne KC-135 refueling aircraft equipped with drogues (baskets) or refueling booms. F-4s and F-105s used "receptacle" refueling (tanker probe inserted into open aircraft receptacle). F-100 pilots inserted a refueling probe to a "drogue" (basket attached to fuel hose) to obtain fuel while airborne

TDY - temporary duty - away from home base

Thud – affectionate nickname for the F-105 Thunderchief aircraft

Tracers - illuminated rounds fired by AAA sites to allow gunners to track aircraft. Normally the ratio of tracers was 1:6 or 7

Truckpark - parking areas for trucks. Usually carved-out in fan-fashion at the end of a road to disperse vehicles, making them harder to hit by attacking fighters

Twenty mike-mike - 20mm ammunition for F-100, F-4 or F-105 guns

UHF - Ultra High Frequency radio - the radio frequency band on which all USAF/USN military aircraft operated. The Army aircraft operated on VHF and FM frequencies

Unworkable - can't put in airstrikes, usually due to poor weather, i.e., "The weather is unworkable today"

Vietcong/VC - the Vietcong – indigenous enemy soldiers in South Vietnam

VFR - visual flight rules - flying in good weather

VR/Vr-ing - visual recce/performing visual reconnaissance

Warp-speed - refers to going fast

Warthog – affectionate term for the A-10 Thunderbolt II aircraft

Wheels-up - refers to raising the landing gear after takeoff

Wild Weasels/Weasels – aircraft equipped as SAM hunter-killers that provide strike force protection by locating SAM radars and firing homing anti-radiation missiles. F-100s were employed as early Weasels in Vietnam, later F-105s assumed the role, now F-16s

Willie Petes - white phosphorous smoke rockets fired by FACs to mark targets for fighters.

WOXOF – military weather acronym for "weather is - indefinite ceiling at zero ft, visibility zero in fog"

WSO – Weapons System Operator, the backseater (navigator) in a two-place fighter such as the F-4. Originally pilots were assigned to the backseat and called PSOs

ABOUT THE EDITOR

Don Shepperd graduated from the United States Air Force Academy in 1962. He flew fighters in Europe and 247 combat fighter missions in Vietnam including 60 as an F-100 Misty Fast FAC over North Vietnam. He flew for the airlines and sold light airplanes in industry. He retired from the Pentagon in 1998 as a Major General and head of the Air National Guard. He formed his own consulting company. He covered the wars in Iraq and Afghanistan for CNN. He and wife, Rose, live in Tucson near their three grandchildren. He is an author and editor, and his books can be found on Amazon.com

"When once you have tasted flight, you will forever walk the earth with your eyes turned skyward, for there you have been, and for there you will always long to return"
– author unknown

Made in the USA
Lexington, KY
30 January 2016